FURIOUS INTERIORS

WALES, R. S. THOMAS
AND GOD

JUSTIN WINTLE

HarperCollins*Publishers*

HarperCollins*Publishers*
77−85 Fulham Palace Road
Hammersmith, London, W6 8JB

Published by HarperCollins*Publishers* 1996
1 3 5 7 9 8 6 4 2

A catalogue record for this book is
available from the British Library

ISBN 0 00 255571 9

Set in Postscript Garamond No 3 by
Rowland Phototypesetting Limited
Bury St Edmunds, Suffolk

Printed and bound in Great Britain by
Caledonian International Book Manufacturing Ltd, Glasgow

For Joe Bain *and* Barrie Williams

But the cormorant and the bittern shall possess it; the owl also and the raven shall dwell in it; and he shall stretch out upon it the line of confusion, and the stones of emptiness. They shall call the nobles thereof to the kingdom, but none shall be there, and all her princes shall be nothing. And thorns shall come up in her palaces, nettles and brambles in the fortresses thereof: and it shall be an habitation of dragons, and a court for owls.

Isaiah 34; 11–15

This party rode out until they reached a great level plain and saw a fortress, the strongest one ever. They journeyed throughout the day, and when they expected to reach the fortress they were no nearer than at first; yet as they travelled along the plain they could see a great flock of sheep with neither end nor limit to it, and a shepherd watching from the top of a mound, a cloak of skins on him, and a shaggy mastiff at his side, larger than a nine-year-old stallion. He had never lost a lamb, much less a sheep, nor did there pass him any company which he did not harm or wound mortally, for his breath had burned every dead tree and bush on the plain to the ground.

The Mabinogion (trans. Jeffrey Gantz)

> We are cleverer
> than you; our nightmares
> are intellectual. But we never awaken
> from the compulsiveness of the mind's
> stare into the lenses' furious interiors.
>
> R. S. THOMAS, 'Probing'

CONTENTS

PERMISSIONS

The author and publishers of this work wish to express their gratitude to R.S. Thomas, and to the following:

Canon A.M. Allchin, for permission to quote his translation of the 'death-bed' poem by Meilyr Brydydd.

Bloodaxe Books Ltd., for permission to quote untitled verses from *Counterpoint* by R.S. Thomas; 'Mass for Hard Times', and 'A Marriage' from *Mass for Hard Times* by R.S. Thomas; and 'Incarnations', 'No Time', 'The Lost', 'S.K.', 'Play', 'Anybody's Alphabet', and 'Geriatric' from *No Truce with the Furies* by R.S. Thomas.

J.M. Dent & Sons Ltd., for permission to quote 'The Small Window', 'Sea-Watching', 'It Hurts Him To Think', 'Epitaph', 'Ap Huw's Testament', 'Welsh', 'Sorry', 'The Boy's Tale', 'Parent', 'Sailor's Hospital', 'Album', 'Looking at Sheep', 'Llanrhaeadr ym Mochnant', 'Anniversary', 'The Untamed', 'Because', 'Marriage', 'The Way of It', 'Seventieth Birthday', 'He and She', 'Cynddylan on a Tractor', 'Country Church: Manafon', 'A Peasant', 'Welsh History', 'On Hearing a Welshman Speak', 'A Lecturer', 'Maes-yr-Onnen', 'A Priest to His People', 'Out of the Hills', 'Affinity', 'Iago Prytherch', 'The Welsh Hill Country', 'The Old Language', 'Wales', 'The Tree (Owain Glyndŵr Speaks)', 'The Minister', 'Memories of Yeats whilst travelling to Holyhead', 'Priest and Peasant', 'In a Country Church', 'A Welshman to any Tourist', 'Song at the Year's Turning', 'No Through Road', 'Border Blues', 'A Line from St David's', 'In Church', 'Temptation of a Poet', 'Green Categories', 'The Dark Well', 'Servant', 'Absolution', 'The Face', 'The View from the Window', 'Poetry for Supper', 'This To Do', 'Burgos', 'Pre-Cambrian', 'The Moon in Lleyn', 'Abercuawg', 'Rhodri', 'Reservoirs', 'Welcome to Wales', 'To Pay for His Keep', 'He Agrees With Henry Ford', 'Ann Griffith', 'Phew!', 'Kierkegaard', 'Once', 'Petition', 'Invitation', 'No Answer', 'Via Negativa', 'Making', 'Other', 'H'm', 'The Kingdom', 'Emerging', 'At It', 'Destinations', 'Poste Restante', 'Souillac: Le Sacrifice D'Abraham', 'Directions', 'Synopsis', 'Balance', and 'The Answer' from *Collected Poems 1945–1990*, by R.S. Thomas.

Faber & Faber Ltd., for permission to quote from Philip Larkin, *Selected Letters*, ed. Anthony Thwaite.

Victor Gollancz Ltd., for permission to quote from *The Welsh Extremist: A Culture in Crisis* by Ned Thomas.

Gwasg Gomer (The Gomer Press), for permission to quote 'How To Write Anglo-Welsh Poetry' from *At the Edge of Town* by John Davies; extracts from *Cymru or Wales* by R.S. Thomas; *Wildlife, My Life* by William Condry; and from *Dafydd ap Gwilym: A Selection of Poems*, ed. and trans. Rachel Bromwich.

Llanerch Publishers Ltd., for permission to quote from *Y Gododdin*, trans. Steve Short, and from *The Black Book of Carmarthen*, trans. Meirion Pennar.

Y Lolfa (Publishers, of Tal-y-bont, Ceredigion), for permission to quote from *To Dream of Freedom* by Roy Clews, and from *The ABC of the Welsh Revolution* by Derrick Hearne.

Macmillan & Co. Ltd., for permission to quote 'That Place' from *Laboratories of the Spirit* by R.S. Thomas; 'Salt', 'The Tree', and 'Covenanters' from *Later Poems* by R.S. Thomas; 'Retirement', 'A Country', and 'A Life' from *Experimenting with an Amen* by R.S. Thomas; and prose and verse extracts from *The Echoes Return Slow* by R.S. Thomas.

Reed Books and William Heinemann Ltd., for permission to quote from Robert Bolt's stage-play, *A Man for All Seasons*.

Seren Books (Poetry Wales Press), for permission to quote from *Ingrowing Thoughts* by R.S. Thomas; *Welsh Airs* by R.S. Thomas; and from *R.S. Thomas: Selected Prose*, ed. Sandra Anstey.

The University of Wales Press Ltd., for permission to quote from 'The Deluge 1939' from *Selected Poems of Saunders Lewis*, trans. Joseph P. Clancy.

A.P. Watt Ltd. and Michael Yeats, for permission to quote 'The Second Coming', 'The Curse of Cromwell', and lines from 'Ben Bulben' from *The Collected Poems of W.B. Yeats*.

Every effort has been made to contact the copyright owners of material included. In the instances where this has not proved possible, we offer our apologies to those concerned.

ILLUSTRATIONS

The portrait photograph of R.S. Thomas is reproduced by kind permission of Howard Barlow.

The photograph of the tennis team is reproduced by kind permission of St Michael's College, Llandaff.

The photograph of R.S. Thomas officiating at the wedding is reproduced by kind permission of Hazel and Michael Boulton.

The photograph of the Penyberth Three is reproduced by kind permission of the National Library of Wales.

The photograph of Cayo Evans leading an FWA demonstration is reproduced by kind permission of Y Lolfa, and is taken from their publication entitled *To Dream of Freedom* by Roy Clews.

All other photographs are the author's own.

PREFACE

THREE THINGS THIS BOOK IS NOT: a formal biography; an academic monograph; or the outcome of any collaboration between its author and its subject, the Welsh poet and erstwhile priest R. S. Thomas. Rather, it is an attempt to size up a prodigious and controversial figure before he is berthed in whatever niche, or grave, literary history is destined to provide him; before, that is, he is rendered either impotent, or harmless, or both; before he is reduced to that state of judicious veneration with which time and academe conspire to embalm humanity in its more striking individual manifestations.

Thomas, however, was not my starting point. Initially, after coming to live here, I had in mind to write about Wales, as a respite from what I usually write about, which is the conflicts that have beset the peoples of south-east Asia. But the more of Thomas's poetry I read and re-read, the more I succumbed to its uneasy, brittle spell; just as, the more I thought about Wales in the light of that work, the more I realized that, west of Offa's Dyke, any respite is cosmetic.

The result reflects perhaps my deflected purpose. Elements of biography and criticism have been combined with social observation and history. I have also used Thomas as an excuse to visit parts of Wales previously unfamiliar to me, and recounted such journeyings. Yet the man lends himself to a hybrid approach. Great praise has often been bestowed upon the poet. The biographical notes that accompany his books inform us that he won the Heinemann Award in 1955, the Queen's Gold Medal for Poetry in 1964 and the Cholmondeley Award in 1978. He has, too, frequently been honoured by the Welsh Arts Council. Then, mid-way through 1995, came the news that he had been nominated for the 1996 Nobel Literature Prize. It is commonplace to hear him described as the finest living poet in the English language; even, I have heard it said, the finest since Wordsworth. Among some he is regarded as a prophet – though this, as will be seen, is an ambivalent soubriquet. Yet Thomas has as regularly evoked bewilderment and dismay. A craftsman who combines modernism with many of the traditions and aspirations of an increasingly obsolescent high culture, and a pacifist who embraces an ardent patriotism, he has often appeared to the public as an eccentric, even perverse figure: a fully paid-up member of the awkward squad, no less.

While much of the hostility towards Thomas is ill-informed and ungenerous, it is scarcely difficult to see how the caricature has come about. Anyone who is a poet *and* an Anglican priest *and* a Welsh nationalist must, to the casual contemporary English or anglicized Welsh onlooker at least, seem definably odd: someone condemned to inhabit only the peripheries perhaps of British society; someone, as it were, with a great deal of ground to make up. Nor, very often, does Thomas himself seem either willing or able to make up such ground. On the contrary, he can appear to delight in his isolation from the common ruck. In particular, his championing of the Welsh language, an entirely honourable objective in itself, is sometimes taken to such lengths that it becomes hard not to detect at best a bloody-mindedness, at worst a racism. And this, his opponents say, from a man of the cloth!

Yet out of the manifest peculiarities and tensions inherent in Thomas's collective persona comes an avalanche of poetry that is as creatively mainstream as it is idiosyncratic.

How can this be? Through my investigation I hope to provide a few clues that may not have been spotted before, and bring together in one place others that have already been suggested, not least by R. S. Thomas himself, in his Welsh-language autobiographical writings. I am aware though that my approach, quite apart from the matter of its execution, is likely to provoke disappointment, indignation and wrath in several quarters.

The disappointment will be among lovers of straight biography, and also among academic critics who are more painstaking than I. The indignation I anticipate from some Welsh readers, for presuming as someone who is seven-eighth's English to discuss their country and their culture. And wrath, perhaps, from R. S. Thomas himself.

I should here clarify my relations with the poet. This book was researched without either his approval or his blessing. Rather the opposite in fact. In April 1994 I wrote to R. S. Thomas, providing a preliminary outline of what I intended and requesting that we meet. Thomas replied immediately, courteously and pithily. He did not, he said, 'wish' for a biography, adding: 'If ever one gets written, it will be essential for the biographer to be Welsh speaking.' I wrote back declaring that it was not my purpose to write a formal biography, rather that I wanted to explore Wales and his poetry together. I also stated that while his surmise that I was not a Welsh-speaker was correct, I had 'every intention to rectify that shortcoming'.

These entreaties, I hoped, would break the ice; after all, R. S. himself did not begin learning Welsh until late in his twenties. To this second letter, however, I received no reply. At the beginning of July Mr Philip Gwyn Jones, my editor, kindly wrote to Mr Thomas on my behalf. The answer was not unexpected. Mr Thomas reiterated that he did not want me to write a 'biography', adding that it was 'unwise' that my book should have been commissioned without ascertaining his 'views on the subject'. Whereupon, in a further endeavour to convince the poet that biography was not my primary objective, and that I had no desire to invade his privacy, I wrote a third letter. But to this, as to my second, came there answer none.

No doubt R. S. Thomas, then entering upon his eighty-second year, was irritated by my persistence. Nonetheless, I made one last attempt to win him round. In the second week of September 1994 I wrote a fourth letter, as conciliatory as I could make it. I also mentioned that from the end of that month I would be abroad, travelling in Laos, 'a country I have been trying for a very long time to enter, and whose government has only recently given me permission to do so'.

By now I was taking it as read that the Reverend Thomas would not respond. Indeed I had taken to telling him that there was no need to reply to my letters, but that they were written as a courtesy, to keep him posted on the general development of my researches. The next thing I knew, a half-page article, put together by Marianne Macdonald, appeared in the *Independent on Sunday* on 25 September. This was headlined: 'Biographers: They Can Go To Hell'. It began:

The first biography of the reclusive retired priest whom many regard as Britain's greatest living poet has just been commissioned – but true to form, R. S. Thomas refuses to have anything to do with it.

'I haven't given my consent, so if it goes on it will be entirely without my co-operation,' he said last week. 'I don't want fingers poked into my life. I don't know what they can unearth. I've never murdered anybody or robbed a bank.'

The interview went on to mention me by name. I wondered for a moment whether, if Mr Thomas ever did decide to murder someone, I might not be the preferred candidate. On the other hand he might have chosen Ms Macdonald herself, for the rest of her piece was hardly complimentary. His long and professional involvement with Christianity, she wrote, 'has not modified his malice'. Nor did she refrain from glossing R. S. Thomas's 'studied boredom' in her presence. Not for the first time the poet had peeped his way into the press, only to be caricatured as a high-octane model of all that is disingenuous and cantankerous.

At the time I felt keenly that I had been caught on the hop. Ms Macdonald's interview may have been arranged some while before Thomas learned that I was travelling abroad, or it may have been fixed as a result of that knowledge. Either way the poet had used the press to wrongfoot me. However, when I had told him that I was leaving at the end of the month, I meant it quite literally. Before catching my flight I had time, just about, to make my own representations to the *Independent on Sunday*. These were published in the correspondence column the following weekend. Taking Ms Macdonald to task for not having sought out my own views, my letter continued, in its more substantive part:

She also failed to address the key issue in the relations between writers and their commentators. Of course we would all like to control what is written and said about us. But have we the right when we ourselves have taken active and wilful steps to disseminate our opinions and ideas as widely as we can? What interests me about Thomas is the nature of his views, as well as how he has expressed them. When those views are only explicable in terms of the life, then the life becomes a legitimate object of enquiry.

By these words I was prepared to stand or fall; for it was hardly the case that R. S. Thomas is a blushing violet hidden away from the world. The bulk of his poetry has, at his own choosing, been published by London houses; while much of his prose, whether in English or in Welsh, is nothing if not polemical. If Thomas finds himself in the public eye, it is because he has put himself there.

It is also the case that much of Thomas's work is strongly autobiographical. Indeed the poet's relentless self-scrutiny, as a poet, as a Welshman, as a priest and as a human being, is one of the conditions of his poetry, and lends to it an air of undecidability: is the man self-obsessed to a degree? or, should we say that Thomas's own investigation of himself is one of the great literary voyages of self-discovery, comparable with those of, say, Freud, or Kierkegaard, or W. B. Yeats, or Samuel Beckett?

My solution to this riddle is provided in the pages that follow. After I had finished a first draft of them I again wrote to the poet, in March 1996. Partly (I suspect) as a result of the kind offices of Professor M. Wynn Thomas of Swansea University, R. S. Thomas now seemed prepared to countenance my activities. He had, he wrote back, 'no objection to a critical study of my work by a competent critic'.

Whether this book and its author meet that requirement is for others to decide. Towards myself, Mr Thomas has, in the end, acted with uncommon fairness, even generosity. Nor did he ask, as was his entitlement, to view my manuscript before publication. And in retrospect, it can only be to the good that his collaboration was withheld; for nothing sickens so much as the sycophancy that informs some 'living biographies'. Instead I have had the psychological freedom to write whatever I thought appropriate.

For my persistence, and the annoyance it must have caused him, I offer the poet my sincere apologies. I also offer the following. As suggested above, it seems right to bear contemporaneous witness to the aura of controversy that surrounds a palpable and public figure. Secondly, I have endeavoured to pay homage to that truth that however 'universal' a writer's work may be – and paradoxically Thomas's work is universal in the extreme – it retains and always must retain a specific provenance. Thirdly, if I am committed to anything in life then I am committed to the well-worn yet still scantily acted-upon proposition that friction between cultures can and will only be reduced by a deepening of inter-cultural understanding and exchange. Fourthly, as a writer myself, I have indulged the desire to write about what, for some while, has absorbed and engrossed me. And fifthly, I offer what I consider to be the surest legitimation: that only by reading R. S. Thomas's poetry, on one level, as a prolonged and fragmented autobiography conceived under the double duress of his membership of a culturally threatened minority and of a punishingly severe poetics, can its elusive unity be glimpsed. *Furious Interiors* in this context refers both to what seems to have gone on in the poet's mind for the last eighty years, and to the poet's characteristic method of framing such content.

But of course, I could not have set about this task, let alone completed it, without the help of many others. A list of those to whom I am indebted appears in the Acknowledgements, immediately after the main body this book. Here, I must emphasize my special gratitude to Joseph Bain, M. B. Williams and Philip Gwyn Jones: three very different Welshmen whose friendship and interest have sustained me throughout.

J. W.
Dyfed, May 1996

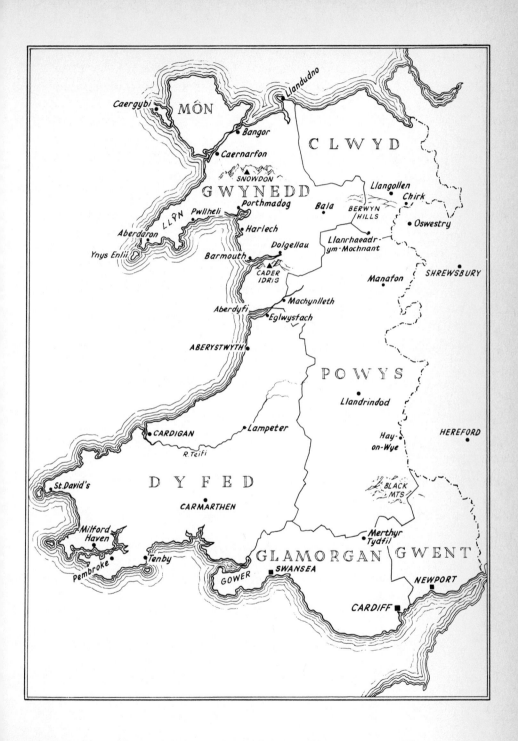

I

THE UNION'S EDGE

We are too apt to confine wisdom and virtue within the
circle of our own acquaintance and party. Our friends, our
country, and in short everything related to us, we are disposed to overvalue. A wise man will guard himself against
this delusion.

RICHARD PRICE,
A Discourse on the Love of Our Country, 1789

MILFORD HAVEN... also known on the road signs and some maps as Aberdaugleddau, though no one who lives there calls it by its Welsh name any more, if indeed they ever did. For Milford is in Pembrokeshire; and Pembrokeshire, in the south-west of the country, has for a long while been known, sometimes affectionately though more usually with scorn, as 'Little England Beyond Wales': one of the parts of Wales where the Normans established an early and lasting foothold. Today, the hills and oil refineries that surround Milford make it look like a cross between Dorset and Saudi Arabia. Nothing very Welsh about that either.

But today is also the last Friday of April, 1994. Upstairs the sun has finally got its act together. Only the blueness of the schoolkids' cerulean sweaters, when they disgorge on to and beyond the streets at 3.25 p.m., is bluer than the water in the haven, which in turn is bluer than the sky above. Probably this is the first day of summer; which means, since it is nevertheless Wales, it could very well be the last. But what the heck! Five of us have elected to walk from nearby Haverfordwest to Nolton Haven, tucked away in the cliffs of the famous Pembrokeshire coastline. Myself apart, there is an Owens, a Morgan, a Griffiths and a Chapman. In other words three Welshmen and two Englishmen. The Welshmen all teach at a nearby comprehensive, which is the common connection: a year before I taught there temporarily, while Chapman, a firearms specialist in the police force, is married to another member of staff.

We convene at Morgan's bungalow, on the outskirts of Haverfordwest: an unexpectedly modest dwelling for someone who, as well as having once been a mayor somewhere, is also a JP. The walls of his kitchen and dining room are covered with moral injunctions, either cut out from newspapers or written neatly on scraps of paper.

On the table in Morgan's kitchen meat pies, crab paste sandwiches and apple tarts have been carefully arrayed by his wife. There is also a small stack of prettily printed paper serviettes.

'A bit like Enid Blyton, all this,' I observe sotto voce to Owens, but Owens retorts loudly: 'Oh stuff Enid Blyton, boy, I doubt that old bird knew what a decent pub was.'

Which is of course the neat point. The nine-mile walk ahead of us might look healthy enough on the map, but it wouldn't be happening if it weren't for the Mariners' Inn at Nolton, not to mention the Preseli Arms beforehand.

The Preseli Arms further explains what to me is an inexplicable delay in starting. Meat pies and apple tarts scoffed, we hang around for no apparent reason. No one's having a second mug of tea.

'Why don't we go?' I ask, seeing a stray pillar of dark cloud teeter above Morgan's garden.

'We're leaving at four fifty, boy, and that's the end of it. Morg's worked everything out in his usual meticulous way.'

I defer. 'Morg' has walked to Northampton via Bosworth, and is known to regard the hundred miles east to Cardiff as a doddle. We are in the best possible hands. At four fifty sharp we leave. At five twenty-nine we arrive at the Preseli Arms, at the very moment a fat white hand turns round the 'Closed' sign.

'What did I tell you? Is this precision or isn't it?'

Morgan winks at me: 'We'll stop for a pint, then move on.'

The pint becomes two. 'Everything in moderation, including moderation.' There is much discussion about an aerial photograph of an early RAF jet. Other photographs depict an assortment of rugby teams. Then the talk turns to school, despite or because of an agreed moratorium on the subject. The question is: Has the Bubble Finally Burst? Can senior management survive another day, or has the will to teach at last been overcome by rampant bureaucracy, as promulgated by an arsehole government and in particular an arsehole Secretary of State for Education?

Nursing my drained half-pint of shandy I listen with only one ear. The anal epithets are not altogether inappropriate, since the teachers' gripe is precisely the amount of added paperwork that has been imposed from the top downwards upon their unacknowledgedly hardworking profession. What it's really about this time, though, is some Mary fight between two senior female staff members.

'Are we having another or what?'

Owens advances with empty tankard towards the bar.

'I think the sun's coming out again,' I counter. 'And anyway, aren't we being met at Nolton?'

It is as well that I table my motion. Wives and other women have been detailed to bring vehicles to the Mariners at a certain hour. A third pint would be the beginning of the end: it would certainly put the kybosh on any further legwork, while later on there would be female fury to contend with.

I receive thunderous dark looks. Nonetheless the acuity of my interception hits home.

'I agree,' says Chapman. 'Let's go.' The will to walk overcomes the beerocracy, and it is the policeman who leads us out of the inn.

We stick to the road. Since there's no other watering hole before the Mariners, the pace picks up smartly. Arms flailing, Morgan strides ahead, and Owens and Griffiths stride with him. Having broached the great educational debate, they are reluctant to relinquish it. I fall back with Chapman, the fittest member of the team.

Chapman impresses me not a little. Though he looks like a boxer from a lighter division, he is scarcely your average intellectually challenged cop. He exudes common sense and intelligence. Over hill and over dale he tells me what it was like to work in London as a bullet-stopper, and also some of the essentials of handling stake-outs and the armed siege. What he thinks is not what he has been told to think so much as what he thinks himself.

'And now you're back in Dyfed?'

'Yes. For the wife's sake and the kids'. I'm an ordinary copper again. Though of course there's scope for a firearms specialist here as well.'

'The IRA?'

Chapman nods warily. This was before the moonshine peace process. 'You'll have heard of the arms cache we discovered at Newgale?' he says by way of answer. 'But they keep a low profile around here. The Welsh coast is too important to them as a conduit to other parts of Britain. That, and I suppose a measure of Celtic solidarity. The

Special Branch has a presence at the ferry terminals, but doubtless there's a lot of traffic that goes through undetected. It's partly a question of manpower resources. The Dyfed-Powys constabulary though is a good force.'

'And the Welsh nationalists?'

The bullet-stopper smiles tightly. He knows, or at least suspects, I have more than a passing interest in this one.

'If you want to ask me how many Sons of Glendower there are, I don't know. They're not a priority problem though, and probably they're not very many. Even the fire-bombers of the 1980s must be getting on a bit now. In any case we're not much affected down here. It's much more mid and north Wales, from Cardigan upwards. At the moment they're pretty dormant. The policy is, when they do mount a campaign, deal with them then. After all, they're not interested in killing people. Rather the reverse. Holiday cottages when they're empty, and the odd town hall dustbin when everyone's gone home. Have you ever tried aikido?'

I take the hint and allow our man off the beat to change subject. Culturally at least I'm curious about the martial arts. It has always struck me as remarkable how the Japanese and other orientals have developed the body as a multi-articulated defensive-offensive weapons system. Something we westerners have rather neglected to do.

'Aikido could be very useful in police work, which is why I have trained myself in it, and encourage others to do so,' Chapman tells me. 'The point about it is it teaches you how to use the mass and violence of your opponent to his own disadvantage. That's very useful when you consider there's no guarantee that the copper will always be stronger than the punter. In many cases he's not, and simply has to rely on his uniform to get him through. Here, let me show you.'

Thus cautioned, I find myself immediately incapacitated as Chapman takes my left hand in a relatively simple hold in both his.

'What's so funny?'

What's funny is that I am walking along a lane in a remote part of the countryside and in effect I am holding hands with a policeman.

Up to that point I had lived in Wales six years, yet still I could not quite get used to it. But then I never can get used to wherever

I am. Existence anywhere is so odd, and if I found myself in similar circumstances in London's Hammersmith, where I was born, or Hanoi's Hong Gai Street, which I love beyond all other streets, walking hand in hand with an off-duty firearms expert, then the incitement to mirth would be exactly and irresistibly the same.

Ahead of us the road snakes up a steep hill, and at the top of the hill Owens, Morgan and Griffiths are silhouetted against the western burn. Like Shadrach, Meschach and Abednego they seem hellbent on something unusual. They are practically cantering.

'They're in sight of Nolton Haven,' Chapman says.

'And unless my name's Jeffrey Archer of the Mariners too.'

The brow of the hill confirms our hunch. When we reach it, the tails of the three best Welshmen ever are seen flicking backwards, fangs-of-a-Smith's-viper-wise, through the entrance of the said hostelry.

But now our party is beset by a double problem. In the saloon of the Mariners there are children playing pool. Kids and pints do not mix. Further, the Mariners, a good touring pub set in a declivity among the cliffs, looks out on a sea fairly aflame beneath a now fulsome evening sun. The coastal path beckons as it has never beckoned before. Ostentatiously I order a second half-pint of shandy, but in fact there is general concurrence with my viewpoint. Everybody is looking at his watch as Morgan suggests we decamp to Druidston and the Druidston Inn, a couple of miles southwards along the ineffably romantic rim of St Bride's Bay. Right boys, let's go.

And this is how it should be. The coastal paths of Pembrokeshire, in no small measure the inspiration of R. M. Lockley, the man who provided Richard Adams with rabbits, are world-class tracks. They add percentage points to any alcohol partaken before or after. The quiltwork patterns of the sea, the clamorous winds, the sweep out to the Atlantic, the Americas imagined beyond, the black vertical cliffs, the gullies and the ravines, the promontories and the headlands, all constitute a magisterial immensity inhabited by, among other aviators, buzzard, kestrel, peregrine falcon, the occasional red kite that has strayed from the north and, lower down among the rocks, oyster catcher, razorbill and kittiwake.

We file out from the Mariners, cross the road and join the path. Another steep climb and we are atop God's kingdom. On our right the sun, now a magnesium disc, hovering above a bruised band of cloud; behind us, beyond Nolton Haven, which is narrow, pocket sized, Rickets Head, beneath Black Cliff itself; to our left, protected by fences and dismal gorse, the unprofitable fields of farmsteads that never will be rich, for all the mechanization and Euro-subsidies that today are to hand; and in front of us, still bright, Madoc's Haven, and further up the shoreline, Haroldston Chins and Settling Nose.

This is a different kind of walking. There is no regularity to it. The path is never even. One eye at least must be kept on your feet, for the unguarded drop beside you is sometimes sheer, and sometimes comes to within inches of your shoes. Wooden turnstiles baldly advise 'Killer Cliffs' – each year claims its fatalities. Some are accidents, some not. It is always well to walk here with those you trust. Even a slight trough is likely to be filled with stepping stones that are caked with potentially lethal mud; while to cross a stream towards the base of a cliff demands goatlike agility. You don't have to fall from the heights for your head to split open like a mackerel.

The order of procession changes. Chapman leads, I struggle to keep up, Morgan and Griffiths bring up the rear, while Owens, his jacket tied around his waist, holds the middle. The two miles take forty minutes. At the end we come down to the beach at Druidston Haven, then take the steepest climb of all, up to the Druidston Inn perched bravely above. Only Chapman contrives not to break into a drenching sweat. But all this makes us a happy band. The Druidston – pronounced 'drew-son' – is as good a place to be as any on an early summer's night. Run by Rod, short and bearded, it is part hotel, part restaurant, part bar and part club. Phone calls to wives and women are made, then we settle in a snuggery, five drinking men, four on beer, myself on Jameson's Irish.

On the walls of the whitewashed parlour we have chosen are simple paintings redolent of the sea. Starfish in a spin, and a phallic mermaid. Even so, with six or seven rounds accounted for, it is not enough. At ten o'clock the women arrive and by half past ten we are travelling by car back to civilization, back to our houses, back to our beds.

'Shall we go to the Taberna and get pissed or what?' Owens nudges me.

'Yes, let's,' I reply, for there are things we must talk about. It'll be just he and I.

The Taberna, in the village of Herbrandston – stress on the first syllable – is, or was, one of those establishments that stay open for as long as its customers want it to stay open. Conversation can be and frequently is rough as rats, and there are sometimes present a couple of hairy unwashed louts whose only mission in life is to judge newcomers solely by their accents and make filthy comments in the very few Welsh words they know. It is also the only place I have seen the one-eared-elephant routine fully demonstrated, and that by a well-equipped if flaccid farmer who at the time was drinking with his sister. But if sensibilities are best left at the door, it can also be a college of alternative enlightenment. No one who wishes to speak ill of the bureaucracies that dominate our waking lives should miss out on a seminar in civic bile held nightly around the Taberna's wooden counter; any political party seriously committed to pulling out of Europe could do worse than instal a sound recorder there forthwith, to catch some handy slogans.

But not tonight. For the first time in living memory both bar and saloon are deserted. Nor is there any sign of either Nick the landlord or Jilly the quietly knock-out bargirl. A stand-in mooches behind the bar rolling a joint. Only John-Boy, who'd never dream of drinking elsewhere, sits with a glass.

'They're gone, gone utterly,' Owens says, impersonating W. B. Yeats. 'We'll go elsewhere instead. Call a taxi, and have one while you're waiting.'

In every session there's the drink that converts light-headedness into the roar of urgent but elusive thought, when truth breaks darkly from the glass.

'Don't you see what they're doing to us? All this crap about democracy and accountability. But it's them that's making us accountable. The situation isn't even symmetrical any more. Talk to the firemen, talk to the teachers, talk to the doctors, talk to the farmers even, everybody's been turned into a pen-pushing paper-bearer. Accountability, my backside. Whitehall rules, OK? Only now it's Brussels rules OK, and it's you and I who are the culprits. Get it?'

Before the taxi comes Owens and I manage two rounds. The stand-in barman finishes his reefer and tells John-Boy he's closing up, because there's a party at the Three Crowns and there's no point in him staying the night in Herbrandston. But at least now we know where to go.

The party at the Three Crowns, on the road back into Milford, is in honour of two local football teams and their molls. On the way in one of these latter endeavours to kiss me, then spoils it by mouthing, 'Fifty quid.' I disengage and scan the two adjoining rooms. Bodies are strewn everywhere, and in a dark area beyond dancers dance to a sodden beat. To my slight chagrin I see Nick the landlord and Jilly the barmaid standing in the middle of it all, hands clasped.

'Bloody hell, boy, have you heard?' Owens comes up, his shout to hand. 'The Tab's been sold!'

What's left of the evening, this threatens to destroy. I glance again at Nick and Jilly, and have a nasty vision of them living comfortably together in Lyme Regis on the proceeds. Still they are holding hands.

'That is bad news.'

'Bad news! It's a tragedy worse than Carthage. Probably it's some brewery. I can see it now, last orders at ten forty and on your bikes the lot of you at five past.'

There is reason for Owens to be shaken. As a teacher, most of the in-town pubs are out of bounds to him. It isn't seemly to be seen getting merry by sixth formers, let alone (as in Milford) third and fourth formers. For Owens the Taberna is not just a favoured watering hole, but a Friday necessity.

'It's the end, boy, I'm telling you, the end of life as we know it.'

His beer sucks down in three strong pulls.

'Here, I'll buy you another.'

I do so, then raft across to Nick and Jilly.

'Congratulations! I hear you've sold.'

Nick smiles down from his not inconsiderable fair-headed height. 'So everybody keeps telling me.'

Jilly says, 'I'm a lazy cow at heart.'

I say, 'But a very lovely one.'

Nick, affecting not to hear, grips her hand more tightly.

'The main thing,' I tell Jilly, 'is make sure you're well looked after.'

'There's always my parents,' she answers.

Has she or hasn't she understood me? Do I want her to understand me? Am I really so interested in her? Am I really so interested in anybody?

Commitment is what we prescribe for others, to provide more space for our own peradventures.

I return to Owens at the very moment he rediscovers his tongue.

'What an arsehole. I mean what a total arsehole.'

'Who? Nick?'

'No. Not 'im. Nor you neither. R. S. Thomas.'

Ianto Owens is a long-time friend who probably likes books more than I do. At any rate it is for each other's libraries that we leave our front doors open. He is also valleys Welsh. That is, he comes from the South, but is not to be confused with the denizens of the seaboard towns and cities, any more than he is to be confused with the predominantly rural, conservatively minded people of West Wales. A significant proportion of the southern urban population are 'incomers': that is, English and Scots, even Italians and Caribbeans, originally drawn to Cardiff and Newport and Swansea and other such places by the opportunities for employment and wealth-making that accompanied the industrial revolution. But the people in the valleys above the towns are more distinctively Welsh: the descendants of those who left rural Wales in the nineteenth century to supply the coal mines and metal factories with sweat and labour, and sometimes blood.

The son of an Ammanford coal man, Owens was brought up in a household that was still Welsh-speaking. He was also brought up on a diet of Sunday Schools and Working Men's Institutes. In his speech are embedded equal portions of the Bible and Lenin. Yet he stands apart from his background. The family was church, not chapel, a curious anomaly for Ammanford. The result? An intense dislike of any kind of cloth. Also, while all his primary-school mates went to the secondary, Owens went to the grammar. Later he was to work in Whitehall, in the Ministry of Defence, and marry an English-woman, the daughter of a wing commander. With his feet in many different camps there was a period of toing and froing before he turned teacher. Within his burly frame the fire remains, in his cups he is a great banger of drums, but daylight tempers his spirits. The futility of causes, including the causes he cherishes, is never far from his thoughts. The class struggle matters to him, in a 1930s sort of a way, but he also senses that sufficient unto the day is the evil thereof. He is full blooded, and at the same time packed solid with remorse.

It was from Owens I first learned the meaning of *crachach*, an all-important Welsh word used to denote, and thereby demean, the typical English or anglicized Welsh master type. Regularly we take the piss out of each other, but only so far. He can call me *crachach*, and I can tell him to stop rattling his leek. We laugh. But if I suggest that, for better or for worse, the Labour Party of Great Britain is the single most compelling reason why in the present century Welsh aspirations towards independence have been thwarted, the conversation is apt to sour. Owens is no nationalist, yet through and through he is Welsh: a mixed condition that, while not uncommon among his southern compatriots, wears the skin off his heart.

Tonight though he has another Welshman in his sights, one whose patriotism is less ambivalent. In our regular exchange of books, I have leant Owens my copy of R. S. Thomas's autobiography, *Neb*[1], meaning 'nobody' or 'no-person'. Because of a historic rift between south Walians and their northern counterparts, I am particularly interested in his opinion of it.

'So you've read it already?' I ask.

'Oh yeah. I'm almost at the end. It's hard work though. The writing's spare like a potato-picker's wage, and his language – well, it's not the Welsh I grew up with.'

'Meaning?'

'There's a lot of Gwynedd in it, but it's also high culture Welsh, BBC Welsh. Very precise, classical, but lacking in sinew.'

Owens looks dolefully at his glass, then finishes its contents.

'It's odd, I tell you. I don't know the man, I don't know many of his poems even, but I smell a rat. Almost a fascist rat, which is odder yet, because by his own admission Thomas is a pacifist.'

'Shall we have another, or shall we walk?'

'Let's walk, boy. I've had enough tonight.'

We leave the Three Crowns and make an unsteady way down the hill into Milford. It is after half past one in the morning, and the whiteness of a moon just past its prime is muffled by fog.

To avoid crossing Victoria Bridge and the climb up to Front Street beyond, we go further down, into the area of the docks. There we are stunned by the apparition of a three-masted schooner, the STA *Malcolm Miller*. Powerful lights from its deck illuminate its super-structure, but nonetheless the light is swallowed by the fog, so that the ship and its reflection might as well be floating in the darkness of outer space.

'Christ, what beauty!'

We lean over a railing to gaze. Then Owens musters breath and mounts a second charge.

'He has no time for the South, that's the trouble. For chrissakes, isn't that where the majority of us live? He likes the head of the Teifi valley, but nothing else. He has no sympathy for the great struggles that went on in Merthyr and Newport and all the other places. Has he never heard of the Fed?[2] I find it hard to trace his humanity, and I can't find any love for his fellow man at all. Jesus Christ, there's about two lines on Hitler, while there's two pages on the winter of 'forty-seven. You know what I'd like to do? Draw a time-line. On one side, all the great and important things that happened down here, and not just down here, but in Europe and beyond. On the other, the things that have preoccupied Thomas. Doesn't he understand how good men sweated and died in the valleys? Doesn't he know that Aneurin Bevan once walked this earth? The great things that were done in our lives, the education and health and housing reforms, and which we were a part of? Oh it wasn't just that we gave our allegiance to Labour. We were internationalists as well. Men went from the valleys to bloody die in Spain. OK, not very many, only a hundred and fifty or so, but how many went from the North? Where's all that in *Neb*? Where is his compassion for the common man? When Thomas goes abroad it's to birdwatch. And he insists on calling us a little people, a small people. And that's another thing. He recounts at one point having to listen to a dying man repeat himself over and over again, and pats himself on the back for it. But that's a priest's job, isn't it? To listen to our mortal repetitions? As if they didn't have enough of their own! The thing he dislikes most of all though is the English language. He says he is familiar with several languages, including Basque and Breton. But his venom is reserved for English. The *iaith fain*, he keeps calling it. The thin language. Well, I've heard that before. And I suppose compared to Welsh English is a bit thin on the ear, but I prefer it to the turkey gobbling I've heard in Bangor. What I can't understand though is, if he hates English so much why does he write his poetry in it?'

'Because he's a modernist,' I sport. 'Therefore consciousness itself is unendurable. I imagine he still thinks in English, therefore he hates it.'

'Oh bollocks, boy, bollocks!'

We continue staring at the schooner, which tomorrow will look plain ordinary, just as the high points of our over-oiled conversation will sink back into mere overstatement.

'Look, I don't know the man, okay? And I don't know the poetry, okay? All I know is that in *Neb* he writes about himself in the third person, which is odd, and he kicks off by saying – and I quote – that he was born a penny short of a shilling. So I shouldn't be saying these things, right?'

And then:

'Oh you're right, boy. We're not Italians in the rain, we're Sicilians in the drizzle. Thomas probably is a genius. Those lines of his that everybody quotes – 'an impotent people,/ Sick with inbreeding,/ Worrying the carcase of an old song'[3] – we're like that, I'm afraid. All of us. We love ourselves not wisely but too well. We won't let go the past. We have *hiraeth* where others have souls. And you know what *hiraeth* really means, don't you? The long hurt. The pain that comes of having a past like ours. Am I afraid to read the poetry? It might turn me into a bloody nationalist. But there was hope once. Oh there *was* hope. And I don't mean in Owain Glyndŵr's time. Not then, boy. I mean after the war, during my childhood, when Jerusalem was there for the taking.'

'Oh not that again!' I groan. In his cups Owens very often waxes torrential on the socialist paradise that could have been, but somehow never was.

'And why not?' Then Owens laughs. 'Have you forgotten already why the Cymry withdrew to Wales? Because we didn't approve of Saxon table manners!'

I look at my watch. Sure enough it is 2 a.m. Whenever Owens and I go drinking, and two o'clock comes round, then so too does the jest about Saxon table manners. Spot on the hour.

We thread our way through the docks towards our separate houses. Or rather I thread, while Owens, maddened with mirth, does a version of the soft shoe shuffle, Zorba in sneakers, endeavouring as he does so to teach me an old Welsh song about goats.

Three weeks later, 20 May, I drive through South Wales to Hay-on-Wye, for the opening day of the international literature festival there. For some years R. S. Thomas has inaugurated proceedings by reading his poems. This year, it is rumoured, may well be his last appearance. He is eighty-one and cannot continue these things indefinitely. To mark the occasion, two Thomas events are to be staged: a critical forum in the afternoon, and in the evening a double act with Lord Gowrie, Chairman of the (then) Arts Council of Great Britain.

By an unhappy coincidence, this 20 May is also the day of the funeral of the Labour Party leader John Smith. Taking the slow but entirely beautiful A40 from Carmarthen to Brecon, via Llandeilo and Llandovery, in preference to the faster and mainly loathsome M4, I am full of mixed feelings, divided loyalties. Smith, one thought, was exactly the man to furnish a resounding left-liberal triumph over stale and despotic Conservatives. He was sincere, unextremist, but persistent in what he believed right. He was also eminently clubbable. He was a lawyer with the common touch who nonetheless retained such virtues as the better of that profession have. He had what both his party and the country needed: the ability to bring people together. But now he was gone, and I felt the sort of queasy sorrow reserved for passing friends.

Should I have stayed at home, to rue the day? Smith's political and human qualities sharply contradict those of the man I am journeying to see. Still at the outset of my investigation into R. S. Thomas, I have already encountered aspects I strongly dislike. One poem in particular, as I drive along the often wooded and narrow road, keeps running through my head: 'The Small Window',[4] contained in his 1968 collection *Not That He Brought Flowers*. It is a short piece, just fourteen unrhymed lines varying between six and eight syllables in length; an example in fact of a Thomasian sonnet, a paring down of the traditional pentameters, arranged on the page as an octave followed by a sestet, with an abrupt and shocking gear-change between the two:

> In Wales there are jewels
> To gather, but with the eye
> Only. A hill lights up
> Suddenly; a field trembles
> With colour and goes out
> In its turn; in one day
> You can witness the extent
> Of the spectrum and grow rich
>
> With looking. Have a care;
> This wealth is for the few
> And chosen. Those who crowd
> A small window dirty it
> With their breathing, though sublime
> And inexhaustible the view.

Anyone who has spent any time at all in almost any part of the Welsh countryside will recognize at once the power and accuracy of Thomas's description. Because of the hilly and mountainous nature of Wales, extending in places to the very edge of the sea, there usually is a movement of clouds that generates a play of light that is wondrous to behold. This Thomas, rightly regarded as an exceptionally fine nature poet, captures with unerring precision and economy. The traditional props of formal rhyme are rendered wholly unnecessary. But it is the business in the sestet that causes the upset. The word 'chosen' tilts the whole poem violently onto a different plane. One moment we are admiring the view – indeed have been invited to do so. Our eye has been specifically directed. The next we are plunged into a vortex of political passion. In the context of other poems written at the same period, Thomas's first objective would seem to be the preservation of the Welsh landscape from the incursions of the tourist. The small window is unspecified, but could be the window of a bus or a train or a motor car or a caravan. And with that there is no great problem. Let the unspoilt remain unspoilt by all means. But it is the rest of it that gives offence. The 'chosen' few are presumably – although again Thomas declines to be specific here – the local residents, i.e. the Welsh-speaking Welsh whom Thomas habitually champions. Again, no very great problem with that, if everything were strictly on a first come, first served basis – though historically that is always likely to be a dubious proposition. But the word 'chosen' goes way beyond that. If someone is chosen, then they are chosen by someone, or at least by some entity (one can be chosen by a computer, or a lottery machine). But in fact the phrasing is near Biblical. It suggests a people chosen against all others (whose breath is dirty) by a markedly Old Testament God. And this sense is confirmed by the closing words: 'though sublime/And inexhaustible the view'. What is on offer is a version of paradise reserved for some and denied all others not even on any moral basis, but simply according to birth and provenance. As in the Bible, parts of the New Testament as well as the Old, God's favour is reserved for the members of one race only. And that sort of thinking, though it may be acceptable to some Bosnian Serbs, for most of us is not. Hence the implicit inhumanity of the poem. Thomas appears to be suggesting that paradise does after all exist, at least in an earthly manifestation; but that there is no point in the outsider contemplating it, because by his own breath the vision will be obscured. The outsider is damned ab initio.

Conversely, it is very difficult not to admire the compactness of the poem itself, the way the words are chosen and lie on the page.

Delicacy and wrath are superbly combined. Thomas, one must assume, knows what he is up to in every respect. Control of that calibre does not happen by chance. Considered purely as a *poem*, 'A Small Window' is a fine example of good workmanship.

And that is the problem, not only with Thomas, but with other poets as well: T. S. Eliot, for example, or Ezra Pound. At what point do we insist that what a poet says is at least as significant as the manner in which he (or she) says it?

Some schools of criticism, notably the structuralists and their progeny, downplay any overt or objective meaning in a work or corpus of work. Rather, examples of literature are seen as more or less sealed units which exhibit, as through a glass encasement, their own mechanism, their own dynamics. Meaning is internalized, so that it becomes no more than the hum generated by the interactive parts. While certain literary artefacts lend themselves to this approach more than others, if we protest that, where words are employed, this cannot be, for words have meanings outside of a poem, then we are likely to be told: to be sure, that is correct; but language itself is just such another example of an enclosed system. Outside of itself, or outside the community that uses it, it has no objective meaning. Everything is a matter of interactive dynamics. Further, each reader, each human, has his or her own value or meaning system, so that a poem is never the same in two sets of different hands. Why bother, therefore, to elucidate its 'meaning'?

This regression can go on a long time, until finally it becomes futile. In the end the whole of the observable universe is reduced to a self-contained language laboratory, where no meaning can ever have more than relative purchase. While there may be some descriptive accuracy in that, indeed there must be, I prefer a more realist view. Languages, whether verbal or constructed out of a sign system, are conventions. They may change, they may admit of nuance, they may be susceptible to all sorts of bending of their rules, but they are essentially compacts agreed to by the individuals who use them. Otherwise they would not exist. But it is the fact that they can be used, and are used, that gives the lie to the more extreme claims of the structuralists.[5] Inevitably, between readers, with their different backgrounds and different experiences, there will occur differences of response to a given text. But there will be many more similarities, and humanity itself is demeaned (choose your sense here!) if we preclude the possibility of actual transactions mediated through the written, or for that matter the spoken, word.

I can imagine a world in which structuralist and post-structuralist shibboleths do hold good, but I do not imagine it is the world I inhabit; nor is it the world I would choose to inhabit. Linguistic and cultural 'systems' certainly exist, but they are prone to interpretation and interference by other such systems. They are finally limited only in the sense that they belong among the human race.

This realist interpretation of language and literature however imposes two obligations. It imposes the obligation to acknowledge areas of uncertainty in the matter of meaning, generated precisely by differentiated reader responses; and it imposes the obligation to articulate our own character as readers; or, for that matter, as writers.

These obligations determine perhaps the legitimate scope and necessary application of criticism. Without such criticism we will indeed live in a world crowded with mutually unintelligible sign systems masquerading as languages.

So it is with a cultural 'artefact' such as Thomas's poem 'The Small Window'. We are at liberty to respond to it as we may. This includes giving it a response based on what is apprehended as its primary or direct meaning. But we are also constrained to look further into it. What cultural traditions, we should ask, are at work? What is the psychology behind it? Is there a possibility that the meaning the poet attaches to his words is radically different from the one we attach? Is 'The Small Window' in fact and necessarily as odious as it seems? Or is it the case, as often is the case in poetry, of halfway houses?

From Brecon I take the Hereford road. I am now in the heart of the Welsh Marches, the borderland between Wales and England, here and in May a landscape of unsurpassed languor. Later, in the evening, thin mists nudging against trees and woodlands dressed in their finest muslins will suggest something oriental in their watercoloured delicacy.

When I arrive at Hay-on-Wye it is still only lunchtime. This is my first visit to the mother of all secondhand book marts, and the effect is disconcerting. There is no joy in browsing among several hundreds of thousands of items, when you know that what you are looking for must be there somewhere, and that if you don't find it then the fault is entirely yours. There can be no conceivable valour in telling your friends, Look what I found at Hay; only the not finding of anything would be remarkable. With its dumpy castle and inflated prices, it is worse even than Bath, say, or Pisa, at the height of the season.

It is also my first visit to the festival. Above the town many marquees, all of them white, are sensibly laid out in a field. The logo of the sponsoring newspaper, *The Independent*, flutters everywhere, and there is no shortage of bar pavilions. About it all is something medieval, though the serious jousting takes place under canvas. Since I had half-expected that events would be staged in decommissioned chapels, I am, in this respect, agreeably surprised.

At 2.30 p.m. I file into a middle-sized marquee. In all there are about forty people in the audience, seated on hard wooden seats banked up on scaffolding. These include, at the high rear, R. S. Thomas himself, accompanied by two women who cannot be much younger than himself. Although his face is obscured by shadows, it is instantly recognizable from the photographs on account of its cragginess, its tension, and the seeming absence of humour.

There are three speakers on the small, lit platform. These are M. Wynn Thomas, a senior lecturer[6] in the English department at Swansea University, and an acknowledged academic authority on R. S. Thomas; to his right, Jason Walford Davies, a younger lecturer in the Welsh department at Bangor; and to his left John Davies, a gifted 'Anglo-Welsh' poet.

It would perhaps have been more daring to have had at least one non-Welsh speaker on the podium, someone to represent either the English view of R. S. Thomas, in both its negative and positive aspects; or, since Hay purports to be an international festival, the wider international response. Because of this oversight on the organizers' part the session, through no fault of its participants, is a little constrained in its horizons. Yet as M. Wynn Thomas will later tell me, the business of conveying Thomas's stature to the world outside Wales very often is a thankless task. 'Sometimes', he said, 'I feel I can do no more than listen to my own voice inside an echo chamber.'

What he doesn't say is that the poet himself scarcely makes his task any the easier. Literary genius and uncompromising attitudes not infrequently go together, but seldom in the stark doses administered by R. S. By dwelling almost incessantly on Wales as a small country he makes it difficult for his fellow countrymen publicly to discuss his work without themselves appearing restricted. It shouldn't be so, and yet it is. The gold of contemporary Anglo-Welsh letters is also its liability. To cherish that gold can too easily become to guard that gold.

On this occasion however the Swansea heavyweight leaves his woes at home. M. Wynn Thomas is a gifted presenter. He has the ability not only to steer debate productively, but he is also good, exceedingly good, at speaking *ad lib*. He disarms dissent by drawing attention to it at the outset. He kicks off by in fact quoting a number of mainly hostile English repsonses to R. S. Thomas, as though to warn his audience to beware of literary establishments of any nationality. These include Peter Reading's well-known bitch from his review of *Ingrowing Thoughts*[7] in the *TLS* of 3 October 1986: 'The work is nicely, and probably expensively, produced by Poetry Wales Press with the financial support of the Welsh Arts Council – a measure of parochial wealth and chauvinism.' Donald Davie's remark about R. S. having gone out of his way 'to disappoint and offend the reader's ear' is also recalled. But the purpose of these quotations is in fact antiphrastic. M. Wynn Thomas, black haired and bespectacled, reads them out with a wry smile, then dismisses them with a smile even more wry. As if to say, Well really! I am quite prepared to be open minded about our subject, I am a neutral chairperson, but if this is the best that R. S.'s adversaries can come up with, then . . . let's get on with the real business!

The real business is absorbing. John Davies, fifty years old and a teacher in Prestatyn, is particularly impressive. He was born in the south though, in Glamorgan. The face is large and reddish, almost that of a sergeant-major. The accent is slightly burred, the result of a long stay in America. He scores immediate points by declaring his inability to find much meaning in most of Dylan Thomas's verse. R. S. Thomas, he rightly insists, carries meaning on his sleeve. His theme is R. S. Thomas's bird imagery.[8] The poetry, we are reminded, is riddled with birds, and Thomas's observation of them is always precise. We should note, for instance, how R. S. very often distinguishes between males and females of bird species. Birds for Thomas are never mere poetic ornaments. In the end rather Thomas's birds become so much a part of his quest for God that at times God perhaps is a bird, or most like a bird, as in the poem 'Sea-watching':

> Ah, but a rare bird is
> rare. It is when one is not looking,
> at times one is not there
>   that it comes.[9]

But Davies's address is not that of the scholar who has carefully annotated every instance of bird-occurrence in the work of R. S. T. and printed out a concordance. It is the address of a man at once passionate and coherent about his subject. The proof of this is when, closing his eyes and swallowing great draughts of air, he recites two or three exemplars of Thomas's poetry from memory, injecting real blood into lines usually prized for their sparseness, their intellectually contrived anaemia even.

That is refreshing. M. Wynn Thomas gently chides him for his animadversions towards Dylan Thomas, saying he is being 'perhaps discourteous', but Davies stands his ground. His reason for mentioning Dylan at all, he says, is to draw our attention to the overwhelming virtue of R. S.: 'It is rare to come across a poet who is at once so suggestive and so visually clear.'

I know I shouldn't, but even so I do. I sneak a quick glance over my shoulders to see how the man himself reacts to this compliment. But R. S.'s expression hasn't changed one iota. It is still completely adamantine.

The younger academic, Jason Walford Davies, son of a well-known professor, spruce in jacket and tie, makes a few interesting points about *Neb*, Thomas's 1985 autobiography, which the programme notes tell us he is translating into English.[10] The Welsh word, *neb*, doesn't only mean 'nobody' or 'no person', it can also mean, like the French '*ne personne*', anybody. The book therefore combines universality with humility. This, however, neatly evades the question as to why R.S. wrote an autobiography in the first place. In fact, like most literary autobiographies, *Neb* is a species of special pleading, of personal propaganda, however rarefied. Nor does Jason Walford Davies consider adequately the book's real idiosyncrasies, which are that it is written in the third person, that at several points R.S. delivers himself of his rancour against not only the English language but also the English people (despite the fact that the childhood described was an exclusively English-speaking childhood); and that also vigorously attacked is the poet's mother. In respect of which last the platform, after some light-hearted deliberation, opts for the psychoanalytic recipe that R.S. Thomas's 'fierce independence of mind' can be accounted for by the young poet's ability to stage a successful rebellion against a dominating parent.

Thomas's most celebrated, and most distasteful, assault on his mother is, however, far more interesting than that. This occurs in the poem 'It Hurts Him to Think'.[11] One by one the English arrive in Wales to destroy its language, and one by one the Welsh submit. Thus the 'heiresses' fall for the 'velvet businessmen/ of the shires'; thus the peasantry is boxed in by fences made of 'the bones of heroes'. Finally, the vampire industrialists are discovered

> burrowing
> in the corpse of a nation
> for its congealed blood,

But Thomas does not leave this strongly worded lament for the demise of the Welsh language at that. He concludes with an equally forceful personal statement:

> I was
> born into the squalor of
> their feeding and sucked their speech
> in with my mother's
> infected milk, so that whatever
> I throw up now is still theirs.

In a way these are brave lines, because Thomas is acknowledging that what he laments is not unequivocally his to lament. To be robbed of a language before one is born is a strange state of affairs, and the poet does not shy away from its implications. There is something too of Joyce's description of Ireland as 'the old sow that eats her farrow'.[12] But if it is Thomas's intention to personify Wales as a mother, *the* mother, it fails. The word 'my' takes us off in another direction, and we are left wondering whether the poet might not have found some other means to express his wound. As it is we are given the subliminal, though admittedly powerful, image of his mother's breast discharging poison. As the lines stand, Thomas's willingness to sacrifice his parent's integrity on the altar of a compromised nationalism does discredit to his views about the unquestionably tragic decline of the Welsh tongue.

In fact, the mother's 'infected milk' may very well refer to an episode in Thomas's infancy. As he tells us in the opening paragraph of *Neb*, he contracted meningitis soon after birth. But there is nothing in the poem itself which tells us this. If the reference is to this illness, is it fair of Thomas to resort to a scrap of personal history that remains concealed? Is it not hubris to expect the reader to have read his autobiography, which is in Welsh, before coming to the poem, which is in English and was in any case written before *Neb*? Instead, in the unmediated poem, the 'infected milk' becomes a pejorative reinforcement of the 'sucked' speech. The English poison is extruded by the mother, but ingested by the son. By such means Thomas achieves a conflation of two strong dislikes: his dislike of English, for all that it is the tongue he writes his poetry in; and, here, an equally strong dislike for his parent, whose child he nonetheless is. Had his mother been properly Welsh, the inference is, and had she been able to suckle the poet with the Welsh language, then all might have been well.

As it is, even in his sixty-first year, when the poem was published in the collection *What is a Welshman?*, the outcome of Thomas's alleged rebellion against his mother is still uncertain. Indeed, expressed in the conflationary terms supplied by the poet, and given that Thomas's publicized anxieties about the Welsh and English languages have continued to the present day, it may be more apt to suggest that any such rebellion has been an on-going and finally unresolved affair; an aspect, indeed, of the poet's furious interiors.

But today in Hay we have come to cherish Thomas. The afternoon session comes to a halt after two hours, which leaves three-and-a-half before the evening event. Part of this time I spend in Hay itself, but inevitably I am drawn back to the literature encampment rather before I need return there. In a beer tent two young men from Cardiff sit at my table, engineers I think. Like me they have come to the festival specifically to see R. S. Their enthusiasm for him knows no bounds, yet is also entirely innocent. When I ask them what it is about his poetry that appeals to them, the more talkative replies: 'He uses words so simply and so powerfully.' But does it go beyond that? What about Wales, the Welsh language, all that? They shake their heads. No. It has nothing to do with that. It is just the quality of his lines. The fact that they are in English, but often about Wales, is neither here nor there. And they are so pleasant, these two young fellows from Cardiff, that I cannot imagine they are telling me anything other than their real feelings.

My drink finished, there is still time before the evening show. I walk across therefore to the tent that is a temporary bookshop. There is a shelf-ful of Thomas, but to my annoyance all the titles it contains are ones I already own. Since the bookshop knows its festival business however, I am not entirely disappointed. Also for sale are one or two volumes by John Davies. Having been impressed by his performance on stage, I open a book to see if I am as impressed by his performance on paper. But before I can be impressed, I am startled:

'How to Write Anglo-Welsh Poetry'

It's not too late, I suppose . . .
You could sound a Last Post or two,
and if you could get away with saying
what's been said, then do.

First, apologise for not being able
to speak Welsh. Go on; apologise.

Being Anglo-*anything* is really tough;
any gaps you can fill with sighs.

And get some roots, juggle names like
Taliesin and ap Gwilym, weave
A Cymric web. It doesn't matter what
they wrote. Look, let's not be naive.

Now you can go on about the past
being more real than the present –
you've read your early R. S. Thomas,
you know where Welsh Wales went.

Spray place-names around. Caernarfon.
Cwmtwrch. Have, perhaps, a Swansea
sun marooned in Glamorgan's troubled
skies; even the weather's Welsh, see.

But a mining town is best, of course,
for impact, and you'll know what to say
about Valley Characters, the heart's dust
and the rest. Read it all up anyway.

A quick reference to cynghanedd
always goes down well; girls are cariad;
myth is in; exile, defeat, hills . . .
almost anything Welsh and sad.

Style now. Nothing fancy; write
all your messages as prose then chop
them up – it's how deeply red and green
they bleed that counts. Right, stop.

That's it, you've finished for now –
just brush the poems down: dead, fluffed
things, but your own almost. Get
them mounted in magazines. Or stuffed.[13]

One Welshman to another? Davies satirizes far more than just R. S. Thomas; a whole school of writing, no less, as the title implies. Nonetheless, it is Thomas who sits in the centre of the squib, and, aside from the girls who are *cariad*, nearly everything in it can be made to refer to something or other in the Thomas canon.

Not for the first time I pause to ask myself: is Thomas really worth the pursuit? One of his more salient characteristics is his utter *seriousness*; and it is this, inter alia, that Davies's stanzas hit at so palpably.

Thomas cannot leave anything alone, but worries it to the bone. This is the central compulsion of his literary personality. Although he is not bereft of wit, indeed Thomas as an old man sometimes displays an astonishing agility in that department, seriousness is the sea he sails and the air he flies.

This is another aspect that distances him from the contemporary world, the common ruck. There, the serious isn't altogether outlawed but, in literary culture at least, it is constantly cut down to size. Poets should be humorous betimes, and few 'serious' novelists can afford not to be. Thomas, by contrast, abides by a high-mindedness that is modernist, but is not post-modernist. What interests him is all-important; if it doesn't, or isn't, he banishes it from his attention. He is the very opposite of someone like, say, Anthony Burgess, who was prepared to be interested in anything.

It occurs to me, as I re-read John Davies's 'How to Write Anglo-Welsh Poetry' in a tent in Hay, that I may have made a quite appalling error by contracting to spend the next year or two of my life endeavouring to learn something about someone who probably would have nothing but contempt for many of the things that furnish me with at least a passing joy: the music of Louis Armstrong, for instance, or dining out in Soho, or watching a well-scripted sitcom on telly.

On the other hand: Exile the serious, and I banish my deeper self. Such depth may be illusory, a mere will-o'-the-wisp phantomed by the lenses of the poet or poets I read; but to act upon that negative assumption – as so much contemporary culture encourages me to do – is also a form of deprivation. Two thousand years on from the best of the Greeks, we still haven't unravelled who was right: the Epicureans or the Stoics, the Dionysians or the tragedians.

The Midland Marquee, named after the bank, is packed out when I re-enter it shortly before 7 p.m. Outside the temperature has fallen, and a fine Welsh mist is unfurling; but inside is warmer than before, thanks to the heat generated by three or four hundred bodies. I am lucky to find a seat a few rows from the platform. Behind me a woman with a refined voice actually says, 'I do like poetry readings – people don't go to them to be seen', while in front of me, amid a clutch of celebrities, I observe that the best-groomed is John Birt, Director General of the BBC. This is no poems-and-pints affair at a pub down the road, but an occasion for cultural mandarins to scrutinize a living legend.

Beneath the lights there are just two chairs now, one for Thomas, the other for Lord Gowrie, who, as supremo of the Arts Council of Great Britain, is cultural mandarin-in-chief. Gowrie, an Anglo-Irish aristo, enters first. Despite the Robin Day bow-tie, he is the very image of your noble dashing lord. He is also claret-voiced, a little eggy even. One recalls that he is himself a poet. How it is that Thomas can share a platform with this member of the Establishment beggars belief, except that – and here is another 'contradiction' – old R.S. is known to quite like social elites. It is the middle classes he cannot abide.

About Gowrie the individual I know nothing. In one respect at least, however, he commands my admiration. He is prepared, this evening, not only to read some of Thomas's poems with the poet sitting just a few feet away from him, but also to challenge Thomas on some of his perceived contradictions. He doesn't read Thomas particularly well: the way he treacles some of the lines suggests he hasn't entirely got the measure of the man; and some of his questions are a touch too diplomatic, as though they had been prepared by a civil service secretariat apprised of the possible consequences of rubbing Thomas up the wrong way. The overall impression he creates is one of blandness. But courageously he has a go. Some of the distinguished audience have come a long way to be here, and Gowrie won't let them depart empty-handed.

By contrast Thomas betrays no eagerness to please whatsoever. His projected persona is exactly as anyone who knows anything about him would anticipate. Therefore he pleases. His face, while always concentrated on whatever issue is to hand, is thoroughly implacable. He is the stone man in a flannel suit. He acknowledges those who have come to see him and listen to him without so much as a glance.

28

Conceivably he is monumentally shy. Sometimes, when he shifts in his chair, he exhibits the ungainly movement of the truly old. His legs are long and incredibly thin. His hair is wispy and very white. The ears though, in their hugeness, are blazing red. As is his tie. His blazing red tie must have been chosen. *Y ddraig goch?*

As well as the two chairs there is a lectern. Thomas and Gowrie will take it in turns to read some of Thomas's poems. Then they will sit in their chairs and discuss broad themes. Gowrie gets up and addresses us. Thomas stares at his feet. He has heard or read this patter too often before. Sometimes the muscle twitches in his jowl. Then it is his turn. He shuffles some loose papers in his hands, and stands. With a minimum of introductory comment he recites some recent poems. Poems that have yet to be published in a collection.

But of course it is impossible to focus on the poems. The voice is what we have been waiting for. And the voice astonishes.

It astonishes not because it is either particularly strong or particularly rich. On the contrary it is a palpably aged voice, a dry leaf of a voice. There is fine cadence, but the cadence is the cadence of weariness, of exhaustion. But this is not why it astonishes. It astonishes because its pedigree is so utterly . . . English. And I mean an upper-middle-class English of thirty or forty years ago. It is like listening to Alec Guinness reading late Eliot.

The topics are lined up one by one. Wales, poetry, the countryside, science, his ministry in the church, God, love. And Thomas's responses are the obiter dicta of a sphinx. Granules of granite. 'Wales? Wales has become something of the mind. I am a romantic. Wales began as something tangible, but it became under modern conditions something of a wraith. Which is why I turned to bird-watching.' 'We have nothing else but our language.' And he quotes T. H. Parry Williams: 'God help me, I cannot escape from Wales.'[14]

Gowrie: 'But you can be pretty politically incorrect about the English?' Thomas: 'If you are defending a minority you have to be extreme. If you start prevaricating you collapse into amorphic . . .' (Someone behind me coughs.) 'I think Yeats and Joyce were a disaster for Irish culture. They did more harm to the Irish than the English would ever have done.'

Science? 'I find it very difficult to fit a previous concept of God into this context.' 'We need to be more austere.' 'There is a need for clear questions.' 'I find it very difficult to believe in a personal God. I have been too influenced by certain thought. Hinduism, Buddhism . . .' And love? 'I don't know what love is. It was never one of my priorities. It's there, obviously, but I don't know I was ever taught what love is. So there is always a certain bitterness or irony when I deal with it.' 'We can be so terribly self-conscious in the late twentieth century. I imagine love is without self-consciousness.'

And: 'A poet is allowed to contradict himself.'

Thomas is the last of the modernists. But whereas Yeats and Pound and Eliot and Beckett are dead, Thomas is not. Liveth the youngest ancient yet.

In Rome once I watched Alberto Moravia endeavour to hold court in similar fashion. The circumstances were rather less formal. We were in a warehouse, and all we had to sit on were packing-cases. Moravia's audience, young Italian poets and writers, boys and girls, were ranged around him in a circle. They fired questions at him, and he attempted the lapidary reply. After a while though Moravia grew fed up with proceedings, or ran out of answers. So he began giving the same answer to every question. What did he think of the theatre of the absurd? 'O, le banalità convenzionali.' But what about Pinter? You know the work of Harold Pinter? 'O si. Signor Pinter. Le banalità convenzionali.'

Perhaps Moravia had decided to dish up an example of the theatre of the absurd by way of explication. What he achieved was less than any banality, conventional or otherwise. He came across as being, on that occasion, merely lazy-minded; a view several of his critics would endorse apropos his novels.

But not so Thomas. On the surface, through the tones of his voice, laconic to the point of entombment. But inside, one felt, he was still wrestling away. Never giving an inch unless he had to, and even then as often as not not giving it.

A seeker after truth? Of course. But also a dissimulator of sorts. 'I don't know what love is. It was never one of my priorities.'

I quote the last poem contained in his *Collected Poems*, which is also to be found in *Mass for Hard Times* (1992), and called 'A Marriage'. It was written some time after the demise of his wife, which occurred in 1991:

> We met
>> under a shower
> of bird-notes.
>> Fifty years passed,
> love's moment
>> in a world in
> servitude to time.
>> She was young;
> I kissed with my eyes
>> closed and opened
> them on her wrinkles.
>> 'Come' said death,
> choosing her as his
>> partner for
> the last dance. And she,
>> who in life
> had done everything
>> with a bird's grace,
> opened her bill now
>> for the shedding
> of one sigh no
>> heavier than a feather.

Since the Romantic epoch at least it is taken as granted that the self and its responsive aspects are allowable literary subject-matter. Were it not so, our literature would be denuded of much that is best in its poetry; the finest productions of Wordsworth, Byron, Shelley and Keats, for example, or of Yeats and Emily Dickinson, would be disallowed. Of the Romantic movement itself, relatively little of worth would be left.

Of course, there is also a great and glorious tradition of public, impersonal poetry: the epic poets apart, one has only to think of Dryden, Swift, Pope, most of Tennyson, Robert Graves, W. H. Auden. Without their major work too the language would be disastrously impoverished. But what is also true is that few poets of either category are immune to displays of hubris. Indeed, hubris seems part of the poet's stock-in-trade, whatever mode or genre he or she writes in. But particular problems arise when the poet assumes a licence if not to parade himself before his reader, then at least to assume that his self and his life are objects of particular interest, whether or not the self revealed is a true self, or an adopted, even fabricated, persona – and in most cases the poetic self would seem to lie somewhere between these two. The poetic character may be at odds with the known personality as he or she is actually perceived by others: the poet located in daily life. But within the creative process the self that the poet 'projects' is also the self that is discovered; and the whole personality therefore becomes germane to the interest that the poet, and not the reader, has originally proposed by the act of publication.

With Thomas, this issue is acute. Take for example 'A Marriage', the poem quoted in its entirety above – by no means the most egocentric of Thomas's poems. Indeed its surface feel and mood are almost fiercely anti-egotisitical. Its ostensible theme is the transience of human love, even humankind, within the passage of time; and the poet's presence is balanced and reduced by the poem's descriptive concentration on the woman and the marriage itself. The only suggestion of particular character occurs when the departed woman is remembered as one who comported herself 'with a bird's grace' – a beautiful compliment regardless of whether the reader is aware of the poet's lifelong obsession with and passion for birdlife. But the phrase has more than elegaic potency. It sets up the metaphoric imagery for the poem's climax, or denouement, the death no less, while also returning the reader to the opening proposition:

> We met
> > under a shower
> of bird-notes.

The entire marriage is presented within a wholly natural comprehension: the substitution of one species by another reinforces the central idea of the tyranny of time, acting through nature; or the tyranny of nature acting through time. In addition, there is the contraction of two different time-spans into one. There is the human time-span:

we are told that the duration of the marriage was 'Fifty years', and this certainly implies participants of a yet greater longevity; while 'grace' suggests a species of bird far more short-lived; so that one subliminal import is the notion that it actually doesn't matter how long a life or a marriage is, it is still over in the twitch of an eye.

One could say a great deal more about 'A Marriage'. There are touches of assonance and consonance and alliteration; but the only formal prosodic device is the alternation of short lines, each second line indented to give a push-and-pull effect. And then there is the burning brevity of the piece: twenty-two lines, but a mere seventy-three words, almost as though the poet's lifelong dedication to economy of expression had been a preparation for this one defining outburst of superbly controlled anguish.

By any standards then 'A Marriage' is a remarkable composition, not least because, regardless of whether all its nuts and bolts are taken apart and reassembled, it is its power to move that marks it out as one of the great love poems. Yet why is this so? Partly I think because, unlike the great run of love poems, it does not idealize the woman at a particular stage in her development, either at the adolescent flowering of her beauty or during a midlife fulfilment of that beauty and its attendant personality. This is not an address to Chloë, or Amaryllis in the shade (or, these days, the shed). It is an elegy to an actual woman known over a period of time. Beauty is there, in the 'bird's grace', but so too are 'her wrinkles'. Rather, the true object of the love expressed is the constancy and abidingness of the relationship. There is the feeling that for once the vows have been kept; that the marriage really has endured for better or for worse, in sickness and in health; even, that to talk of love outside such parameters is an error; that love is the end-product, and not an enabling initiator.

That is not to say 'A Marriage' is in any overt or narrow way a religious poem, according to conventional Christian mores. On the contrary it is only religious if we allow a certain pantheism of attitude on the part of the poet. But what can be remarked is the poem's sincerity, a sincerity that is vouched not, as is the case with so many love poems, by an overflowing of affective emotion, but by the retention of the poet's intellectual self. The deceased woman is not reified as an object of desire; rather she is reified as an object of the mind. The final tone of the poem is a coming together of an almost classical coldness, an abstraction into art, with a revelation of utter privacy, so that one does indeed wonder why it is published.

After the evening event at Hay-on-Wye I took the A40 back to Dyfed. By night the pleasant wooded road became something else. It was a long phantasmagoric channel I navigated principally by adhering to the tail-lights of the car in front. Sometimes we hit a wad of fog. My impression was that I was travelling a great deal faster than when I had taken the same route in the morning. Whenever I looked at the speedometer, though, I saw that I was going a great deal slower. The journey therefore had a ghastly interminability about it. Surely, I thought, this is the work of a local sorcerer, or *swynwr*. More, the sorcerer was obviously at the wheel of the vehicle ahead. Soon after Brecon he lowered his exhaust pipe, so that at the slightest unevenness on the road a burst of sparks flew towards my windscreen. Was this a ploy to get me to back off? But if I backed off I would be swallowed up in a wad of fog with no way out. Then the sorcerer's three most dreadful accomplices, summoned from Black Mountain, would spring out of briars big as ferris-wheels and gobble me up.

The real mischief however awaited me at home. The poet James Fenton had left a message on my answering machine. Or rather, a command. 'Okay, Wintle,' the message said, 'you're coming to a party in Oxford on June 14th.' Although Fenton and I were up at Magdalen College together in the late '6os, our post-Oxford encounters have been few and far between. Until I returned Fenton's call therefore I was puzzled by the invitation. Fenton asked whether I had ever collected an MA.[15]

'No,' I replied. 'I didn't bother with my BA either.'

'Never mind. Come to the party anyway.'

The penny dropped. Fenton was hoping to become Professor of Poetry and he was canvassing votes. Several thoughts passed swiftly and feelingly through my mind. The first was, You've got a nerve, mate. The second was: If I were standing in the same election then probably I too would invite all my college contemporaries to a party on election day. Thirdly: Is this a party I want to miss? Fourthly: Is this a party I can afford to miss? For if *i glitterati* weren't handsomely represented chez Fenton then it was difficult to imagine where else they might be so represented. It would be a good opportunity to sound out current thinking about R. S. across the border.

Thus I soon found myself taking the A40 eastwards again, on my way to Cumnor, three or four miles outside Oxford. Fenton's election junket was a very large do indeed, commensurate with the multi-acre site that, blessed with a seven-figure fortune derived from *Les Misér-ables* the musical, he has been busy turning into a formal garden. The riddle of which of two similar stone houses belonged to him was quickly resolved. They both did. One was his residence, the other his library. On a lawn between them stood another marquee, my second of the summer. There was good food and wine everywhere, and an awful lot of *i glitterati* chewing and swilling. I had come to the right place. Clearly Fenton had decided to spend the whole of his first year's stipend as Professor of Poetry on feeding the loyal cohort, even though the result of the contest was not due to be declared until later in the day.

I begin to circulate. As I do so, the gathering bifurcates; or rather, trifurcates. Among Fenton's guests are several of my contemporaries whom I have kept up with, and whom it is always a pleasure to see again. Then there are the worthies, people with names like Malcolm Bradbury and John Carey and Jonathan Miller. And thirdly there is another tranche of contemporaries, whom I have not kept up with, and whom, as I now rediscover, it is not such a pleasure to meet.

In a sense I am back where I belong. I am among those by whom and with whom I was educated. Yet the more I circulate, the more a feeling of outsiderhood encroaches upon me. All the time at the back of my mind is Wales, or at least the south-western part of Wales I live in. Culturally as well as geographically Oxford is at the centre of England, and therefore by extension of Britain. But Oxford is also a hothouse of vanities. The egotism of its denizens is meticu-lously rehearsed. Their exotropic eyes roam restlessly on each other's shoulders as they scan the scene for bigger names. And this I never cared for. It was one of the factors, conscious or otherwise, that took me westwards across the border. Saxon table manners, you could say.

35

Paradoxically it is the actual bigger names who make the afternoon tolerable. The Bradburys, Careys and Millers of this world are, or at least appear to be, unaffected by the more visible symptoms of the Oxford distemper. I ask them their views on R. S. Thomas – of course, what or who else? – and they respond willingly and gladly. Their eyes do not look through you or beyond you, but at you. Figures who in my youth were unapproachable deities turn out to be companionable and fun.

And so, nursing an inner discombobulation, I conduct and advance my inquiry. The most telling exchange is with a former tutor, the poet and novelist John Fuller, whom I find sitting on a bank of grass a little apart from the throng.

'What's your opinion of him then?' I ask.

'Thomas? Some of the poems are very good . . .'

'But?'

'I feel threatened by him.'

Just that, no more, no less. But then I should have remembered. Fuller owns a holiday cottage in north-west Wales, and Welsh holiday cottages owned by the English are among R. S. Thomas's most cherished bêtes noires. His refusal to condemn outright the fire-bombers of the 1980s has been understood by some as tacit condonement.

The result of the election was announced shortly before 4 p.m. Fenton had won by a mile. The three other candidates were nowhere. All afternoon he had played the joyous host, his massive, bald head, balanced precariously on top of an increasingly curious physique, beaming in every direction. Now those around him beamed back. He had conquered, he had triumphed. He *was* the Oxford Professor of Poetry. He had even cocked a snook at his acknowledged mentor, W. H. Auden. Auden was forty-eight when the same honour befell him. Fenton was forty-five.

Auden, however, was scarcely Fenton's only illustrious predecessor. Immediately before him was the Irish poet Seamus Heaney, and in our time as undergraduates the Professor of Poetry was Roy Fuller, John Fuller's father. Auden himself had been succeeded by Robert

Graves, in 1961. But perhaps the figure most enduringly associated with the chair is Matthew Arnold; and it was a series of lectures Arnold gave during his ten-year tenure,[16] published in book form in 1867 as *On the Study of Celtic Literature*, that finally brought Welsh-language literature within the pale of English academic respectability, after more than a century of antiquarian interest. But if the way had already been prepared by Lady Charlotte Guest's appealing three-volume translation of the *Mabinogion* (1846), as well as by Thomas Stephens's *The Literature of the Kymry* (1849), and if Arnold's lectures led, as they were intended to lead, to the creation (in 1877) of a Celtic chair at Oxford, the first of its kind in Britain, *On the Study of Celtic Literature* was a curious, even distasteful performance for a luminary whose ideas and theories still provide points of departure in contemporary literary and cultural curriculae.

The writing of *On the Study of Celtic Literature* occurred during the period when Arnold was in the throes of his campaign against 'Philistinism'. Prefiguring the 'two cultures' debate prompted by C. P. Snow a century later, in *Culture and Anarchy* (1867) Arnold deplores the materialism of his age, brought about by the Victorian middle classes' eagerness to embrace the benefits of industrialization. In particular he argues for a return to, or recreation of, the 'sweetness and light' that in his view had informed the best of earlier culture. But whereas he also argues for a greater awareness of the virtues of European literature, especially as they are summated in the works of Goethe, Arnold's principal concern is with the well-being (or otherwise) of the English soul.

So strong is this concern that, when he turns his attention to the Celtic heritage, his assessment is framed by it. The value to him of Welsh, Irish and Scottish cultures is precisely their potential as purgatives for his own people's distemper as diagnosed by himself. Simultaneously, Arnold indulges an invective against the use of Welsh as a living language. While this was a stock English prejudice of the time, Arnold's resort to it scarcely enhances his overall strategic insistence on critical independence.

'My friend Mr Godwin Smith says, in his eloquent way,' Arnold writes near the beginning his Celtic essay, 'that England is the favourite son of Heaven. Far be it from me to say that England is not the favourite of Heaven; but at this moment she reminds me more of what the prophet Isaiah calls, "a bull in a net". She has satisfied herself in all departments with clap-trap and routine so long, and she is now so astounded at finding they will not serve her turn any longer!'

It is from this base that Arnold develops his theme. What is essentially at fault in the contemporary English character, he suggests, is that it lacks an understanding of its heterogeneous constituents. The English, he asserts, are indeed a Teutonic race, but they are not exclusively Teutonic, any more than they are exclusively Roman, exclusively Norman, or . . . exclusively Celtic. Rather the English should recognize and appreciate in detail the diversity of their make-up; and from this comes the exhortation to study the Celtic past. For Arnold it is first and foremost a matter of Know Thyself. By understanding his Celtic antecedents (Arnold himself had a small amount of Welsh blood in his veins), by assuming certain Celtic virtues, the Englishman will conquer the disease of Philistinism.

To support this position, Arnold invokes the then disproportionately popular goddess of philology. Both English and the Celtic languages are, he says, members of the Indo-European language group. Therefore is there not an underlying bond between them? Indeed, 'philology,' he writes, 'carries us toward ideas of affinity of race which are new to us.'

Lurking within this prescription is, nevertheless, a racism. Having confused race and language, Arnold lets the Celts in, as it were through the back door. The implication is that were the Celts to belong to any other language group, then affinity would be denied, and they would not be allowed anywhere near the English estate. Modern linguistics, however, as developed by Noam Chomsky and others, renders Arnold's position here untenable. *All* languages reflect an affinity between all human beings. Hence, in theory at least, any member of one race is equipped to learn the language of any other race. The conjunction of particular languages with particular races is incidental. Individual language is a secondary, not a primary characteristic.

But only in theory. For it is exactly the capacity of language to dominate consciousness that gives it primary status as regards cultural identification among the discrete peoples of the earth. How can I call myself English or German or French or Welsh unless I can not only speak the language, but think in that language too? And if I do happen to think in English or German or French or Welsh, is that not sufficient grounds for determining if not my nationality, then at least my cultural and social belonging?

Here we have two entirely separate and probably irreconcilable ways of regarding the role of language. One is Darwinian, the other social-realist. On the one hand, perceived primarily as a means of communication, language is observed to have evolved differently in different places among different peoples, but from a universally shared biological skill, or instinct.[17] On the other hand, language is perceived as a definitional specific. For actual human purposes, social, cultural and political, the universal heredity is neither here nor there. What matters is how things are. I speak English, you speak German, he speaks French. We are different. Destroy my language, and you destroy my essence.

To pitch Chomskyan linguistics against Arnold may seem unfair. By the time he published *On the Study of Celtic Literature* Darwin had indeed published his *Origin of Species*, but the anthropological ramifications and applications of that watershed still lay in the future. Even Darwin's own stab at this, *The Descent of Man*, did not appear until 1871. In terms of where and when he lived Arnold is a progressive of sorts when it comes to matters of race and culture, but only of sorts. He does not look beyond Europe, but at least he looks at Europe; as at least he looks at Wales. That said, however, and apropos of Wales and the other components of the Celtic compact, he fails to abide by standards he himself sets. His attitude towards Celtic culture turns out to be purely opportunistic – 'great nation chauvinism combined with tomb robbery',[18] in the words of one Anglo-Welsh critic. Celticism is enlisted by Arnold on a mercenary basis, to combat the enemy within that has infected the English body. But once the enemy has been crushed, the hired army can be dismissed. What in fact we are given is a kind of born-again antiquarianism.

Arnold pursues his theme by exploring the angles. Turning

his attention to religion, he finds that the English – *toujours les anglais* –

> hold a middle place between the German and the Welsh; their religion has the exterior forms and apparatus of a rationalism, so far their Germanic nature carries them; but long before they get to science, their feeling, their Celtic eloquence catches them, and turns their religion all toward piety and unction. So English Protestantism has the outside appearance of an intellectual system, and the inside reality of an emotional system: this gives it its tenacity and force, for what is held with the ardent attachment of feeling is believed to have at the same time the scientific proof of reason. The English Puritan therefore (and Puritanism is the characteristic form of English Prot-estantism), stands between the German Protestant and the Celtic Methodist; his real affinity, indeed, at present, being rather with his Welsh kinsman, if kinsman he may be called, than with his German.

But much of this is merely garrulous. Of the many objections that might be raised to Arnold's analysis here, the most serious is that, with regard to the history of Christianity in Wales, he simply flies in the face of the greater historical record. To be sure, Methodism – originally an English style of worship – did take peculiarly strong root in Wales during the eighteenth and nineteenth centuries. But equally, during the Civil War of the seventeenth century, much of Wales remained peculiarly Catholic, as well as royalist. Methodism and its fellow nonconformities may indeed be associated with the Welsh during a certain period of their history, but to associate Methodism and Celticism is historically absurd.

Arnold gets himself into another fine mess when he schematizes the Celtic influence in English literature. Having characterized English poetry as a hybrid organism, he pays his Celts three great compliments:

> If I were asked where English poetry got these three things, the turn for style, its turn for melancholy, and its turn for natural magic, for catching and rendering the charm of nature in a wonderfully near and vivid way, I should answer, with some doubt, that it got much of its turn for style from Celtic sources; with less doubt, that it got

much of its melancholy from a Celtic source; with no doubt at all, that from a Celtic source it got nearly all its natural magic.

Again though, Arnold is disingenuous. While the qualities he imputes to Celtic writing may indeed be found in great abundance in, for example, Welsh poetry, it is entirely another matter to affirm a historic influence when there are rival candidates with stronger claims. Thus what Arnold terms style, melancholy and even natural magic can with equal ease be located among the Latin poets, with whom most English poets up until his day were familiar in a way they were simply not familiar with Welsh or Irish verse. Indeed there is an alternative argument, most forcefully put forward by Ted Hughes,[19] that the history of English prosody in the three centuries leading up to Arnold reflected nothing so much as the imposition of classical metres and a classical sensibility upon English poetry. According to this view, English verse would indeed have benefited from a knowledge and understanding of Celtic exemplars, but in fact did not. Instead it was suborned by an alien custody; and it was only after Arnold's death that English prosody emerged from its long captivity.

Again, we have to recognize here Arnold's true purpose. The Celtic virtues he identifies in *On the Study of Celtic Literature* are virtues he wishes to reinstate in the English mind, for its own good. And it is in this context that he makes his prejudice wickedly clear:

> By the forms of its language a nation expresses its very self. Our language is the loosest, the most analytic, of all European languages. And we, then, what are we? what is England? I will not answer, A vast obscure Cymric basis with a vast visible Teutonic superstructure; but I will say that that answer sometimes suggests itself, at any rate, sometimes knocks at our mind's door for admission; and we begin to cast about and see whether it is to be let in.

Yet – and here is the great contradiction that reduces Arnold's supposedly path-breaking essay to a heap of untidy opinion – can he bring himself to extend his nostrum that a nation expresses itself through the forms of its language to the Celts themselves?

In a famous passage Arnold does make at least one beneficial intervention on behalf of Welsh studies. He comes down very heavily in favour of regarding early Welsh texts not as the creations of the Christian Middle Ages, but as redactions of a much older literature:

> The very first thing that strikes one, in reading the *Mabinogion*, is how evidently the medieval story-teller is pillaging an antiquity of which he does not fully possess the secret; he is like a peasant building his hut on the site of Helicarnassus or Ephesus; he builds, but what he builds is full of materials of which he knows not the history, or knows by a glimmering tradition only – stones 'not of this building', but of an older architecture, greater, cunninger, more majestical.

Unwittingly perhaps, since Arnold could neither read nor speak Welsh, but of necessity relied on translations, he indicates a direction which, pursued energetically ever since his death, has recovered the bedrock of the first Welsh classics. Not only has the *Mabinogion* been shown to incorporate at least vestigially a complex belief and myth system; but the work of several outstanding early poets, including Taliesin and Aneirin, once stripped clean of later monastic interpolation, has been allowed to stand in something like its true splendid light. But equally famously, *On the Study of Celtic Literature* contains a sustained and savage onslaught on Welsh as a spoken, living language. In his introduction Arnold quotes himself, in a letter previously written to *The Times* on the subject of an eisteddfod held at Chester: 'The Welsh language is the curse of Wales. Its prevalence, and the ignorance of English, have excluded, and even now exclude the Welsh people from the civilisation of their English neighbours . . . The sooner all Welsh specialities disappear from the face of the earth the better.' No matter that English civilization is itself the subject of Arnold's hostile scrutiny, the text proper returns vehemently to this theme:

> I must say I quite share the opinion of my brother Saxons as to the practical inconvenience of perpetuating the speaking of Welsh. It may cause a moment's distress to one's imagination when one hears that the last Cornish peasant who spoke the old tongue of Cornwall is dead; but no doubt Cornwall is the better for adopting English, for becoming more thoroughly one with the rest of the country. The

fusion of all the inhabitants of these islands into one homogeneous, English-speaking whole, the breaking down of barriers between us, the swallowing-up of separate provincial nationalities, is a consummation to which the course of things irresistibly tends; it is a necessity of what is called modern civilisation, and modern civilisation is a real, legitimate force; the change must come, and its accomplishment is a mere affair of time. The sooner the Welsh language disappears as an instrument of the practical, political, social life of Wales, the better; the better for England, the better for Wales itself.

This diatribe continues for several pages.

In 1910 – three years before the birth of R. S. Thomas – Ernest Rhys, the distinguished Anglo-Welsh man of letters who made a career for himself in London, chiefly as the editor of the immensely popular Everyman Library, who was also a friend of W. B. Yeats and with him founded the Rhymers' Club, who did much to promote an awareness of Welsh literature outside Wales, and who was an important figure in the mainly Irish 'Celtic Twilight' movement of the 1890s, set himself the task of writing an introduction to the Everyman edition of Arnold's book. 'At times,' he wrote, 'he appears confused by the thickets of Welsh and Irish philology, and then his adventure is apt to suggest nothing so much as Oxford in person trying to break into the wilderness.' But if we look at the last passage from Arnold quoted above, and its terminology, Rhys's assessment was restrained understatement, perhaps with an 'Anglo-Welsh' psycho-pathology of its own. The 'moment's distress', the 'Cornish peasant', the 'fusion' of inhabitants leading to a 'consummation', 'nationalities' that are 'provincial', 'modern civilisation', 'legitimate force': these and other phrases, and the way they are deployed, constitute nothing less than the bludgeoning rhetoric of a cultural hegemonism.

Arnold presents a striking example of a critic blinded not by the finer nuances of a prejudice, but by its core force. And the same prejudice is, to the abiding chagrin of R. S. Thomas and other leaders of Welsh and Anglo-Welsh culture, endemic among the English. From Shakespeare's portrait of Fluellen in *Henry V* onwards the Welshman has been the butt first of Anglo-Saxon wit, then of Anglo-

Saxon rancour. While the poet Charles Cotton (1630–87) could describe his Welsh guide as having

> A voice like a cricket, a look like a rat:
> The brains of a goose and the heart of a cat[20]

'E.B', a slightly later author, lampoons Wales as 'the fag end of Creation: the very rubbish of Noah's flood; the highest English hills are as cherry stones to the Welsh Alps, so that there is not in the whole world a people who live so near to and yet so far from Heaven as the Welsh do'.[21] The eighteenth-century antiquarians and the earlier Romantic poets did something to refurbish Wales's image, but Wales as a source of easy jest persisted, as for example in the ballad of the Widow of Wycombe, in Sir Walter Scott's *Ivanhoe*:

> Sir David ap Morgan ap Griffith ap Hugh
> Ap Tudor ap Rhice, quoth his roundelay:
> She said that one widow for so many was too few,
> And she bade the Welshman wend his way,

To a degree Victorian piety moderated customary malice, but such malice remained latent, and has repeatedly found expression in the twentieth century.

Even in post-war times, having a go at the Welsh has been a hobby of the articulate. Take, as a recent example, Kingsley Amis. Having spent ten years as a lecturer in the English department at Swansea University, it comes as no surprise that he should devote a chapter of his *Memoirs* (1991) to Wales.[22] For a few pages we feel him practically bending over backwards to be complimentary about the Welsh. But if momentarily he recoils from his habitual spleen, it is in order to deliver what he hopes will be a spatter of knock-out blows. Thus, while he recognizes the separate identities of North and South Wales, Amis exploits this division for comic purposes that kept him bankrolled throughout a long career:

> I shall never forget the charming delicacy with which our hosts at dinner once explained that we would be meeting the Caradocs later. They're very nice people really you know, charming. Very cultivated.

They're, er ... (Nudists, I wondered? Mithraists? Cannibals?) ... North Walians. And whatever the immediate reasons, I shall never cease to find it odd that a state on the other side of the world should end up with the firmly dissociative title of New *South* Wales.

Clearly, from Amis's point of view, if different Welsh are prepared to have a go at one another, then all Welsh are fair game for his own brand of barb. In the next paragraph the old sour-puss tackles that perennial English theme, the supposed dishonesty of the Welsh. Again, while appearing to be fair-minded about his quarry, his real intention is to plunge the knife in deeper:

I am fond of the English and also admire and approve of them. Nevertheless, I cannot help noticing that Welsh people are friendlier and easier to get on with. Their reputation for deviousness is very largely undeserved – by which small caveat is meant that the commonness of this failing is no greater in Wales than in England, but just that there is something *about* the Welsh variety I find specially repulsive. Their appearance of, their name for greater direct dishonesty means nothing more than that they will skin you no more nor less than the English will, but they are more likely to look pleasant as they do it. I wish I could remember which fabulously rich man it was that moved a few miles from the south of France to Italy in his last years, saying in explanation that he preferred to be cheated with a smile. He would have had a similar case for moving from England to Wales.

But Amis's special vendetta is reserved for Welsh nationalism, which, on his own admission, he appears neither to understand nor to want to understand very much:

The next matter is no business of mine and I do not, as before, pretend to anything like a knowledge of the full facts, but I admit to mild irritation whenever Welsh nationalism makes one of its deservedly rare appearances in news or talk. It presents a false picture, both on purpose, so to speak, and unconsciously. In no case can it or does it speak for Wales. It is an entirely peripheral movement, indeed not a 'movement' at all. Its supporters tend to be ministers of religion, college people and schoolteachers, members of the Welsh BBC.

According to one theory the thing would not have got off the ground even a couple of inches if the BBC, setting itself up in Wales about 1920, had not understandably but mistakenly stipulated that all employees should be Welsh-speaking, thus at once confining itself to what in South Wales had for decades been a minority and, among the better educated, often a faction. The classical kind of Welsh it has pledged itself to revive is not the impure kind, full of English loan-words and loan-constructions, still naturally spoken in parts of the country. The bilingual public signs that infest an English-speaking town like Swansea were not there in my time, when there were still quite a few genuine Welsh-speakers about. The bloody things are a joke, with TACSI set up next to TAXI and even BEICS next to CYCLES. The words that matter, like DANGER and STOP and NO RIGHT TURN, are in English only . . .

Why the animus? one is tempted to ask. Why the stew of associative insinuation? Perhaps for the reason another idol of the English funny brigade, Evelyn Waugh, puts into the mouth of one of his characters in *Decline and Fall* (1928): 'We can trace almost all the disasters of English history to the influence of Wales.' And the disasters of Welsh history? But where Amis is in fact leading us, as he leads us so many other times in his autobiography, is towards the debunking of, if not the great and the good, then of a writer significantly better than himself. But before he buries Dylan Thomas – 'a pernicious figure, one who has helped to get Wales and Welsh poetry a bad name and generally done lasting harm to both' – Amis enlists Dylan's services to deliver the final and presumably to his mind ineffably analytic coup de grâce against the nationalism whose motivation he so scrupulously refuses to consider. Recalling an interview the 'Rimbaud of Cwmdonkin Drive' gave to 'that old windbag Miron Grindea' for the magazine *Adam*, Amis writes:

Dylan Thomas was asked his opinion of Welsh Nationalism. Here, for the first and only time, the fog of suffocating solemnity was penetrated by Thomas's reply, for which the interviewer fell back on reported speech: Mr Thomas answered the question in three words, of which the second and third were 'Welsh Nationalism'. He never again rose to such heights.

Curiously, in the present context, Amis was one of the earliest of the English literati to acknowledge, even salute, the power of R. S. Thomas. Reviewing Thomas's collection *Song at the Year's Turning* for the *Spectator* as long ago as 1956, his verdict was that the Welsh poet 'reduces most modern verse to footling whimsy'.[23] It is difficult to credit that Amis can have been unimpressed by the articulacy of Thomas's Welsh views as expressed in that volume, or ignorant of the need to express them; but in 1954 Amis was only five years into his tenure, and, as the saying goes, one learns to forget.

Other contemporary examples of Welsh baiting spring readily to mind. There is, for instance, that scene towards the end of Robert Bolt's stage and screen play *A Man For All Seasons* when Thomas More, on trial for his life, confronts his former henchman, Richard Rich, for betraying him to Thomas Cromwell:

MORE: I *have* one question to ask the witness.
   [*RICH stops*]
That's a chain of office you are wearing.
   [*Reluctantly* RICH *faces him*]
May I see it?
   [*NORFOLK motions him to approach,* MORE *examines the medallion.*]
   The red dragon. [*To Cromwell*] What's this?
CROMWELL: Sir Richard is appointed Attorney-General for Wales.
MORE: [*looking into* RICH's *face: with pain and amusement*] For Wales? Why, Richard, it profits a man nothing to give his soul for the whole world . . . But for Wales – ?[24]

Or again, the multiple jibes in the immensely popular recent television comedy series, *Black Adder*:

BLACK ADDER: Have you ever been to Wales, Baldrick?
BALDRICK: No, but I've often thought I'd like to.
BLACK ADDER: Well don't. It's a ghastly place. Huge bands of tough sinewy men roam the valleys terrifying people with their close harmony singing. You need half a pint of phlegm in your throat just to pronounce the place names. Never ask for a direction in Wales, Baldrick. You'll be washing spit out of your hair for a fortnight.[25]

Here, it is partly the English attitude towards the Welsh that is lampooned. Black Adder himself is too comically opinionated a figure for it to be otherwise. But on the small screen, the lines are delivered with a relish and a gusto that also exploit the abiding prejudice. Like the mother-in-law and the lecherous milkman, like the dark gentleman and the Paki, Wales and the Welsh are a part of the fixtures and fittings of any self-respecting comedian's repertoire.

What is said in jest, it is sometimes advocated, most often by comedians themselves, is best left as jest. 'Look,' the argument goes, 'we all feel these things, otherwise the jokes wouldn't be funny, so let's bring them out into the open and make light of them.' But the obverse rings truer. By so airing our prejudices we reinforce them. Not only that, but by rebedding them in laughter, we make them acceptable. Comedy, far from defusing prejudice, licenses it.

And so prejudice is eased back into the system, to be perpetuated at other levels. A case in point is Philip Larkin. The publication in 1992 of Larkin's *Selected Letters* did a determinedly middle-brow poet's posthumous reputation at best an ambivalent favour. Page after page the reader is introduced to a world of apparently peerless malevolence that in fact has its tap-roots in less than literary humour. More or less everyone Larkin ever met is besmirched by an uncompromisingly acidic lavatory brush. And lo! – among his secret victims is R. S. Thomas, who earns several entries in the index. Larkin is unable to resist subjecting Thomas's initials to phonetic elision. But it is in a 1962 letter to Robert Conquest that the old, racial sneer crystallizes: 'Our friend Arsewipe Thomas suddenly was led into my room one afternoon last week, and stood there without moving or speaking: he seems pretty hard going. Not noticeably Welsh, which is one comfort.'[26]

Of course, not all the traffic has been one way. There is for instance the Welsh proverb, first recorded (as well as loosely translated) by James Howell in a 1659 compilation:[27]

> *Sais Sais a gach yn ei bais,*
> *Y Cymro glan a gach allan –*

> (The Saxon shites in his breech,
> The cleanly Briton in the hedge).

Welsh comedians playing to Welsh audiences in Welsh clubs are just as adept at inciting racial mirth as their English counterparts. Yet there is an essential imbalance. If it is true that the root of all laughter is fear, then two very different kinds of fear are represented by the aspersions that the English and Welsh regularly fling at each other. On the Welsh side, the underlying fear is that of the conquered towards the conqueror; the feeling, if you like, of inadequacy. On the English side, the fear is more complex. Partly it is a fear that the conquest is insufficient, that the conquered may yet strike back; but partly too it is a fear of conscience, even a fear of the lack of conscience.

To stall his very English fears, Larkin robs Thomas of the residual power of the conquered to disturb the conqueror – 'Not noticeably Welsh, which is one comfort' – by co-opting him among his own ranks. Yet simultaneously he finds R.S. 'hard going'.

And R.S. is hard going, as anyone caught in the eye of the hornets' nest that constitutes English–Welsh relations is almost bound to be. This comes across particularly in a poem such as 'The Small Window' (see above, p. 16) There, the contempt directed at the English can, at one level, be read as an inversion of aggressors and aggrieved. In the long set-to between the Welsh and the English, mirrors play an important role.

But the story is not without its moments of light. Ironically, around the time Matthew Arnold was turning his lofty attention towards the Celtic heritage, 1862, another book was published that expressed a more tolerant, and more informed, view of Wales and its people. This was George Borrow's *Wild Wales*. But being by George Borrow, it was marred by an eccentricity that veils its real intelligence.

Borrow was a Victorian alternative, a gifted linguist with an eye for the picaresque, a taste for ale, but also a proneness to manic depression. He was, or became, a low churchman, with an avowed distaste for anything Romish at a time when the Anglican church was moving in that direction. His adventures, like those of other good travel writers, need also to be seen as a critique of the 'society' that bred him. Born in 1802 at East Dereham in Norfolk, he spent part of his childhood in Edinburgh. His adolescent schooling was completed at Norwich Grammar School, and it was in Norwich that he became articled, in 1820, to a local solicitor. Soon afterwards however he fell under the influence of another Norfolk man, William Taylor, a professional translator, mainly of German authors, and a friend of the poet Robert Southey. Taylor recognized Borrow's literary gifts, and encouraged him to abandon law in favour of the quill. Accordingly, in 1826, having already published two volumes of his own translations, one of F. M. von Klinger's *Faustus*, the other of *Romantic Ballads* from the Danish, Borrow moved to London.

But London was only the beginning of Borrow's escape from the confines of a small town in East Anglia. Over the next three decades he travelled extensively in Russia and Europe, as well as throughout his native Britain. For a while, he earned a living in Spain as the agent for the British and Foreign Bible Society. Out of this experience came his classic *The Bible in Spain* (1834). From the perspective of his age though, his most startling writings were his sympathetic accounts of gypsies and gypsy life: *The Zincali* (1841), *Lavengro* (1851) and *The Romany Rye* (1857).

Borrow clearly had an affinity for Romany culture. His narratives are an admixture of observation, fictionalizing and autobiography. But to many of his readers gypsies were outcasts, the lowest of the low, worse than Irish tinkers, and anyone who associated with them was suspect. When Borrow came to write and publish *Wild Wales* therefore, he was, as an author, perceived by some as damaged goods, which perhaps explains the relative failure of that book, for all its flair and industry, to transform English attitudes.

After the imaginative excesses of some of its predecessors, *Wild Wales* represents a return to the more conventional disciplines of the travel genre. In it Borrow recounts his journeyings through the mid, north and west of the country. In the already industrializing south he spends little time, although *Wild Wales* does contain a memorable description, falling only just short of the apocalyptic, of an iron foundry at Merthyr Tydfil (then the largest, indeed the only really large, town in the Principality):

After breakfast I went to see the Cyfarthfa Fawr iron works, generally considered to be the greatest wonder of the place. After some slight demur I obtained permission from the superintendent to inspect them. I was attended by an intelligent mechanic. What shall I say about the Cyfarthfa Fawr? I had best say but very little. I saw enormous furnaces. I saw streams of molten metal. I saw a long ductile piece of red-hot iron being operated upon. I saw millions of sparks flying about. I saw an immense wheel impelled round with frightful velocity by a steam-engine of two hundred-and-forty horse-power. I heard all kinds of dreadful sounds. The general effect was stunning. These works belong to the Crawshays, a family distinguished by a strange kind of eccentricity, but also by genius and enterprising spirit, and by such a strict feeling of honour that it is a common saying that the word of any one of them is as good as the bond of other people.

In Wales, however, for the main Borrow follows his natural bent. His nose is for topography, local history and for people. No village is too small to discourage his interest, no journey between small villages too arduous not to be relished. But above all he has the trait of the true travel writer, which is that not only is he prepared to stop and talk to anyone, but he has the knack of being able to glean at least something from each of them.

In this way Borrow builds a picture of Wales which is very much a picture of Welsh-speaking Wales. His diligence in recording all that he sees and hears is astonishing, to the extent that sometimes he dulls us with detail. But either by design, or as a result of his painstaking method – every night he must have written copiously by candlelight – he succeeds in conveying the essence, not just of nineteenth-century Wales perhaps, but of any rural heartland: that it is composed of any number of communities that are centred upon themselves, and are repositories of their own peculiar character.

The key to this was Borrow's fluency in the Welsh language. In the areas he travelled, many of those he encountered were still monoglot Welsh speakers, and had he not had Welsh he simply could not have written as informatively as he does. Yet it is in this respect that his own eccentricity of character breaks out and sometimes spoils the outcome. Not only does he speak Welsh, but too often he is determined to parade this skill, as well as his considerable knowledge of Welsh literature and history, under the noses of his collocutors. The following, between Borrow and a hay-scyther on the slopes of Dinas Brân, is symptomatic of too many of his reported dialogues:

'You speak very good English,' said I, 'have you much Welsh?'
   'Plenty,' said he: 'I am a real Welshman.'
   'Can you read Welsh?' said I.
   'Oh yes!' he replied.
   'What books have you read?' said I.
   'I have read the Bible, sir, and one or two other books.'
   'Did you ever read the Bardd Cwsg?' said I.
   He looked at me with some surprise. 'No,' said he, after a moment or two. 'I have never read it. I have seen it, but it was too deep Welsh for me.'
   'I have read it,' said I.
   'Are you a Welshman?' said he.
   'No,' said I; 'I am an Englishman.'
   'And how is it,' said he, 'that you can read Welsh without being a Welshman?'
   'I learned to do so,' said I, 'even as you learned to mow, without being bred up to farming work.'

Even this idiosyncratic Victorian drop-out betrays a trace element of racial chauvinism; and Borrow's eagerness to patronize his Welsh witnesses is also a way of patronizing the reader, so that to get through the five hundred pages of small print that constitute the average edition of *Wild Wales* becomes a chore. But set against this is Borrow's memory of how he first learned his Welsh, from a groom, during his days as a solicitor's clerk in Norwich:

A queer groom he was, and well deserving of having his portrait drawn. He might be about forty-seven years of age, and about five feet eight inches in height; his body was spare and wiry; his chest rather broad, and his arms remarkably long; his legs were of the kind generally known as spindle-shanks, but vigorous withal, for they carried his body with great agility; neck he had none, at least, that I ever observed; and his head was anything but high, not measuring, I should think, more than four inches from the bottom of the chin to the top of the forehead; his cheek-bones were high, his eyes grey and deeply sunken in his face, with an expression in them, partly sullen, and partly irascible; his complexion was indescribable; the little hair which he had, which was almost entirely on the sides and the back part of his head, was of an iron-grey hue. He wore a leather hat on ordinary days, low on the crown, and with the side eaves turned up. A dirty pepper and salt coat, a waistcoat which had once been red, but which has lost its pristine colour, and looked brown; dirty yellow leather breeches, grey worsted stockings, and high-lows. Surely I was right when I said he was a very different groom to those of the present day, whether Welsh or English? What say you, Sir Watkin? What say you, my Lord of Exeter? He looked after the horses, and occasionally assisted in the house of a person who lived at the end of an alley, in which the office of the gentleman to whom I was articled was situated, and having to pass by the door of the office half-a-dozen times in a day, he did not fail to attract the notice of the clerks, who, sometimes individually, sometimes by twos, sometimes by threes, or even more, not infrequently stood at the door, bareheaded – misspending the time which was not legally their own. Sundry observations, none of them very flattering, did the clerks, and amongst them myself, make upon the groom, as he passed and repassed, some of them direct, others somewhat oblique. To these he made no reply save by looks, which had in them something dangerous and menacing, and clenching without raising his fists, which looked singularly hard and horny. At length a whisper ran about the alley that the groom was a Welshman; this whisper much increased the malice of my brother clerks against him, who were now whenever he passed the door, and they happened to be there by twos and threes, in the habit of saying something, as if by accident, against Wales and Welshmen, and, individually or together, were in the habit of shouting out 'Taffy', when he was at some distance from them, and his back was turned, or regaling his ears with the harmonious and well-known distich of 'Taffy was a Welshman, Taffy was a thief: Taffy came to my house and stole a piece of beef'. It had however a very different effect upon me. I was trying to learn Welsh and the idea occurring to me that the groom might be able to assist me in my pursuit, I instantly lost all desire to torment him, and determined to do my best to scrape acquaintance with him, and persuade him to give me what assistance he could. I succeeded; how I will not trouble the reader with describing: he and I became great friends, and he taught me what Welsh he could. In return for his instructions

I persuaded my brother clerks to leave off holloing after him, and to do nothing further to hurt his feelings, which had been very deeply wounded, so much so, that after the first two or three lessons he told me in confidence that on the morning of the very day I first began to conciliate him he had come to the resolution of doing one of two things, namely, either to hang himself from the balk of the hayloft, or to give his master warning, both of which things he told me he should have been very unwilling to do, more particularly as he had a wife and family.

The moral movement in this passage, for all that it is motivated by Borrow's appetite to acquire the Welsh tongue, surpasses anything suggested by Arnold, just as it surpasses much, if not most, of what has been written and said about Wales and the Welsh by other Englishmen down the ages. But then Borrow also had an appetite for Welsh history.

The history of Wales is a tortuous affair. One reason for this is its topography: a centre occupied by high hills and mountains, with the fertile flatlands confined to a coastal apron. Its population therefore has never been concentrated on one great river basin or one great city; and indeed Wales as such only came into being because England did. Up until the invasion of Britain by the Saxons and the Angles and Jutes, beginning in the fifth century, after the departure of Rome's legions, there was no real distinction between Wales and the rest of the island. It was inhabited by a number of tribes – the Deceangli in the north, the Ordovices in the north-west, the Demetae in the south-west, the Silures in the south and south-east, and north of the Silures the Cornovii – each of which may be regarded as 'Celtic' in culture, if not in origin.

The Celts had arrived probably in the seventh and sixth centuries BC. Before the Celts, there were Bronze Age settlements of 'Beaker Folk', and perhaps another distinct group, sometimes called 'the small dark people'. To what extent the Celts displaced these tribes, or were assimilated by them, is unclear. Nor is it known who were the first settlers in what has become Wales. Archaeology has uncovered widespread Stone Age remains going back many thousands of years.

Of particular interest in this regard is the fact that part of Stonehenge was quarried in the far-off Preseli Hills, in north Pembrokeshire. How the blue stones came to be transported from the one site to the other, somewhere around 1800 BC, is an abiding mystery. The project, however, indicates a civilization that may have had a technological thing or two to teach the advanced metal-worker Celts. Also suggested is a network of trade and exchange between the tribally differentiated inhabitants of 'pre-historic' Britain. Undoubtedly though the Romans, with their roads and their townships and their taxes, greatly stimulated the social and cultural cohesion of the 'Britons' during their three-hundred-year occupation. By the time of their departure it is reasonable to suppose that with the exception of the Picts living in the Caledonian north, everyone spoke broadly the same Brythonic language. Politically, however, the people of Britain were not integrated. The power vacuum left by the Romans was filled by a number of sometimes warring chiefs or princes; and it was this disunity that more than anything else enabled the Teutonic Saxons and Angles to establish their own territories, later consolidated under a single rule as England.

The Anglo-Saxons were essentially lowland types. Whether by strategic intent or by tactical happenstance, they drove a number of wedges into the Brythonic population. The most significant of these was through what is now Yorkshire and Lancashire, connecting the east and west coasts. The people of the north became permanently separated from the people in the south and west. Ironically some of what is now regarded as the earliest Welsh literature was not written, or rather composed, in Wales at all, but in southern Scotland, Cumbria and Northumberland. Pushed out of England, a part of the Celtic remnant resettled among their cultural and linguistic cousins in Wales, sometimes ejecting Irish communities in the process. Another enclave formed in Cornwall. The political structure however remained unchanged. Instead of combining into one larger unit to resist the strong kingdoms of Wessex and Mercia, and then England, the Cymric leadership continued fragmented. In the sixth and seventh centuries there emerged the rival princedoms some of which have survived in the names of contemporary county authorities: Gwynedd, Ceredigion (Cardigan), Powys, and, until 1996, Gwent.

Until the end of the eighth century, warfare between the Cymry, as the Welsh had begun calling themselves from around 630, and the Anglo-Saxons continued on a sporadic basis. Very often it was as a result of allegiances formed between rulers. A Welsh prince would agree to help, say, the King of Mercia or the King of Northumbria against his Saxon rivals, and suffer punitive incursions as a result. But the mountainous interior of Wales, combined with native belligerence, spared the Cymry from being fully invaded. Gradually both sides realized that a stalemate had been reached. In the 780s this was given physical expression by the digging of Offa's Dyke, a continuous earthworks running north to south, and which still survives in places as the border between Wales and England.

By then another threat to Wales had emerged. From bases in Celtic Ireland the Vikings, or Norsemen, had begun raiding the western coast. Thus, although Offa's Dyke is named after the then King of Mercia, most of the Cymric princes were only too happy to see its construction. Indeed, the evidence suggests that what is probably the world's longest trench was in fact a co-operative effort. By then too, there was a tendency within Wales to create, through dynastic as much as military means, larger amalgamated kingdoms. The first such attempt had in fact already occurred, under Rhodri Mawr (Rhodri the Great) of Powys, who succeeded in adding Gwynedd to his titles. In the tenth century Hywel Dda – Hywel the Good – created an even larger bloc, that comprised, as well as Powys and Gwynedd, Dyfed, Seisyllweg and Brycheiniog. Only Gwent and Morgannwg (modern Glamorgan) lay outside his pale. Later in the same century Maredudd ab Owain achieved a similar hegemony; but it was not until the eleventh that Gruffudd ap Llywelyn managed to bring the whole of Wales under a single dominion, starting out from the enlarged principality of Deheubarth in the south-west. Even this, however, was shortlived. Cymric law, famously encoded by Hywel Dda, did not recommend primogeniture. When a larger kingdom did emerge, almost inevitably it broke up into its constituent parts once the hegemonizing prince or king himself was dead. The sons of the great princes preferred, more often than not, to divide their inheritance, sometimes according to the law, sometimes by scheming, and sometimes by battle. Nor was there any natural impulse towards cohesion. The men of Gwynedd were different from the men of Powys who were different from the men of Deheubarth.

In the end, this was to be the undoing of Wales. In 1066 there came to Britain a new set of conquerors, the Normans. These brilliant warriors and ruthless administrators, limited only by their relatively small numbers, quickly overcame the Anglo-Saxons. Where the Anglo-Saxons offered more than token resistance, as in the north of England, the ferocity of Norman reprisals was of a magnitude hitherto unknown. Nor did the Normans have the scantest regard for Offa's Dyke. While early on in his reign William I paid a courtesy visit to St David's, the centre of Catholic Christianity in west Wales, he also established the 'Marcher lordships': semi-autonomous fiefdoms designed to create a buffer zone between England and any fractious Welsh princelings. At the same time, the Normans began extending their tentacles into Welsh territories. As early as 1100 the first Norman fortresses were constructed in Gwent and Pembrokeshire, then elsewhere. At first these were wooden structures, sometimes with a stone keep. But soon enough they began to be replaced by the awesome castles that are now cared for by Cadw, as part of the 'Welsh heritage'.

Until the late thirteenth century the Norman conquest of Wales was irregular and piecemeal. The areas they most wanted they took by force, but like the Anglo-Saxons before them they recognized that the mountain fastnesses would be more trouble to subdue than they were worth. Provided they offered at least nominal fealty to the Norman monarch, therefore, the Welsh princes were allowed, even encouraged, to continue their rule. If trouble did arise, then a policy of divide and conquer was pursued. Norman kings usually found they could defeat one 'rebellious' Welsh prince by enlisting the support of a rival. At a time when the concepts of nation and nationality were virtually non-existent, the Welsh nobility could be relied upon to behave the same as every other European nobility. Provided they posed no threat to the King himself, they could be left to their own devices. And to some extent at least, via the marriage bed, the Welsh nobility began fusing with its Norman counterpart. But the Norman nobility was, in turn, infiltrated by English elements. Hence it was that the *Sais*, Welsh for Englishman, having been beaten by a band of Nordic Frenchmen, regained his former potency in the Welsh mind.

While nation and nationality were virtually non-existent concepts, the idea of the 'state', under Norman care, developed formidably. From the Domesday Book onwards, the Normans displayed their genius for administration. They too were a small people, but charged with the running of a large kingdom. Soon, the more alert Welsh princes took notice of this, and began dreaming of a state in Wales that would be quite separate from whatever went on in England. This culminated in the two 'Wars of Welsh Independence', of 1277 and 1282, both led by Llywelyn ap Gruffudd, known variously as Llywelyn the Last and Y Llyw Olaf, the Last Prince. Prior to these, Llywelyn had been acknowledged as the 'Prince of Wales', by the Treaty of Montgomery in 1267. But the title meant less than it implied. Many lordships within Wales remained the property of the King of England, and a wide band of land across the south was excluded from the terms of the treaty altogether.

It was to make good his title that Llywelyn took up arms. He lost the first war, and was killed in the second. Thereupon the victor, Edward I, decided there should be no return to the pre-war status quo. Instead he set about 'pacifying' Wales, as he thought once and for all. In Gwynedd particularly, a new line of fortresses was built. These included such blunt monuments to Norman, or as it had now become, Plantagenet military prowess as Caernarfon, Conwy and Beaumaris castles. At the same time the Statute of Rhuddlan (1284) imposed a whole machinery of English rule on Wales. Welsh criminal law, today regarded as an exceptionally enlightened framework for its time, was abolished, and a system of Justices created. Henceforth Wales was parcelled up not only into shires, but also, far more definably than before, into 'Englishries' and 'Welshries'. Those living in the former were granted special privileges, while those living in the latter became, in effect, closely observed colonials.

This settlement lasted until 1536. Periodically there were 'Welsh Uprisings', but always they were crushed. The most spectacular was led, from 1400 onwards, by Owain Glyndŵr, whose name has fired Welsh hearts ever since. Among historians, however, opinion about Glyndŵr is divided. Some see him as a patriot who responded to a real sense of solidarity among his countrymen, while others have rated him an opportunist who masterminded a reign of terror. He spent at least part of his youth in court circles in London, and was married to an Englishwoman. What, according to the legend, turned him was a snub delivered by Parliament when he pressed a petition concerning a land dispute. 'What care we for those barefoot rascals?' was the famous and not untypical English response. For several years thereafter he raised the standard of revolt throughout Wales, capturing Harlech Castle in the process, and setting up a 'parliament' of his own at Machynlleth: in fact little more than an assembly enabling other Welsh leaders to pay him homage. Once again, though, the final outcome of rebellion was failure. Partly the enemy was within. Some other Welsh lords, far from assisting Glyndŵr, opposed him, and over a fifteen-year period the will to fight dissipated. In 1415 Glyndŵr himself 'disappeared', thus adding to the legends that surround him.

On one point historians have tended to concur: Glyndŵr's uprising came too late. A century or even half a century earlier it might have succeeded. This however is perverse. If one is to speculate, then his chances of success must have been much greater later on in the fifteenth century when England was debilitated by the internecine Wars of the Roses. In those circumstances, playing the traditional game of temporary alliances with warring factions, Glyndŵr might very well have carved out a lasting kingdom.

As it was, the long-term fall-out of the same dynastic conflict in England ushered in a very different kind of revolution for Wales. In 1485 Henry Tudor ascended the throne. As well as half his name, half his descent was Welsh. But while the Tudors took statecraft beyond what even the Normans had envisioned, breaking the power of the 'over-mighty' barons and replacing it with a proto-nationalism based on elevating the English middle class to positions of ever greater responsibility, by virtue of their lineage they treated Wales less despotically than their predecessors. In 1536 and 1542, in the reign of Henry VIII, two 'Acts of Union' were placed on the statute books.

The intent and the consequences of this legislation are washed in permanent controversy. In as far as they mark the formal beginning of a recognizably 'British' history, the Acts have always been applauded by unionists, including those many Welsh who prefer to participate in the quantitatively bigger English commercial, cultural and bureaucratic environment. In this reading, attention is drawn to the fact that the statutes specifically granted all Welsh people technical equality before the English law, and so enabled them to benefit from opportunities they would otherwise not have had. Conversely the same Acts are seen by others as having shackled Welsh history to English history, to the extent that Welshmen have frequently been expected, and sometimes required, to fight in 'English' wars. But worse, the 1536 Act disqualified any Welshman who did not speak English from holding public office – not that many had done so before. Indeed, according to the terms of its preamble, it sought to 'extirpate' all Welsh usages and customs that were not consistent with those of England.

The Acts of Union were complex instruments designed primarily to enhance and extend the style of Tudor rule. Other clauses finally abolished the Marcher lordships which, over the centuries, had too regularly been a thorn in the royal side. From the same perspective it made sense to bring all the king's subjects under the sway of one commonly administered legal system. And if that meant granting the same rights to all his subjects, then so be it. At the time, the language clauses could only affect, and perhaps were only intended to affect, a small band of individuals. These were the middle classes – the gentry and the squirearchy – upon whom the Tudors depended so much for the upholding of their power. The actual extirpation of the Welsh language – and at this time at least ninety per cent of the Welsh population were still monoglot Welsh-speaking – was a programme that belonged to the future.

But the future was born of the present. One immediate consequence of the Acts was that many of those Welsh who could afford to learn English did so, and a significant number began migrating to London, to take advantage of employment opportunities there. To the educated Welsh elite the repressions of the past belonged exactly there: in the past. Ironically, one of the professions Welshmen excelled at was law. Their names also frequently appear on listings of academics and higher churchmen. In time too, after the Tudors had been replaced by the Stuarts, Welsh merchants began making reputations and fortunes for themselves in cities across the whole land.

It was only when, much later, the social compact itself began to change that the negative side of the legislation became apparent, at least to some. The industrial revolution, beginning in the last decades of the eighteenth century, unleashed hitherto unsuspected social forces. The Welsh underclasses were no longer confined mainly to the land, but were increasingly herded into towns and cities, where, needing to acquire the skills of literacy previously restricted to folk above them, they also came under pressure to abandon their mother tongue just to survive. Welsh was under fire as never before.

What British governments required from the mid-nineteenth century onwards was not only a literate workforce, but a workforce literate in one common language. Yet such literacy brought its own hazards, even in England. The Chartist movement in the 1840s showed that a reading and writing workforce, or at any rate a workforce whose leaders could read and write, was also a thinking workforce, and one prepared to challenge established authority for political rights. In Wales, where there were also Chartist troubles, the situation was further complicated by a religious revolution. Evangelical methodism and other nonconformisms had taken strong root there, largely because the Anglican Church failed to provide a linguistically adequate ministry. Too many rectors and pastors, schooled in England, belonged to the anglicized English-speaking elite created by the Acts of Union. In the chapels, however, Welsh was offered, and with it a clear if ultimately stultifying morality.

Then, in 1847, there occurred what has gone down in Welsh history as the 'Treachery of the Blue Books'. The Blue Books were the three volumes of a government inquiry into the 'condition of education' in the Principality (so named because, since the time of Edward I, the heir apparent to the English throne first became the Prince of Wales). The 'condition of education' was specifically defined as 'the means afforded to the labouring classes of acquiring a knowledge of the English tongue'. Three monoglot English-speaking London lawyers duly toured Wales, and duly submitted their findings. The 'means afforded', they concluded, were wholly inadequate.

More or less their finding was that education didn't exist in Wales. What they had ignored was the Welsh-language literacy teaching that went on in Nonconformist circles. The Welsh workforce, far from being dismally uninstructed, was in fact better educated than its English counterpart.

Yet by and large it was not the workforce that took umbrage at the Blue Books. Broadly, the 'labouring classes', who did not read government reports, but who nonetheless got wind of what they took to be government censure, responded by redoubling their efforts to learn English, since that was what seemed required of them. Paradoxically the Treachery of the Blue Books lessened resistance to the use of the 'Welsh Not': a piece of board with either the words 'Welsh Not' or the initials 'W. N.' inscribed upon it. This was placed around the neck of any pupil heard speaking Welsh at school. At the end of the day, the child unlucky enough to be caught wearing it was punished, sometimes with a flogging. Rapidly the populations of the main conurbations, unless as incomers they spoke only English anyway, became bilingual. And from there, in the twentieth century, it was but a step to English monolingualism.

Those who did take umbrage, or who articulated their umbrage most strongly, were the mainly Nonconformist Welsh-speaking intelligentsia, another 'class' thrown up by the growth of the cities that accompanied industrialization. The scandal of the Blue Books brought home to them acutely, and in a general way for the first time, the extent to which the Welsh language, and with it a whole culture, would become endangered, if it were not already so.

By definition almost, an intelligentsia likes to have something upon which to exercise its intelligence, and in so doing oppose the prevailing order of things. Cultural revolution of some kind is perpetually on the minds of its members. If they fail in this they are either out of a job, or they lose their identity. Intelligentsias that work for governments are intelligentsias in name only. On the other hand intelligentsias who do not work for the government, either in the bureaucracy or in education, may find it hard to earn a living. The sort of books they write are seldom money-spinners; while, if they work for newspapers, they must unwisely trust to their editors if they are not to be suborned into hacks.

To some extent, the arts and social science departments of the modern university or college provide such individuals with a congenial, well-paid refuge; although, in the long term, the congeniality and the pay are apt to undermine radical, independent thought. But in Wales, largely on account of the majority Nonconformist tradition, the situation is a little different. Throughout the nineteenth century the chapel, as more rarely the church, provided a home and a platform for anti-authoritarianism. Nonconformity also nurtured the emergence of the newly literate classes. Thus by the end of the century, when Wales began acquiring colleges of its own, those who took up teaching posts within them often had cultural and political affinities wholly distinct from their English counterparts. By the same token, schools and the burgeoning bureaucracy were also staffed by men and women who did not readily identify with the establishment.

By such means 'dissent' is more institutionalized in Wales than across the border. Government in Wales has had to draw upon the human resources available to it, regardless of whether such resources are sympathetic to its purposes. At least, that is the underlying score, one by-product of which has been to make the Welsh intelligentsia unusually vulnerable to public criticism, even public scorn. Its members are sometimes perceived to be here, there and everywhere, constantly expressing their opinions, and never allowing a sleeping dog its forty winks. Like members of other intelligentsias they argue, often acrimoniously, among themselves; but because of their increased exposure in Wales, such audible bickering reduces their chances of being taken seriously. And of no issue is this more true than of the language issue.

A well-known joke the Welsh tell about themselves goes as follows. A Welshman is marooned on a desert island. After many years a ship appears on the horizon. The longboat comes ashore. The officer in charge greets the castaway, but asks him why, on the sands of the island, he has built three separate huts. 'Oh that's easy, mun,' replies the Welshman. 'The one in the middle is my house, the one on the left the chapel I go to, and the one on the right the chapel

I don't go to.' Assuming for the moment, however, that a spectral consensus as regards the Welsh language can be extrapolated from at least a moiety of the Welsh-speaking Welsh intelligentsia, its defence of Welsh is roughly as follows. 1. The Welsh nation has been hijacked by history. 2. The principal agents of the Welsh-having-been-hijacked-by-history are the English. 3. Is it right therefore that we should have to speak their language? 4. Especially when we have a language of our own that's just as good as theirs? 5. Moreover, the Welsh language is a lot older than English, a hybrid tongue that didn't begin to settle down until the Middle Ages. 6. Whereas Welsh is of pure Celtic descent, and therefore one of the oldest languages in Europe. 7. What's more, Welsh is the only Celtic language still used on anything like a widespread basis, so special care should be taken to preserve it. 8. To prove all these things, take a look at Welsh literature. 9. And anyway, as I was saying, it's our job to engage in cultural politics.

Living in Wales, one is sometimes tempted to conclude that the language question is tailor-made for a deracinated intelligentsia that nonetheless subsists under generally favourable conditions. But the eighth point especially is irresistible. If the intelligentsia feels itself to be deracinated, then that is not out of some passing intellectual fad, but because, as the literature manifests, something of inherent value is at stake. The poetry in particular encapsulates a consciousness not to be found elsewhere.

To the outsider, mention of 'Welsh poetry' is likely to signify, if it signifies anything at all, bards, the National Eisteddfod and a prosody legendarily more complex than any other. But while each of these terms has a place in any understanding of Welsh poetry as a broad cultural phenomenon, they occlude rather than illuminate its actual character.

The first useful thing to be said about Welsh poetry is that it *is* very old, though just how old nobody for sure knows. Mainly this is because it must have begun as it continued: as an oral practice. Probably therefore the tradition of Welsh poetry is coterminous in its origins with known, but only scantily recorded, Celtic traditions of verse-making. In this context the figure of the bard shades into and grows out of the priestly class (or caste) of the Druids, described by, among other classical authors, Julius Caesar and Tacitus. One possibility is that a bard, or *bardd* (after *bardus*), was a particular kind of Druid, with particular 'verbal' responsibilities. But whereas the Druids did not survive the Roman occupation – famously the Druids of Anglesey were collectively massacred in 61 AD – bards did. At the courts of the post-Roman Welsh princes and chieftains they held honoured places. Indeed, any court worth its salt maintained a chamber of poets. At their head was the *pencerdd*, or chief poet, whose place at the prince's table was two down from the *edling* or heir: that is, above most if not all the prince's most valued warriors. Under this man's charge were the *beirdd teulu*, or household poets, whose rights and rewards, like those of the *pencerdd* himself, are detailed in the Laws of Hywel Dda. And finally there was a third class of poet, the *cerddorion*, wandering minstrels who, although they might not enjoy the permanent patronage of a court, could nonetheless expect payment for their recitations as of right.

Poets, one might say, have never had it so good. These arrangements continued up to 1282 and the defeat of Llywelyn the Last. Thereafter, with the demise of the princedoms, patronage of poets passed to the houses of the richer gentry and landowners. The richer gentry and landowners however did not baulk at this inherited responsibility. Rather they fostered what is regarded as a second great flowering of Welsh poetry, which included, in the fourteenth century, the work of Dafydd ap Gwilym. In marked contrast, the two Acts of Union, enacted under Henry VIII, did bring about a severe curtailment of the courtly tradition, as many of Wales's wealthier patrons either gravitated towards London, or became more self-consciously anglicized. Although poetry continued to be written in Welsh, there was, for two centuries at least, a dearth of genuinely outstanding poets. In Wales, a 'high' culture that had lasted a thousand years was at an end.

The revival, when it occurred, was largely the fruit of antiquarian researches in the eighteenth century. As classical Welsh poetry was rediscovered, coinciding with an English endeavour to trace England's 'British' roots, so Welsh poets once more began writing verses that adhered to the 'strict metres' of the past. But it was in regard to this mini-renaissance in Welsh letters that the features by which

'Welsh poetry' has become popularly known among outsiders dropped into place.

The blithe villain of the piece was Edward Williams (1747–1826), better known as Iolo Morganwg. Jumping on the antiquarian bandwagon, this Unitarian, who was also a laudanum addict, proceeded to forge whatever he could not uncover. He thought nothing of augmenting Dafydd ap Gwilym's work with compositions of his own. But his coup de grâce was the creation – or as he would have it, re-creation – of Gorsedd Beirdd Ynys Prydain, the Council of the Bards of the Island of Britain. This met for the first time in 1792 in London, the hotbed of antiquarian activities. Its particular flavour was Druidic; among those who attended was William Blake. Through fair means or foul, Iolo was determined to attach the bardic tradition to its priestly, and vastly more hazy, antecedents.

Iolo was a prime exponent of what has been dubbed 'the invention of tradition'[28]: a pathology that affected many nineteenth-century proto-nationalisms. Having made entirely bogus claims about the historicity of the Gorsedd, he fused it with the far more authentic tradition of the eisteddfod. In Welsh, an eisteddfod need mean no more than a gathering of poets and/or other kinds of artists to discuss and perform their work. A competitive element may or may not be present. But out of Iolo's activities has grown the whole paraphernalia of the modern National Eisteddfod, with its Chair (a genuine revival) and its Crown and its robes and its Archdruids.

By the time Iolo's forgeries were finally rumbled, the Eisteddfod had become too permanent a fixture to be abandoned. While it has sometimes incited the mirth, even ridicule, of the uninvolved, there is much to be said in favour of Edward Williams's perpetrations. Apart from the obvious fact that all traditions have to be 'invented' some time or other, the modern National Eisteddfod is a real festival that provides a regular focus for Welsh arts and, indeed, the Welsh community. It is also the case that, although the poetry competitions which are the festival's ostensible raison d'être have enshrined prosodic rules that may have been natural to a medieval court or household but which are hard to align with the style of contemporary society, and have therefore overly encouraged the production of pastiche, the Eisteddfod has sometimes provided a platform for more energetic and more thoughtful poets. The twentieth century has seen a third flowering of Welsh-language poetry. Nearly every one of its leading figures has competed, usually successfully and usually at the outset of his writing career, at the Eisteddfod.

But what of the first flowering? The earliest known Welsh-language poetry dates back to somewhere near the beginning of the seventh century. Precise dating however is hazardous, as the texts that have come down to us are generally redactions made by monks from the tenth century onwards. The same is true of the great prose work of the Welsh peoples, the *Mabinogion*: a retelling of Celtic myths and legends, elements of which are undoubtedly far older still. Invariably such transcriptions have been prone to the errors, and sometimes to the explicitly Christian emendations and interpolations, of the copyists themselves.

A further source of 'textual corruption' is the nature of the oral tradition itself. As with other oral poetries, what was composed by one generation of Welsh bards may have been subject to the revisions and embellishments of subsequent generations working under changed circumstances. The disciplines of oral poetry were strenuous in the extreme. A bard went through an apprenticeship lasting many years, during which he learned his craft not only by practising it under the supervision of, say, a *pencerdd*, but also by memorizing the poems of previous poets. When he came to compose his own poems for public recitation, he had to do this entirely in his head. A modern equivalent might be for a novelist to retain the text of a novel in his memory, ready for regurgitation upon request. But for the bard, one sign that he had attained proficiency in his craft was his ability to re-render known poems in his own manner. Another sign might be his ability to deliver an original poem in the style of a predecessor, as though it were an older composition than in fact it was.

These obstacles aside, modern scholarship has demonstrated that the redactions that have come to us in a series of early medieval manuscripts – for example, *The Black Book of Carmarthen* – must in some cases be the vestigial remains of poems composed far earlier. In particular this would seem to be true of two outstanding poets of the early seventh century, Aneirin and Taliesin. *Y Gododdin* ('The Gododdin') is contained in the *Book of Aneirin*. This great sequence of linked elegies gives an eye-witness account of the deaths of three hundred warriors defeated in battle by the Angles at Catraeth (modern Catterick) in *c.* 598. In lyric after lyric it is heroic failure that is celebrated, so that *Y Gododdin* becomes a hymn to that most Welsh of all emotions, *hiraeth*:

> Sooner as wolf's meat
> than to a wedding breakfast;
> sooner a crow's gain
> than to the altar; he would
> sooner go to war
> than be buried.[29]

By contrast, the work of Taliesin is more varied, but also more difficult to disentangle from later impositions. Many poems ascribed to Taliesin cannot possibly be by him. Those that are authentic include 'praise poems', addressed to several Brythonic chieftains. But in a way those that are not 'authentic' are just as important, as they express other main preoccupations of Welsh poetry, for example the themes of prophecy, and of the magical or semi-divine status of the poet himself.

Prophecy is also the concern of a group of poems attributed to Myrddin, better known east of Offa's Dyke as Merlin. Since the historic Myrddin, if he existed at all, may have lived as early as Roman times, the dire warnings against the Saxons that issue from his mouth are almost certainly the inspiration of later bards. But this too is indicative of how the oral tradition worked. Myrddin was a potent figure to invoke, and the actual quality of many of the Myrddin poems is not in doubt. Similarly, in another collection, most probably composed in the ninth century, a series of compelling laments are projected on to the two figures of Llywarch Hen (Llywarch the Old) and the princess Heledd, in the manner of dramatis personae; yet the actual authorship of the pieces is unknown. In an age when poetry was performed, not written, copyright, like authenticity, was not an anxiety.

Inevitably long gaps in the oral tradition occur. The tenth and eleventh centuries seem relatively barren, but this may simply be down to the accidents of loss and survival. The twelfth and thirteenth centuries, however, suggest not only a revival of Welsh poetry, but also fresh departures. Leadership, war and death in war continue as staple themes, but now the feast is enriched by poets who turn their attentions upon love and nature, and also upon God. There is strong evidence that external influences were at work: the semi-classicism of the 'twelfth-century renaissance', and also the traditions of the European troubadour. Yet the decisive event, that permanently turned the course of Welsh poetry, was the defeat of Llywelyn in 1282, marked at the time with ominous foreboding by Gruffudd ab yr Ynad Coch:

> Why, O my God, does the sea not cover the land?
> Why are we left to linger?[30]

Thereafter, as literacy among poets became the rule, not the exception, they found themselves working for patrons of reduced means, or at any rate reduced estates. But far from spelling the death knell of Welsh poetry, 1282 inaugurated its second golden age.

Welsh prosody also underwent a sea-change, though this, in the nature of such things, was more gradual. Welsh verse forms became progressively more intricate, until, in the fifteenth century, the 'twenty-four metres' were codified by Dafydd ab Edmwnd. The rules of *cynghanedd*, an extraordinarily complex system of alliteration, consonance and internal rhyme, were extrapolated once and for all time. Even so-called permissible 'free verse' was, by the standards of English prosody, anything but free.

In social terms, this development, or apotheosis, was in part defensive. Historically, through bardic practice, Welsh poets always had been highly professionalized, and their subsequent insistence on technical virtuosity was one way of maintaining their guild. But *cynghanedd* and the twenty-four metres were also defensive in another plane. In the hands of the outstanding poets, Iolo Goch (*c.* 1320–98) for example, or Siôn Cent (*c.* 1400–40), or Tudur Aled (*c.* 1465–1525), but most memorably Dafydd ap Gwilym (*c.* 1320–70), Welsh prosody became the means of maintaining Welsh values against English domination. Bewilderingly arcane to the outsider, to the insider it was a place of rest.

Many of the things Dafydd ap Gwilym wrote about have become synonymous with the ideals of a certain sort of 'Welsh Welshman', among them R. S. Thomas. Always ready to castigate the *Sais*, he was also dismissive of towns and town life. Conversely he extolled, if not always the virtue, then certainly the beauty of Welsh womanhood; and he immersed himself in the natural world, both as a means of escape and as a route to God. Thus his *Offeren y LLwyn*, or 'Woodland Mass':

> *Mi a glywwn mewn gloywiaith*
> *Ddatganu, nid methu, maith,*
> *Darllain i'r plwyf, nid rhwyf rhus,*
> *Efengyl yn ddifyngus.*

> (I heard there, in language loud and clear
> a chanting, long and without cease,
> and the gospel read distinctly,
> to the parish – no unseemly haste.)[31]

These are lines of a profound joy, but also of a profound retreat, the correlative perhaps to Aneirin's warriors, rushing out to certain death.

Often it is said that the Welsh language is all that the Welsh have left to call their own. For this reason the works of Dafydd ap Gwilym and the best of his contemporaries, together with the *Mabinogion* and the earlier poets, are prized as the very embodiment of a people and its culture. For all that the same poetic culture too often seems by its own inclinations embarked upon defeat, at the edge of a spurious union that has become modern Britain it still offers a political resistance.

II

BORN LOST

A child's memories
are of the womb, the sleep
by unearthly waters;
his dreams are of a happiness
unfounded.

R. S. THOMAS,
'Incarnations'[1]

BOTH THE HISTORY and the literature of Wales strongly suggest a people blown off course, culturally at odds with their dominant English neighbours, but often equally at odds among themselves. Conversely, the commonalty of Welsh enjoy a greater aggregate of security, rights and opportunities today than at any point previously. The era of the independent Welsh princes, effectively brought to a close with the death of Llywelyn in 1282, like the doomed uprising of Owain Glyndŵr a century later, may be looked back upon by some as a golden age, but it would take a brave scholar to argue that life was then better for the ordinary adult than it has been during most of the twentieth century, quite apart from the advances made in technology and medicine. On the contrary, from before and after the time of the Norman conquests, the Welsh grandees behaved very much like the grandees not just of England, but of all Europe. In their courts they may have encouraged and sustained a high culture that was peculiarly Welsh, but their abiding aspirations were dynastic, their means military and feudal. If it suited their purposes to join forces with their Anglo-Norman counterparts, either on the battlefield or in the nuptial chamber, then generally they did so without hesitation.

This is not to say that the twentieth century has been uniformly benign for Wales. One has only to visit the desolated collier valleys of Gwent and Glamorgan to realize that. They compare with the blighted inner city districts of (for example) Liverpool. As, in common with all other post-industrial societies, Wales has steadily diversified, so too have the fortunes of its differentiated communities varied. But set against the unevenness of prosperity and decay, there is the bald fact that the only substantive political disadvantage the Welsh suffer collectively in comparison with the English is numeric.

73

In every other respect, the Welsh enjoy political equality with their supposed oppressors. They partake of the same representative demo-cratic system, they are subject to the same laws and benefits, they have equal freedoms of movement and expression. Of the many Welshmen who have risen to high office, David Lloyd George became Prime Minister, while Neil Kinnock was for much of the 1980s an intermittently brilliant leader of the British Labour Party. And further down the ladder, for every holiday home purchased by an English person in Wales, several jobs at least are filled by Welsh persons in England.

Very largely the two countries are merged. Transport, economic and communications systems are all shared. Some Welsh may feel that with less than 10 per cent of parliamentary seats in their hands, their views can never be adequately reflected in the prevailing politi-cal agenda; but the reverse of that is that in several twentieth-century elections the party returned to power, Liberal early on, Labour during the 1960s and 1970s, was returned precisely because it was the majority party in Wales, and without the Welsh constituencies the English would have had governments more of them had voted for. The system is not perfect, but its imperfections affect both peoples alike. Arguably the introduction of proportional representation would enhance Welsh aspirations where they differ from normative British aspirations, and would give more point to voting for Plaid Cymru, the Welsh National Party, just as perhaps it would enhance Scottish or, say, north-of-England aspirations. But until PR is introduced, everyone is similarly vulnerable to the vagaries of an antiquated first-past-the-post machinery; and in fact the campaign for PR has if anything been pursued rather less vigorously in Wales than else-where in the UK.

Or, look at Wales through the kaleidoscope of the European Union. The same numerical disadvantage pertains. As matters stand, Britain as a whole is gradually being merged with her European partners. About this process there is something seemingly ineluctable. In the Maastricht negotiations, John Major and his fellow elected oligarchs achieved a number of 'opt-outs' from the Europe-wide treaty. Nobody seriously doubts, however, that in the long term if the European roller-coaster continues gathering momentum then Britain will have to toe the common line, just as in the event that other European governments decide to adopt a common currency, then Britain too will be propelled willy-nilly into monetary union. The only true alternative is to withdraw completely from the EU: a potentially disastrous strategy unless at least one other front-line, and several second-line, European states were prepared to adopt the same course, in which case the European Union as such would disintegrate.

In this context, Wales waits upon the deliberations of the British government, in which, through the ballot box, it exerts, or may exert, some influence. Were Wales to attain sudden independence, however, either through orderly devolution or, as seems far less likely, through a unilateral declaration, its position vis-à-vis Europe would be little altered. While Plaid Cymru argues, perhaps correctly, that as a separate member state of the EU Wales could gain more benefits, particularly in the form of European subsidies, economically there is a zero-sum equation. Those subsidies would only replace what in effect are subsidies internally provided by Whitehall, and the only real gain would be in Wales having 'a voice of her own'. But in Strasbourg and Brussels that voice would be correspondingly diminished by not being joined with the larger English or British voice. There would be no more Welsh Euro MPs in the European parliament, and probably even fewer Welsh mandarins within the Euro-bureaucracy, which is where, quite undemocratically, most of the decisions that matter are made. In fact the only way Wales could expect to have any impact on European decision-making processes would be for its spokespersons, whether or not they are elected, to join hands with non-Welsh representatives on the basis of party or ideological affiliation; the same, in other words, as happens now at Westminster; and indeed happens at Strasbourg.

For some Welsh, including presumably the higher echelons of Plaid Cymru, the idea of being continually bigfooted by the European community is preferable to continuing to be bigfooted by the English establishment – a view shared by a not inconsiderable number of English themselves – even though in each case the net result is more than approximately equivalent. Again the true alternative – an independent Wales that was not a member of the EU – is largely unthinkable. If only because of geographic proximity and the land frontier, in this circumstance Wales would probably find itself bigfooted by its neighbour on a scale not experienced since the Cromwellian revolution, though the means would be predominantly economic.

Wales, then, is lumbered with the disadvantages conferred upon it by its size for the foreseeable future. All in all, looked at dispassionately from the point of view of political economy, the overwhelmingly reasonable course for the Welsh to take would seem to be to acknowledge the reality of their union with England, indeed to exploit it for every kind of commercial and social gain. To say: we may not have started off as one people, but we are becoming one people, and so let us benefit from this increment to our size. Together we can still be a large nation in Europe; together, we can win.

And why not? In unity is strength, and all of that. But there are other ways of regarding Wales, of regarding nations. The dispassionate political-economy vision is precisely that: a dispassionate vision, arguing what should be from what is. Or rather, from what has come to be. It insists that culture and custom are subordinate to government and market structures, that content follow form. Whereas in reality should it not be the other way round? Should not form follow content? Should not a people's and a nation's institutions reflect their culture, their character?

The point is made very expressively as regards the Welsh language. Language is both content and form, and what has been excluded from much of the Welsh landscape since the Treachery of the Blue Books is precisely that thing that Matthew Arnold identified as being the essence of a nation: its mother tongue. Even parliamentary democracy, however fine in itself, or however much it at least excels its rivals, if in its particulars, which include the language spoken in its representative chambers, it is an organism that has evolved outside a people and its culture, and been imposed upon them, how much legitimacy can it claim? Could not Wales and the Welsh have been relied upon to develop their own democratically accountable institutions, in keeping with their custom?

Perhaps. Almost certainly yes, since that has been the experience of every other western nation-state. But of course it is too late. The damage, if damage it is, has been done. The political and economic structures that Wales is encumbered with have had time to affect Welsh culture, Welsh thinking, above all, and to its certain detriment, the Welsh language. After a while, content does follow form. Live long enough in a brothel or a bank and anyone will adopt the posture of a whore or a clerk. It is no longer possible even to talk of Wales. Dialogue rather must take account of at least two broad-brush crudities, not one: 'Welsh' Wales, and its more populous corollary, 'non-Welsh' Wales. The 20 per cent of the population who can speak Welsh, and the 80 per cent who can't.

Non-Welsh Wales! Surely there is a cognitive dissonance here? A schizophrenia even. But because of the numbers situation, because of the demography, because even within Wales itself Welsh speakers are in a minority, it is the Welsh-speaking Welsh, and not their counterparts, who are more likely to be rated as misfits or outsiders, to be castigated as mentally aberrant.

So was it ever, we might say, among nations and their peoples. There are majorities and minorities, and further minorities within both. In time though, the differences are or will be ironed out: by the sword, by assimilation, by the encroachment of a common, global lifestyle; by death.

In the meantime we are stuck with the circumstances we are born into, and the circumstances that evolve around us. From the inside looking out, the numbers game is not irrelevant, indeed it must affect us, one way or the other, but it will certainly be misleading, and at worst an excrescence. So what if I share my language and my culture with a hundred million others, or with only a million? With several hundred thousand, or just a few hundred? It would still be my culture, still be my language, the preconditioning of my creaturely existence:

> We are the lost people.
> Tracing us by our language
> you will not arrive where we are
> which is nowhere. The wind
> blows through our castles; the chair
> of poetry is without a tenant.

We are exiles within
our own country; we eat our bread
at a pre-empted table. 'Show us,'
we supplicate, 'the way home',
and they laughing hiss at us:
'But you are home. Come in
and endure it,' Will nobody
explain what it is like
to be born lost?

from 'The Lost'

If we have any mind at all for these lines, published by R. S. Thomas in his collection *No Truce with the Furies* as late as 1995, we will recognize the limitations of the prescripts of political economy. We might even go further. We might allow the Welsh Welsh what they have always wanted: their own land, governed by themselves. Not the whole of Wales, of course – realistically it simply is too late for that; and in any case, within an independent Wales the Welsh Welsh would still be a minority, English would still be the lingua franca. But a smaller republic, an enlarged Gwynedd perhaps, taking in, as well as the north-west of the country, parts of west and mid-Wales, of Powys and Dyfed: that might be realistic.

Other than its natural beauty, such a republic would have few resources to depend upon. In Europe its only asset would be its charm. Or perhaps with Eryri, Snowdonia, at its centre, Welsh Wales could follow the way of Switzerland, steer clear of the EU, and become fabulously rich on banking.

Who knows what might happen? In any event, the Republic of Gwynedd would be an interesting project. The Welsh Welsh might fail, but the right to fail is, or should be, everyone's.

'The Lost' is a late, uncompromising statement by R. S. Thomas of the agony endured by a minority long threatened with linguistic extinction. But it is other things beside. It is as much a personal elegy as a public one. Indeed, part of what it says is that, in matters of language, there is no separation between nation and individual. It is also about old age, and the disappointment of a religious expectation. From the point where we left it, 'The Lost' continues:

> We have our signposts
> but they are in another tongue,
> If we follow our conscience
> it leads us nowhere but to gaol.
> The ground moves under our feet;
> our one attitude is vertigo.
> 'And a little child,' the Book tells us
> 'shall lead them.' But this one
> has a linguistic club
> in his hand with which, old as we are,
> he trounces and bludgeons us senseless.

The identity of the child with the 'linguistic club/ in his hand' is not revealed. Conceivably, since the poem was written while the youthful Conservative John Redwood was Secretary of State for Wales, it refers to Redwood, reported to have refused, during his tenure of that office, to sign any document written in Welsh. More probably it either refers to Charles Windsor, in his role as Prince of Wales, or more loosely to today's Welsh schoolboy, reared to speak English. Whichever or whoever was in the poet's mind, the closing image is striking. What could be more cowardly than mauling the aged? But, by building his poem towards a closure couched in a biblical image, Thomas says much more than 'Look how the weak are driven to the wall!' Also driven to the wall is an entire morality, the morality of Christendom, which, as it happens, is also the vestigial morality of the persecutor, so that the crime perpetrated is not only a crime against humanity, but a crime against God. Suddenly, what looked like an entirely secular issue –

> If we follow our conscience
> it leads us nowhere but to gaol

referring to a number of prison sentences meted out to Welsh nation-alists for their acts of civil disobedience – takes on a different, some would say enhanced, complexion. The 'conscience' is transfigured, from the sublunary political into something almost Christological.

79

More, the light thrown back through the poem by its ending begins to explain the otherwise opaque two lines that follow:

> The ground moves under our feet;
> our one attitude is vertigo.

Unless this means that the matter of Wales is in some way a holy matter, indeed primarily a holy matter, then it is far from clear what can be meant.

Like many other of Thomas's poems, 'The Lost' weaves a number of different imageries and themes into a compelling whole. As so often, on a single page we have the measure of the poet, and the measure of his art. Yet the two conflict. The poet, one senses, is driven by a depth of feeling towards his subject-matter that insists on expression. He is not a writer of either occasional or ornamental verses. He rejects the Aristotelian concept of the poet as one kind of artificer among many. That is why the poem gets written. The art, on the other hand, is conflationary, is indeed art. The personal and the political, history and the divine, are cocktailed together. It conjures unity among elements others might consider disparate; elements indeed some would say Thomas has no licence to compound.

And this is the challenge Thomas sets the reader. He returns poetry to its tap-roots. He provides us, albeit via modernist techniques, with a species of tribal propaganda, in which ancestors, customs and gods are run together. He is like Homer in a thousand fragments, shorn of narrative concern, or Isaiah in an hour-glass. At times he is blindingly good; at others, three thousand years on from the inception of such a project, awesomely suspect.

But that is only the beginning of R. S. Thomas. What he does he seldom does unwittingly. His own critical eye is kept open, and trained on his own manoeuvres, as summarized in an earlier poem, titled simply, and most prematurely, 'Epitaph':

> The poem in the rock and
> The poem in the mind
> Are not one.
> It was in dying
> I tried to make them so.[2]

Whatever the precise application of these lines – 'the rock', for instance, could refer equally to the natural world, or to religious faith, both key concerns throughout Thomas's writings – there can be no doubt that they evince an absolute synthesis between the poet's life and the poet's work, so that the life is the work and the work is the life.

And this is not a pose, even though 'Epitaph' could equally be taken to refer to Christ.

Yet had Thomas never written a line of verse the externals of his life might be little changed. Born in Cardiff in 1913, but raised and schooled in Holyhead, he attended the University College of North Wales at Bangor, taking a second class honours degree in Classics (Latin). From Bangor he returned to Cardiff, to prepare for ordination into the Anglican Church in Wales at St Michael's College, Llandaff. Ordained deacon in 1936 and priest in 1937, he held curacies at Chirk (Y Waun) in Denbighshire and at Hanmer in (old) Flintshire before being installed as the Rector of Manafon, Montgomeryshire, in 1942. After twelve years at Manafon he moved to another living, at Eglwysfach, on the boundary between Cardiganshire and Meirionnydd, close to the west coast of Wales. Then in 1967 he transferred to the vicarage of Aberdaron, at the end of the Llŷn peninsula in the far north-west, almost, but not quite, opposite the wind-washed holy island of Enlli (Bardsey). Finally, in 1978, he retired from the ministry. For fifteen years he continued living in Llŷn, but after the death of his wife he returned to the scenery of his childhood, taking up residence near Holyhead in Môn (Anglesey), where, in his eighties, he may still be found.

And in all, a not especially distinguished clerical career, but rather one pursued by many hundreds of other Anglican priests for whom country livings provide a secure if not overly glamorous or lucrative niche. Along the way Thomas might or might not have acquired the Welsh language, might or might not have concerned himself with issues raised by Welsh nationalism, and might or might not have fallen out with some of his parishioners. Again, he might or might not have undertaken a searching personal quest for God. But towards the end of an outwardly uneventful life, only his surviving family, a handful of colleagues and a thin flock would have any particular reason to remember him.

Such is the biography of many a contemporary parson, against a background of decimated congregations and cultural values that have become as secular as they are urban. As it is however, while still contained within the seemingly narrow confines of such a parabola, R. S. Thomas's life, through his poetry and other writings, has emerged as something of an exemplary critique of everything considered modern or contemporary, so that it is probable he will be remembered, in Wales and beyond, in legendary terms; as indeed he is already regarded by many of his countrymen.

Thomas's first volume, or collection, of poetry, *The Stones in the Field*, was published in 1946. Prior to that, several poems had appeared in magazines. Thereafter, and continuing to the present day, his poetry has appeared at more or less regular intervals. Poems published at first individually in periodicals are gathered into books, along with other poems previously unpublished. To date, across a span of fifty years, twenty-five such volumes, of varying thickness, have found their way into print. Of late, more rather than fewer poems are being published, so that Thomas rivals Hardy's fecundity in old age. In addition, there has been a *Selected Poems*, first published in 1973, and a *Collected Poems 1945–1990* (1993). The latter by no means contains all Thomas's published verse. Many poems from the earlier volumes are excluded, while well over a hundred poems that appeared in magazines have never found their way into any collection. Indeed, the *Collected Poems*, containing roughly five hundred poems, represents less than half what there is. Establishing the dimensions of the true canon, which must also include unpublished verses as well as the fugitive will probably occupy Thomas's bibliographers well into the twenty-first century.

Thomas then has been an unusually prolific poet. Assuming that the final tally approximates to somewhere in the region of 1200 items, the mathematics imply that, on average, Thomas has produced one poem per fortnight for fifty years: a prodigious performance. But that is only an average. Inevitably even Thomas will have experienced, as in fact he has testified, lean as well as fat periods, so that when in full cry it is probable he has written several poems per week, perhaps for months on end. We must also take into account, again on his own testimony, that it is not unusual for him to devote much of the day to a composition which he then abandons; and at least one fellow Anglo-Welsh poet has conveyed his suspicion that Thomas probably does write something every day of his life.[3]

Characteristically the R. S. Thomas poem is relatively short, fitting on to a single page. The usual length is in the region of twenty to forty lines, while many poems, including a large number that may be classified as pseudo-sonnets, are a good deal shorter. Conversely, there are a dozen or so longer poems, usually made up of prosodically diversified sections. The 'Complete Thomas', when eventually it appears, may fail to match the bulk of the 'Complete Browning', 'Complete Milton' or even 'Complete Byron'. Yet compared to most other leading English-language twentieth-century poets – Auden, for example, or Yeats, or Eliot, or Dylan Thomas, or Philip Larkin – Thomas remains significantly ahead in terms of volume.

But productivity in itself means little or nothing. What daunts some readers of Thomas's poetry is its consistently high quality. It very nearly is the case that he is incapable of writing, or at any rate of publishing, a 'bad' poem. In the complete editions of Coleridge's verse, or Byron's, or Shelley's, or Wordsworth's even, there is much that is undisputedly second-rate, so that reading their *Selected Poems* is often an intelligent compromise. We are grateful when editors have done their work efficiently. But in Thomas's case, the obverse applies. The fewer poems of his we read, the less we are inclined to acknowledge his stature. Whereas if we read many, or even most of his poems, then it becomes almost impossible to deny his mastery, regardless of whether we in fact *like* what we read; and indeed the *Collected Poems* of 1993 is virtually a minimum requirement.

This is not to say that individual poems by R. S. Thomas do not stand and work in their own space. Most of them do. Rather it is to draw attention to their cumulative effect, and their habit of virulently rubbing up against, and thereby enriching, each other: an aspect of some other poets, notably Yeats, but one Thomas brings to a pitch. Nor is it to suggest that his poetry is *uniformly* of the same high standard, or interest. Of course there are variations – troughs and peaks – in the poet's energy or imaginative levels. Some mannerisms do intrude; and one question that has to be addressed as regards some of the later verse is whether it is poetry at all, rather than philosophical inscription. But overwhelmingly, the more Thomas we read, the more convinced we are likely to become that we are some-how in the presence of a born poet; that he is, for better or for worse, the lifelong prisoner of an endlessly exacting muse.

But there is also a body of prose writings. Thomas's non-poetic output may be tranched into the critical, the polemical, and the autobiographical. There are reviews he has written, and introductions to verse selections he has supplied. There are fighting patriotic articles contributed, mainly in the Welsh language, to a range of predomi-nantly Welsh magazines, as well as the pamphlet *Cymru or Wales?* (1992). And, as well as the book-length memoir *Neb*, and its con-densed version prepared for the American *Contemporary Authors: Auto-biographical Series*,[4] there are other deliberately autobiographical excursions, including *Blwyddyn yn Llŷn* ('A Year in Llŷn', 1990), the late *ABC Neb* (1995), and the idiosyncratic mixed-prose-and-verse book *The Echoes Return Slow* (1988); to which may be added, down the years, a fair number of media interviews and talks.

In fact, for a man renowned for a tetchy reticence about his personal life, there is a surprising amount of evidentiary material to hand, most of it supplied by the poet himself, making conventional biography in a way superfluous.

As already suggested, outside the poetry the principal source for R. S. Thomas's life is the 130-page *Neb*, edited by Gwenno Hywyn, and published by the Gwasg Gwynedd (Gwynedd Press) in 1985. This was one of a series of autobiographies by different writers. Written in a somewhat stilted, correct Welsh, *Neb*'s primary characteristic is that Thomas narrates his life in the third person – a time-honoured if relatively uncommon literary device, used, inter alia, by some Old Testament prophets, and to devastating effect by Julius Caesar, in his histories of his Gallic campaigns. But while Caesar's purpose was to enhance his reputation within the Roman Republic by reifying his own achievements, Thomas's intentions are less unambiguous.

The book's epigraph is taken from the French poet-dramatist Paul Claudel: '*Et de ce néant indestructible, qui est moi,*': 'About this indestructible nothingness, which is me.' This accords well with Thomas's title. The Welsh word *neb* means nobody, or no-person; 'just anyone' perhaps, or 'nobody special'. The proposed posture of the memoirist is therefore one of existential humility. The nothingness with which Thomas equates his being is a nothingness defined by its relations with the more enduring, and physically daunting, natural world, and by his perception of God. Yet that humility is mitigated by two factors. Firstly, we may fairly ask whether, whatever the device or devices used, the simple act of autobiography does not imply some degree of vanity? Secondly, Thomas's particular handling of the third person humble in fact enables him to pursue some peculiarly virulent prejudices, but in such a way that they are cloaked within an objective, even minimalist outlook. Through a seemingly even-handed deprecation of himself. Thomas is set at liberty to deprecate much else, including, at times, the rest of humanity. As with Claudel, however, his ultimate drift is religious, or spiritual. The inconspicuousness that Thomas adopts in the face of human affairs is often ironic; but brought up against his own final and oddly bleak vision of the greater human realities, the humility is reasserted as being philosophically proper.

Thus the end-point, the pay-off if you like, of Thomas's autobiographical journey. Yet at once it plunges us deeply in a dilemma, which is the dilemma of nearly all autobiography. *Neb* was not written during the whole course of the life it narrates, as that life unfolded, keeping pace with it as a diary or journal might, but from the point of view of an accrued, even idiosyncratic, state of consciousness. There must be, therefore, an incorrigible bias – in this case the bias of a sustained patriotic misanthropy. If we go back to the beginning and examine the very first paragraph of *Neb*, describing the poet's birth, we find thoughts and perspectives that no infant could conceivably entertain:

Man is a fecund creature; he has enveloped the face of the earth. Why then fear sterility? At this moment womenfolk are giving birth in every corner of the world. And so it was in Cardiff, on the 29th

March 1913, one birth among thousands. Augmenting the pain of the world, a girl cries, then a baby howls, and continues to howl for a long time. There are illnesses in this world, and little children fall prey to them. Meningitis! The photographs show a child only half-sane. But his clothing is pretty.[5]

Life, Thomas tells us, is in itself undesirable, not just his life, but all life, at least all human life. Human life is a world of pain, harsh, unremitting physical and mental pain. But about his particular life there is something especially unwholesome. Some time after birth he contracts meningitis. But when exactly? This he does not tell us. Only that the earliest photographs show a child who is 'half-sane'; or to translate the Welsh words literally, one who is 'short of a yard', a penny short of a shilling. But such is the telescopic energy of this paragraph — no name, for example, is given to the place of birth, the hospital or nursing home — that the causal relationship between the illness and the symptomatic condition is not quite spelled out. The one could be the consequence of the other; but the opposite of this conclusion, that the very young R. S. Thomas was in some way naturally demented, is not entirely excluded. In fact, just the sort of elliptic manoeuvre Caesar indulges in his campaign histories.

Three years after *Neb* Thomas published his second attempt at an extended autobiography, the 121-page *The Echoes Return Slow*, this time in English. Here, on each double-page spread, a paragraph of prose on the left is complemented by a poem on the right. The sense of selective distillation is even greater. Again he begins with the matter of his birth:

Pain's climate. The weather unstable. Blood rather than rain fell. The woman was opened and sewed up, relieved of the trash that had accumulated nine months in the man's absence. Time would have its work cut out in smoothing the birth-marks in the flesh. The marks in the spirit would not heal. The dream would recur, groping his way up to the light, coming to the crack too narrow to squeeze through.

And from the poem across the page:

... Charity
spares what should be
lopped off before
it is too late.

So we learn that Thomas was a breach baby, that he was 'plucked
untimely from his mother's womb', though not, as some commentators have supposed, by Caeserian section. But are we to believe
that the nightmare of his birth is repeated in his dreams? Or is this
an allowable metaphor wrought by the seventy-five-year-old poet,
based on a knowledge of his birth and not a memory of it? And why
nightmare? For the mother certainly; but for the newborn? In many,
if not all, cultures birth is regarded as an adventitious miracle, a
renewal of the life cycle, or at the least a cause for celebration.
Exceptions are when the child is born deformed in some way.

Is Thomas deformed? Physically, certainly not. At school and
college he will become something of a sportsman. As a priest, he
will be noted for his rugged strength. All his life he will walk and
climb mountains. Indeed, he develops an attitude of intolerance
towards the unmanly. But mentally?

Mentally it is hardly creditable that Thomas is wanting. He is
articulate, both in speech and on paper, to an uncommon degree.
His serious utterances are intensely pruned and pared – edited in
the brain box, we might say – before they are issued. In fact, he has
been unusually fortunate. Although he does not specify what kind
of meningitis he suffered as an infant, we must assume a viral, not
bacteriological, variety. Even with the help of modern antibiotics,
bacteriological meningitis kills. In the early years of the century it
was invariably fatal. Viral meningitis, still difficult to treat, offered
a choice of outcomes. It could kill, or it could leave the victim
mentally impaired, or there was full, spontaneous remission. Where
mental impairment occurred (and continues to occur) the result could
be anything from a relatively mild disorder, the 'clumsy child' syn-
drome, to persistent vegetative state. But once a clumsy child, always
a clumsy child; and the known dispositions of Thomas do not suggest
the clumsy child. He was lucky.

What the evidence does suggest is that at an unspecified point in his early childhood Thomas did indeed experience viral meningitis, but that he was granted full remission. Nevertheless for a while he would have been acutely ill, and this is what seems to be remembered, so that many decades later the mature poet, probing the root causes of what he acknowledges to be an inherent idiosyncrasy in his personality, elects to give pride of place to an early and transient affliction by placing it at the centre – *Meningitis*! – of the first paragraph of his prose autobiography.

I am not suggesting that Thomas is deliberately disingenuous here; merely that he reclothes his past with perceptions borrowed from the present. His exertions at total recall may have been less than Proustian, but in that respect Proust is the exception that proves the rule. As regards his despondent attitude towards human life in general, Thomas had very good reasons to feel as he did when he wrote both *Neb* and *The Echoes Return Slow*. On the one hand, his own situation then was that of a fit man in the decline of his years; on the other, and probably more critically, his wife was gravely ill, and known to be dying.

Still the point is made. Thomas as he looks back on his life does seem unusually overcome by pessimism, by accidie, so that the question becomes: was he always like that, a fish out of water, a born nay-sayer, or did he merely become so? To what extent, for example, did his acute identification with Welsh minoritism bring about his characteristic mental outlook, or did that mental outlook lead him towards Welsh minoritism?

These questions are the mysteries of an interior landscape. And because the landscape is interior, short of discovering a psychologist's report, assembled over a period of time, we in fact have little choice but to rely upon Thomas himself as our guide.

That we should want to traverse such a landscape in the first place has to do with the poems Thomas has written. And in this respect it is we who are fortunate. Not only are many of the poems specifically about that landscape, but unlike *Neb* they were composed along the way, contemporaneously. They are soundings taken during the voyage; so that if we combine the two, poems and autobiography, something like a reliable marine topography can emerge.

*   *   *

88

The poet Ronald Stuart Thomas was born in Cardiff, on the eve of the First World War, but was soon removed by his parents to Liverpool. His father, T. H. Thomas, was an officer in the merchant navy, and went where he was ordered. In an interview conducted in 1990 for the Anglo-Welsh periodical *Planet*, R. S. acknowledges that 'there was an air of the Thomases as having come down in the world'.[6] A great-grandmother was a gifted singer and there had been talk, when she was young, of sending her to Italy to train as a soprano. The paternal grandmother, née Miles, was also of upper-middle-class stock, as was the grandfather. A cousin went to Oxford, gained a cricket Blue and bowled out Bradman. One of his great-uncles owned Lanelay Hall. Thomas's grandfather too was a man of property; for a while the Porth Hotel in Llandysul was his. But he was also a spendthrift, and died young, leaving behind eleven children and little money, forcing T. H. to go to sea.

In Wales in the nineteenth century, many boys did end up working on trawlers, coastal tramps and ocean-going steamers. There were the traditions of the great ports in the south, the fishing industry all around the coastline, and the Menai schooners that flew across the Atlantic to both the Americas. The sea took care of the surplus male population, those for whom there was not enough land to offer employment, and who, for whatever reason, opted not to labour in the coal mines and metal works not just of the south, but also of the north-west – Deeside. By the same token, the sea also offered a profession to those whose families had fallen on hard times.

There were seafarers on the mother's side as well, although Margaret Thomas's father seems to have worked as a cashier in a colliery 'in what the Welsh call Merthyr Vale'. He however died even younger than Thomas's other grandfather, so that Margaret was brought up by a relative, an Anglican priest, in the days before the disestablishment of the Church in Wales. Unlike T. H. Thomas, she did not speak any Welsh, even as a child. Rather she came from a background that was both self-consciously genteel and anglicized.

In the divide between Welsh and non-Welsh Wales therefore, R. S. had a foot on either side. In his childhood, however, it was the English-speaking maternal camp that predominated, by virtue of the fact that his father, T. H. Thomas, known as Huw, or Hugh, was usually away at sea. The boy Ronald did not learn Welsh, except later at school in Holyhead: lessons that did not interest him then, and which he quickly forgot. Instead he was groomed by Margaret Thomas, if not a clergyman's daughter then a clergyman's ward, in the expectation that he too would one day enter the Church. And so, in time, it came to pass. R.S. became an Anglican priest, after disestablishment, thus fulfilling his mother's ambitions for him: one cause, perhaps, of his enormous chagrin. For R.S. Thomas, while a mother's boy in his childhood and youth, wanted to be his father's boy in adulthood.

But the father was usually away. Only in his teens, living in Holyhead, does R.S. begin to see more of Huw Thomas, and then only because T.H. is working on the Holyhead–Dublin ferry. But T.H. Thomas by then is a broken man. He will never make captain, he will never command his own ship. First mate is as far as he will advance. He is becoming deaf, and deafness will force him into early retirement; one consequence of which is that the father–son conversations which might have occurred cannot. Even when the father is there, he is absent.

In a sense T.H. Thomas is fortunate. In his misfortune he has a wife to look after him, as well as a clever son who will go to college and who is well capable of making his own way in the world. But his son, the future poet, does not see it like that. The son is seized by a profound sense of guilt in this matter, a guilt which transmutes into an antipathy towards the mother. But far more than that, and about which R.S. Thomas is never explicit, the father becomes the prototype of the great emblem of the poet's later work: of the *deus absconditus*, the God who is there by not being there, and whom R.S. Thomas will wait for by the sea's edge.

The thesis Thomas does develop is that his mother trapped his father. She was the girl in port who waylaid the seafarer, and seduced him from a noble calling, the spiritual union of sailor and ocean. And having seduced him she kept him, by means of the son she bore.

Directly and obliquely, several poems, published with many years between them, give witness to this version of the family history. The earliest is 'Ap Huw's Testament'[7] from *Song at the Year's Turning*

(1955). 'Ap Huw' is of course R. S. Thomas himself, the son of Huw, and the poem is as good an example as any of the poet's ability to compress and distil feeling and experience into a series of unadorned statements. In this case, the poem is organized into five partly rhymed triplets, giving an account of the 'four people' in Thomas's life: father, mother, wife and his own 'one child'. The wife, 'her of the immaculate brow', is considered first, and disposed of first. Thomas offers a statement of affection. But not his affection for her, rather her affection for him: '. . . she loves me. I know how', suggesting a burden, a guilt, which is at once repeated as regards his mother:

> My mother gave me the breast's milk
> Generously, but grew mean after,
> Envying my detached laughter.

Later, as we have already seen, the mother's milk will be apprehended as a form of poison. But here the poet's detachment, his inability to repay her original bounty, is explained in the stanza that follows:

> My father was a passionate man,
> Wrecked after leaving the sea
> In her love's shallows. He grieves in me.

No hint is given of the father's malady, no suggestion that he would have had to leave the sea in any case. Only that he is wrecked in his wife's 'shallows'.

'Ap Huw's Testament' concludes with the hope, the prayer, that Thomas's own son may be kept 'free of the world's net'; presumably, in the context of what has come before, free from shipwreck by women.

The same misogynist attitude (it is difficult to know what else to call it) resurfaces eight years later, in a poem called 'Welsh',[8] from the collection *The Bread of Truth* (1963). 'Welsh' though, while being one of R. S. Thomas's classic Welsh airs, is not necessarily autobiographical; or rather is autobiographical at one remove. The themes, which now include the matter of the Welsh language, are recognizably drawn from his own life as recorded in *Neb* and elsewhere; but the poem is deliberately pitched in a self-mocking,

self-accusatory voice that has too much of the boyo in it to be
Thomas's own:

> I'm Welsh, see:
> A real Cymro,
> Peat in my veins.

Not at all the delivery of the Vicar of Eglwysfach, as Thomas then
was. Yet, as the poem unfurls, it is thrown off course by a real passion
one suspects can only have its source in the poet's own antecedents.
The speaker describes how, although he has been brought up 'nice',
he must endure the 'one loss'. He cannot speak his own language.
Instead he is obliged to 'gather' alms from 'blonde strangers', i.e.
the English. And no sooner are the English introduced than the poet
gives vent to his spleen. As this happens, the speaker's self-mockery
vanishes, to be replaced by a vision of Wales close to the poet's own:

> I want the right word
> For the gut's trouble.
> When I see this land
> With its farms empty
> Of folk, and the stone
> Manuscripts blurring
> In wind and rain,
> I want the town even.

The 'stone/ Manuscripts'? Not at all what one expects from someone
who introduces himself by proclaiming 'I'm Welsh, see: . . .' Instead,
it is an educated metaphor for gravestones, and the poem has gone
through a somersault, hijacked by the poet's semi-private obsessions.
The real sting though is in the 'town'. Towns R. S. Thomas generally
has no use for whatsoever. But not so here. In this town he hopes to find

> The open door
> Framing a slut,
> So she can speak Welsh
> And bear children
> To accuse the womb
> That bore me.

In other words, a city slut would be a better mother than a genteel countrywoman, so long as the latter cannot speak Welsh, and the former can.

The savagery of this astonishes, as it is intended to astonish. There is a deal of antiphrasis involved in Thomas's working, but even so the poem falls short of the gold standard of Swift's 'savage indignation'. Rather 'Welsh', as the bald title implies, is a directly political, inflammatory piece, written at the height of Thomas's involvement with Welsh nationalism, in which any attempted ambivalence is swamped by an insistence that has its wellsprings in circumstances that are private to the poet. Further, that some few readers will find themselves fired by such lines, while most will be persuaded only of their poor taste, is very much the point of 'Welsh': it is written for those Thomas considers a 'chosen few', from which elect the English-speaking, English-inculcating mother is conspicuous by her exclusion.

The Bread of Truth contains other 'parental' poems. In 'Sorry'[9] Thomas offers a somewhat condescending truce to the still living ghosts of his childhood. 'I forgive you my life,' he tells his father and mother in a direct address:

> Begotten in a drab town,
> The intention was good;

He acknowledges that he was raised up decently enough. What went wrong was his own 'mind's weight'. It is not their 'fault' that the poet inflicts wounds on himself that are mental, intellectual. 'The Boy's Tale',[10] on the other hand, pursues pithily the same misogyny implicit in 'Welsh', making it clear that the poet, far from overcoming what at heart is a not uncommon emotional trauma of male adolescence – the rejection of the mother – is still pained by it. The sailor returns home to his Welsh valley, and takes a girl 'from the tip'. At first his intention is not to marry her, but eventually she entraps him. Having caught him in 'her thin hair' she endeavours to hold him. When she fails, she resorts to another stratagem:

> She went fishing in him;
> I was the bait
> That became cargo,
> Shortening his trips,
> Waiting on the bone's wharf.
> Her tongue ruled the tides.

Again, the woman, who is also the poet's mother, is presented as procreative snare. Thomas attempts to distance himself by resorting to a universalized title, 'The Boy's Tale': but the manoeuvre is merely transparent. In another poem, the pseudo-sonnet 'Parent',[11] the process of artistic detachment is taken further. In lines reminiscent of Yeats's 'Leda and the Swan' Thomas retells how the Greek world is engendered from a single act of divine rape. The earth becomes peopled by a 'confusion of persons', each bearing a grudge

> Rooted in the enormous loins
> Of the first parent.

– a poem that could have been written, and can be read, without reference to the biography of its maker, except that this would be to exclude any kind of interior motivation, and propose instead a model of creative gestation that is plainly alien to the Thomasian method. In any case, we have the baldly and boldly suggestive title itself, 'Parent'. What is obvious, but nonetheless interesting, about the poem as displaced autobiography is the elevation of the father to godlike status. Other poets, for example Ted Hughes, may follow the lead given by Robert Graves in his pursuit of *The White Goddess*,[12] the all-fertile queen of heaven who visits earth in many shapes and forms, sometimes as muse, sometimes as mother, sometimes as unobtainable beauty; but the world R. S. Thomas inhabits and builds is strongly, relentlessly masculine. The feminine does occur in Thomas's poetry: there are the poems written to his wife, there are references to the Welsh mythological figure Rhiannon, and there are explorations of the eighteenth-century mystic hymn-writer Ann Griffiths; but in contemporary parlance Thomas can be characterized, or caricatured, as the archetypal unreconstructed male.

This can be seen in other verses that fall within the parental

category. Two years after *The Bread of Truth* was published T. H.
Thomas died, in hospital in Holyhead in 1965. 'Sailor's Hospital',[13]
from *Not That He Brought Flowers* (1968), commemorates the father's
dying. It is also, and unusually for Thomas, beguilingly tender at
the finish.

The poet describes a visit to the ward. Again, the town, the urban
thing, is woven into the poem's constructive imagery. Outside the
hospital are birds, caught up

> In the brambles' old,
> Jagged iron, with one striking
> Its small song.

One bird however, in Thomas's universe, is usually enough to betoken
grace, and the bird here, cast among metal, sings as a bell; a funeral
knell maybe, or the sort of hazard bell hung by the sea, but perhaps
also the bell used by a priest. And hearing it, the poet contemplates
the houses of the town (which is Holyhead):

> Who first began
> That refuse; time's waste
> Growing at the edge
> Of the clean sea?

At once, in responding to this question, he returns to the idea already
adumbrated in 'Ap Huw's Testament', 'Welsh' and 'A Boy's Tale'.
A sailor may have been who; some sailor ensnared by a woman or
women on the shore, and the ancestral progenitor of all the 'sick
men' who are his descendants.

This is the Fall all over again. Only in place of Eden is the sea,
and the first man a sailor, not a gardener, with women there only
to breed from, to spawn ungodly towns and cities. In literal terms,
a ridiculous tale. Whence, we may ask, the clothes, whence the ships?
But in the terms of what may be presumed about Thomas's interior
psychology, as compelling a creation myth as any:

> Every day
> Regularly the tide

Visits them with its salt
Comfort: their wounds are shrill
In the rigging of the
Tall ships.

By an extraordinary inversion of a commonplace the sailors marooned
in their hospital beds are restored to their dignity. When rubbed –
by the wind? by the waves' sound? – into their wounds, the healing
salt returns the men imaginatively to their best sea vehicles.

But the poem doesn't end there. There is a coda. The poem
becomes specifically about the father, and the poet's leave-taking.
Inside the hospital ward, his thoughts 'clenched', Thomas observes
the helplessness of the nurses

                                   tugging
At him, as he drifted
Away on the current
Of his breath, further and further,
Out of hail of our love,

The sea reclaims its own, a sea that the poem as a whole depicts as
a worthy bourn. Not only, most unlike the mother, is the father
loved by the son; he is also redeemed.

Ten years on, in 'Album',[14] from *Frequencies* (1978), R. S. Thomas
picks up where in 'Sailors' Hospital' he leaves off. In this shorter,
more formally controlled poem – there are four five-line stanzas –
the poet simultaneously attempts a more direct description of what
he takes to be the essential grievance of his childhood family, and
its resolution. In his hand he holds a photograph of the parents and
their child. Immediately he invokes the special bond between himself
and his father:

My father is dead,
I who am look at him
who is not, as once he
went looking for me
in the woman who was.

Once again the mother is introduced as no more than the means of reproduction, and through reproduction, the harbinger of pain. But now Thomas seems more prepared to consider his own role in the tightly contrived equation:

> There are pictures
> of the two of them, no
> need of a third, hand
> in hand, hearts willing
> to be one but not three.

A different kind of Eden, of bliss, than the one that went before, and more conventional by far. It is as though, for the first time, Thomas acknowledges the propriety of man and woman, that the need between his father and his mother may in fact have been mutual. And what spoils this need, what upsets the Edenic applecart, is not the serpent, but Thomas himself, seeking knowledge, leading his parents to the forbidden fruit. In the third stanza he depicts himself as an instrument his parents use for hurting each other. Through this pain, however, comes the possibility of reconciliation, and the salving of the poet's peculiar guilt.

And then, another five years on, there is 'Salt',[15] from *Later Poems* (1983): one of Thomas's most ambitious poems, and also one of the most deliberately Romantic in tone. Running to almost two hundred lines, and crafted into sections controlled by varying metres, 'Salt' glamorizes the severities of life at sea, conflating his father's experiences with those of other members of his family. Yet if Thomas senior is initially presented in nothing less than heroic terms –

> The centuries were without
> his like; then suddenly
> he was there, . . .

– the build-up is there to effect a greater drop, a drop that is quickly introduced in non-metaphoric terms. The sailor patriarch falls from the rigging and is hospitalized – an actual episode from the grandfather's life:

Past four
decks, and his bones
splintered. Seventeen weeks
on his back. No Welsh,
no English; but the hands
of the Roumanians
kind.

But was this not also, R. S. asks,

the fall
of the soul
from favour?

Inevitably the sailor is prized from the element that tempers him
by a woman, easily identified as Margaret Thomas by the allusion
to a 'vicarage garden' – 'the cramped harbour/he came to.' Only here
R. S., in this extended homage to his male progenitors, cannot leave
it at that. The point is hammered home. There are the slippers
waiting by the hearth that will 'destroy him'. And then,

'The hard love I had at her small breasts;
the tight fists that pummelled me;
the thin mouth with its teeth clenched
on a memory.' Are all women
like this? He said so, that man,
my father, who had tasted their lips'
vinegar,

Of the female parent, a vastly unflattering portrait, made the more
acid by having the father give the description as reported speech,
although R. S. adds his own jaundiced verdict when he presents his
view of the man and his marriage:

a navigator
without a port; rejected
by the barrenness of his wife's
coasts, by the wind's bitterness
off her heart. I take his failure
for ensign, flying it
at my bedpost, where my own
children cry to be born.

As one would expect from a poem of its period, 'Salt' also contains a measure of *hiraeth* for the passing of things Welsh, and a splenetic assault on the details of urban environments. Indeed, R. S. Thomas seems hell-bent on super-loading his father with all his own concerns and obsessions. The poem concludes with a drawn-out, and moving, account of the sailor's land-stricken decline into age and death, and the final images of T. H. Thomas boxed in his grave –

> the bone's anchor too
> heavy for your child spirit
> to haul on and be up and away?

– are finely piteous; but it is difficult to contemplate 'Salt' in its entirety without sharing the poet's own uneasiness of mind.

Move on another five years, to *The Echoes Return Slow* (1988), and we find the uneasiness persists, albeit the poet is now into his seventy-fifth year. In a prose paragraph, R. S. recapitulates the agony inside his father's coffin, although he again concedes that perhaps there was love between his parents. But this does not deter him from a further snipe at his mother:

> He was buried in a grave in a town by the sea. Seven years he waited
> for his wife, dragging the bones' anchor in the colourless fathoms.
> And then it was her turn, too feeble to speak. The woman, who all
> her life had complained, came face to face with a precise ill.[16]

Across the page, the accompanying poem unburdens the poet of his chill emotions. At the end of her life Margaret Thomas is brought to the poet's household

> with her appeal
> to die, and we made her live
> on, not out of our affection
> for her, but from a dislike
> of death.

Eventually the ambulance comes to 'rescue' Thomas from 'the issues/ of her body', and to deliver her from the 'incompetence/of our conscience'. In yet another hospital ward, however, the poet finds it within himself to take her hand in his, making

> a tight-rope
> of our fingers for the mis-shapen
> feelings to keep their balance upon.

Marie-Thérèse Castay, a Welsh-speaking friend of R. S. and a lecturer at the University of Toulouse-Le Mitrail, writing about the autobiographical elements in Thomas's poetry in *The Page's Drift*, a collection of essays published to celebrate the poet's eightieth birthday in 1993,[17] observes: 'As has been repeatedly noted, R. S. Thomas's poetry is characterised by a great reluctance to speak about himself and even when he does the emotion is always under control.' The parental poems contradict this view. The emotions may seem bottled up in the extreme, but at more or less regular intervals, and with Pandoric consequences, Thomas does remove the cork. In particular, his portraits of his mother, regardless of whether they are direct or oblique, break a widely respected taboo: a taboo not so much against a frank and intimate discussion of parental relations – these fairly often find their way into print – as against revealing a level of personal animus that, however psychologically acute, only questionably has a place in literature.

As has been noted by some other of Thomas's commentators, the poet, always ready to deplore modern mores, somehow fails to take cognizance of basic Christian chivalry. With the burning exception of his wife, his dismissive attitude towards women generally is Old Testament, not New. Again and again Adam is undone by Eve. In this respect, his having been a priest for forty years, a role that will have included preparing sermons centred on readings of Isaiah and other prophets, may explain as much as it gives cause of surprise. Yet with regard to the poetry, it need not be a matter of unmitigated censure. One response to Thomas's outspokenness, not just with regard to his mother, but towards every other topic he touches, is to commend him for a certain kind of courage. Either he is not bound, or he does not allow himself to be bound, by polite convention. Indeed, his poetry often has been applauded for its 'honesty'.[18]

That may be putting it too strongly. A person who bares their soul may do so from a number of motives, psychological compulsion among them. What the parental poems, as I have called them, do show is the characteristic method Thomas has of dealing with his subject-matter – or the characteristic method his subject-matter has of dealing with him. He gnaws at it, it gnaws at him. This is what sets him apart as a poet, and above most other poets. Sometimes accused of narrowness in subject-matter, he more than makes up the alleged defect by the persistence and depth of his explorations. Without resorting to the full panoply of psychoanalytic interpretation, it does begin to appear that Thomas's poetic personality is enchained and empowered by perceived and powerful childhood forces. His revulsion at his mother's breast is such that even strenuous mental mastectomy cannot rid him of its spell. In its willed absence it is still there.

Conversely, another continuous presence of the early years, the Welsh landscape, survives unscathed, and joins forces with the sea to sustain what, in the poet's imagination, becomes a version of cargo cult. Out of the sea, somewhere from the land, grace may come.

The father's profession meant that the family moved around a lot. Thomas's earliest years were spent in a variety of ports, most of them in England, including London, Liverpool and Goole. But at the end of the war, in the autumn of 1918, T. H. Thomas was given a job on the Irish ferry, and the Thomases settled in Holyhead – Caergybi in Welsh – in the far corner of Anglesey, or Ynys Môn, the island of Môn. There R. S. grew up; there he went to kindergarten, to primary school and secondary school, the last being one of the County Schools, the equivalent of a grammar school. And from the County School he proceeded, in 1932, to college in Bangor, to read Classics (Latin) on a church scholarship, prior to entering the priesthood.

By then his father, though he would survive another thirty-three years, had already been forced into retirement from the sea by his loss of hearing: a disablement that was soon compounded by a stress disorder of the stomach. The ferry company gave him a shore job, but at a reduced wage. From being relatively well-to-do – all Ronald's schools were, in local terms, 'superior' – the family was impoverished. But during his childhood, although Thomas sometimes mixed with children from conspicuously richer homes, there is no suggestion of any great hardship; nor indeed of any untoward suffering, other than his intermittently experiencing mainly unspecified illnesses, and being an only child, a mother's boy in a society where fathers were expected to exert a forceful presence. Yet out of this upbringing emerges a writer frequently identified by his insistence upon the anguish of life.

Thomas's prose account of his boyhood, as given in *Neb*, as well as other texts, and inevitably coloured by the seasoned sensibility of his adulthood, oscillates between the bitter and the idyllic, but is thin on outwardly climactic events. Too much is sometimes made of too little, and were this passage of his memoirs by and about someone unknown, it would excite scant interest. But simply by virtue of being Thomas's memoir, it carries a peculiar moral charge, a hidden didactic. In what is primarily an address to Welsh readers written in Welsh, Thomas seems to be saying to us, this unglamorous boyhood, though it may seem provincial and inconsequential, is in fact of the essence. It was not, like so many other childhoods, a false childhood; and if you find it lacklustre, then that is your shortcoming.

In *Neb* the poet makes no particular effort to reconstruct an exact chronology of his earliest years. His narrative, though broadly linear, is impressionistic, and, for all that Thomas employs the third person, sometimes solipsistic in its phrasing. 'Doctors came into existence,' he writes: 'nasty men who used to push spoons down the throat.'[19] After the trauma of birth and meningitis, supplemented by a broken arm, the result of a maid's carelessness, the earliest memories are of wartime Liverpool, of the gas-light in the bedroom he shares with his mother suddenly contracting one night to 'a small blue speck in the glass ball'. Next day there is talk of a German zeppelin having approached the city. But to the child this means little or nothing: '*Dim ofn yn absenoldeb deall.*' No fear in the absence of understanding. The child is innocent. There are no horrors of war, only the horror of things that may happen to his body.

Taken to the park one day, an insect crawls into the child's nose when he smells a flower; indeed, in the boy's imagination, crawls 'almost to the brain'. *Neb* continues:

> Fear seized him and he ran screaming for his mother. Isn't the world nasty to a child? And why was it necessary for an older boy to attack him and hit him? Was this a symbol of the hatred people bear toward a coward, toward a poet in preparation?[20]

On another occasion, little R. S. is taken by his mother one evening on board his father's ship. While she dines with her husband in the officers' mess, he rests on a bunk in his cabin, only to be terrified by a cockroach.

> Eugh! . . . And the parents busy enjoying themselves! Thus fear came to be a part of his experience. Yet from time to time kind faces appeared in the doorway, members of the crew checking to see whether he was all right. But how could a child get grown-ups to understand the horror of a cockroach?[21]

In *The Echoes Return Slow* (1988) this will become: 'The cockroaches should have been a reminder. The shadows from which they crawled were as dark as those where the submarines lurked.'[22] But as Thomas also recalls in *Neb*, his mother had begun feeding the boy's imagination not by telling him about the war, but by reading him stories of ogres and dragons, of princes and princesses. At night he imagines the house to be full of the roaring of a giant. When he is older, he sees a gorilla enter his room. Rushing in, his parents find him on the floor.

A further episode, or brace of episodes, is more puzzling. It seems to be recounted both in *Neb* and in *Y Llwybrau Gynt, The Paths Gone By*, a radio talk given in Welsh and published in 1972[23] – therefore the earliest of Thomas's autobiographical excursions in prose. But whereas in the later account the incident takes place in Holyhead, in the earlier it is located in Liverpool:

> Another time, going to one of the parks: it is the middle of winter and the lake there is frozen over. A crowd of people are sliding on it. Near to the bank, there is a patch which has not frozen. A clergyman comes into view, sailing along like a ship with the wind behind

it. Suddenly, to my astonishment, he disappears into the pool. Others come straight away to pull him out, dripping wet. He goes off, crestfallen.[24]

In *Neb*:

It was winter, and although Holyhead is quite a mild place, a mountain pond, surrounded by some snow, had frozen over. The three of them [R. S. and two school chums] were there late in the afternoon, when it was beginning to get dark. In the middle of the pond was a small unfrozen patch. Two of them were on a branch looking down, the third out of sight somewhere behind them. Suddenly a figure appeared before them and started running for the clear water. The two in the tree started shouting at the same time to the other to be careful. But the next moment he joined them from a completely different direction. Simultaneously the apparition vanished. The two would have been prepared to agree that it was a dream, except that they both shouted at the same time.[25]

In neither account is any further comment added. In the one, we have the almost slapstick spectacle of a priest getting a ducking; in the other, a far more sinister spectre appears and vanishes God knows where. Are the two stories in fact based on one episode? If not, it seems strange that Thomas should not have made more of their relatedness. If they are, either the memory of childhood plays extraordinary tricks upon the man, or the man plays extraordinary tricks with his memory.

But there is light as well as shadow in Thomas's recollections of Liverpool. The ambience of sail and steam, the smell of the docks and the smell of beer are recalled if not with emotion, then without distaste. Often he is taken by his mother across the Mersey to Hoylake, or New Brighton, where he remembers a one-legged man diving off the quay for coins. There were holidays, there was fun. And there were the rare appearances of his father, who told the poet about his own boyhood in Llandysul, Cardiganshire, and how he fished in the Teifi 'with his back on one of the gravestones in the cemetery'.[26]

It is on the Wirral Peninsula that the real awakening in the poet's life occurs. He is taken to play on a beach near Hoylake by his parents. In the distance, across the waters to the south-west, his father points to a range of blue-grey mountains and declares: 'That's Wales!' – *Dacw Gymru*, though said in English.

Other towns and cities are recalled, but only phantasmagorically. In Cardiff he sees a huge crowd and policemen on horseback. In London, he watches trains go by, and waits, inexplicably, with an uncle outside Wandsworth Prison. Somewhere else, his father advances towards him in 'white clothes', most likely at a cricket match. In Goole, a river floods its brown mud banks. But these are fleeting images that mean nothing, that have no purchase.

Sut mae'r cof yn gweitho?[27] How does the mind work? Thomas asks. Some things it retains, others it condemns to forgetfulness, he answers simplistically. Had his family not returned to Wales, would he still recall those two words spoken by his father on the beach? Or would the tide have washed them away along with so much else?

Conversely, why was it that the few stored images of Cardiff, Liverpool and London did not germinate some longing for the city, with its thoroughfares and immense human activity? Why in fact, through time, the reverse?

Thomas does not attempt an explanation, psychological or otherwise. He prefers to maintain his posture as an innocent. Being an only child, there are none of the enriching complications of a sibling relationship. Albeit through the lenses of his mature concerns and prejudices, he provides a minimalist account of his first years. Thus, and perhaps wisely, he avoids engagement with the interminable and insoluble debate between the rival claims of nature and nurture; of what in our character we owe to ourselves, and what we do not.

At the end of 1918 the Thomases settled in Holyhead, on Holy Island, separated from the rest of Anglesey only by the narrowest of channels, a kind of half-island, rather as Anglesey itself – Ynys Môn, sometimes called the 'Mother of Wales' – is separated from mainland Wales by the wasp-waisted Menai Strait. Archaeological remains indicate Celtic and pre-Celtic settlements. Seafarers have used Holyhead as a natural crossing-point to Ireland since time immemorial.

The landscape, like the landscape of the rest of north-western Anglesey, is barren and rugged; few trees, gorse-covered hills, and a lot of
rock. Jonathan Swift, finding himself there in September 1727, wrote:

> Lo here I sit at holy head,
> With muddy ale and mouldy bread:
> I'm fastened both by wind and tide,
> I see the ships at anchor ride.
> All Christian vittals stink of fish,
> I'm where my enemyes would wish.[28]

It was, he added, a place 'Where nature hardly seems alive'. But
during the succeeding century the town of Holyhead – its Welsh
name means St Cybi's fort – grew and prospered. In 1801 it was
officially designated a port of trade with Ireland, and by 1820 the
main road to London via Shrewsbury, still graced by Thomas Telford's
suspension bridge over the Menai, had opened. Soon too the railway
arrived, from Chester, and in 1873 the safe harbour area was greatly
expanded by the building of a mile-long breakwater.

Today, Holyhead, bearing all the scars of ad hoc town planning,
is one of the largest ferry-ports in Europe. The A5 and trains from
Euston feed vehicles and passengers on to vast vessels that resemble
nothing so much as floating warehouses. The RTZ aluminium factory, an RAF station at Valley and tourism help sustain the island's
commercial life. In the 1920s the steamships were smaller, but the
town itself busier, more human. Instead of the contemporary sanitized
housing estate, rows of workers' cottages ratcheted the surrounding
slopes: 'small houses full of very large families'.[29] The quayside and
centre bustled with chandlers, boiler-makers, sail-weavers, copper-
smiths and all the other artisans and apprentices needed by the twin
labour-intensive industries of rail and navigation.

Yet the essential contrast of Holy Island, between town and
countryside yonder, remains unchanged. Half an hour's walk from
Caergybi takes you among ancient stone walls dividing one field
from another, crumbling farmhouses and string-tethered goats in the
yards. By the sea are rugs of land too threadbare for cultivation and
which have never been put to any use. At Trearddur in the mid-south,

and around Four Mile Bridge, retirement chalets and holiday hotels of the kiss-me-quick kind have spawned, but about the rest there is still an air of bleak forgottenness.

The five-year-old boy's first impressions were negative. 'I remember the day we arrived: a dark wet day in December. Is there any town worse than Holyhead on a day like that?'[30] And indeed for the town itself Thomas has never expressed any affection. As recently as October 1995, responding to a question put by Naim Attalah for an interview published in the *Oldie*, he declared Holyhead to be 'a terrible little town'. But, he added, 'all around was the sea and in the distance were the mountains of Wales.' The morning following his advent his attitude changed. The sea was 'as blue as could be', and everywhere glistened with light. Henceforward the 'sickly' child would venture out by himself, often without his mother's knowledge, early in the day, before school, exploring the beaches, exploring the rocks, exploring the landscape. As though he were in his element; as though he had come home to roost.

Thus begins the idyll, Thomas's lifelong romance with the natural world, and in particular the natural world of Wales, attested in and by his poetry in all its phases. Dark questions will be asked, Tennyson's characterization of nature as 'red in tooth and claw' does not escape him, but in the main Thomas's attitude towards it is centred in respect, empathy and wonder. Nature is not only God's creation, but the channel we must tune in to if we are to receive the divine broadcast. Just as children born to the South American Kōgi people are shielded during their first years from visual contact with anything outside, and are thereby inculcated with a near-visionary sense of trees and flowers and fauna when eventually they are led from their birthing huts, so too perhaps in a lesser way with R. S. Up until his sixth year, a highly impressionable age, his experience is confined to townscapes. He knows about the sea, but largely the sea is associated with the father, a companionable man more loved because of his long absences. And then suddenly, at the very time he can begin creating a little independence of thought and movement for himself, he is transported to a compellingly alien environment.

What initially engaged his attention in Holyhead was the extreme changeableness of the weather. To express his wonder at that first morning, in *The Paths Gone By* Thomas quotes from one of the old *penillion* – verses composed for synchronized singing against the accompaniment of a harp. '*Ar noswaith ddrycinog mi euthum i rodio . . .*' In his own translation, 'One night I arose and went . . .'[31] No matter that the boy could not speak Welsh: Thomas anoints the occasion with traditional Welsh verse. More, in his radio talk he introduces them with the words, 'You must know the old penillion . . .' An expression he repeats several times. 'But the problem with a fast winger as you know . . .' 'As you know, the line from Cardiff to Shrewsbury runs through the Marches . . .' As you know. As you and I know. As we Welsh know. As anyone who is part of an intimate and elect circle knows:

> But on the morrow, when I passed that way,
> On Menai shore the hush of heaven lay;
> The wind was gentle and the sea a flower,
> And the sun slumbered on Caernarfon tower.

What applies to Menai applies equally well to Holyhead, as indeed it applies to most parts of the western Welsh seaboard. To a significant childhood memory Thomas again adds the layering varnish of a clearly apprehended adult identity.

Or, to put it another way: in the twentieth century particularly, goaded by magazines and films and television, children growing up in the back of beyond, as outside of Caergybi Holy Island was and still is, have often hankered to abandon their roots and seek more glittering lives in towns and cities. It is only later in life that people feel drawn back to their roots. With R. S. Thomas matters stand a little differently. The desire to return affects him much sooner. For him the back of beyond is more like a version of Eden, from which later on, as a college student and then a priest, he is removed, but with this twist; as a child, as an innocent, he never properly belonged there in the first place. He didn't speak Welsh – in the 1920s still the language used on the Holy Island farmsteads. To effect a return therefore, not only must the physical displacement be annulled, but the mind itself must be set aright. Acquiring the Welsh tongue becomes the necessary means of re-entry, of accomplishing the life task; a matter not so much of reconstituting childhood, but of repairing its original defect.

The sea particularly becomes a part of the young boy's life. In *Neb* Thomas tells of the excitement at living so close by it. At night the light from the lighthouse darts into his room like the sails of a windmill. When there is a storm, the small harbour fills up with a 'forest' of masts – an image he retains to be deployed later on in three or four poems of his maturity. If a ship is in trouble, sailors in their fishing boats are out at sea before the lifeboat is readied and launched. Storms also create apprehensions about the safe arrival of the Irish ferry – a sustained panic, doubtless communicated by the mother, to which the first mate's son must have been especially prone. 'A kind of panic attack spread through the town . . .' And then there are the calm days, when the ferry-boat's captain calls him down to the quay, jokingly inviting the lad to come aboard for the ride.

At other times Thomas goes blenny-fishing, or idles in the fields. As much time as he can he spends outdoors: 'The weather was king in Holyhead. It ruled all my activities.'[32] But another transformation takes place as well, a more ambivalent increment to his existence. He begins to socialize. At school he makes friends, in the circumstantial way children do. In particular there is a family living two miles outside the town, at Penrhos Feilw: two boys, around Thomas's age, and their sister, three years older. At first he visits with his parents, then sometimes stays over on his own. Their house, Bryn Awel (Breeze Hill), a slightly grand dwelling, becomes the savoured destination of the young explorer. The boys show him tunnels in the surrounding gorse, and in early November collecting gorse for a bonfire on Guy Fawkes' Night becomes an annual rite. But walking back from Bryn Awel to his own home by night was also a part of the magic, with the stars above, and the sounds of the sea, and the gorse-bush 'squeaking and fidgeting in the night wind'.[33]

Yet memories of a more foreboding solitude still find their way into Thomas's autobiographical narratives. 'Some evenings,' he writes in *Neb*, his parents wanted to go out. 'Will you be all right on your own?' Of course he would be! He hated to admit the opposite. After they had gone though silence would possess the house. Slowly he would realize that he was alone. And yet was he? A house is not a dead thing. It moans and it squeaks and it whispers. He listened. Was there somebody upstairs? What *was* that noise, like a man breathing? He goes to the foot of the stairs and turns on a light. Yet the far end of the loft remained in shadow. He calls. No answer. Step by step he would climb the staircase, then pause to listen again. Suddenly he would leap forward, and, stamping his feet, shout: 'Boo!' But there is nothing there. Nobody. He would return down the stairs with a feeling of relief, and sat reading by the fireplace until his parents came home.[34]

But what exactly is the 'feeling of relief' here? Is it disappointment at finding himself after all alone, or is it a sense of the foolishness of his fright? Thomas doesn't explain. Instead he is laconic, and mildly sententious. The human personality, he tells us at the beginning of the following paragraph, is a strange thing that works in strange ways. He continues:

Where did the boy get the idea of making the image of a figure, clothing it, and putting it on a chair at the top of the stairs? And when the parents came in there it was, waiting in the shadows. And of course, it was his mother who was the first to climb the stairs and get the shock of her life. Screams followed by a big fuss, with the father scolding him for such foolishness. And yet it was all harmless. The parents would quite happily have stayed at home, except that he had assured them there was no need.[35]

Given Thomas's subsequent emergence as a poet, and the themes of isolation and God-searching he pursues, it is tempting to read into this passage more than it can sustain. Thomas himself takes a contrary direction. Not for the first time in *Neb*, nor for the last, he picks up a memory thread, begins to make something of it, then lets it collapse into utter inconsequentiality. It is as though he had never read anyone else's biography or autobiography. Yet this, one suspects, is very much his purpose. The child and adolescent is a self-professed nobody, and to a nobody nothing very much does happen.

A sense of personal failure pervades *Neb*. 'On the whole,' he tells us, unconvincingly, 'he was a happy boy.' Immediately he qualifies this: 'At least, that's what he told himself when he reached manhood. The country made him so. Despite the nervous, worrying nature of his mother he was free to roam the island from sunrise to sunset.'[36] But inevitably there was more to childhood than that. As he matures, Thomas finds that, although he is attracted by girls, he cannot easily overcome an instinctive shyness towards them. The poet's adolescent sexuality is introduced and disposed of swiftly. Comparing his young life to a film that consists of 'thousands of small events, most of them gone to forgetfulness by now', he assembles a mini-montage:

> He is crying, after a beating by a stronger boy. Over there he is singing at the top of his voice as he sees waves racing over the sands on a stormy day, and the foam flying like a flock of gulls. He is at the cinema; he is on a playing field; he is eyeing a girl but not daring to say a word to her, nor touching her like the bolder boys did.[37]

In *The Paths Gone By* Thomas is a shade more forthcoming, though again his awareness of sex is adversely highlighted by the activities and attitudes of his male peer group. To his mother's express displeasure, young Ronald develops a friendship with a town-boy, Rhodri. He was not one of the 'local yobboes', Thomas tells us, yet, unlike himself, had no fear of them. His accent is impure. In Holyhead terms circa 1925 Rhodri is streetwise. He is a boyo in the making and can show Ronald things his more refined companions cannot. Together they get involved in scrapes, of the cricket-ball-through-someone's-window kind. Rhodri is also addicted to the cinema. His head is full of fights, and he has no timidity addressing girls. Out walking in a threesome, with another boy of Rhodri's ilk, Thomas is challenged: when a girl smiles at him, why doesn't he say something?

The very idea frightens him. 'And yet,' Thomas goes on, 'the little armed god was waiting for me.' There is another house in the country his parents take him visiting, a house full of youngsters of both sexes. On one such visit a daughter takes him aside and chats to him 'amicably'. 'Gradually I lost my shyness and began for the first time to bask in female company.' Indeed his world is transformed.

When he walks home with his mother it is as though 'in a dream'. But true to form, this second awakening peters out. For a while the boy takes to walking along the road near this girl's house, in the hope of seeing her 'by chance'. When she fails to materialize he at last plucks up the courage to knock on her door. A maid answers, and he is invited to join the family for tea in their orchard. He becomes a frequent visitor, and begins writing her name upon the strand. But, although he can refer to this as 'his first love', it leads nowhere. 'Certainly we didn't quarrel or fall out in any way. The whole thing just gradually receded from my mind, its place taken by other things, in particular sport.'

How old was he then? we want to know. What did she look like? What were her interests? What was her name? Thomas tells us nothing, and at college his sexual diffidence survives intact.

He is equally unforthcoming about any scholastic achievement. He gives the impression, which cannot quite be right, of merely muddling through the County School. In retrospect he decides that it was probably not a very good school in any case, although he praises the headmaster, Derry Evans, for his teaching of Latin. Parsing Latin sentences, and learning to attach a precisely correct syntactic and semantic value to each word, was an important aspect of the training of a poet whose prosody depends absolutely upon a similarly exacting handling of English words. 'By having to search for the right word to translate Latin he learned the need to do this in poetry as well,' as he puts it in *Neb*.[38] That Thomas, even in his youth, was interested in writing poetry is apparent from one of the few self-congratulatory, though sardonic, anecdotes he tells of his childhood. 'In school he composed a song, and passed it to his neighbour at the adjoining desk, and he, after reading it, in turn passed back, whispering "Poet Laureate" . . . The fledgling accepted this praise as his right.'[39] Winning a class prize, the book Ronald selects is a biography of Tennyson. 'The Lady of Shalott' was already a favourite with him.

But, in hindsight, his primary and secondary education let him down in two respects, both of which form central planks in his mature polemics. He was not taught systematically about the natural world; for example, how to identify the bird-calls he was already familiar with, though only by sound. Holyhead was 'a special place to watch the birds go by in the autumn on their way south, if only he had known it at the time'.[40] Nor was there anything more than a half-hearted attempt to impart the Welsh language. He took Welsh in his first year at the County School, 'one subject among many others. Nothing stayed in his head except one tiny verse about an apple . . .'[41] Indeed, the only time he heard Welsh spoken at school was on St David's Day, when a concert replaced ordinary lessons. Then those among the staff who had Welsh spoke it, to the surprise of many of the pupils: 'They sounded very funny to children used every day to hearing them speak the "thin" language.'[42]

Again, with regard to religion, the poet's childhood suggests little about his future. Although a visit to some chapel-going relatives of his mother living in South Wales instils in him a dislike of Nonconformity, his attitude is scarcely pro-church:

> He was not a regular worshipper at the church by a long chalk. In fact his mother had the bad habit of setting off on a walk at exactly the time the congregation was setting out for church on a Sunday evening. This caused the boy embarrassment. And it was the same when he did go to church with his mother. She was sure to be late, with the result they had to walk the whole length of the church in order to get a seat.[43]

Throughout the service Thomas felt that everyone was looking at him, so that he blushed compulsively. One Sunday the sense of shame is so acute he is physically sick, and has to leave. But this, Thomas tells us, was actually a blessing, because he was not obliged to attend services for several weeks afterwards.

The church he attended was not the early medieval and immensely picturesque St Cybi's, overlooking the harbour, but St Seiriol's in the centre of town, since demolished, as has been the original brick building of the County School. At St Cybi's services were conducted in Welsh, at St Seiriol's in English. Therefore the Thomases attended St Seiriol's. A contemporary of Ronald Stuart's, Mrs Ethel Jones, born in 1910, the daughter of one sea captain and later the wife of another, told me she remembered the family well.[44] The father tall and cross-looking, but morose because of his hearing difficulties; the son, a little ungainly, gauche, unassertive; but most of all the mother, 'a small bony woman with a terrible tongue'. One December afternoon Ethel was rehearsing in a children's play for the Christmas fête, put on at the town hall under the patronage of Lady Dent, the wife of the then resident admiral. The cast of *The House That Jack Built* were drawn from the younger congregation of St Seiriol's, and included Ronald Thomas. Midway through the rehearsal Margaret Thomas burst in, walked up to her son and 'proceeded, in front of everyone, to give him an absolute dressing down. I can't recall the cause of it, except that it was something minor. Nor was it the only time. We all felt sorry for the boy. That man's had a cross to bear on his shoulder all his life.'

Were such episodes the origin of the poet's long love-hate affair with silence? George Herbert, Byron, Browning, G. M. Hopkins and Oscar Wilde were also the sons of overbearing mothers, so at least, had he but known it at the time, he was in distinguished company. Long before his schooldays finished Thomas's future career appears to have been settled for him. As the poet himself has frequently conceded, the decision to enter the church was Margaret Thomas's. Margaret Thomas – who was not by all accounts an especially religious or even pious woman, but who had been educated at an English church school, as well as being brought up by an Anglican cleric; and who recognized that, in the conventional pecking order, a vicar was a respectable enough figure in Welsh society.

'Who knows,' R. S. Thomas questions wryly in *Neb*, 'how destiny has its way with us?' – *Ond pwy a ŵyr fel y mae tynged dyn yn cael ei ffordd?* God doesn't always employ shock tactics to gain converts. His mother, R. S. told the *Oldie*, 'obviously had these secret ambitions for me. I was at a malleable stage in my teens and I didn't raise any resistance. God moves in mysterious ways.'[45]

In Thomas's case, if we accept the various versions of his autobiography, the initial summons to the ministry was motivated by considerations of status, and perhaps money. In the 1920s many Anglican incumbents in Wales enjoyed good livings. The Vicar of Llanelli's stipend, for example, was, at £800 p.a., two to three times what any school-teacher could hope to earn – and that was before taking into account fees for baptisms, weddings and funerals. By Thomas's last year at school T. H. Thomas had already quit the sea; the family, small as it was, would have been hard-pushed to fund him through college. A church scholarship was the answer.

Duly, the young R. S. began learning a little Greek as well as Latin. He travelled south to the theological college at Lampeter, to sit the examination. Duly too he won a bursary – 'Who ever heard of anyone failing?' For the moment, the idyll of his Holyhead child-hood, if idyll it was, was over.

'The clouds towered,' R. S. Thomas writes in *The Echoes Return Slow* of this latest alteration to his life, the transition from boyhood to studenthood: 'Their shape was prophetic, but there were no prophets.' And across the page, the verse counterpart:

> With cash in the one,
> no harm in the other,
> they persuaded all
> but the child, who knew
>
> with a child's roguery
> whichever he touched
> of the hands held out
> would always be empty.[46]

In a manner reminiscent of Wordsworth's 'shades of the prison house' Thomas's life had been mapped out for him. Resistance, when eventu-ally it surfaced, took several forms. These included Welsh nationalism and, more perversely perhaps, given the circumstances of his entry into the ministry, a sustained vigilance towards God. But the young R. S. was, in post-war parlance, a slow developer. Even by the rela-tively static, and certainly more sober, conventions of his day, before the eruptions of youth and student culture, his abiding character, as it is handed down in the poetry, endured a slow gestation.

Conversely, when that character, or poetic persona, does emerge, there is nothing impetuous about it, nothing ill-conceived in haste. He is not a poet of idle flirtations. The ideas he addresses are, within the framework of the development of his own consciousness, perma-nent. Late juvenilia exist, tucked away in college magazines; but his first collections beg attention as urgently as the most recent.

*   *   *

The student register at Bangor University – the University College of North Wales, to give it its proper title, UCNW – records that Ronald Stuart Thomas arrived there in October 1932, and departed in the summer of 1935 with a '2nd class Div II' honours degree in Latin. The three lower boxes on the columned page, designated 'Particulars as to career after leaving College', 'Present Address' and 'General Remarks' are each blank. Thus the official notice of one of Bangor's more illustrious alumni.

Thomas's own summary of his student days, as distilled in the prose paragraphs of *The Echoes Return Slow*, is only slightly less reticent. His fellow undergraduates seemed 'wiser' than he, and more confident. They saw college as a rung on a ladder, 'that life was a thing meant to be climbed', whereas R. S. himself was 'half prepared for everything but life'. 'In long trousers, with no money in his pockets,' he writes, 'he pretended to forget the black gown he wore was a kind of mourning for his dewy boyhood.' But always there was the salvation of the Welsh landscape. In the verse counterpart:

> He rationed his intake
> of knowledge. On fine days
> with the mountains leaning
> over him to whisper
>
> there were other picnics
> beside the musty sandwiches
> in the library.[47]

And there was another boon: 'He tasted freedom in a parent's absence.' In *Neb*, Thomas recounts how he does not arrive at Bangor unattended:

And his mother came with him! Her excuse was that she wanted to make sure he had good lodgings, and so on. She came too to share his first day away from home. Mercifully, because he was completely unknown, the other students were in no position to make fun of the little baby arriving with its nurse. Those were his feelings at the time.[48]

The previous night, at the Thomases' house in Garth Road, his mother had wept, and his father had endeavoured to quieten her. 'Then in his bed, after falling asleep, he awoke to find someone kissing him over and over.'[49] Fortunately, however, Margaret Thomas had to catch the evening train back to Holyhead, and at last R. S. was left alone.

The following day he enrolled at UCNW. The college had been independently founded in 1884, but was federated into the national university in 1893, along with similar colleges at Aberystwyth (1869) and Cardiff (1883). Before these dates Wales had no non-denominational degree-giving bodies. Indeed the only institution chartered to award degrees was St David's College at Lampeter, established in 1822, and that was effectively an Anglican seminary. Any Welshman wishing to go to university had to travel to England, most usually to Jesus College at Oxford – always known there as the Welsh college. But the university movement in Wales during the latter stages of the nineteenth century was, from a patriotic perspective, at best a mixed blessing. Although Aberystwyth, Cardiff and Bangor all had small Welsh departments by 1900, their primary function was to provide higher education in standard subjects in English. The university colleges can therefore be seen to have been part and parcel of two processes: the creation of new universities as happened in any case in most parts of Britain in Victorian times; and the spread of English as the educational and therefore accepted lingua franca in Wales during the same period.

In this second respect, the 'non-denominational' status of the colleges was a slap in the face for the nonconformist majority more than it was a distancing from the Anglican establishment. It was after all the chapels that kept the Welsh tongue wagging in the nineteenth century. Although the original Welsh departments in particular tended to gather in one place well-educated and often high-minded devotees of the Welsh cause, it was not until the 1960s, when some departments began offering Welsh-medium instruction in subjects other than Welsh language and Welsh literature, that the University of Wales began in any formal way to achieve what many of its teachers saw as its proper role, the encouragement of nationhood. By then, however, various other bodies had been incorporated, including the University College of Swansea and the Welsh National School of Medicine, and increasingly students were being drawn from further afield – not just from England and Scotland, but also from various parts of the Commonwealth, as well as some from the United States. It has also been the case that the majority of Welsh students attending the University of Wales have in any case been non-Welsh speaking, and therefore the argument for an exclusively Welsh-medium curriculum, though sometimes propounded with passion, has tended to appear quixotic.

Bangor, being in the heart of Gwynedd, and therefore in the heart of 'Welsh' Wales, has emerged as the second most Welsh-minded of the university's various constituent colleges, after Aberystwyth. Periodically the language issue has disrupted academic life. At the end of the 1970s especially there was a strong and vociferous group of students and some younger teachers prepared to demonstrate on behalf of their demands for a purely Welsh university – a prospect not enhanced by the continuing federal structure of the University of Wales. Inevitably perhaps, R. S. Thomas became one of their mascots, and R. S. himself returned to his alma mater to participate in at least one student sit-in; so that today collegiate staff opinion about the poet is sharply divided.

But in 1932–5 such events were well over the horizon. Thomas was headed for the altar, not for the barricades. After a year in digs, he moved into the Church Hostel, a property held on trust successively for the Clerical Education Committees and then the Boards of Finance of the two northern dioceses of Bangor and St Asaph.[50] But although the University of Wales's statutes stipulated that the college at Bangor be non-denominational, the hostel, Craig Menai, a red-brick house just a few hundred yards away from the main college complex on the side of a hill overlooking the Menai Strait towards Beaumaris, and later destined to become UCNW's Anglican Chaplaincy, was even then something more than a simple hall of residence. The inspiration of H. T. Edwards, Dean of Bangor between 1873 and his death in 1874, it first opened its doors in 1886. By 1933 it had been extended to accommodate up to twenty-one students, its warden and a few domestics. Its purpose was to assist in the rebirth of Anglicanism in Wales by enabling ordinands and would-be ordinands attending UCNW, whether they were graduates or undergraduates, to live together in an Anglican community; to give them, in the words of one Principal of Bangor College, Emrys Evans, 'a second loyalty'.[51] In a sense therefore it was a college within a college. Its values, particularly during Thomas's stay there, were strongly Anglo-Catholic, or High Church – 'bells and smells'. The warden then was Glyn Simon, later Archbishop of Wales, and the most able Welsh churchman of the mid-century. Under his aegis a strict discipline, approximating to the quasi-monastic regime of a theological college, was imposed. Matins and Evensong were compulsory, as was a daily Eucharist, after which communicants were expected to observe twenty minutes of prayerful silence. When Mass was said, it was said in Latin. There was also a quiet study period in the evening, after compline. The hostel doors closed at 10 p.m., and lights went out at eleven.

Glyn Simon was also responsible for commissioning the hostel's finely airy chapel. Designed by H.L. North, this is regarded as an architectural high point of the Arts and Crafts Movement. Previously services had been held in a makeshift chapel in the hostel's basement. The new chapel was consecrated in November 1933, a month or so after R.S. Thomas took up residence. At an opening service the sermon was preached by A.G. Edwards, Bishop of St Asaph and Archbishop of Wales,[52] with the Sulfrayan Bishop of Maenan as well as the Bishop of Bangor in attendance.

Whether R.S. was also present goes unremarked by the poet. In *Neb* he comments that Glyn Simon was effeminate in his manner but strong in his convictions; that he would tell the students what the score was, without any hair on his tongue. Each Sunday he chose two of the young men to assist him during Mass. When it was Thomas's turn, he was 'angered' by Simon's habit of hurrying through the opening sentences, leaving his assistants no time to catch up. But the warden preached well: despite a 'poor' delivery he usually gave Thomas 'something to chew on'.

In the dining room were two long tables, one for English-speaking ordinands, the other for Welsh speakers. R.S. 'sat with the English, because that was his language'. Sometimes, however, he sat at the other table, where he would be invited to try out Welsh words difficult to pronounce, for example *llwy*, 'spoon'. If he failed there would be laughter at his accent. At the time, he recalls, the warden himself was learning Welsh, and occasionally conducted a chapel service in 'the old language' – *yr hen iaith*: a feel-good phrase Thomas frequently uses, when he writes about his country's past, in antithesis to *yr iaith fain*, the thin language, or English. But although a good many of UCNW's five hundred-odd students were bilingual, when Thomas did mix it tended to be with monoglot English speakers. At the time 'the boy felt no inclination' to learn Welsh. His background was 'too much' for him.[53]

Indeed, applied learning of almost any kind seems to have been an unwelcome burden. Thomas consistently deprecates his academic performance. He did not read outside his syllabus, but stuck to the prescribed texts. As the final examinations neared, even these seemed at times beyond him. At the age of twenty-two, he can do no more than 'much unintelligent swotting'.[54] What kept him going was a guilt towards his parents, for the sacrifices they made to keep him at college, and the knowledge that unless he passed his exams an intended church livelihood would slip through his hands. Certainly there is no remembrance, and no sense, of any intellectual ferment. Thomas's time as a student was not like, for example, his near contemporary Anthony Burgess's.[55] Whereas Burgess used his time at Manchester University to explore unashamedly as many ideas as he could lay hands on, Thomas remains cocooned. Bangor in the 1930s may not have been a premier seat of learning, but even so such societies and clubs as the college possessed he generally refrained from joining. The exceptions were the choral society – Thomas sang as a second bass – and, intermittently, the College second rugby fifteen. He was a keen sportsman, but even in that respect he was not quite good enough.

This explains something. Thomas's intellect, when later on it does develop, is no mean instrument. His poetry will graduate quite rapidly into a poetry of ideas. But the ideas, and the intellect controlling them, are alike subordinate to forces that are primarily psychologically affective. Thomas uses only what is of use to him; he passes everything through the eye of a spiritual quest – for God, for Wales, for the self – and what is considered of no relevance to that quest is jettisoned. Things do not interest him in themselves; either they are worked into an existing pattern, most usually as metaphor, or they are ignored. There is room for subtle humour, but none for comedy.

Unlike Burgess, and for that matter unlike the great majority of his other contemporaries, Thomas has little capacity (and also no liking) for journalism. He is a powerful commentator on the bare bones of life; he has something too to tell us about the flesh; but the clothes people wear, the constantly changing apparel of everyday living and the crowded mantle of immediate public event, will largely leave him cold; disengaged; the enemy of ephemera.

Yet ferment of a kind there was for R. S. Thomas at Bangor; or rather, a continuation of the ferment already observed in his childhood. Behind the small town wrapped around a hill on the southwestern side of the Menai Strait rose the great mountain majesty of Wales: Eryri ('the abode of eagles'), in English, Snowdonia.

Socially, Thomas appears to have made little progress. Women still perplexed him. At the end of his very first week the College held a 'welcome dance' for newcomers, a sort of freshers' ball. Thomas stands with a group of other diffident males watching 'with envy' the more self-confident whirl about the floor. 'How long,' he asks, 'before he learned to push a long-suffering girl up one side of the hall and down the other, and ask for the last dance as an excuse to walk her back to the girls' hostel?'[56] The first time he succeeds in this ploy, he writes to his parents to tell them he has met someone 'magical', even though he has failed to discover her name. 'Whoever agreed to consort with me soon dropped me.'[57] And again, as regards the rugby team, he seems not to have been fully part of it. When he plays in the second fifteen more often than not it is at an away match: he was prepared to pay the travel expenses where others were reluctant, but this did not earn him a regular place. Nor does his refusal to play cards with his team-mates, once he has convinced himself that he is being cheated, endear him to them.

But all was not lost. At Bangor he discovers beauties of nature different from those he knew on Holy Island. 'One evening he went for a walk to Felin Esgob. The moon was full and the stream sparkled by her light as it flowed past the small railway line that led to Mynydd Llandygai.'[58] Returning late to his first-year lodgings, it does not occur to him that his landlady might think he has been out with a girl. Thereafter he makes a habit of going on long solitary walks. He will take a bus to the foot of one mountain, climb over it, and take another bus home. Eryri opens up before him. 'The first time he did this, after ascending some hillock and seeing the crests in their glory before him, he burst out singing "Land of My Fathers", throwing his puny voice against the majestic surrounding mountains.'[59] And why not? Yr Wyddfa (Snowdon) is but one of a dozen peaks that rise over three thousand feet. The Alps or the Pyrenees are higher, but scarcely more dramatic. At almost any time of the year what mesmerizes the Welsh mountain hiker is the devastating play of light across threadbare green slopes, pockmarked with rock and sheep, and leaning steeply over valley floors picked out by thin glinting rivers and old, mainly disused, stone dwellings.

How much should we make of this? Most people at some point in their lives take to some or other mountain range, if only for a few hours. The experience usually is of a different order of existence, but is then tucked away among whatever other images are stored in the memory, where its pristine power slowly diminishes. With Thomas though there is patently much more to it than that. Later he will write what is perhaps the most effective of all his prose works, *The Mountains*.[60] The different order of experience is gathered into the self as a permanency. The first time he sees the mountains he bursts out with 'Land of My Fathers' – *Hen Wlad fy Nhadau*, the national anthem of Wales. *Old* land of my fathers, rather. And presumably he burst out in Welsh, which, even if he didn't speak the language yet, he would have learned by rote from his Welsh-speaking, Welsh-singing rugby team-mates.

Was this the beginning of the patriotic attachment? In *Neb*, persisting in the third person narrative, Thomas immediately continues: 'Another time, in February during an unusually warm spell, bathed in sweat he climbed the northern slopes of Carnedd Llywelyn. But once he reached the saddle between Llywelyn and Dafydd he saw that the furthest slope was white with snow, and the wind blowing at him was sufficiently icy to take his breath away.'[61] And then, with a clear recollection of disappointment, he comments that, while climbing, he has the notion that he is 'the only living thing', until, reaching the summit, he spots two other figures – 'black specks'

– also labouring in the 'great snow'. Unless the almost didactic nomenclature of the peaks in question is taken into consideration, here is another passage that threatens to fall flat on its face. But Carnedd Llywelyn and Carnedd Dafydd are named after the two last indigenous princes of Wales, Llywelyn and his son, and that, for Thomas's Welsh readers, must be what gives the paragraph purpose.

There is also the embryonic solipsism. Until he discovers otherwise, Thomas believes himself to be alone in one of the vast arenas of Eryri. One speck of rat's dung, as the Chinese say, destroys the whole pot of rice. Though he doesn't quite say so, the intrusion of others, their mere existence even, spoils the feast. And indeed, encroachment upon Welsh landscapes by outsiders – but particularly English outsiders – will become a theme of the mature poetry.

'Compared to experiences like this,' he writes, 'there was something unreal about his attempts to pursue college activities.'[62] Behind his back he sometimes overhears fellow students taunt, 'Who does he think he is?' His own answer is that he doesn't know, he is a nobody, a *neb*. But again, there is more to it than that. One may very well imagine what sort of figure he cut. Like that of anyone possessed of diffidence, but especially a tall young fellow such as Thomas was, his manner could easily have struck others as aloof. It is the old Freudian sore about the interfusion of inferiority and superiority complexes, and never quite knowing where the one ends and the other begins.

Freudian, but also quintessentially Romantic. Who are we, and what is the significance of our strong emotions? In one respect Thomas did partake of college life more fully than the majority of his fellows. Regularly he contributed poems to the college magazine, then called *Omnibus*, though not under his own name. He employed two pseudonyms: the anglophile, belletrist 'Curtis Langdon', and then 'Figaro'. Of the former he has commented, in the 1990 interview published in *Planet*, that 'it was revelatory of my home background. My mother often used to ask the Boots librarian if she had anything nice for her to read. So coming from an atmosphere of Ethel M. Dell and Warwick Deeping it was not unlikely I should choose the pen name I did.' When a new editor took over, however, R. S. overheard him swearing that so long as the job was his there would be no more poems by 'that bloody Curtis Langdon' printed in the magazine. Thomas therefore resorted to the simple expedient of changing his name and getting a friend to copy out further poems, so that their authorship wouldn't be identified by their handwriting. Duly, 'Curtis Langdon' continued to be published.

'Was this,' the then seventy-seven-year-old poet asked, 'my first experience of literary prejudice?' A superficial reading of the poems themselves leads one to confirm the editor's reservations. They are mostly not even pseudo-Georgian, but sub-Shelleyan stuff, composed by someone whose poetic horizons, as Thomas himself has acknowledged,[63] were bounded by an over-familiarity with Palgrave's *Golden Treasury*. Yet what in hindsight is interesting about them is precisely their contrived Romantic sensibility. In the most ambitious of the Curtis Langdon verses, 'The Singer',[64] Thomas tells of an imagined Italian country poet who is wooed away from 'his native clime' by the promise of gold. But arrived in the city, his art deteriorates, until he is easily pushed aside by a rival:

> So thus forsaken and of men forgot,
>   And being too poor to reach his native land,
> His reason failed, and, weary with his lot,
>   He sought a wretched death by his own hand.

In 'Loneliness'[65] the young poet from Holyhead listens self-piteously – his own gloss – to curlews during a sleepless night:

> . . . I am far, far lonelier than they,
>   For all their shrill and doleful clamouring.

Nature is similarly exploited in other poems to mirror and magnify the poet's sense of self-apprehension and anomie. Yet in 'Romance'[66] the mood switches to a Christian pantheism, as though Thomas had abruptly alighted upon Wordsworth:

> Life must be Disillusionment
>   To him who, in the surge of sea,
> Finds little that's magnificent;
>   Who, in the symmetry of tree
> Sees no divinely noble plan;

Whose heart is not attuned to Love
Or grand complexity of Man;
    Who cannot, will not, look Above.

Perhaps Thomas's conscience had been pricked into thinking that an ordinand should not give way to despair too wholeheartedly. Dylan Thomas, born a year after R. S., and whose poetic instincts were also rooted in Romanticism, had by this same time already drafted 'Fern Hill' and other conspicuously modern, conspicuously successful poems. But in the timing of a poet's emergence there is no book of rules to say what should occur and when. What is germane is that Dylan, having mastered Romanticism in a contemporary idiom, never really went beyond; whereas slow-breeding R. S., when he does find his voice, uses it to launch an oblique but sustained critique of Romanticism's elements. To a degree, the themes of R. S. Thomas's publicly known poetry are consistent with the themes explored with only borrowed panache by Curtis Langdon/Figaro. It is in their treatment that the radical, even subversive, emerges.

Meanwhile the injunctions to acknowledge God's hand as issued by the three stanzas of 'Romance' may have been rather less unctuous than they appear on the page. In the 'Autobiographical Essay' Thomas relates one further, and perhaps the most curious, episode from his student days. Bangor is visited by Pastor Jeffreys, a faith healer. Thomas persuades his father to attend a meeting. 'Never had I prayed so hard. Kneeling in the Hostel chapel, I lifted my eyes time and again to the large wooden crucifix that hung before the altar.' In the marquee, T. H. Thomas approaches the healer. The healer puts his fingers in the father's ears, says something, then sends him back to his seat. Afterwards, Thomas's father announces he can hear a bird singing, 'something he had not done for years'. But any restoration of the man's hearing was short-lived. Within a week he is deaf again.

'My mother,' R. S. Thomas concludes tersely, but without indicating an exact sequence of cause and effect, 'was foolish enough to accuse him of having lost his faith.' R. S. on the other hand seems to have found his, though this in turn will be subjected to the same critical scrutiny that he directs at the mainsprings of his earliest known verses. In his religion and poetry alike, sentiment and sentimentality will be rigorously outlawed; as in his persona, diffidence is slowly remoulded into the vatically assertive.

In October 1935, after spending the summer at his parents' house in Holyhead, Thomas set off for Cardiff, the city of his birth, and later described by him as 'the capital of a fake nation'.[67] His task now was to prepare for ordination. Duly he enrolled at St Michael's Theological College, in the leafy cathedral suburb of Llandaff. But although the course offered was supposed to last two years, R. S. left after only one. Feeling trapped inside an urban environment, and not especially enamoured of his fellow ordinands, who for the most part were south Walian, Thomas gladly accepted the offer of a curacy from the Vicar of Rhosymedre.

The college was furious: its function, from before the Disestablishment of the Church in Wales, was to ensure that new priests were adequately trained, in matters pastoral as well as spiritual. There were efforts to persuade the young man from Anglesey to review his decision. When he wouldn't, the under-warden intervened to repair at least some of the damage. For whatever reason Rhosymedre was adjudged an unsuitable parish for Thomas to work in, and instead he was found a curacy at Chirk, in St Asaph diocese. The then Vicar of Chirk, Canon John Walter Lloyd, appears to have had the ear of his Bishop, William Thomas Havard, who agreed, as was his prerogative, that the troublesome priest-to-be should be ordained as an archdeacon forthwith.

Thus Thomas got his way. About Llandaff he has little to say. *Neb* devotes scarcely a page to St Michael's, and the 'Autobiographical Essay', the sanitized or emasculated version of *Neb* prepared for an American readership, a single paragraph. Again R. S. found his warden, Edward Williamson, subsequently Bishop of Swansea and Brecon, 'effeminate' in manner, 'yet a scholar and able to lay down the law every bit as sharply as Glyn Simon'[68] – a view partly at odds with others' characterization of St Michael's at the time as 'Williamson's Rest Home'.[69] But R. S.'s main gripe was that living in Cardiff deprived him of the Welsh landscape. 'There was nowhere to walk except along a main road. There were no mountains, and no open countryside.'[70] Worse, because the college year was divided into four ten-week terms, he had to spend part of his summer away from Holyhead. 'Neither the college nor this arrangement', he summarizes sniffily, 'appealed to him.' After Bangor he found the buildings 'old-fashioned', and life 'uninteresting'.

Once a term there was a day of silence, when the college tradition was to invite an outside preacher to address its inmates. But only one of these, the Rev. R. O. P. Taylor from Ringwood in Hampshire, made any impression, and then perhaps for all the wrong reasons. He spoke of a colonel in his parish who was always a 'nuisance', but who was 'actually a very frightened man': a type Thomas himself was to encounter during his own subsequent ministries, particularly at Eglwysfach, and guaranteed to infuriate the author of 'The Small Window' and other devotedly anti-English and anti-establishment poems.

As part of their preparations, ordinands were expected sometimes to take services in local parish churches, but this was not absolutely compulsory, and 'with his customary cowardice'[71] R. S. succeeded in ducking his turn. Only three recollections associated with Llandaff give the memoirist any pleasure. The first was attendance at a concert given in Cardiff by the virtuoso violinist Fritz Kreisler: an experience transmuted into poetry twenty-five years afterwards, in the somewhat overreaching lines of 'The Musician'[72]: Kreisler suffering on his instrument becomes Christ suffering on the Cross. The second was attendance at the rugby international between Wales and the All Blacks at Cardiff Arms Park in December 1935, famously won in the dying moments by the home side. The third, the train journeys back to Holyhead. 'As you know,' Thomas tells us in *The Paths Gone By*,

the line from Cardiff to Shrewsbury runs through the Marches, with the plains of England on one side and the Welsh hills on the other. I was often stirred by the sight of these hills rising in the west. It sometimes started to get dark before we reached Ludlow. In the west, the sky would be aflame, reminding one of ancient battles. Against that light, the hills rose dark and threatening as though full of armed men waiting for a chance attack.[73]

But a chance attack by whom? By the English upon the Welsh, or
the Welsh upon the English? In another poem of Thomas's maturity,
'Looking at Sheep',[74] the mood is bitter, not wistful, though in its
cleverly contrived conclusion the underlying fantasy is similar:

> Seeing how Wales fares
> Now, I will attend rather
> To things as they are: to green grass
> That is not ours; to visitors
> Buying us up. Thousands of mouths
> Are emptying their waste speech
> About us, and an Elsan culture
> Threatens us.
> What would they say
> Who bled here, warriors
> Of a free people? Savagely
> On castles they were the sole cause
> Of the sun still goes down red.

'Elsan' here refers to the manufacturer of portable lavatories, popular
with English campers in the 1950s and '60s, and therefore reducing
their language to semi-treated sewage.

More needs to be said about St Michael's, however, than R. S.
Thomas is prepared to tell us. Even if he did spend only one year
there, it was the eye of a needle he more or less had to pass through
if he was to become a priest.

Today St Michael's is the only residential theological college in
Wales, St David's Lampeter, originally established along the lines of
an Oxford college and offering a variety of courses besides theology,
having become fully integrated with the University of Wales. Its
motto is *Goreu meddyg, meddyg enaid*, 'The best doctor is the doctor
of the soul'; its tradition strongly Anglo-Catholic. Founded on
St David's Day 1892, St Michael's was very much a product of the
nineteenth century and the Anglican Church's endeavours to reform
itself. It was not just in Wales, during the course of the preceding
century, that the Church had become vulnerable to its Nonconformist
rivals. The root of failure was identified in the laxity of the clergy.
Too many rectors and vicars had neither the training nor the aptitude

for the posts they held. Livings were largely in the gift of the landed gentry and awarded to younger sons. A bachelor's degree from either Oxford or Cambridge was deemed sufficient preparation for the ministry. Ordination was determined by the bishops and their chaplains; but in general bishops and their chaplains were swayed principally by considerations of class. The clergy were a part of the gentry, and a part of the gentry they would remain. If a young man seemed a decent sort, and unlikely to embarrass the club by unruly behaviour, then his membership followed as a matter of course.

This pleasant absence of enforced piety, though well suited to shire life before the industrial revolution, and which Jane Austen was still able to witness in her country novels, could not continue indefinitely. It made no provision for the spiritual and pastoral needs of the newer kind of community growing up in the factory shadows of the late eighteenth and early nineteenth centuries. And it was here, in England's rapidly expanding towns and cities, among populations still at the threshold of political expression, that Methodism and Nonconformity made their deepest inroads.

The picture was further complicated by the demand for Catholic emancipation. Since the days of the Glorious Revolution (1688–9) Catholics had been subject to a number of restrictions that effectively barred them from public life. Concurrently the established Church, endeavouring to compete with the new heterodoxies, shifted, for a while at least, in a Protestant direction. Between 1828 and 1832 Parliament, attempting to be even-handed, enacted laws that removed several of the prohibitions against Catholics while also lifting such 'Anglo-Catholic' requirements as the obligatory receipt of the Eucharist on Sundays by holders of government office and members of municipal corporations.

In Wales the situation was exacerbated by the language divide. Not all, but too many Anglican incumbents were unable even to speak to their congregations, whether in town or country. For this reason Nonconformity enjoyed its model successes not just in the urban south, but also, even especially, in the rural west and north, so that by the 1830s Anglicanism was already a minority denomination.

Across Britain, it was no longer assumed that Anglicanism would survive as the established state religion. It was, however, in England that the Church's efforts at self-reform were concentrated. This took two forms. A number of theological colleges were founded to address the shortcomings of the Anglican ministry, indeed to professionalize the clerisy; Wells and Chichester in or around 1849, Cuddeston in 1854, Lichfield in 1857, and others to follow. Secondly, the Church re-examined its doctrinal foundations, with the result that a powerful Anglo-Catholic movement emerged, centred on a group of Oxford clerics, and variously called the Oxford Movement, Tractarianism and Antidisestablishmentarianism. Its luminaries were John Henry Newman, Richard Hurrell Froude, John Keble and Edward Pusey. Creating an essentially reactionary church-within-a-church, they emphasized the ritualistic elements of the liturgy. By underlining what they conceived to be the all-importance of the Eucharist they insisted on the special status of the officiating priest as a mediator between his congregation and God. While Nonconformists and 'protestants' within the Anglican communion, later to emerge as the Church's evangelical wing, preached atonement as the necessary means to salvation, the Tractarians advocated the efficacy of grace.

The Oxford Movement did revivify the Church, although its long-term legacy has been division. For many clergymen the Tractarians harked back to the days of Archbishop Laud and the 'Beauty of Holiness': a response vindicated when Newman converted to Roman Catholicism; for which apostasy he was (eventually) rewarded with a cardinal's hat. In the present century the influence of the Anglo-Catholics, as the Tractarians became known, has waned dramatically, so that the Church today, at least in England, is composed mainly of middle-of-the-roaders, evangelicals, 'liberals' and charismatics. In Wales, where the Church has gone its own way since Disestablishment in 1920, doctrinal debate has tended to play second fiddle to maintaining and expanding Anglicanism's minority share in a more fragmented and fast contracting religious market. It is probably also the case that while the ruling body of the Church in Wales has been careful to present a united front, traditional social values have allowed for a greater tolerance of doctrinal difference among parishes. What happens in one community is not seen as being any of the business of the next.

At the close of the nineteenth century, however, the Church in

Wales was still a part of the Church of England, and the Oxford Movement far from being a spent force. Like other Anglican theological colleges, St Michael's was consciously Tractarian. Its most important early patron, Olive Talbot, belonged to a High Church family. Indeed, her father, Christopher Rice Mansel Talbot, a man worth six million at his death, had been a student at Oriel College at the same time as Newman and Froude. She provided St Michael's with its first home, a country house belonging to the Talbots outside Aberdare, together with the moiety of its initial endowment. The buildings it presently occupies in Llandaff, however, were purpose-built from 1905. These consist of an Oxbridge-type quadrangle in the Gothic revival style, using red Forest of Dean Stone.

The college was founded on a non-diocesanal principle; that is, it was intended to prepare ordinands for any and all Welsh dioceses. It was governed by its own College Council, although the Bishop of Llandaff has usually been its chairman. The warden too was granted unusual powers, particularly as regards staff appointments and the selection of students. The then Archbishop of Canterbury, Randall Thomas Davidson, initially agreed to attend an inaugural service of dedication in August 1907, the date set for the opening of the new buildings, but changed his mind when he learned how limited the local bishop's authority was.

Tractarians keenly supported the status of the bishops, but at St Michael's academic freedom was set above even episcopalianism; one reason why for some years student enrolment was low, since it was the bishops who recommended would-be ordinands. And St Michael's was beset by other crises. In 1915 all college activities were suspended as its students enlisted for service on the front, and the much prized new buildings were handed over to the St John's Ambulance Association for the duration of hostilities. In July 1919, however, St Michael's reopened, with all of five men in residence. Nor was the new warden, F. W. Worsley, an inspired choice. An able scholar, Worsley lacked the will to enforce the semi-monastic discipline that was supposed to lie at the heart of St Michael's ethos. Although a high churchman, he was also affected by the vogue for 'muscular Christianity'. In college photographs he appears heavily adorned with medals picked up during the Great War. These included an MC. A keen sportsman, he preferred those ordinands whose behaviour conformed to his own 'gentlemanly' outlook.

Inevitably Worsley fell foul of the Council. As his son T. C. Worsley was to write, 'Golf once a week they would have found acceptably modern, but golf every day raised very natural suspicions about the time left over to administer the college's affairs.'[75] The trouble was he was unsackable, and by an adroit manoeuvre in 1926 he succeeded in getting himself appointed Dean of Llandaff, which further strengthened his position as warden. In the end, however, Worsley got rid of himself. Among the priest's penchants was a taste for women. Before the war he had put a maid in the family way. During the war, his son suggests, he struck up with a 'little widow in Genoa'. One morning in 1931, without a word of explanation, he informed his wife he was leaving, and vanished altogether. Years later, he resurfaced at the Admiralty, working as a clerk.

Under Worsley, however, student enrolment had improved, largely because, after Disestablishment, the Church in Wales was determined to rely upon its own human resources. Widespread unemployment outside the college walls – this was the era of the General Strike – also ensured that student numbers reached something like a full complement. When R. S. Thomas arrived, in the autumn of 1935, St Michael's was already embarked on a period of stability. Worsley's replacement, E. W. Williamson, a bachelor and classics scholar, had steadied the boat. Although more quietly committed to the values of prayer and the sacrament than his own successor, Glyn Simon, Williamson restored discipline. Once again ordinands were required to wear robes during services. They were also required to attend those services, three times a day. Slowly the college returned to being what had always been intended: a community of Christian men living, studying and praying together. At night, a more or less strict curfew was maintained, starting at 10 p.m.

About St Michael's communal activities Thomas has nothing to tell us. The college register shows he spent only four terms there. It wrongly gives his place of birth as Holyhead, but does record that, at the time, his knowledge of the Welsh language was non-existent.

He is also absent from the annual collegiate photograph for 1936; Thomas absconditus, perhaps. Other college photographs, however, show that he was a member of its rugby, cricket and tennis teams. But his main purpose in being there was to prepare for and sit the General Ordinand Examinations. These were set in England by the Central Advisory Council of Training for the Ministry. No further record survives of which papers Thomas sat and when, or how he fared, but a look at the GOE for 1936 gives some idea of what R. S. was obliged to study. There were separate papers on the Old and New Testaments, on Christian Doctrine, Christian Worship, Christian Morals and Church History. Ordinands were also expected to offer unprepared translation from either Latin or Greek.

Some of the questions posed by the Church examiners,[76] at this distance in time, do little more than raise a weary smile. 'Discuss briefly the function of women in the life and work of the Christian Church', for example; or 'State what you conceive to be the merits and defects of the Greek view of life.' There is even 'Estimate from the Christian standpoint the merits and defects of the "British character"'. Battle lines are drawn when it is commanded: '"The Romish doctrine concerning Purgatory . . . is . . . repugnant to the Word of God." Discuss this.' But other questions, especially those from the Doctrine and Morals papers, point unerringly to the religious and spiritual concerns that dominate much of R. S. Thomas's poetry. For instance:

Do you consider the profession of soldier to be compatible with the precepts of the Sermon on the Mount?

'Pray without ceasing' (I Thess v. 17). Can this injunction have any meaning for modern man?

How, in dealing with simple minds, would you answer the question, 'Who is God?'

Draw out the witness of conscience to the existence and character of God.

What do you consider the most valuable considerations in facing the problem of evil?

What do you understand by Pelagianism, and why is it thought to be peculiarly attractive to Englishmen?

More broadly, questions of both types help define the religious climate that, for better or for worse, Thomas wedded himself to when he became a priest in the Anglican communion. But at St Michael's, Anglicanism was given a double spin. First, there was the Tractarian outlook, which had also been the outlook of the Church Hostel in Bangor; second, Anglicanism in Llandaff was tailored for perceived Welsh needs.

By way of example, take the last of the six questions listed above. Since the General Ordinand Examinations were contrived by a committee in England, and adopted by most Anglican theological colleges at the time, the reference to Englishmen is not prima facie pejorative. Rather, since the Pelagian heresy involved the doctrine that salvation can be attained by individual virtue rather than through either grace or atonement, the question becomes a sort of back-handed compliment paid by the examiners to themselves. What is suggested is the morality of self-sufficiency that was the product of a particular kind of muscular Christianity that flourished in England in the interwar years. A Welsh Anglo-Catholic, on the other hand, may have come up with a different answer: Pelagianism appeals to the arrogant English because they think they can get by without God's grace.

Thomas's very fine poem 'Llanrhaeadr ym Mochnant'[77] written in praise of Bishop William Morgan, who translated the Bible into Welsh in the latter stages of the sixteenth century, and included in his collection *Not That He Brought Flowers* (1968), contains these lines:

> There is no portrait of him
> But in the gallery of
> The imagination: a brow
> With the hair's feathers
> Spilled on it? a cheek
> Too hollow? rows of teeth
> Broken on the unmanageable bone

> Of language? In this small room
> by the river expiating the sin
> of his namesake?

Morgan is pictured working in the vicarage at Llanrhaeadr ym Mochnant, close by an unusually musical brook that is fed by the famous Llanrhaeadr cataract four miles away, in the heart of the Berwyn mountains. But who is Morgan's namesake? One critic suggested Thomas meant Henry Morgan the pirate, and was roundly censured by the poet, in the *Anglo-Welsh Review*:[78]

> The Morgan to whom I refer is, of course, Pelagius. There is a legend to the effect that Pelagius was a Celt and that his name was a Latinisation of Morgan. This is the namesake whose sin William Morgan was expiating. And please note that had I been referring to Morgan the pirate I would naturally have used the word crime not sin, a necessary distinction these days!

That this Morgan, father of a heresy considered peculiarly attractive to Englishmen, was in fact Welsh is a cruel irony; but the association suggested in the examination paper was and is an old chestnut among churchmen, and it is not beyond speculation that Thomas intends a sly dig at the *Sais*, as well as an affirmation of the importance of grace. Legend also has it, quite improbably, that Pelagius, a.k.a. Morgan, was decisively refuted by St David; and of course one of the points where Welsh history is perceived to have been suborned by English history is when the church established by David was crushed by the Henrican Reformation and the puritanism that followed.

Thus by the deftest of touches R. S. Thomas reinforces Bishop Morgan's claim to be a Welsh hero: not only on account of what he did for the language, but also as someone in league with Wales's patron saint. But it would be wrong to pronounce too strongly that 'Llanrhaeadr ym Mochnant' fixes Thomas within a Tractarian tradition. Doctrinally Thomas is notoriously difficult to pin down. Extreme Catholics see him as something of a Protestant, while Protestants see him as something of a high churchman. One priest told me he is very much the 'cat that walks alone' in this respect. The poem does, however, attest the poet's ingrainedly religious mindset. 'Llanrhaeadr ym Mochnant' also attests the same mindset from another perspective. In purely poetic terms, its prosody is conspicuously modern. There is no rhyme, and both the stress and syllable patterns are irregular. There is some assonance, some consonance, but no more than one might expect to find in, say, a piece of carefully crafted prose. The most effective device is the line-break, not least because where a line-break, or even a paragraph-break, occurs, it seems at first sight arbitrary. And yet for all this the prosody works, as it works for so many other poems written by Thomas in the same manner. It shouldn't be poetry, but in fact it is.

How can this be so? One answer, perfectly correct, is that Thomas has mastered the prosody of English verse to such a degree, and borrowed so subtly from Welsh prosody, that he can proceed without any of the usual props. The cat that walks alone walks without crutches. So well tuned is his ear he can write as though there are no rules, or invent them as he goes. But perhaps it is not simply a matter of his familiarity with the poetic conventions and the poetic canon that enables him to do this. A church or a chapel, a pulpit or a prayer-rail, is also a forum that exposes any falsity in the choice and rhythms of words employed.

When Thomas leaves St Michael's it is to begin a forty-year ministry. The Christian religion in Wales considered purely in its physical dimension – those acoustically severe stone rooms of varying sizes, where every word spoken is weighed in the balance – must have played its part in making Thomas the kind of poet he became: a technical modernist, yet drawing upon reserves of language scriptural in their centredness.

The two roles, priest and poet, also reinforce each other in another way. Customarily the churchman, but especially the churchman prepared in High Church circles, addresses his congregation with special authority. His vestments bespeak a privilege reserved to himself. He has the word of God up his long sleeve. So too with Thomas the poet. However great the doubts that beset him personally, towards his reader his attitude frequently is one of assurance, and sometimes of superiority, even condescension. The mythology of the poet as seer will become incorporated in his poetics.

*　　　*　　　*

From Llandaff he goes to Chirk, Y Waun in Welsh, meaning meadow or moor, but in the mid-1930s an English-speaking mining town, built on a coalfield straddling the border; a flat country, pitted with Marcher villages since grown prosperous with an influx of London and Manchester types: great houses and small castles; and churches far larger than those to the west. To the south is Oswestry, and a dozen miles to the north Wrexham, with Offa's Dyke crossing Chirk itself.

As curate, Thomas was in effect, for the four years he was there, Canon Lloyd's assistant. That is, he did not have a church of his own, but was expected to help out wherever there was need in the parish. His first sermon was preached at the colliery church in nearby Halton. His duties included sometimes conducting services at the main church, St Mary's, a double-aisled edifice dating, in its oldest parts, from Norman times, and sometimes called *Eglwys y Waun*. Before then the site was occupied by another church, or holy compound, originally dedicated to the seventh-century Welsh saint Tysilio. Chirk Castle, still maintained as a residence, was constructed in the wake of the Edwardine conquest of Wales by Roger Mortimer, whom Edward I created Lord of Chirkland, in 1282. After changing hands several times, the castle and its accompanying title were sold to Sir Thomas Myddleton, a grote millionaire grocer and founder member of the East India Company, in 1595.[79] The same family owns and inhabits it today. The interior of St Mary's is also something of a Myddleton preserve: the main altar is flanked by two large statuary memorials, designed by John Bushnell, one to the second Sir Thomas (d. 1660) and his wife Mary Napier, the other to Elizabeth Wilbraham, wife of the third Sir Thomas. Indeed, with other Myddleton memorials abounding, in stained glass and brass as well as stone, the place has the air of a family chapel.

What R. S. Thomas thought about the striking yet faintly daft Myddleton memorials can only be guessed. Possibly he was revolted by them; less likely, but still conceivably, he was charmed by their foppish aristocracy: the bust of the second Sir Thomas sports a Richelieu-type hairdo or wig, but only the shallowest of foreheads to go with it. In the 'Autobiographical Essay' he comments briefly that he found Chirk to be 'a fairly stratified parish from two earls at the top through a residential class to the miners at the bottom, as it were'.[80] This was of a time before he began giving vent to either his romantic affinity for the Welsh hill farmer, or his distaste for the English middle classes. The other aristocrat in the vicinity was Lord Trevor, who may or may not have been instrumental in Thomas's eventual departure from Chirk.

In *Neb* Thomas relates that soon after his arrival in Chirk he discovered that his predecessor had been 'chaplain' to the local branch of Toc H: a Christian society formed in 1915 to help combat the effects of bereavement and other forms of isolation incurred during the Great War. The name Toc H derives from Talbot House, the organization's first headquarters at Poperinge in Belgium. Although now a charitable body committed to working with young people in run-down urban environments, its early reputation was for stimulating self-recovery through moral re-armament. The expression 'queer as a Toc H lamp', prevalent in military circles up until the 1970s, with or without the sexual connotation, denotes how the society's meetings earned mixed reactions among outsiders. Mainly, though, such meetings were simple discussion groups, but culminating in a group prayer session, with the symbolic lighting and extinguishing of a candle (the 'lamp').

Thomas willingly agreed to continue his predecessor's role as prayer leader, and soon found himself giving talks on 'a variety of topics', not just in Chirk but also at other branches of the society in the area. It was, however, as much a learning experience for Thomas as it was for his audiences. The mainly middle-class male members he encountered included 'those who had lived for a time overseas' and who were ready to discuss 'things out of the ordinary'. Their remarks were peppered with examples of social and spiritual life drawn from distant parts, and Thomas 'enjoyed' listening to them.

Perhaps in his relative inexperience of the world the still young poet-priest allowed himself to be carried away somewhat, but in one respect at least his attendance at those meetings had a lasting outcome. It was largely through his involvement with Toc H that Thomas became a committed pacifist. Early on he was steered towards theosophy – another broadening of his then limited intellectual horizons – to the extent that he made one or two prose contributions to a theosophical magazine in India. But of greater importance was his reading in 1938, during the preparation for one of his talks, of a pamphlet by the then Dean of Canterbury, Hewlett Johnson, commonly known as the 'Red Dean'. Already it was widely believed that it was only a matter of time before Hitler and German Nazism once again plunged Europe into war, but Johnson, more a pacifist than a Marxist, argued that in the modern era wars are invariably the product of capitalist machinations.

Hewlett Johnson's analysis came as an 'awakening' to Thomas. The talk he gave to his Toc H group, based on the Red Dean's ideas, went down so well that the following Sunday he preached it as a sermon at St Mary's. Canon Lloyd was ill-amused. 'Don't you preach that stuff here,' he told his curate a couple of days later.[81] But it may not have been only Canon Lloyd. In Chirk it is remembered that Lord Trevor himself had been singularly taken aback 'by a sermon given by the Toc H man'.[82]

Even if Thomas did incur a local grandee's displeasure, he may not have known about it at the time. He left Chirk in August 1940. The reason given for his departure in Neb was that Canon Lloyd 'didn't want a married curate'.[83] Thomas had by then met and married the artist Mildred E. Eldridge, usually referred to by Thomas as Elsi. But that may have been only the immediate pretext. By then too the Second World War had begun, and Chirk 'society' may have been looking for a suitable excuse to dispense with the services of an unpatriotic priest.

Would Thomas himself have disputed the charge? In Neb the depth of his remembered feelings is manifest. Canon Lloyd's injunction not to preach 'that stuff here', he writes, 'opened his eyes to a fact he later became more conscious of: the Church was not prepared to condemn war, only to urge young men to do their "duty" and to pray for them afterwards. For a young fellow with ideals to uphold the situation was clear enough. Christ was a pacifist, but not so the Church established in his name.'[84]

But as ever there was more to it than that, quite apart from the problematic assertion that Christ was de facto a pacifist. That rather depends on which Gospel you read, and how; while the Book of Revelation places Christ at the centre of a universal cataclysm (Armageddon) in which all but a chosen few (144,000 male members of the tribes of Israel) are condemned to a violent and everlasting perdition. An uncharacteristically, even dangerously trite sentence about the coming of Hitler's war in *The Echoes Return Slow* reads: 'The first peace had but sown dragon's teeth, not the Welsh dragon's.'[85] This antithesis only really works if we concede that the Welsh dragon is in some way opposed to war, a difficult gloss to establish historically.

During the four years at Chirk, to an astonishing extent, the elements of Thomas's known persona begin to coalesce. The altercation with Canon Lloyd marks the beginning of a quest for religious or spiritual identity that will be protracted for the remainder of his life. As well as the pacifism, there are the first stirrings of an intense concern with the individual experience of pain, his almost single-minded awareness of the human condition as being essentially one of suffering. There is also a deepening of, even an arrival at, his feeling of being fully Welsh: a condition that will sometimes threaten to place his pacifism in jeopardy, as the cause of Welsh nationalism gathers momentum. And poetically, though relatively little is published, there is a similar sense of a future grasped. His voice begins to emerge.

Thomas's duties included pastoral outwork: visiting the ill and the old and the lonely in their homes. 'Some of the parishioners were very sick and merited frequent visits.'[86] Some of these Thomas lists: a paralysed wife who mistakenly thought she was getting better; another wife, married to a collier, who would take minutes to answer the door on account of her rheumatism; a miner who couldn't eat because of a stomach tumour. Though his pity is aroused, he gives the impression of not really knowing what to do in the face of suffering. 'Very slowly, through reading and thinking, he came to understand that this was one of the greatest problems that has perplexed man since he began using his brain.'[87] Already the conventional comforts offered by institutionalized Christianity appear inadequate to their task.

And the reading? This would have included the theosophical and other more or less 'serious' magazines Thomas became familiar with through his association with Toc H. But at Chirk he also began

building a personal library. Ever dismissive of his academic achievements as a student, Thomas presents himself, not altogether inappro-
priately, as an autodidact who came alive at Chirk. As a reader he
will often convey the impression that he comes to other authors
with unpremeditated eyes, as though he had chanced upon them by
accident. Yet he will also become a harsh, even implacable critic,
maintaining rigorous standards as to the admissibility of any particular author into what eventually becomes very much a high culture
pantheon; a further trait maybe of his high church nurturing.

Impressed by Canon Lloyd's collection, Thomas arranges through
a firm in London to buy 'fifty books' on hire-purchase. Thus, 'for
the first time in his life' volumes of poetry came into his possession.[88]
The same ingénu quality informs Thomas's descriptions of the first
excursions made beyond Wales as an adult: to Scotland and to Ireland,
more or less predictable destinations given his increasing absorption
with things Celtic. Although to begin with at Chirk Thomas is fully
occupied with settling into his new environment and learning the
ropes of his profession, inevitably the day comes when he rues being
so close to the English border in an un-Welsh part of Wales. October,
when he first arrives, greets him with trees 'in their glory' turning
colour. But within a few weeks the weather changes to cold rain and
grey mists. 'The boy suddenly and fearfully realised where he was.
Thus started the *hiraeth* for Ynys Môn and the sea; a longing that
affected him through the long years that followed.'[89]

What made it worse for him perhaps, though Thomas tells us at
the time it was a comfort, was the proximity of the Ceiriog Valley
to the west, and of the Berwyn mountains. In Llangollen and other
more obviously Welsh towns and villages the flat Shropshire accent
prevalent in Chirk gives way to something more sonorous. In Llanar-
mon he befriends the vicar and meets there with other Welsh-minded
priests. Soon he begins exploring further afield, travelling as far as
Bala, at the head of Lake Tegid, with Eryri in view. Little by little,
the interior of Wales opens up to him. Yet, as he puts it himself,
his poetic response to this landscape was still tenderly, or meekly,
lyrical. He had by now, among the Georgians, started taking serious
notice of Edward Thomas, a lasting if, *pace* the endeavours of some
Welsh critics to enlist him as an Anglo-Welsh writer, curiously

English influence. But the more overtly 'modern' poets – Gerard Manley Hopkins, Wilfred Owen, Ezra Pound and T. S. Eliot – were still unfamiliar territory to him. Even of Yeats, whose presence can be strongly detected throughout Thomas's first half dozen or so printed collections, and beyond, only the earlier 'Celtic Twilight' poetry had penetrated his attention.

But the figures who influence a poet are not restricted to other poets. Thomas's verse would certainly have been vastly different had the literary encounters with Edward Thomas or Yeats never occurred. But equally important to both his life and work was the woman he met and married while curating in Chirk.

The extraordinarily tender poem 'A Marriage', which is also a poem about age, has already been discussed and given in quotation. Down the years, either directly or obliquely, Mildred E. Eldridge is the subject of many other poems. As with his mother, R. S. does not refrain from exploring a central relationship in print. Yet very often the particular colouring he gives to his marriage is one of intense privacy. The reader is invited into the poet's hallway, but is told he can advance no further than the foot of the staircase.

Some of these poems are placed, with strategic gallantry, at the end of a collection. 'A Marriage' itself is placed as the last item in the *Collected Poems*, and is in fact the only poem contained within that volume from the late collection *Mass for Hard Times*. It is as though Thomas cannot let a book rest unless his wife's presence is acknowledged. But gallantry, implying a want of final sincerity, is therefore the wrong word. When R. S. writes about Elsi Thomas, invariably it is with a profound concern. The earliest poetic reference to her occurs in 'Ap Huw's Testament'[90], (see above, p. 90):

> . . . Let me begin
> With her of the immaculate brow
> My wife; she loves me. I know how.

Nothing more. But in the first marriage poem proper, 'Anniversary',[91] from *Tares* (1961), Thomas opens the door on their privacy just a little wider: three eight-line stanzas, each beginning with the line 'Nineteen years now', cast a cool, almost clinical eye on the relation-ship, as though there were something inherently odd about it being there in the first place:

> Nineteen years now
> Under the same roof
> Eating our bread,
> Using the same air;
> Sighing, if one sighs,
> Meeting the other's
> Words with a look
> That thaws suspicion.

Love, one might deduce, under some duress, love clung to amid not plenty but an almost contrived frugality, although 'bread' carries with it, in the context of other poems in *Tares*, overtones of the Eucharist. At table, the second stanza tells us, Thomas and his wife are

> Careful to maintain
> The strict palate.

The third stanza endeavours to continue this habit. The nineteen years are spent 'Keeping simple house', and opening the door to 'friend and stranger' alike. What threatens the equilibrium is the arrival of a child,

> Opening the womb
> Softly to let enter
> The one child
> With his huge hunger.

On a first reading the child's appetite – for food? knowledge? love? – is a little shocking. It is as though the poet were resentful of the boy's intrusion. But the word upon which these closing lines hinge is 'softly'. After the stark, clinical expression 'Opening the womb' we are at once put in mind of a corresponding tenderness, and it is this tenderness that balances the 'huge hunger'. With an absolute economy of expression – another poet might have made an untidy and far more distasteful meal exploring the same tensions – the equilibrium, poetic as well as domestic, is in fact preserved.

Thereafter there are a dozen or so poems that are either addressed to Elsi Thomas, or seem to be about her. 'The Untamed',[92] from *The Bread of Truth* (1963), may or may not be numbered among these. The poet contrasts two gardens: one is the wild sea that belongs to him, the other a cultivated enclosure looked after by a woman, and where

> Despite my first love,
> I take sometimes her hand.

But who is this 'first love'? Is it in fact his wife, or is it some girl dated in adolescence? The poem was written while Thomas was vicar at Eglwysfach, and other sources indicate that while there he developed a platonic friendship with another woman. Again, there are hints in some of his very late writings that he may have formed a youthful attachment that went rather deeper than any of the failed flirtations described in the earlier writings, up to and including *Neb*.

A weaker ambiguity informs 'Because',[93] in *Pietà* (1966), a praise poem clearly addressed to a female whose ability to 'See . . . things' incites the poet's envy. The things seen include

> . . . the starved fox and
> The obese pet . . .

– doubtless referring to Elsi Thomas's incarnation as a gifted nature artist. But at the poem's end there is a bleakness that seems almost to contradict Thomas's admiration:

> The flowers wither
> On love's grave. This is what
> Life is, and on it your eye
> Sets tearless, and the dark
> Is dear to you as the light.

With a hideous irony, not long after the publication of this poem Elsi Thomas exhibited the first symptoms of the long illness that would rob her of her eyesight, and eventually, in 1991, of her life. Yet even before the knowledge of this, there is an absence of blitheness in Thomas's expressed marital affections that places what is nonetheless a compelling love poetry at the polar opposite of conventional Jack-and-Jill-ism. As Milton famously has it at the conclusion of *Paradise Lost*,

> Some natural tears they dropp'd, but wip'd them soon;
> The World was all before them, where to choose
> Their place of rest, and Providence thir guide . . .

But for Thomas there is seldom such solace. The comfort that female companionship brings only underlines the terror of mortality. What he captures so well, and which again is an unconventional topic for poets to dwell upon, is the sense of growing old together, of being caught in each other's company almost. Thus in 'Marriage',[94] from *Laboratories of the Spirit* (1975), and not to be confused with the later 'A Marriage', while declaring his wife to be more deserving of praise than any hallowed queen, he nonetheless writes:

> because time
> is always so short, you must go by
> now without mention, as unknown
> to the future as to
> the past, with one man's
> eyes resting on you
> in the interval of his concern.

In 'The Way of It',[95] the title poem of a 1977 collection, the same sense of isolation on the part of his wife is repeated, though now Thomas adds in a measure of his own guilt:

> With her fingers she turns paint
> into flowers, with her body
> flowers into a remembrance
> of herself. She is at work
> always, mending the garment
> of our marriage, foraging

145

like a bird for something
for us to eat. If there are thorns
in my life, it is she who
will press her breast to them and sing.

The bird imagery, so central by then to Thomas's metaphoric value system, and which he nearly always has resort to in his marriage poetry, is extended into the poem's second half, when he describes himself as having once spread 'his feathers' to draw her toward him. Yet this leads at once into a curious admission, amounting almost to a confession. The woman was not 'deceived' by the poet's display, but accepted him

as a girl
will under a thin moon
in love's absence as someone
she could build a home with
for her imagined child.

Elsewhere R. S. goes further, suggesting that he was not Elsi's first choice. Yet is this merely another example of his cultivated diffidence, and his insistence that disappointment lies at the heart of things? Commemorating Elsi's 'Seventieth Birthday',[96] in *Between Here and Now* (1981) – born in 1909 she was four years his senior – Thomas can discover a maddened lyricism in the most unlikely of places:

Made of tissue and H_2O,
and activated by cells
firing – Ah, heart, the legend
of your person! Did I invent
it, and is it in being still?

And again, echoing the farewell to his father in 'Sailor's Hospital':

You are drifting away from
me on the whitening current of your hair.
I lean far out from the bone's bough
knowing the hand I extend
can save nothing of you but your love.

To look at these and other poems addressed to Elsi Thomas is to take soundings from the whole span of Thomas's poetic career. What we find is that the image of her is regularly updated to keep pace with the poet's changing attitudes and preoccupations. As Thomas progresses ever further into his search for the divine, his wife is not left stranded behind, at least in his thoughts. In 'He and She',[97] from *Destinations* (1985), he clothes the marriage if not in images of eternity, then in images of the quest for eternity, the quest for faith.

> Were there currents between them?
> Why, when he thought darkly,
> would the nerves play
> at her lips' brim? What was the heart's depth?
> There were fathoms in her,
> too, and sometimes he crossed
> them and landed and was not repulsed.

The 'fathoms' here are not merely an extension of the sea metaphor implicit in the 'heart's depth', and punningly suggested by 'currents'. They signal also, as the word always does in Thomas, the '70,000 fathoms' of the Danish Christian existentialist thinker Søren Kierkegaard: the dark waters of doubt and philosophical conundrum that necessitate (for Kierkegaard) the all-important 'leap of faith'. That 'There are fathoms in her' therefore is not just a way of saying she is as 'deep' as the poet imagines himself to be, but rather a way of saying that in her own way she shares his spiritual anxieties. More, the implicit 'leap of faith' becomes, in the poem, a leap of trust, of love; but expressed in a concealed religious allusion.

What 'He and She' also conveys is a sense of the poet's dependency, despite or because of the increasing abstraction of his intellectual obsessions; as though indeed she is his strong anchor in an otherwise intolerable swell. Such at least is what the opening five-line stanza tells us:

> When he came in, she was there.
> When she looked at him,
> he smiled. There were lights
> in time's wave breaking
> on an eternal shore.

Here as elsewhere, there is the profound feeling that, however great or narrow the ostensible gap between them is at any one point in time, either as husband or wife, or more simply as discrete human beings, R. S. and Mildred E. Eldridge are fastened on parallel tracks that must meet eventually. The vanishing point however is just that: where life vanishes. In another powerful elegy written after 1991, 'No Time', published in *No Truce with the Furies* (1995), Thomas observes how

> She left me. What voice
> colder than the wind
> out of the grave said
> 'It is over'? Impalpable,
> invisible, she comes
> to me still, as she would
> do, and I at my reading.
> There is a tremor
> of light, as of a bird crossing
> the sun's path, and I look
> up in recognition
> of a presence in an absence.
> Not a word, not a sound,
> as she goes her way,
> but a scent lingering
> which is that of time immolating
> itself in love's fire.

At one level, these distinctive lines are a direct expression of the disbelief that accompanies bereavement, particularly bereavement in old age. Thomas as the poet of longevity can and sometimes does speak to and for all humankind in a manner that too often eludes him as a younger man. The momentary remission from grief, given here as a tremor of light 'as of' a passing bird, is, I hazard, not at all an uncommon experience among the elderly widowed. And of course, in that there is necessarily an eschatological element. They are not gone, but passed away, passed over . . . Yet here Thomas's affirmation of a faith is more precise than simple geriatric whimsy. The 'presence in an absence' leads back to an entire theology of a *deus absconditus.* But this theology, of the *via negativa*, which also and again has its points of contact with the writings of Kierkegaard, is overturned by an infinitely more suggestive communion. Time immolating itself in love's fire is not just a pretty way of asserting that human love is somehow more permanent than the conditions that shape and constrain it. It is an image drawn precisely from the writings of the Christian mystics, most especially Meister Eckhart, for whom God's reality, and therefore true reality, exists outside and quite independently of time.

More or less the same apotheosis is crafted in another poem from the same volume, 'The Morrow'. Cold fish as he may often appear, in his own terms, or the terms he has adopted, Thomas nonetheless attempts his utmost on behalf of the woman he married, and was married to for fifty years and more.

They met in Chirk. Local memory has it that they were in fact living in the same building, Bryn Coed, opposite St Mary's; but as it is a long building, they would not necessarily have had anything to do with each another for a while. According to the 'Autobiographical Essay', Elsi was 'one of the girls from a neighbouring house'. Thomas was on his way to catch a train one day when a car containing two women pulled up. They asked whether he would join them for a game of golf. Thomas declined, but accepted a lift to the station. For once the Lothario in him cast aside his habitual shyness. 'The daughter of the house was driving, but my eyes were on her passenger. I gave her that look which a man gives to the woman of his choice.'

To some she has seemed an odd choice. Mildred E. Eldridge was upper-middle-class English. People have sometimes wondered how it is R.S. can rail against her compatriots quite as often and quite as vehemently as he does. It is, they say, one of the contradictions in his make-up. But, when he met her, it was before his love of the Welsh landscape acquired its nationalist stridency. She was even then, as Thomas himself puts it, an 'established' artist, although the reason she was in Chirk was that she taught art at a school in Oswestry. Trained at the Slade, she had also studied in Italy, and some of her work had been exhibited in London galleries. At their best her paintings, water-colours and drawings, always technically assured, are sensitive but unsentimental studies of the natural world. Indeed, they exhibit the same detachment so often found in her husband's work.

Elsi's feeling for nature must obviously have endeared the young poet-priest to her. She also actively encouraged R. S. to develop his own artistic skills. According to *Neb*, her example inspired him to take the writing of poetry more seriously. 'He was eager to prove himself in his own field.'[98] As a result, he began submitting poems to the *Dublin Magazine* and other literary periodicals, and so became a properly published poet. But more than that, Thomas discovered that Elsi 'shared my inner dissatisfaction with modern society. We dreamed of breaking away, and going to live in a cottage, "on water and a crust".'[99]

Eventually, in the village of Rhiw towards the end of the Llŷn Peninsula, that dream became a reality. At Chirk, however, they satisfied their craving for an alternative lifestyle by making as many trips as they could into the Welsh hinterland, usually in Miss Eldridge's Austin Seven. Elsi also acted as chauffeuse to Thomas on his journey to Scotland, or at least for part of that journey. Thomas had fallen under the spell of the Celtic Twilight novelist Fiona Macdonald – the nom de plume of William Sharp (1855–1905). In general, R. S. does not present himself as a reader of fiction. Rather the opposite. Apart from one delicately felt sonnet to Henry James in *Frequencies* (1978), an abiding respect for the Welsh novelist Kate Roberts, and glancing references to Dostoievsky, Tolstoy and D. H. Lawrence, in the poet's considered roll-calls of literary honour novelists are conspicuous by their absence. They are too routinely middlebrow for him perhaps, and in any case they write in the 'inferior' medium of prose. But William Sharp, with his Celtic credentials, was an exception. *Pharais, The Mountain Lovers, The Sin Eaters* and other of Fiona Macdonald's novels published in the 1890s furnished a romanticized, even mystic picture of Gaelic crofter life on Scotland's west coast and among the Hebridean islands such as Thomas could or wanted to relate to.

They travelled in August 1937, Thomas deliberately setting out his stall to explore Macdonald's Scotland for himself. Spending the night in the highlands, next day they set out for Mallaig, to take the steamer for Barra, the most southerly of the larger of the Outer Hebrides. But the road between Fort William and Mallaig was under repair, and they arrived to see the boat pulling out to sea. Since in those days crossings were a once-a-week affair, it all looked rather hopeless until Thomas found a fisherman willing to take him over to Soay, a smaller island that nestles off the coast of Skye. It is unclear, however, from the parallel accounts of this Scottish expedition provided by *Neb* and the 'Autobiographical Essay', exactly what happened next. Within half an hour Thomas finds himself bidding a somewhat 'ungallant' farewell to Elsi on the quay and setting off in the fisherman's boat. Whether the fisherman had room for only one passenger, or felt the crossing too hazardous to take a woman on board, or whether Thomas and Miss Eldridge had some altercation is left to the reader's imagination. At any rate, R. S. set off alone.

On Soay he did not have a particularly joyous time. The idyll he went in search of eluded him. Mostly it rained. One of a handful of crofter families took Thomas under its roof, and did its best to make him comfortable. His only pleasure seems to have been listening to the soft 'swish' of spoken Gaelic in the early evenings, a language that even had he known Welsh at the time would have remained almost completely unintelligible to him, Gaelic occupying a different branch of the Celtic language tree. However, when he joined his hosts, they courteously switched to English. They also endeavoured to lay on a 'ceilidh', or merry evening, for his benefit, but that too was a desultory experience. For half an hour a neighbour stopped by and discussed the weather in front of a peat fire, then he left and the evening was over. One wonders whether or not Thomas wore his clerical collar.

After a week he decided he had had enough, and returned to Mallaig. There he discovered Elsi had taken herself off to Canna, another of the Inner Hebrides, presumably with her easel or drawing pads. At once he telegraphed her, 'selfishly' asking her to rejoin him immediately. When she responded, he persuaded her to spend the rest of their holiday back in Wales. So much, one might conclude, for crofter life in the Scottish islands. But the acute sense of disappointment at being unable to find the vanished folk-life described by Fiona Macdonald was, we may suppose, a lesson in itself. Within three or four years Thomas will begin describing the lives of the Welsh hill farmers, not a little romantically, but also with a keen perception that their way of life is rooted in a fragile past, so that even as he studies them they seem sometimes to be disappearing from his view.

His first trip to Ireland, undertaken later the same year, was altogether more propitious. At Christmas Canon Lloyd tells Thomas that he can have a week off from his duties. Thomas jumps on his bicycle and sets off for Holyhead, and thence across the sea to Dublin. There he calls on his editor at the *Dublin Magazine*, Seamus O'Sullivan. Armed with an introduction to the noted Celtic scholar and patriot Liam O'Briain, then a professor at Galway University, Thomas heads across Ireland by bus to the as yet undeveloped west, and succumbs to the traditional hospitality of the people living there. Arriving in the middle of the morning Thomas is at once presented by O'Briain with a sizeable glass of whisky. When he indicates his desire to push further west still, having caught a glimpse of the Aran Islands, O'Briain accompanies him a part of the way on foot, and provides him with another introduction, to the painter Charles Lamb.

Thomas records how, on the way to the Lambs, he passed a number of seaweed carts standing in 'the fields of Galway', and these, together with the smell of peat in his nostrils, and the Gaelic address of a carter returning west, 'lifted his heart and filled him with new hope'.[100] This was a land he could recognize from such Yeats as he had read, Celtic in custom and Celtic in tongue. Likewise, staying with the Lambs on New Year's Eve, he is able to observe the local celebration: 'hundreds of candles shining from the windows of the cabins around the loughs and beaches'[101] offering a welcome to whatever spirits were abroad in the night.

Thus began 1938, and with it the events leading up to Neville Chamberlain's moral surrender to Hitler at Munich in the autumn. Back in Chirk, Thomas notices the increased amounts of military traffic, but writes to his new friends in Ireland that war will never happen, that God will not permit it. But God's intentions were otherwise, and soon enough Thomas finds himself helping to distribute ration books while the wives of Chirk scavenge materials to black out their windows.

Under these circumstances, burying any differences that may have lain between them, R. S. and Elsi decided to marry, precipitating the need to move to another curacy. The ceremony itself took place in 1940 at the small church in Llanycil, on the western shore of Lake Tegid. Anxious to observe Welsh custom, Thomas requested the owner of the hotel where they stayed to supply a harpist to sing for their parents at a pre-wedding dinner the night before. 'But the proprietor was English and failed to find anyone', even though the curate had been told by Euros Bowen, then Rector of Llangywair and Llanuwchllyn, and to become in time the outstanding Welsh-language poet of his generation, that there were plenty of musicians in the vicinity 'so long as you went about it in the right way'.[102]

With Europe plunging into war, Thomas the pacifist was already preparing for other battles.

In the event Thomas was found a curacy in the parish of Hanmer, several miles to the east of Chirk, also in the diocese of St Asaph, and in 'Maelor Saesneg' – the 'English plain': a corner of Wales bulging across Offa's Dyke, and supposed to have been given to Owain Glyndŵr as part of his marriage settlement with Margaret, daughter of David Hanmer. This time, however, Thomas was to be no vicar's assistant but a priest-in-charge, with his own church and his own vicarage, at Talarn Green, to the north of the main village, and right up against the border. Indeed, the minor road running through Talarn Green, no more than a straggle of houses and farm buildings, is the border.

In Hanmer itself, the disproportionately large Church of St Chad, a triple-aisled 300-seater rebuilt after a devastating fire in 1889, rests on a slight hill commanding the best views of Hanmer's principal attraction, its forty-five-acre mere; hence indeed the name of the place, Han's or Hana's Meer, reflected in St Chad's former name, the 'church on the shining meer'.[103] At various times of the year migratory birds settle on this lake, including Canada geese, grebes, teal and cormorant. As well as Glyndŵr, Dafydd ab Edmwnd – the late medieval poet who codified the twenty-four meters of Welsh prosody – is reputed to have resided in the village. In August 1940, when R. S. came to Talarn Green, the then Rector, T. J. M. Morris, had four curates at work under him; today, the Vicar of Hanmer has none: evidence either of religious decline, or of improved productivity among incumbents, or both.

The church at Talarn Green, dedicated to St Mary Magdalene, is best described as an example of Victorian Cosy. It was built under the patronage of the local grandee, Lord Kenyon, and consecrated in 1873. The adjoining parsonage, designed by John Douglas and dating from 1882, is, in its subdued mock-Tudor outlook, of marginally greater architectural interest. It was also the first, and smallest, of a succession of well-to-do homes that the Thomases lived in. At the time though, neither building had electricity.

Thomas stayed at Talarn Green less than two years. Parish records show that his ministry there ended on the last day of May 1942. About the curacy itself he has nothing to say except that it lay more or less directly beneath the Luftwaffe's flightpath to Merseyside, twenty miles to the north and a key target for the Germans. As the 'phoney war' drew to a close, bombing missions began in earnest. Soon the relentless drone of German aircraft played on the young priest's nerves. Once at least, standing in his doorway and watching flames light the sky, he 'felt the wind from the bomb blast move through my hair' and 'stir his wife's skirt'.[104] On another occasion a bomb fell nearby, next to a zinc-roofed cottage in which an elderly couple lay sleeping, but failed to detonate. The thought that what he heard overhead signalled the death of innocents kept the problem of pain and unnecessary suffering uppermost in his mind. It also inspired him to do what he could to protect his bride. At the back of the Talarn Green parsonage he banked a wall with earth to provide safe shelter below the staircase inside. And with good cause: as the air defences around Liverpool improved, German and soon Italian bomber pilots began depositing their cargoes as best they could before returning to base.

Thomas's response to this was to begin learning Welsh. If he acquired Welsh then he could apply for a job in a Welsh parish. Petrol rationing meant that fewer and fewer journeys could be made into the Welsh interior. But Elsi Thomas now had a part-time teaching post in a school outside Llangollen, and once a week he accompanied her to take Welsh lessons from a gentleman called Iorwerth Roberts. The pity of it was that there was no one else, either in Talarn Green or in Hanmer, he could practise the language with. What with the war and the difficulties of travel and the distance of the nearest Welsh mountains, Thomas's *hiraeth* became near unmanageable. But 'mercifully', as he puts it, he heard of a living that had become vacant in Montgomeryshire, and thus effected his escape.

A problem with R. S. Thomas's pacifism is that it is never adequately defined. Although he may embrace the arguments of Hewlett Johnson and others, he seldom rehearses them. The pacifist position, however laudable in itself, is too often taken as granted, as though the particular horror he may have felt in, say, Hanmer must be universal. Nor does he debate the obvious but powerful contention that unless regimes of the sort perpetrated by the Nazi Wehrmacht are contained, there will be more not less ugliness in the world. That after all is what makes war and peace a true dilemma. But for Thomas all war is unthinkable, all war is dreadful, period. Or rather not period, because Thomas is, or soon will be, also capable of writing in praise of Owain Glyndŵr and other warrior leaders of the Welsh against the English. Thus, as will be seen, a fault-line emerges in the poet-priest's outlook. His response to violence is and remains essentially Christian pacifist, but is vulnerable at moments to the poet's equal hunger for Wales.

Yet without these tensions, Thomas would be nothing as a poet. Even in the 'Autobiographical Essay', although he forbears to comment on the responsibilities of a priest to his flock, he explains his departure from Talarn Green as a combination of the desire to live in parts more conspicuously Welsh *and* personal cowardice.[105] Naive in some respects he may be, but it is never the naivety of a soul at ease. What strikes one again and again is the contrast between the almost contrived simple-mindedness of *Neb* and the sophistication of the poetry's agonizings. A poem contained in his first collection, *The Stones of the Field*, 'Homo Sapiens 1941', but strangely excluded from the *Collected Poems*, deserves a place in any Second World War anthology. Clearly written out of his Hanmer experience, it depicts a fighter-bomber pilot at work, caught by a searchlight:

> Murmuration of engines in the cold caves of air,
> And, daring the sunlight above the stiff sea of cloud,
> Deadly as a falcon brooding over its prey
> In a tower of spirit-dazzling and splendid light,
> Pedestrian man holds grimly on his way.
> Legions of winds, ambushed in crystal corries,
> Conspiring to destroy him, and hosts of ice,
> Thronging him close, weigh down his delicate wings;
> But loud as a drum in his ear the hot blood sings,
> And a frenzy of solitude mantles him like a god.

A quarter of a century later, the isolation of the military aviator, his physical insulation from the war of destruction he wages, became a cliché of the Vietnam War as American pilots blithely ravaged the Annamite mountains and their inhabitants. Here, Thomas empathizes so well with his subject – note how the beam of the searchlight is 'spirit-dazzling' – that there is a danger the poem's intentions will be misunderstood. The point of it, however, is manifest in the last line. The pilot does not in fact achieve apotheosis, he is only 'like' a god. He remains 'Pedestrian', incapable of reading the message of the heavens he scours. Nonetheless, the poet's imaginative resources include the possibility of beholding glory in the devil's work: hence the poem's mock-Miltonic grandeur.

This trick of extended antiphrasis was deployed a few years after the writing of 'Homo Sapiens 1941' in 'Cynddylan on a Tractor',[106] perhaps Thomas's most widely anthologized piece, much used in school classrooms and contained in his second collection, *An Acre of Land* (1952). Here the tone is mock-heroic:

> Ah, you should see Cynddylan on a tractor.
> Gone the old look that yoked him to the soil;
> He is a new man now, part of the machine,
> His nerves of metal, and his blood oil.
> The clutch curses, but the gears obey
> His least bidding, and lo, he's away

Out of the farmyard, scattering hens.
Riding to work now as a great man should,
He is the knight at arms breaking the fields'
Mirror of silence, emptying the wood
Of foxes and squirrels and bright jays.
The sun comes over the tall trees
Kindling all the hedges, but not for him
Who runs his engine on a different fuel.
And all the birds are singing, bills wide in vain,
As Cynddylan passes proudly up the lane.

The new farmer is blithe about his business as Chanticleer is blithe; but in reality his mechanized liberation from the hard toil of the earth has dehumanized him. Flesh and blood are replaced by metal and oil, and he cannot be kindled by the sun. Finally, the seemingly halcyonic scene is arrested by the wide-open bills of the birds – the bright jays – powerless to halt the march of a technology that does not tend nature so much as ruin her.

Thus the conventional reading of a famous poem. To an extent, our understanding of 'Cynddylan on a Tractor' is dependent on knowledge of ideological values present in Thomas's work at large: his particular emphasis on 'the machine' as a harbinger of woe, his approbation of a life yoked to the soil, his use of birds to signal a divinely purposed order. But there is another level of possible meaning that adds to the poem's dialectical and ironic complexity. 'Cynddylan' is not just any old Welsh name. To the reader versed in Welsh history it cannot fail to suggest the tragic seventh-century figure Cynddylan Prince of Powys, memorialized in an immensely stirring cycle of saga *englynion*, composed probably in the tenth century, and a classic expression of *hiraeth*:

Cynddylan's hall is dark tonight,
There burns no fire, no bed is made,
I weep awhile and then am quiet.

Cynddylan's hall is dark tonight,
No fire is lit, no candle burns,
God will keep me sane.

Cynddylan's hall. It pierces me
To see it roofless, fireless.
Dead is my lord, and I am yet alive.

Cynddylan's hall is desolate tonight
Where once I sat in honour.
Gone are the men who held it, gone the women.

Cynddylan's hall. Dark is its roof
Since the English destroyed
Cynddylan, and Elvan of Powys.[107]

In Thomas's poem, once this echo is allowed, the poet's scope is seen
to be much broader than at first appears. 'Cynddylan on a Tractor'
is not just a satire about the spiritual destitution of contemporary
agriculture; it is also a Welsh lament. Where once proud princes
bestrode the land, now there is only the deceived labourer.

This extra layer of meaning tilts the balance. 'Cynddylan on a
Tractor' is not ostensibly polemical. It is a great deal more subtle
than that. But the concealed identity of Cynddylan leaves the
informed reader in no doubt as to Thomas's loyalties. It may be that
the absence of an equivalent lining in 'Homo Sapiens 1941' explains
that poem's exclusion from the *Collected Poems*. Nonetheless, it is a
remarkable specimen to find so early in Thomas's output. A touch
over-written it may be, but there is an oddly mature precision in
much of its diction. Like many of the poems to come, it is homo-
centric, an aspect of the priest's concern with the image of Christ
on the Cross; but it also prefigures one of the most distinct strands
of middle and late R. S. Thomas: the endeavour to fix the character
of mankind at discrete moments of its history.

Other poems written or at any rate inspired by his two-year stint
at Hanmer show Thomas crossing his true poetic threshold. Mention
has already been made of contributions to the *Dublin Magazine* while
Thomas was still at Chirk. These continued.[108] Two or three of them,
including the exquisitely spare nature poem 'Cyclamen',[109] were to
find their way into *The Stones of the Field*. But even at Chirk, the
signs are there. Called simply 'Fragment', and published in the *New
English Weekly* on 13 July 1939, the following were the first lines
by Thomas to appear in print since his student days in Bangor:

Deep in the blue of April skies
I have seen the cruel pair
Hawk and kestrel pierce the air
With needle eyes,
Stitching to the ground with unseen thread
The tender shrew-mouse as it sped.

The rhyme is cumbersome, and there is a superfluity of adjectival description. In no time at all Thomas will have realized the redundancy of the phrase 'with unseen thread'. But the word 'Stitching', with or without the antecedent needle, is quintessentially his own.

III

MANAFON

The outward shows of sky and earth;
Of hill and valley, he has viewed;
And impulses of deeper birth
Have come to him in solitude.

WILLIAM WORDSWORTH,
A Poet's Epitaph

The flag of morn in conqueror's state
Enters at the English gate;
The vanquished eve, as night prevails,
Bleeds upon the road to Wales.

A. E. HOUSMAN,
A Shropshire Lad xxviii

MANAFON WAS THE MAKING OF THOMAS. The twelve years he spent there as rector, from the age of twenty-nine in 1942 to the age of forty-one in 1954, defined his temperament and gave to his poetry a compelling and enduring edge. The fugitive from Talarn Green, appalled by such evidence of the war as had come his way, discovered in a Montgomeryshire valley, and in the hills above that valley, the materials of what he perceived as more permanent conflicts; or at least, conflicts he could with better conscience engage in. Daily he witnessed signs of the evaporation of Wales and Welsh culture; the struggles of a diminishing band of upland farmers to wrestle a living from an ungenerous soil; and the encroachment of suspect technologies. Each of these impinged sharply on the poet-priest's consciousness. But just because he was a poet and a priest, his observations became entangled with the search for deeper resolutions. Could Wales in fact be preserved, even revivified? In the unequal contest between peasant and the elements, taken as a metaphor for the human condition, what part did God play? And what good was mankind doing to itself in its pursuit of the machine's easier options? At Manafon, the patriot, the countryman, the obdurate anti-cosmopolitan and the troubled divine come into focus. These are the personalities that will inform whatever Thomas writes; and which between them begin to dispel the lingering gaucheries of his child-hood and youth.

Yet Thomas's early diffidence is never quite dissipated. Rather its scar stretches across his entire work. He may indeed learn well enough how to inhabit a high moral ground; but there usually is a counter-vailing tendency, in which life, and most particularly life as R. S. Thomas encounters it, is projected as an unmanageable siege. His opinions may often seem precarious and exaggerated; but they are fashioned under a psychological duress. As with other modernists, notably Samuel Beckett, the quest for expression, and the perfectibility of expression, is predicated on a capacity, even an appetite, for disquiet.

Manafon is not so far from Chirk and Hanmer – in fact no more than twenty miles to the south. It is still in the Marches, with the border town of Welshpool six miles to the east, and English Shrewsbury, sometimes called the Gateway to Wales, another twelve beyond. Further to the south is Newtown, and to the west, pursuing a line that bisects Wales at its narrowest point, outcrops of the Cambrian mountains, then the Cambrians themselves, before coming down into Machynlleth, and the coast, a mere thirty miles or so distant as the crow flies, though a great deal further by any of a choice of wending highways. But the landscape at Manafon is quite different to what Thomas had become accustomed to, and appreciably more 'Welsh'. The village lies on a road, the B4390, that passes along the floor of a considerable, even, in the lights of spring and autumn, grandiose valley. Parallel with this road is the river Rhiw, a tributary of the Severn, in summer no more than a trickling stream. On each side of the valley, north and south, with large arable fields hanging on them like flags below barren sheep runs, thousand-foot hills rise, while to the west is the yet higher, and more barren, Mynydd Waun Fawr – Great Moor Mountain.

To reach Manafon from Talarn Green the Thomases would have come via Welshpool, on the Oswestry road. In those days, the village proper consisted of only a handful of buildings: the church, an adjacent primary school, the rectory, a general store, an inn and a scatter of mainly farmhouses along the valley floor. There was no electricity, and water was still drawn from wells and hillside springs. Then as now, however, it was an English-speaking parish. In the hills some were still bilingual, but there were no Welsh speakers on the new rector's doorstep, and Welsh had not been used in the church since the turn of the century. Indeed, as early as 1832, records show that Sunday services were conducted alternately in both languages.[1]

Fifty years on, Manafon has grown. Today it boasts a caravan site, and there are two or three clusters of trim modern houses and gardened bungalows. These are either retirement dwellings, or, as the array of up-to-date motor-cars parked in their drives indicates, the homes of professionals. And Manafon is more anglicized than ever.

I came, in July, not from the north, but from Cardiff, via Brecon and that extraordinary, faded assemblage of late Victorian and Edwardian spa architecture, Llandrindod Wells. First though I had to drive through the Vale of Merthyr, once the powerhouse of Welsh industrialization and the pride of Labour, but looking now as though some vast garbage can had been emptied from the skies. Yet at the head of that valley the road immediately takes one into the relatively unspoilt beauty of the Brecon hills, and beyond those the Black Mountains. Only the road itself, unusually well maintained, denotes the intrusion of the modern state: there is an army barracks at Brecon, the Welch Fusiliers, and in Wales wherever the army is nearby the country thoroughfares are better.

Who, one might ask, would be so careless as to make the same journey in reverse? Yet that it would seem is the direction time and history have steered, with mankind at the helm. Merthyr, Ebbw Vale and the Rhondda, to name but three of many huge crevices comprehensively ransacked for their coal and iron deposits, have proved, to any eye halfway nurtured on nature's varied feast, dismal mistakes; though others will assert that amid such carnage priceless blooms of communitized humanity have flowered.

But that again is Wales for you; a place of dramatically quick contrasts. Too quick, perhaps, and too dramatic, stimulating rowdy, and eventually internecine debate. For who is right? Those who will not suffer any incursion on the landscape? Or those, like my socialist friend Owens, who see such incursions as the necessary means towards a more egalitarian society?

'Come on, boy, what do you want? To be penned in a hovel forever at the beck and call of a feudal master? No matter whether he was Welsh or English? Oh stuff Glyndŵr! Give me Aneurin Bevan any day.'

The pity of it is that neither the dreams of the conservatively minded nationalists nor the aspirations of the socialists have been vouchsafed. Instead they have stymied each other. But if those dreams and those aspirations should one day fuse? Then for sure the *Saesneg* wedding party would be wrecked . . .

Heading towards Manafon, and seduced by the cool sensuality of the Brecons, my expatriate sensibility inclines if anything towards the conservatives. The landscape *is* the best support for the views of R. S. Thomas and his kind. In any case, I am determined to give him as fair a hearing as possible. But when I do get to Manafon, will I find anyone to remember him? And if so, how?

I arrive a little before lunchtime. A score of children swarm in the playground, filling the village with the cries of an irresistible innocence; but otherwise the place is deserted, the church locked. Nor is there any joy or food to be had at the Beehive, the old Tudor-style inn that was once the home of Samuel Roberts, a famous clockmaker. That too is closed. So I return to the school and wait for the appearance of an adult. Duly the dinner lady tells me that the person to help me is the churchwarden, a Mrs Hazel Boulton, living opposite in the Old Post Office. But when I cross the road and knock on the door, Mrs Boulton's husband tells me his wife is no longer the warden. That honour, he says, now belongs to Mrs Ruth Hall, living in a house near the Beehive. Nonetheless, I should return later, because Hazel's father was also a churchwarden, during Thomas's ministry.

I amble back down the road. Being July, it is warm, without any wind to disturb the hot air bottled in the valley. There are too many flies, and even the distant bleating of sheep has a suppressed, enervated ring to it. But Ruth Hall is at home, and insists on accompanying me to the church. There is, she hints, something in the belfry I absolutely have to see.

Ruth is in her late fifties or early sixties. She grew up in the village and entertains me with such memories of R. S. as she has. He was, she says, a reserved man, but a good priest. Sometimes he could be very aloof, walking straight past you as though you weren't there. But at other times he would stop for a chat, and it was known he spent much time visiting parishioners who lived outside the village proper, particularly those up on the hilltops. Even then people knew he was a poet, and made allowances for the 'do not disturb' sign he sometimes hung on his face.

'And of course,' Ruth Hall continues, 'he was a physically strong man too. At harvest time he could be seen helping out, manhandling the heavy bales with ease. He would have been useful on any farm. And when the belfry needed a fresh coat of paint, he got up on the roof himself. His brush could be seen from all points of the valley.'

We come to the church, St Michael's, set back from the road, which is graced with a simple lych-gate. Although repeated restorations make it difficult to date the present structure, it goes back at least to the sixteenth century, while a church of some kind or other has occupied the site from before Norman times. Its thick walls, inset with narrow side windows, are reputedly built from stones drawn from the Rhiw – a legend that inspired R. S. Thomas to compose the rhymed quatrains of 'Country Church (Manafon)',[2] memorable both as an early example of the poet's inclination to deploy sea imagery in his description of a landscape, and for the poem's internal consonance ('stands . . . stone,/Brittle . . . breath' etc,) that may or may not have derived from Thomas's growing familiarity with *cynghanedd* and other aspects of Welsh prosody:

> The church stands, built from the river stone,
> Brittle with light, as though a breath could shatter
> Its slender frame, or spill the limpid water,
> Quiet as sunlight, cupped within the bone,
>
> It stands yet. But though soft flowers break
> In delicate waves round limbs the river fashioned
> With so smooth care, no friendly God has cautioned
> The brimming tides of fescue for its sake.

We are left, of course, to imagine for ourselves the reasons why God has not intervened to stem the flow of grasses – or, for that matter, why his appointed agent the rector did not in his great manliness do the job himself. Most likely the tidal metaphor is intended to denote the spread of godlessness across the Welsh fabric, although it also tells us something about the perceived character of God, as a being already caught in the act of detachment: in Thomas's later work a major theme. But, since the publication of these lines, which first appeared in the magazine *Wales* in the autumn of 1946, the literal fescue (coarse grass) has not advanced. Rather the churchyard, viewed in the summer of 1995, was no more, though no less, unkempt than one might expect at that time of year, while the path around the church was cleared, and the single yew standing by the porch clipped. The square wooden belfry, surmounted by a working weather vane, had again been repainted. As Manafon becomes yet another middle-class enclave in the Marches, its more prosperous denizens have a care for their acquired heritage.

Inside, St Michael's was a peculiar mixture of high and low. There was no stained glass in the windows, even behind the altar, but the distinguishing features were a reredos and rood screen, both Victorian. Hanging from the simple wooden barrel-vaulted roof were the original oil-lamps used before the installation of electricity – at the very end of Thomas's ministry.

Most of the other furnishings are more recent, gifts of the Henllys Williams family. The real money in the area belonged to the Dyson-Perrinses, of Lea & Perrins fame, but the Williamses and Perrinses had intermarried. It was the belfry loft, though, that Ruth Hall was most anxious for me to examine. Getting up there was not an easy business. First the trap door, dropping downwards, had to be opened, then a loose ladder only just long enough for its purpose had to be climbed. The loft itself was hot and musty, and caked with bird droppings, and I was not at all sure what I was doing there.

'Can you see them?' Mrs Hall called up.

'See what?' I cried.

'On the big beam to your right.'

I looked at the largest of the old oaks, and then saw the three deeply and boldly carved initials: R. S. T.

'Who put them there?' I asked as I climbed down.

'He did, of course. Who else?'

I suggested someone might have carved the letters as a prank, but Mrs Hall was adamant. The initials were a Manafon legend. They were certainly the work of the rector's hand.

'You see, the water for the vestry basin has to be taken up there and put into the tank. There's still no pipe. Mr Thomas always did it himself. He wouldn't let anyone else. Now my husband does it. It's the churchwarden's responsibility, but I couldn't possibly manage the ladder *and* five gallons of water.'

Mrs Hall takes me back to her house. On the way I ask about Elsi Thomas. Oh yes, she says, she is remembered too, a fine lady who sometimes helped out with art lessons at the school. Indeed, when we reach her house, she shows me a small picture executed by Elsi Thomas, sent to her as a gift twenty years ago. The drawing, of smaller winter birds, is charming, but wilfully childish. Mrs Hall smiles. 'It was after her sight began failing. She was reduced to doing Medici Christmas cards. But she was a kind person, and it was nice of her to send me something she'd done herself.'

Back on the road I encounter Hazel Boulton, a younger woman with a faintly Irish accent she swears is local. She is waiting for me with a clutch of papers in her hand. These are pamphlets relating to the histories of St Michael's and the school. To my surprise I learn that not many people come to Manafon on the Thomas trail, indeed that besides an American post-graduate I am the first. Again though, I am invited into the home. Like nearly everywhere else in Wales, nobody at Manafon stands too much on ceremony. Rather they insist upon hospitality. In the Boultons' well-cultivated garden I am offered tea and cake. We are joined by Hazel's husband Michael, an Englishman.

The Boultons confirm Ruth Hall's recollections. R. S. was well respected, although he could be a little distant, a little cold at times. When the Boultons married, because Hazel's father had been Thomas's churchwarden R. S. himself officiated, making the journey from Eglwysfach. Out come the photographs, and a couple of letters. But then I am shown another letter. Even in Manafon, Thomas's subsequent reputation has caught up with him.

This third letter concerned the school, which, after 163 years, was about to close. There were only twenty or so pupils, and the education authority had calculated it would be cheaper to bus Manafon's children to Newtown. The effect of closure on the village would be severe. The school was a natural focal point, and the elderly took comfort from the sights and sounds of the midday playground. But a closing day had been organized, a 'celebration' to mark the end of a tradition. Former pupils and teachers had all been invited. So too had former rectors, since the rector of Manafon had always sat on the governing body. Thomas, though, had declined to come – just as, indeed, he had declined to attend a previous celebration in 1983, to mark the school's 150th anniversary. And the reason he gave was not that he lived too far away, or had another engagement that day, or that he was too old, but rather that Manafon had become 'too Anglicized'.

'What has upset people,' the Boultons add, 'is that only a year ago he gave a poetry reading just up the road, at Gregynog. He spoke openly and engagingly about his life then, so why now the bee in his bonnet?'

But the resentment is short-lived. 'It's a small parish matter, and perhaps we expect too much.' Both Hazel and Michael acknowledge that the poems of Thomas they have read they admire. Then they direct me towards the rectory, now called Manafon Grange, and owned by a family of wealthy incomers, the Greeson-Walkers.

Once again I am offered tea and cake on a lawn. David Greeson-Walker, his wife Lorraine and their daughter Verity seem determined not to be outdone in the Manafon hospitality stakes. What most impresses me, however, is the size of the former rectory: a large, three-storeyed late-eighteenth-century house (it was built in 1793) that once had stables, coach-house and a paddock attached. Set amid its own yews at the end of a proper drive, its grounds bank down to the Rhiw, while inside is a full set of high ceilings.

'R. S. wouldn't approve of my living here at all,' David Greeson-Walker smirks as he shows me around. 'I'm a businessman, computers mainly, who has taken time out to write a pulp novel. I expect my word-processor is in more or less the same position that Thomas had his typewriter. Mind you, I've spoken to a few of the older farmers around here, and they weren't too pleased with the Iago Prytherch stuff. So things even out in the end.'

An hour or two later Greeson-Walker's assessment is dramatically confirmed. After photographing the Grange née Rectory, I drive into the hills, to take a look at Adfa and Cefn Coch – two upland villages Thomas refers to in his autobiography as places where he discovered some of his remnant peasants. On the way I pass more caravan sites, and at Cefn Coch find little else besides a pony trekking station. Outside Adfa, however, I espy what I have been looking for: an ancient farmhand chewing grass.

'Do you remember R. S. Thomas by any chance?' I ask, getting out of my vehicle with a hopeful smile.

The labourer gobs pointedly on the ground between us.

'There was never any Thomas here.'

'The poet? The rector of Manafon? Ronald Stuart Thomas?'

'He wasn't here I'm telling you!' the labourer retorts. Then he turned and stalked off.

I had the impression he knew exactly whom I was enquiring about.

Since I was in the area, I took the opportunity to visit Plas Gregynog, a few miles back along the road to Newtown. Although I had heard and read about this house, nothing prepared me for its jocund splendour. Set in an impeccably maintained seven-hundred-acre woodland park is a 'black-and-white' timbered mansion of imposing dimensions. Built in the mid-nineteenth century, it was once the property of David Davies of Llandinam (1818–90), a coal and steel magnate second only to the Marquis of Bute, and known variously as Davies the Ocean (after his Ocean Coal Company), Davies the Railway and, out of deference to an early apprenticeship in a timber mill, 'Top Sawyer'. But as well as an industrialist Davies was a strict Calvinist Presbyterian and a munificent philanthropist, donating considerable sums to the new university colleges of Wales towards the end of his life. His grand-daughters, Gwendoline and Margaret, continued Davies's devotion to Welsh culture and the Welsh nation. In the 1920s and 1930s Gregynog became a noted concert venue, featuring Welsh alongside international composers and musicians. It also, from 1923, became home to the specialist fine art printers, the Gregynog Press. In the 1940s and 1950s its cultural activities declined, but in 1964 Plas Gregynog was bequeathed to the University of Wales.

Since then it has once again functioned as a showpiece of Welsh high culture.

Strikingly well-groomed as its external appearance was, however, Gregynog did not especially appeal to me. The inside, with its stately seminar rooms and library, was equally immaculate. What was transmitted was not so much intellectual or artistic striving as social pretence. On a different occasion a man in Holyhead, the author and naturalist Edwin Roland Owens, put it to me, by way of a ribald jest, that 'The Cymraeg academics are more dangerous than the Tory Party.' The strangely unrevolutionary flavour of the Welsh cause as propounded by many of its more articulate spokesmen is highlighted by this and other like-minded comments. On the one hand, there is no shortage of scholars and writers determined to identify Welsh culture and Welsh tradition as something entirely separate from its English counterpart. On the other, the idea that Welsh culture emanates from the whole of the Welsh people is often absent.

In this respect, Welsh nationalism in its cultural aspect is at odds with the twentieth-century stereotype of nationalism as a necessarily revolutionary movement. No great social levelling is proposed; no root-and-branch back-to-basics let's-start-again-from-scratch and mobilize-the-whole-nation strategy. Rather, *those* sentiments, where they occur, do so, with diminishing frequency, among the industrial populations of the south, whose allegiance, as already remarked, is as much (though not necessarily more) to British socialism as it is to Wales.

Where R. S. Thomas fits into this admittedly simplified scheme of things is part of what has to be shown. For the moment, I was puzzled why he should have chosen to revisit Gregynog, a pile raised ultimately on the back of the poet's abiding bête noire, the Machine, but not the parish where he had served as priest for a dozen years.

Having seen Manafon, and having seen the rectory, I could well imagine the temptations that must have beset anyone coming by such a residence. By the age of thirty Thomas had what many educated men of his generation aspired to: security of professional occupation, status, and a fine house to live in. In the sense that on his father's side at least, the Thomas family fortunes had declined, R. S. had made up lost ground.

A lesser individual must have succumbed to such a life of relative, low-profile ease; in which case the blandishments of Gregynog, just around the corner, might well have sufficed to appease a vestigial patriotism. But not so R. S. Though there was no strict necessity for it, the idea of Wales, and in particular a de-industrialized Wales, burned a much angrier hole in his soul.

For a priest, at least nominally committed to Christian values, Thomas was soon cast upon stormy waters.

After I had done with Manafon, I decided to return home the long way round, and so set out for Bala. The route I had chosen would take me, via Llanfyllin, into the wondrous Tanat Valley; then, on the B4396, up along the commanding heights of the Berwyn Hills. But also on the way was Llanrhaeadr-ym-Mochnant, where Bishop Morgan translated the Bible. I wanted to hear for myself the mountain torrent as it hurried, in Thomas's words, 'Not too furiously by.'

Sure enough, at the bottom of the church enclosure, a stream gurgled its measured phrases. Inside the triple-naved church itself, however, was an altogether different message. A prayer had been posted on a placard, for every visitor to read:

> PRAY for peace and understanding between this nation and her neighbours and for all people who have responsibility for interpreting one nation to another. PRAISE God for the Cross of Christ, which brings together Latin and Welsh and Saxon, and all the languages of the world.

Here was another, presumably Welsh voice clamouring to be heard. Although I am not myself Christian, other than in a cultural sense too diluted to warrant the name, I could recognize in these words, for all their contrived accommodation of superstition with the politically correct, what many people would take as the essence of Christian doctrine; or if not the essence, then that part of Christian doctrine which deserves to survive. Yet I also recognized that, on the evidence of much that he has published, the same words did not and do not begin to reflect the opinions and attitudes of my quarry.

*   *   *

In fact, the figure of the seemingly idiosyncratic literary parson is a tradition in Wales, as indeed it is in other parts of Britain. In Wales though, the Anglican priest in particular, especially when he has been the incumbent of a rural living, has generally had a surfeit of time on his hands to pursue his studies and shape his thoughts. From the late seventeenth century onwards, the success of Nonconformity reduced the size of his flock, and therefore the extent of his pastoral duties. Thomas himself subscribes to this, when, in his autobiography, he summarizes one of the advantages of a rural as opposed to an urban living as being precisely the time it afforded him to write his poetry. But even before the Nonconformist era the Church beneficed a number of oddball authors.

Of these the most famous, and arguably the most infamous, was Rhys Prichard (1579–1644), known as *Yr Hen Ficer*, the Old Vicar. Like many of his clerical colleagues he attended Jesus College, before returning, in 1602, to Wales and the living at his native Llandovery, in Carmarthenshire. By then this neo-Puritan had already begun to compose the Welsh verses that, later collected as *Canwyll y Cymru* ('The Welshman's Candle'), established his reputation on a par with John Bunyan's. Prichard's purpose was to repair the piety of his degenerate compatriots, and his poems, based on Bible stories, were as didactic as they were direct. The legend is, however, that Prichard himself was a degenerate, until reproved by an unlikely quadruped. George Borrow takes up the tale:

> His conduct for a very considerable time was not only unbecoming a clergyman, but a human being in any sphere. Drunkenness was very prevalent in the age in which he lived, but Rees Pritchard [*sic*] was so inordinately addicted to that vice that the very worst of his parishioners was scandalized, and said: 'Bad as we may be we are not half so bad as the parson.'
>
> He was in the habit of spending the greater part of his time in the public-house, from which he was generally trundled home in a wheel-barrow in a state of utter insensibility. God, however, who is aware of what every creature is capable of, had reserved Rees Pritchard for great and noble things, and brought about his conversion in a very remarkable manner.
>
> The people of the tavern which Rees Pritchard frequented had a

large he-goat, which went in and out and mingled with the guests. One day Rees in the midst of his orgies called the goat to him and offered it some ale; the creature, far from refusing it, drank greedily, and soon becoming intoxicated, fell down upon the floor, where it lay quivering, to the great delight of Rees Pritchard, who made its drunkenness a subject of jest to his boon companions, who, however, said nothing, being struck with horror at such conduct in a person who was placed among them to be a pattern and example. Before night, however, Pritchard himself became intoxicated, and was trundled to the vicarage in the usual manner. During the whole of the next day he was very ill and kept at home, but on the following one he again repaired to the public-house, sat down and called for his pipe and tankard. The goat was now perfectly recovered, and was standing upright. No sooner was the tankard brought than Rees taking hold of it held it to the goat's mouth. The creature, however, turned away its head in disgust, and hurried out of the room. This circumstance produced an instantaneous effect upon Rees Pritchard. 'My God!' said he to himself, 'is this poor dumb creature wiser than I? Yes, surely; it has been drunk, but having once experienced the wretched consequences of drunkenness, it refuses to be drunk again.'[3]

Drawing the inevitable lesson, Prichard reformed his ways and became a beacon to his people. According to another, unfounded legend, he is credited with the ruination of Maesyfelin, a hall outside Lampeter. Prichard's son Samuel was betrothed to Ellen, the daughter of the house. Ellen's four brothers, fearful that their share of the eventual inheritance would be diminished if the marriage went ahead, resolved to murder their sister's fiancé. Thus Samuel Prichard was dragged along the road from Lampeter to Llandovery, and his body thrown into the Tywi. When she saw what had been done, Ellen died of grief, and the Old Vicar laid a formal curse on those who had slain his son. Some short while afterwards a fire destroyed Maesyfelin. Worse, three of the murderous brothers were butchered by the fourth, who then, either out of remorse, or because there was nothing left of the estate, or because he was lonely, hanged himself from a tree.

Whatever the truth of these and other stories that have clung to the name of Vicar Prichard, in his own lifetime they did him little harm. In 1614, with the backing of a powerful group of

Pembrokeshire landowners, he became chaplain to the Earl of Essex. Later still he was preferred as prebendary of Christ Church College, Brecon, and ended his career as Canon of St David's. At his death he was sufficiently rich to endow a school at Llandovery.

Such good fortune singularly failed to animate the career of one of the succeeding century's foremost literary clerics. Goronwy Owen (1723–69), sometimes known by his Welsh nom de plume Goronwy Ddu o Fôn, was another Jesus College man. Born in Anglesey, Goronwy has been described by one Welsh writer, Jan Morris, as being 'too Welsh for promotion'.[4] On leaving Oxford he worked as an assistant schoolmaster before taking orders and serving as a stand-in curate in the parish of his birth, Llanfair Mathafarn Eithaf. But this arrangement lasted only a year, and the hunt for a benefice of his own, at a time when bishops favoured ordinands of independent means and dependent attitudes, proved fruitless, so that in 1757 Goronwy accepted a teaching post in Virginia. Losing his wife and youngest child on the Atlantic crossing, he adopted the mores of a drunk and libertine. He next lost his job, and passed through a period of personal destitution before, at last, he acquired the parish of St Andrew's, Brunswick County. He also acquired a small tobacco plantation, but died, more or less penniless, at the age of forty-six. Yet the survival of the bardic tradition of Welsh poetry can be credited, in no small measure, to this reprobate. Both his father and grandfather had composed poems in the strict metres, and his own verses, first anthologized in *Diddanwch Teuluaidd* (1763), written in the classical *awdl* and *cywydd* forms, became models for contenders in the later Eisteddfod Crown and Chair competitions. Often considered the Welsh Augustan par excellence, Goronwy Owen had an unfulfilled ambition to write an epic in Welsh that would rival Milton's *Paradise Lost*; and his failure, in this as in so many other respects, became, in its Celtic proportions, the source of an abiding regret among his Welsh-language successors.

But it was not just poets who looked to the Church for material sustenance. Theophilus Evans (1693–1769), a Breconshire priest, is rightly regarded as the father of Welsh historiography, in that his many publications explored Welsh history as a thing in itself, and not just an adjunct of English history. Again, his namesake, Evan

Evans (1731–88), also known as Ieuan Fardd, and who served in many different parishes, gained fame throughout Britain as the antiquarian who rediscovered the ancient texts of Aneirin and Taliesin. Indeed, it was Evans's researches that inspired Thomas Gray's 'Pindaric Ode' *The Bard* (1757), which in turn stimulated the literary obsession with Celtic culture that was to become one of the more positive aspects of the English Romantic Movement.

As it happened, one of the parishes Evan Evans ministered in was Manafon. He was curate there from 1755 to 1757, the hired deputy of the pluralist and therefore often absent rector, William Wynne. Wynne too was a poet, though of no great repute. Yet even if we confine our attention to that one parish, other more imposing names beckon from the past. Among several distinguished predecessors R. S. Thomas could, and indeed in *Neb*, has singled out Walter Davies (1761–1849).

Davies – Gwallter Mechain – was rector of Manafon between 1807 and 1837. He was also a leading light among *Yr Hen Bersoniaid Llengar*, 'The Old Literary Clerics': a coterie of conservatively minded, at times fiercely anti-Nonconformist, Anglicans who deliberately set out to preserve and promote Welsh culture, sometimes at the cost of incurring their bishops' displeasure. The group's lay associates included Lady Charlotte Guest, translator of the *Mabinogion*. Gwallter's own contributions to this movement were various. He was, as well as a poet and an author, a compiler and editor of anthologies. His interests extended to topography, and he is best remembered both as a defender of exacting standards at local *eisteddfodau*, before Iolo Morganwg created a National Eisteddfod, and for two books about the agriculture and economy of North and South Wales.[5]

By the middle of the century, Anglicans had been widely usurped by Nonconformists as the standard-bearers of Welsh culture; or at least, the preservers of the Welsh language. Indeed, Nonconformity was by then already on its way to becoming the conformity of Wales. But a hundred years after Gwallter first ascended the pulpit at Manafon, another incumbent, William Morgan – 'Penfro', to give him his bardic appellation – was already gaining a reputation among eisteddfod circles. R. S. Thomas therefore, in 1942, although he had as yet little Welsh, and would in fact never succeed in writing more than two short poems in that language, could derive some succour from the literary pedigree of his parish. He could also align himself with the broader tradition of priestly writers in the Welsh church (as well as with priest-poets in the English church, most obviously George Herbert); just as he could pursue what were often heterodox opinions with relatively little fear of episcopal censure, which, in the wake of Disestablishment, has lain at times strangely dormant.

Well within a year of moving to Manafon R. S. Thomas had written, and published, what is regarded as, to use the American expression, his first seminal poem. 'A Peasant' appeared in the March 1943 number of the 'little' London literary magazine *Life and Letters Today*, at the time edited by Robert Herring. The issue was specifically devoted to 'Cambria', as it was subtitled. Thomas's contribution stood alongside others by well-known Anglo-Welsh poets: Henry Treece, Vernon Watkins, Alun Lewis, even, in a translation by Keidrych Rhys, Vicar Prichard. There was an article, 'Notes on the Welsh Short Story Writers', by Glyn Jones, and an introductory essay, 'Evolution of a Nationalist', by Walter Dowding.

Dowding can be described as one of those lesser writers whose work is forgotten almost as soon as the print is dry. The few poems he wrote are never anthologized, and he fails to gain an entry in that indispensable vademecum, *The Oxford Companion to the Literature of Wales*.[6] In 1943 he was a WEA teacher in his native Brynmawr. His 'Evolution of a Nationalist', however, merits our attention: not only because it was written in simple straightforward language, and probably reflected the experience and attitudes of many of his contemporary compatriots, but because of its particular affinity with aspects of R. S. himself.

It begins – conventionally enough until it is remembered that at the time Britain was engaged in hostilities against Hitler under the banner of democratic liberty – by setting out what, in the 1940s, was still the Welsh citizen's abiding grievance:

Men who are born members of a self-governing society – how fortunate they are! And for those not born free, how unfortunate that their free-born brothers should have so little understanding of the measure of their own good fortune. That they should not know how their lives have been simplified and made easy to a degree, by the accident of their place of birth. A clear example: John Watts, born at Lydney, decides to go abroad, and is filling in his passport application; or he is getting married and giving particulars of his birth to the registrar, or doing one of the other multitudinous things which entail a declaration of nationality. John Watts will not hesitate. Or, if at all, he will have a merely whimsical hesitation about whether to register 'British', or 'English'. It will not be a serious matter this. 'English' and 'British', as the result of ill-advised Scottish propaganda, will be interchangeable terms. But twenty miles away, at Wysg (Usk), at precisely the same moment of time, Evan Watkins, having decided to go abroad, or to get married, etc, etc, will not find it so easy to fill up his forms. 'Nationality?' 'Well, Welsh, of course.' But can he so describe himself on an official form? His nationality has no legal status, is not officially recognized – outside Eire . . . It is a situation quite impossible to a free man in a free country.

To this cri de coeur, the crudely obvious rejoinder was: Learn English, mun, and then you will have all the rights enjoyed across the border. But that of course was precisely the trap the English state had set ever since the 1536 Act of Union. Dowding however avoids taking dialectic issue. His essay becomes not the anticipated political harangue, but an autobiographical résumé that ends on a note of reconciliation. Further, he has some explaining to do. His own situation is the reverse of his prototypical Welshman Evan Watkins's. Born of mixed Welsh and English parentage, Dowding was raised as a monoglot English speaker. It is the idea of Wales as his cultural and social provenance that leads him, over a forty-year period, to embrace Welsh nationalism; and which gives the essay its psychological momentum.

Interestingly, like R. S. Thomas in his much later autobiographical excursion, Dowding writes about himself in the third person: the self-alienated mode, perhaps. 'Very early in life,' he says, 'he was made aware that he did not belong by his playmates.' The reasons for this were his name and his accent, and not that he spoke, as did the other children, English per se. Rather, he did not speak English in the Welsh way. Confused, the child, whose father had died a year after his birth, rushes to his mother:

> 'Mam! Am I English or Welsh?' Now his mother was Welsh, from Llanfair ym Muallt, and most probably had – like all the Welsh – a secret pride of race. For though her answer was always clear, and always the same, it was reluctant. 'You are English, I suppose,' she would say. Then Walter would say, 'But you are Welsh and I was born in Wales!' 'But your *father* was English,' would come the final, crushing reply – said with even more reluctance – 'and so you are English.' Walter, never having considered it possible, or even desirable, to argue with his mother's dicta would then go away, superficially accepting the verdict, but inwardly unsatisfied.

The dissatisfaction lasted a long time, 'Whether or not he was Welsh, he *wanted* to be Welsh!' He plays truant at the English Baptist Sunday School of his mother's choice in order to attend Welsh classes at a Welsh Baptist Sunday School, but is soon rumbled. It is another six years before he again comes in contact with his '"native"' speech. That is at the County School, to which he wins a scholarship. But even there Welsh lessons last only a year, before they are replaced by French lessons, 'greatly to the satisfaction of nearly all the little anglicized snobs in the form, who had already learned that France was a big, important country with a place in world history,' Likewise, 'Welsh History also ceased after the first form and became English History.'

After three years Dowding leaves the County School, almost, but not quite, the desired product:

> You see, nearly twelve years' education in his country's schools had given him no knowledge of that country, had merely turned him into an ignorant little imperialist. It was not that he specially venerated England, or had decided by now that he was English. It was the empire on which the sun never set which had captured his puerile imagination.

By then, the Great War had begun, so naturally Dowding's 'puerile imagination' continued to be fed by the propaganda machine of the British state in full cry. But just because he had left school didn't mean Dowding had finished his education. Again like Thomas, there was an element of the auto-didact about him. What spare cash he has he spends on Everyman books, or volumes in the Home University Library, as well as the *Daily News*. And it is the young man's appetite for knowledge that creates a new disjunction in his mind. He reads about Ireland, and the struggle for nationhood there.

> By the middle of the war he 'burned' about Ireland (as he still does!). He saw no inconsistency at first in his love for the empire and his wild devotion to the Irish cause. This came later. About any 'Welsh' cause he was almost entirely ignorant. Disestablishment and Disendowment he knew about, and the arguments in favour of them, but he was not concerned. They were a cause without romance. After all, how could nonconformity – which he had already begun to loathe and revolt from – ever appear romantic? It was stern, serious, possibly, in many ways, enlightened, but romantic, appealing – No!

In 1917, a convert to socialism, Dowding enlists in the Royal Engineers. As for so many Welsh soldiers in the British army, the experience was salutary. His mess-mates make him aware of his nationality, rather in the same way his first classmates at school had made him aware of an un-Welshness. 'Now he was "Taff" to the other men in his tent, and those in his regiment with whom he palled up. He liked these Englishmen, it must be said, and quickly made friends with them. But he saw, too, that they did not accept him *as an Englishman*, they called him "Taff".'

In 1920 Dowding returned home, only to find the same old complacency about things Welsh that had shaped his childhood. Yet outside Brynmawr there was a sea-change afoot. Others had returned to Wales from the war, to be confronted by the same disillusionment. Viewed alike from valley head and coal-pit, amid growing unemployment, the jingoism that had attended hostilities looked increasingly hollow, especially when, as the 1920s unfolded, unemployment set in. The identity of Welshmen had been nothing augmented. Conditions were ripe for a new movement that would assert the nation's own identity.

That movement came in 1926, with the birth of Plaid Genedliaethol Cymru, the National Party of Wales, later always known as

Plaid Cymru. For a while Dowding, thinking his own thoughts and applying his own analysis, held back. He writes letters, however, and an 'unsuccessful' novel that proposed a 'synthesis of Catholicism, Nationalism, and Socialism'. He also begins taking Welsh lessons in earnest. In 1929 he has a 'five-month breakdown', and then forms a new attachment. He falls in with some Quakers, and experiences yet another conversion. But as well as their doctrine of 'Inner Light', the Quakers present Dowding with a nationalist fellowship. At least, many of the individual Quakers he encounters are Welshmen committed to the idea of self-government:

> Membership of the Party followed. There was reborn zeal for acquiring the language. Agonies of almost unaided study and seeming failure. (Had it been real failure, suicide would almost certainly have followed, because Walter *knew* he could not be a Welshman without Welsh and not to be a Welshman was to be disintegrated.)

But as Dowding's political and cultural activities expand, as he abandons reading books or even writing letters in English, so his ambition, to be a Welshman, a true Cymro, is realized.

The story ends happily, with Dowding's appointment as a WEA tutor in cultural studies. Through teaching, in Welsh, he could 'be finally and completely emancipated inside himself from the dual pull of England and Wales'; could become what 'he had desired to be, with varying stress, from childhood to middle-age – a complete Welshman, in thought and feeling'. The important thing, he recommends, is not simply to know about Dafydd ap Gwilym and other Welsh poets, but to read them with understanding. 'Before "Culture in Wales" . . . could be taught, it must be assimilated. *This* was the baptism of fire! It was entered into with fear of inadequacy, suffered often as a martyrdom, but it gave, in the end, release.'

Dowding's psychology is one of dispossession and displacement. His purpose is not to render a watertight defence of nationalism, in his day a weaker brew than it later became, but to delineate a personal journey, a quest for self-identity from unpromising beginnings. Rather, it is the unpromisingness of those beginnings that provides Dowding, and others like him, with his rationale. It is the confusion, easy to describe but hard to imagine, as to the identity of his social self that sets in motion what to an outsider may seem a tenuous chain of events. In the end it is not simply a question of parentage, or of provenance, or even one of language, that generates the turbulence. It is all of these, and none of them. It is the bald fact of *not* belonging to a readily defined, coherent and consistent framework, such as it is the peculiar genius of the English so often to have provided for themselves.

Conversely, the one strong cohesive element Welsh society enjoyed then, and had done for more than a hundred years, was Nonconformity. It is indeed possible that, at the community level, the reason for Nonconformity's success as a cement was the want of other cements, Nonconformist beliefs were divorced from the state and ancient traditions. It represented an alternative. But because of this, the affinity between religious and nationalist feeling, in a Welsh context, should come as no particular surprise.

Yet between religion and nationalism there exist, and must exist, non-affinitive tensions. Christ exhorts his followers to love one another and adopt passivity before Caesar, while nationalism is by its very nature assertive, and has its own, sometimes violent, way of dealing with Caesar, and those it perceives as being Caesar-like.

Dowding purports to effect a compromise. He specifically disavows any hatred towards the English. By limiting his nationalism to the cultural sphere, to the restitution of and absorption in an existing body of Welsh literature, he can still maintain his Christian posture.

Like Dowding, Thomas became a self-professed pacifist. Thomas however is too alert, too hard even, to adopt Dowding's compromise. Knowing where the logic of patriotism must eventually lead, he cannot deposit it in the safety of cultural studies.

Yet equally, he is loath to put aside his religious principle. Far more ardent in the cause of Wales than Dowding, he is also far more ardent in his pursuit of God. The fudge therefore is denied him. In its place, the Welshman and the pacifist collide head-on.

This is apparent even in 'A Peasant,'[7] which appeared alongside Dowding's essay in *Life and Letters*. Again it is necessary to remember when it was written and published; in the midst of war-torn Britain, war-torn Europe. But a large part of the strength of the poem derives from the fact that Thomas refuses to take the wider arena as his starting point:

> Iago Prytherch his name, though, be it allowed,
> Just an ordinary man of the bald Welsh hills,
> Who pens a few sheep in a gap of cloud.
> Docking mangels, chipping the green skin
> From the yellow bones with a half-witted grin
> Of satisfaction, or churning the crude earth
> To a stiff sea of clods, that glint in the wind –
> So are his days spent, his spittled mirth
> Rarer than the sun, that cracks the cheeks
> Of the gaunt sky perhaps once in a week.
> And then at night see him fixed in his chair
> Motionless, except when he leans to gob in the fire.
> There is something frightening in the vacancy of his mind.
> His clothes, sour with years of sweat
> And animal contact, shock the refined,
> But affected, sense with their stark naturalness.
> Yet this is your prototype, who, season by season,
> Against siege of rain and the wind's attrition
> Preserves his stock, an impregnable fortress
> Not to be stormed even in death's confusion.
> Remember him then, for he, too, is a winner of wars,
> Enduring like a tree under the curious stars.

About these lines a great deal has been written. Their technical assurance, even virtuosity, comes as a quantum leap when compared to their author's previous compositions. The restrained use of rhyme, the almost casual internal assonance, the contrapuntal control of rhythm, the telling enjambement and the sheer power of the diction bespeak an instinctive mastery of form and style. Again, in the context of English pastoral verse, the genre 'A Peasant' most readily attaches itself to, an original and startling turn-about is achieved. But all these attributes are subordinate to what the poem says. One feels, from the deliberately dramatic and abrasive opening words – 'Iago Prytherch his name' – that the poet is intent on making a statement; but that the strength of that statement depends on its compelling admixture of the bold, and the subtly indirect. 'A Peasant' is not ostensibly an anti-war poem, nor does it at first sight seem in any way religious. Yet, in a subterranean way, it is both these things, and more. Thomas seems to be saying, Here is a man who is not a soldier, but who deserves a soldier's honour. Whereas in fact he is saying something quite different.

The boldness consists in the description of Iago Prytherch, the subtlety in the poem's responses to that figure. During the war, farm labourers were generally excused military service on the grounds that their ordinary occupation was too vital to the war effort to be entrusted to feebler hands. A patriotic poet, realizing this, might have been tempted to present the peasant therefore as a willing hero; as at least a noble savage; or, in the terms of conventional pastoral, as a laudable figure in a wider landscape. Not so R. S. Thomas. The view he gives of Iago Prytherch is, initially at least, anything but laudable. His grin is half-witted, his mirth is spittled, at night he gobs in the fire, and there is a vacancy in his mind. What dignity attaches to him is an aspect of the poet's own elevated language. He is indeed a 'shock' to the refined sensibility of the beholder. But here Thomas at once throws everything up in the air. The figure of Iago Prytherch not only affronts the refined sensibility, but forces that sensibility to acknowledge its own affectedness. And in the same line, Prytherch too is abruptly transformed. The assemblage of his person – his clothes and his sweat, his whole off-puttingness – is redefined in the one phrase, 'stark naturalness'.

Yes, Iago Prytherch is at one with the natural order in a manner denied the poet and the reader, with their 'refined,/But affected, sense'. Nonetheless, Prytherch, his image already redeemed by this, is 'your prototype'. But whose prototype? Is Thomas in fact addressing us? Or himself? Already, in his dealings with Iago Prytherch, there is a sense of close interior combat. Already Prytherch has been fixed in his harsh landscape as a mirror-surfaced emblem. But here, in this case, there is an unresolved ambiguity: 'your' could mean both; but in each case there is a different drift. Prytherch is 'our' prototype, the reader's, in that, however educated we are, however distanced from the exacting labours of the land, he represents a common ancestry. He is the magistrate's prototype, the officer's, the professor's, the king's. But as R. S. Thomas's prototype Iago Prytherch stands in a more precise relationship. The clue to this is provided in the second line, 'the bald Welsh hills'. Wales stripped down to its essentials: no ports, no coalfields, no chapels even. Just the hills.

These two applications of 'prototype', if they are valid, unsettle the poem's seemingly easy conclusions. The country is at war, therefore the introduction of martial imagery – 'siege', 'attrition', 'impregnable fortress' – is not only permissible, but in no need of an explanation. Iago Prytherch, seemingly the dumb, idiot peasant, is 'a winner of wars' too. He deserves to stand alongside the soldier heroes in the roll-call of honour. But the weight of the poem, the element of doubt created by the ambiguities latent in the word 'prototype', as well as the derision of the refined but affected sensibility, suggests something other. It suggests that Iago Prytherch may not only be the soldier's equal, but is in fact his superior. He is the son of nature, and it is on him alone – for the whole thrust of his portrait is to view him as an isolated figure – that the curious stars (a metaphor for the heavens, therefore of God) look down. He endures like a tree. Soldiers are blown away.

In time the tree will feature among Thomas's most potent symbols. Again and again it will be associated with the crucifix, as well as with aspects of Celtic culture. In the light of its gathered application, it is tempting to read into this phrase, 'Enduring like a tree', a metaphor that equates Prytherch with Christ. That however may be premature, and in any case is unnecessary. Attention is better focused on the word 'curious', in 'under the curious stars'. In a sense the whole poem swivels on this, as upon a heel. What exactly does 'curious' mean? What does it imply? Is it too literary a word for the conclusion of a poem full of unliterary expressions: 'gob', for example, or 'animal contact'? Or is its very literaryness supremely artful, taking us back to the refined but affected sensibility?

As an example of where refined and affected sensibilities may lead men, we may look no further than the Winter 1990 and Spring 1991 issues of *The New Welsh Review*. Two heavyweights of the

academic establishment, the critic Walford Davies and the philosopher D. Z. Phillips, both professors, indulge in an acrimonious
slogging match. D. Z. Phillips, in an earlier broadcast, had inadvertently misquoted a line from 'A Peasant'. Instead of saying 'Remember him, then,' he had said 'Salute him then'. Spotting this, Walford
Davies went for his jugular. And so the scrap developed. At the heart
of it was a contest between disciplines, each laying claim to truths
unobtainable by its rival. Crucially the debate centred on that
word 'curious', as applied to the stars by R. S. Thomas. Walford
Davies initially favours the archaic meaning of 'curious' as defined
by the OED: 'Made with care or art; skilfully, elaborately or beautifully wrought.' To support this interpretation, he invokes lines
from Andrew Marvell's celebrated seventeenth-century poem 'The
Garden':

> What wond'rous life is this I lead!
> Ripe Apples drop about my head;
> The Luscious Clusters of the Vine
> Upon my mouth do crush their Wine;
> The Nectaren, and curious Peach,
> Into my hands themselves do reach.

Phillips, while not ruling out this reading, questions whether even
Marvell may not have meant something different, the more simple
definition of 'curious' as 'exquisite, choice, excellent, fine' (also from
the OED). His concern is that Marvell would not have wished to
sentimentalize a theistic 'argument from design'.

Rejecting Walford Davies's gloss of 'curious', identified in Marvell,
then transferred to Thomas, D. Z. Phillips develops the notion of
'multivalence': in other words both poets, in the manner of all good
poets, must have been aware of multiple meanings attaching to the
word. And indeed, he quotes Thomas, from their private correspondence: 'All is ambivalence, multivalence even. The same natural
background, which from one standpoint has facilitated my belief in
God, has from another raised enormous problems.' Replying, Davies
vigorously defends his back:

But curiouser and curiouser. As one who confesses that he hadn't even thought of a different meaning for 'curious' in R. S. Thomas's line . . . it is late in the day for Phillips to start setting the ground-rules for the word. (Yet notice how he suddenly starts talking of a 'studied ambiguity!') Generations of R. S. Thomas readers have been discussing the word's deft evocation of intricate pattern. Less than deft is Phillips's attempt to make me say that my 'reading of Thomas's poem is *obviously correct*'. I use 'obvious' only of the word 'curious', and even then call it only the 'main' meaning. But Phillips makes worse misrepresentations here, and they lead him into his futile digression of the argument-from-design.[8]

But what is odd about the whole exchange, which, spread over several columns of small print, becomes progressively more rarefied as it becomes more rancorous, is that neither critic nor philosopher seems willing to consider contemporary common usage meanings. 'Curious' summons up the phrase 'curious to behold', from which derives the monosyllabic synonym . . . 'odd'. Or perhaps, 'strange', not immediately fathomable.

'A Peasant' describes a culture shock. The refined but affected worlds of the reader and priest-poet are confronted by the crude and elemental world delineated in the figure of Iago Prytherch. In the midst of a war, a different kind of battle takes place. And this is the subtlety of the word 'curious'. Multivalency is indeed of the essence, but neither professor spreads his net quite wide enough. In a poem laced with quotidian expression, it can only be appropriate that the word on which the poem's final meaning depends should reflect both the worlds it finds to be in conflict.

So we can look again at that last line,

> Enduring like a tree under the curious stars.

All possible meanings can and should be credited to 'curious'. Whether or not it supports notions of the 'argument from design', there is certainly a theistic undercurrent. Another current might be: by being 'curious' the stars exhibit curiosity, or intelligence. The heavens themselves are interested in this lonely peasant. He may not be as godforsaken as his appearance suggests. Whether they are simply beautiful, or finely wrought, the stars here evoke a human situation more enduring, as also more terrifying, than any passing conflict. *That* is what we should be concerning ourselves with. But at the same time Thomas chooses not to be dogmatic. By allowing a more ordinary usage, supported by the deliberately unrefined diction of the earlier parts of the poem, Thomas also draws to our attention the naked oddness of a man pitted against the cosmos; and thereby to the oddness of the cosmos itself.

This, spectrally at least, suggests a fusion between the beholder and the beheld. From the theistic viewpoint, refinement and affectation are as nothing. Our clean attire is of no more protection than Prytherch's sweaty garments. And so, schematically at least, Thomas, who as a priest must be concerned with such things as the argument from design, finds kinship with a living ancestor. There is no 'main' meaning as such. Only by acknowledging the equality of meanings present in the word 'curious' is the culture shock of 'A Peasant' potentially resolved. And by the same token, the religious, Welsh and even pacifist qualities of the poem push to the fore.

In the matter of meanings, there may be another, equally deft play. There is the name itself to be considered, Iago Prytherch, who will figure in many more of R. S. Thomas's poems. The critic Anne Stevenson, in an essay called 'The Uses of Prytherch',[9] writes:

> The name Iago Prytherch, strange to English ears, is common enough in Welsh. Iago simply means James, pronounced with a short 'a', as in 'baggage' or 'map'; it bears no relation, probably, to the long-aed villain of *Othello*. Prytherch, or Prydderch in Welsh, would be a contraction of ap Rhydderch, or son of Rhydderch. It is not likely that 'Prytherch' has significance as a name, apart from its being a Welsh surname given to an English-speaking hill-farmer, rooting him in Wales and its hereditary Celtic 'tree'.

But there is a temptation to be much less matter-of-fact. In the telephone directory the name 'Prytherch' occurs but rarely, while Iago is an equally uncommon given name. What is odd, even curious, is that having correctly analysed 'Prytherch' into 'ap Rhydderch', Ms

Stevenson declines the offered bait, even though, in the same sentence, she deploys the word 'Celtic'. Yet if we look up 'Rhydderch' in the *Oxford Companion to the Literature of Wales*, we find:

> Rhydderch Hen or Rhydderch Hael (6th cent.) one of the four kings of the Old North who, according to Saxon genealogies incorporated in Nennius's *Historiae Brittonum*, resisted the Anglian king Hussa . . . In the Triads he is listed as one of the Three Generous Men of the Isle of Britain. He became associated with the legend of Myrddin [Merlin] at an early stage in its development and there are several references in the Myrddin poems which suggest that he fought at the battle of Arfderydd in 573. In Geoffrey of Monmouth's *Vita Merlini*, a poem drawing on Welsh sources, Rhydderch appears as Rodarchus, King of the Cumbri, who defeats Guonnolous (Gwenddolau) and his supporter Merlinus (Myrddin) in battle. In the life of St Kentigern by Jocelyn of Furness (12th cent.) Rhydderch is praised for his generosity and portrayed as a patron of the Church.

The involvement of Merlin – not the benevolent fixer of the Arthurian romances, but the wild, sometimes insane, soothsayer of early Welsh poetry – is tantalizing. In the Merlin poems, Rhydderch is Myrddin's tormentor. It is because of Rhydderch's machinations that Merlin flees to a wilderness, and spends twenty years 'mad among his pigs'. From the *Black Book of Carmarthen* (and Carmarthen is derived from Caer Myrddin), 'The Ohs of Myrddin':

> Oh little piglet,
> with your sharp nails,
> discourteous bed-fellow
> going to lie down like that.
> Rhydderch the Generous
> at his carousal
> little does he know tonight
> the extent
> last night
> of my insomnia.
> Snow to my thighs
> surrounded by dingoes,
> icicles in my hair,

my glory gone.
Tuesday will see
a day of violence
between the Lord of Powys
and the Gwynedd lads.[10]

And yet Rhydderch is also a hero. Not only is he honoured among
the Welsh Triads,[11] but he was one of those who withstood the
Saxon horde. The question becomes, who was the better Welshman:
Myrddin, who prophesied the eventual defeat of the Saxons (and also
testified to the internecine squabbles of the Welsh princes, even at
this early, critical stage); or his great antagonist, who (when he wasn't
fighting his fellow leaders) did something about it?

Imagine for a moment that, consciously or otherwise, R. S. Thomas
had this Rhydderch in mind when he fixed Iago Prytherch's name.
Two things happen. First, a resonance between the Welsh Iago and
Shakespeare's becomes possible, for in this case 'Iago' and Rhydderch,
both tormentors, are well matched. Secondly, and far more interestingly, if Iago Prytherch is a version of Rhydderch, then Thomas
stands in the position of Myrddin. He is challenged and vexed by
the mere existence of Prytherch, just as Myrddin was challenged and
vexed by the very existence of Rhydderch.

To put this spin on Iago Prytherch may or may not be fanciful.
Nothing that R. S. himself has said or written warrants it. But literary
artefacts have a life of their own, and the notion of R. S. as being in
some manner *Merlinus redivivus* is peculiarly forceful. Among other
things, 'Myrddin' entertained a holy hatred of the *Sais*, and liked
nothing so much as to dream of their ruin:

> I foretell
> the battle of Llwyfain woods,
> and stretchers
> all red
> before the rush of Owain:
> when dung-bailiffs churn
> our chittle-chattle;
> the country's paltry men
> into perjury and treachery.

> And when comes Cadwaladr
> to occupy Anglesey,
> the English will be wiped out
> in the lands of Britain.[12]

The Owain foretold here was, eight hundred years later, identified
in Welsh folklore with Owain Glyndŵr – the last native Prince of
Wales celebrated in many poems by Thomas. And Thomas too could
turn his hand to similar prophecy, as in 'Welsh History':[13]

> We were a people, and are so yet.
> When we have finished quarrelling for crumbs
> Under the table, or gnawing the bones
> Of a dead culture, we will arise
> And greet each other in a new dawn.[14]

Or as in another, slightly later poem, 'On Hearing a Welshman
Speak',[15] where, by making time run backwards, Thomas irresistibly
combines prophecy with *hiraeth*:

> Stones to the wall fly back.
> The gay manors are full
> Of music; the poets return
> To feed at the royal tables.
> Who dreams of failure now
> That the oak woods are loud
> With the last hurrying feet
> Seeking the English plain?

It would be wrong to push the analogy with Myrddin too hard.
In Thomas there is as much if not more Dafydd ap Gwilym. In 1943
it may have been too early for this level of concealed referral to have
been operative in Thomas's work, although thereafter it certainly is
a feature. But it does offer, besides an additional layer of complex
ironies in 'The Peasant' and other Iago Prytherch poems, an alternative perspective on Thomas, rooting his poetic identity in something
as truly Welsh as it is ancient, and therefore altogether Celtic. And
for this reason I have aired the conjecture.

*   *   *

As regards the immediate inspiration for Prytherch, Thomas has been unusually forthcoming. Introducing 'A Peasant' for a sound recording,[16] he has said: 'My awakening to the possibility of a more robust poetry came with my removal to my first incumbency in the Montgomeryshire foothills in 1942 ... I came in contact for the first time with the rough farm folk of the upland valleys. These were pre-tractor days. Their life was a hard slog in wind and mire on hill slopes with the occasional brief idyllic interludes. Their life and their attitudes administered an inward shock to my Georgian sensibility. I responded with the first of my poems about Iago Prytherch, a sort of prototype of this kind of farmer.' In *Neb*, Thomas is even more specific:

> To him the country and its surroundings were beautiful. He chose to continue writing poems in praise of them. But how could he reconcile the life and the attitudes of the farmers themselves with this? One cold, dark November day, on his way to call at a farm a thousand feet above sea-level, he saw the farmer's brother out in a field topping swedes [i.e. 'docking mangels']. This made a deep impression on him, and after he had returned to his house he began writing 'A Peasant', the first of his poems to confront the reality of what lay around him.

And then:

> Was it because of a hardness in the people and their work, or because of some nice-niceness in himself, that there arose a tension which was to be part of his spiritual and literary problems for so many years? At the time he was too young and inexperienced to know that conflict is a necessary condition of art. And yet two-thirds of him was in sympathy with these people who had to be out in all weather cultivating the land and looking after animals as unmanageable as the people themselves.[17]

The last sentence – *Ac eto roedd deuparth ohono mewn cydymdeimlad â'r bobl hyn oedd yn gorfod bod allan ymhob tywydd yn trin y tir a gofalu am yr anifeiliaid oedd mor anhydrin â'r bobl eu hunain* – is extraordinary. Is the fraction 'two-thirds' merely a figure of speech, or is it a more precise quantification? Either way, it rings hollow. If two-thirds of R.S. Thomas really is in sympathy with his uncouth farm types, then it is difficult to see how he could account for them as being no more manageable than animals (which in itself is a peculiar notion to apply to sheep, say, or cows). But if this is his conviction, then the figure 'two-thirds' looks unnecessarily generous, even self-congratulatory. For what the sentence would then seem most to express is its author's haughtiness.

But against this, we have the evidence of the poem itself, 'A Peasant'. Clearly the spectacle of Prytherch docking mangels in a November field did induce an acutely felt cognitive dissonance, so what appears to be uncharacteristic carelessness on the part of Thomas the prose-writer may in fact be a faithful echo of a truly tectonic event.

Tectonic events do not in the main provide the fabric of what Thomas tells us about Manafon in *Neb* and the other autobiographical writings. Rather the Manafon passages are marked by the same near-inconsequentiality that informs his descriptions of childhood, adolescence and early manhood. Wherever it can be, the larger world of significant event is ignored. Even the use of atomic weapons against Japan in 1945 seems to escape his contemporary notice: a peculiar exclusion given the poet's subsequent involvement in anti-nuclear protest, and his obvious horror at the destructive potential of modern technologies. But possibly Thomas is being peculiarly disciplined here. *Neb* may have been written well after Thomas appeared on the anti-nuclear stage, but to have back-projected later concerns on to the screen of his earlier life would have been misleading. Rather, Thomas's priority is to render the actual progress of his mock anti-hero: no one, nobody, anybody, *neb*.

Yet whether what he in fact writes about himself is necessarily less misleading may be questioned. It is with no little skill that R. S. continues to present himself as a Voltairean naive; as the text unfolds it becomes clear that his self's assumed unwittingness lends credence, functionally at any rate, to overtly moral perceptions and prescriptions that are gathered up towards the end of the book. Innocence is used by Thomas to humanize his polemic.

It is noticeable, in this regard, that the tone of *Neb* is appreciably different from the *entiché* and sometimes belligerent tones of such prose as Thomas produced during the Manafon years. In the autobiography he plays down the highlights of his advancing literary career.

None of his early, and since famous, volumes of poems is mentioned by name; and, 'A Peasant' apart, he has nothing to tell us about the circumstances of their composition.

These considerations, however, help us identify the true intent of *Neb*, which is not so much to furnish the reader with a comprehensive life as to guide us through the long gestation of a Welsh conscious-ness, albeit a particular variety of Welsh consciousness. In this respect *Neb*, and also pieces such as *The Paths Gone By*, are to be seen as Thomas's contribution to the same literature of emergent cultural consciousness as Walter Dowding's essay, 'Evolution of a Nationalist'.

The landscape around Manafon is repeatedly extolled. Not only are the uplands in themselves beautiful, but they are where Thomas can sometimes hear *yr hen iaith*, the Old Language, spoken as a lingua franca. The setting also brings him into contact with chapel communities. As Llangollen is too far away for him to continue his Welsh lessons there, he seeks out a teacher closer by:

> There was also a Welsh chapel at Adfa, and it was to the Minister that he first went for help with his own Welsh. This was D. T. Davies, one from the South, but he soon moved away, and the new Rector went to the Minister at Penarth, a chapel between Manafon and Llanfair, and asked for help there. He was H. D. Owen, born in Penrhosgarnedd. This was a blessing, because it meant the student would come to speak the language of the North.[18]

A small advantage perhaps, until, ten pages later, Thomas returns to his theme of the glories of the Welsh countryside. After the war, and the easing of petrol rationing, he and Elsi resume their explo-rations of the countryside:

> But besides Nanmor, which is one of the most beautiful areas of Wales, there were other places to be visited: Cwm Twrch in Mont-gomeryshire, for example, in the parish of Garthbeibio, where the river runs down in a series of waterfalls to meet the river Banw. Then there was Tal-y-llyn, and the sea itself at Aberdyfi, where they would go sometimes to take Gwydion [their son] for a taste of the waves. And by going around like this, he started to form a comprehensive picture of Wales, her mountains and moorlands, and her frothing streams.[19]

A *comprehensive* picture of Wales? Then as later, large areas of the country will remain off-limits: the north-east, and the southern counties of Gwent, Glamorgan and Pembrokeshire. At Manafon, through a continuing process of self-definition, Thomas's Welshness is confirmed. He becomes, if he was not one before, a patriot. But equally the specificity of his Welshness is defined. The *hiraeth* for Gwynedd begins in earnest.

Neb half weaves, half throws together such strands of his life as Thomas wishes to reveal, making any summary or précis difficult. In the space of a few hundred words, sometimes in a single paragraph, his focus and his attention can shift kaleidoscopically from a description of the bald hills above Manafon and the Rector's spiritual concerns to the more mundane aspects of his work as a parish priest and his domestic life. There is much to be learned about the man and the poet however. Arriving at the Rectory, although he does not quote it he invokes Edward Thomas's poem 'The New House':

> Now first, as I shut the door,
>   I was alone
> In the new house; and the wind
>   Began to moan.
>
> Old at once was the house,
>   And I was old;
> My ears were teased with the dread
>   Of what was foretold.
>
> Nights of storm, days of mist, without end;
>   Sad days when the sun
> Shone in vain: old griefs and griefs
>   Not yet begun.
>
> All was foretold me; naught
>   Could I foresee;
> But I learned how the wind would sound
> After these things should be.[20]

Thomas climbs to the top of the Rectory's stairs and looks out over the river Rhiw to the fields and hills beyond. 'That moment he foresaw the seasons before him, with the weather turning from rain to shine and from heat to snow. And so it was. There was nothing else to look upon but the land and the sky under the changing seasons.'[21] In the summer the Rhiw is nothing, but in the autumn and winter can rise dangerously high. The Rector wonders whether the cellar beneath the Rectory is damp, and takes a look. When he opens the door he discovers water within a foot of the step. Yet, in the same river he would also 'fish for trout, which were numerous. That is why his father was so happy when he heard he had been appointed to the parish, because he liked nothing better than to fish in a river.'[22] And so the river becomes a part of his life, 'sometimes quiet, at other times rushing by brown from the peat where she rose: a place of small cottages and sheep waiting for him to find them'.[23]

As best he may, Thomas depicts the claustrophobia of the place, both the village and the valley containing it. Many of its inhabitants knew no broader horizon. 'Earth from earth they were; their only interests were the farm, their animals, prices and the personal affairs of their neighbours.' In the days before television a hard day's work was followed by an evening in front of the fire before climbing upstairs to bed. So what point, Thomas asks, in talking about spiritual matters to a people 'who lacked the normal conveniences of middle-class life?' But even these can offer scant defence against the weather at its worst. In the legendary winter of early 1947, Thomas, Elsi and their young son Gwydion find themselves cut off by six feet of snow. The rector starts digging towards the road, others start digging from the road, until a trench is cut. But after the snow came the sub-zero temperatures, and the biting winds. In an unusually extended and focused passage, Thomas continues:

> To make matters worse, throughout this period the rector had to keep a fire in the church, to warm it. The bellringer previously had made the fire, but had grown old, and because he was a heavy man and had to go down some stairs under the church to light the fire, the Rector had persuaded him to give up this work in case he had a fall. 'We will get someone else,' he said. But no one had volunteered

and the worst winter of the century had begun. In addition the pipes of the big rectory froze every night, and the whole morning was consumed by his and his wife's attempts to unfreeze them. Sometimes the heavy clouds would move and the sun break through for an hour or two. But the clear sky only made the frost worse than ever. One night the temperature dropped to $-10°F$ – forty degrees of frost. As the frost tightened its grip the house creaked throughout the night, and by morning the windows were adorned with ferns, so that no-one could see through them. The water in the house had frozen and even the river had difficulty in moving. And through all this the little one had to be kept warm and entertained indoors, because it was far too cold to contemplate taking him outside. Then, after a day of expectation, there would come the sound of a snowball hitting the window and there was Roy the nurse's son, returned from school. There were eighteen foot snow drifts in Dolanog that winter, and we heard stories of the moorland people having to walk miles to the next village to buy their bread. The birds came close to starvation and the fields were full of fox tracks. The bark was torn from the trees by rabbits desperate to discover food. When the thaw finally came, and the heavy rain, the ice in the river cracked like gunshot, and great white slabs of it began to gallop past the rectory.[24]

About this passage is a structural significance. The great freeze of 1947, which spread across the whole of Britain and much of Europe, represents the point of greatest physical enclosure in Thomas's adult life. Around it, however, Thomas places a number of growth points. Some of these antedate the freeze, others follow it, either narratively or in time. But these new beginnings, or old beginnings resumed, are in the manner of a springtime flowering. They also show Thomas finding his way beyond the valley, and the restrictions that bound others of its inhabitants; and they reveal how ill cut out he was to be a sedentary country parson.

To start with there was, of course, the son, Gwydion, the Thomases' only child, born on 29 September 1945 and christened Andreas Gwydion Thomas – 'Gwydion' being the name of 'the best of all story-tellers' in the *Mabinogion*. In *Neb*, R. S. tells us that a child was Elsi's idea. 'As hopes grew that the war would soon be over, the Rector's wife expressed a desire to conceive.'[25] Nor, either in *Neb* or in the poetry, is there very much to suggest that the father regarded the birth as anything but a mixed blessing. 'How could a nobody be a father to someone?' he asks. But the fates had decreed otherwise, and after a 'night of thunder' Thomas found himself at the hospital in Newtown looking down at 'the bit of flesh that was lying in a cradle at his mother's bedside'. The rector is struck by the joy on the infant's face, but, back at the house, any joy of his own is soon dispelled by the baby's bawling, the 'huge hunger'[26] which, for two years, murders sleep.

Later, to the delight of R. S. Thomas's enemies, Gwydion will be educated in England, first at a preparatory school in Shrewsbury, then at Bradfield public school, finally at Magdalen College, Oxford. People who want to deride Thomas habitually carp at a hypocrisy. How deep, they ask, does his loyalty to Wales and its language really run when he packs off his own child for superior treatment across the border? Presumably, though, Elsi Thomas had some say in the matter as well, and it is possible that the circumstances of Gwydion's education, far from embodying a hypocrisy, reflect the poet's unwillingness to adopt the role of domestic dictator.

Given Thomas's known penchant for high culture, such an interpretation may be too generous. Even so, we should recall de Rochefoucauld's double-edged definition of hypocrisy as the homage vice pays virtue: the accuser often finds he has swapped places with the accused. What is more disturbing, or at least more questionable, is the poet's readiness to divulge in print his paternal misgivings. Literature is full of children who revenge themselves upon their parents in later life. Edmund Gosse's *Father and Son* is but the exemplar of a genre. But the other way round is uncommon. Thomas doesn't in fact tear Gwydion apart, but he does use him, rather as he uses Iago Prytherch, to sort out some of his own feelings. In *The Echoes Return Slow* we find both prose and verse passages that swerve between the chilling and the lyrical:

The child growing imperceptibly into a boy, the strange plant that has taken root in one's private garden. The apple of the mother's eye. The grudging acknowledgment by the male, so different from the female, that this also is a twig on a branch of the tree of man. The father's share in the promise of fruit and his resentment at canker.

> He was sometimes a bad boy,
> slovenly, vain, dishonest.
> Yet I remember his lips
> how they were soft and
>
> wet, when I kissed him
> good-night, and a shadow
> moving away from the bed's
> head, that might have been God's.[27]

Interestingly, Gosse's father Philip, who was a member of the Plymouth Brethren as well as a distinguished naturalist, also entertained what might be termed a special relationship with God. There is, one fancies, a deal more chapel in Thomas than his Church background would always indicate. It is honest to acknowledge the anguishes of fatherhood. It may even be of some comfort to other fathers suffering male post-natal depression. But to make a known individual the subject of an address which is essentially self-probing from on high is ethically questionable.

That the address in question portends forgiveness or grace is neither here nor there. And yet – and there always is a yet with Thomas – it is just this capacity to unsettle his reader that marks him out as a writer. Cyril Connolly's celebrated aperçu, that, for the creative writer, 'there is no more sombre enemy of good art than the pram in the hall,'[28] is more collected than Thomas's outpouring, but it is also far more genteel. Indeed, it is Thomas's irritation with his own gentility, his awareness of its inadequacy, even falsity, as a literary persona, that generates his art, pram or no pram in the hallway. If the arrival of a son expanded Thomas's universe in ways not wholly congenial to its principal inhabitant, he leaves us in no doubt as to the depth of that change:

> And this little finger says:
> 'I was not there.' And this one
>
> 'I was in somebody else's
> pie.' And the third, pointing
>
> in no particular direction, accuses:
> 'It was you.' And we look up

away from ourselves, encountering
the sky, that sometimes we take,

so inscrutable its expression, for God's
face, venerable with cloud,

staring back at us and enquiring
with bland ingenuousness: 'Who? Me?'[29]

The end of the freeze, like the end of the war (and the one is almost
a metaphor of the other), meant that Thomas, either on his own or
in the company of his wife, could resume exploring the Welsh landscape. The landscape, however, was but an aspect of an even greater
and more dynamic release. At Manafon he develops as a nature poet
and as a pastoralist; but his arrival is cast in the frame of Welsh
nationalism. As in the First World War, so in the Second. Welsh
men and Welsh boys were drafted into the British forces; but inside
the army they discovered their Cymric identity. *Neb* again:

> Even the English-Welsh of south Wales felt they were of a different
> lineage to their fellow soldiers. Some of them wrote to the newspapers
> and magazines to express this feeling. As a consequence, the magazine
> *Wales*, under the editorship of Keidrych Rhys, was revived to provide
> them with an English-language platform. The emphasis though was
> on Welshness: stories with Welsh characters, Welsh sayings, and
> quotations from the classical bards.[30]

In fact, Thomas had been contributing poems to *Wales* for some
time, and the magazine's history is more complex than he here
suggests. Many of its contributors, including Thomas, had not seen
active service. It would be fairer to say that returnees from the war
provided a larger audience for, and more participants in, a diffuse
movement that had its particular starting point in 1936. And Thomas
himself says as much in his 'Autobiographical Essay', when he writes:
'The Anglo-Welsh movement had come to life again as a result of
Welsh people's experiences in the forces.' But from the narrower
perspective of our concern with the one poet, Thomas is certainly
right to draw attention to Rhys's publication, belletrist as much as

patriotic though it was. Through *Wales*, R.S. first established his reputation as an English-writing Welshman. He gained considerably in confidence, the more so as he could now look upon himself not as a loner, but as someone able to speak on behalf of a discernible campaign. And among the leaders of that campaign, whom he now met, he could move, increasingly, as an equal who held his own opinions.

At first though, Thomas allowed himself to be awed, both by the big names of the so-called Anglo-Welsh movement, and by those established Welsh-language writers who endorsed the movement's aspirations. In *Neb*, at several points, Thomas presents himself, with reason enough, as the willing but untutored acolyte of Welsh culture. But by doing this, he also enhances the importance and glamour of the club whose membership he craves. Thus,

> He read in *Y Faner* ['The Banner'] an article by Saunders Lewis that closed with the words 'O flodyn y dyffryn, deffro' ['O flower of the valley, awake']. It moved his whole being. He went to Llanfarian to visit Saunders without a word of introduction. He was kindly received, and began to speak in English about his ideals and plans; but in no time he was led by Saunders to continue in his scrappy Welsh.[31]

and

> To help him in his efforts to learn Welsh he frequented the meetings of the ministers of Llanfair with others of the area – the Brotherhood ['y Frawdoliaeth'] as they were called. Later, Islwyn Ffowc Elis[32] came to Llanfair. The rector called one day to invite him for a walk through the moorlands around Cwm Nant yr Eira, but Islwyn refused. He was too busy serving his Wales. Were the two Waleses the same? He had met Euros Bowen[33] once or twice, and he now wrote to him for help with his Welsh. He received a kind invitation to stay at Llangywair for a week. Whilst walking on the shores of Lake Tegid, he described how the light fell differently on the slopes of Arenig to the way it did at Manafon. Euros stopped, and said in his convincing way: 'That proves you are a Welshman'. Euros was one for staying on his feet until the small hours, but his guest learned much about Wales and the Welsh that week. Euros was also keen to take him to see Llwyd o'r Bryn [Robert Lloyd],[34] but after further consideration

decided that his torrent of Welsh would be too much for the learner.[35]

Thomas, however, gives no clear indication as to when exactly these meetings, half-meetings and non-meetings took place. In his narrative, the encounter with Islwyn Ffowc Elis comes immediately after a short paragraph about the Scottish nationalist Douglas Young, which in turn immediately follows the description of calling on Saunders Lewis:

> Later, Douglas Young, a nationalist from Scotland, came to address a meeting at Rhosllannerchrugog. The rector attended, and met him after his speech. Later, following a review by him [i.e. Thomas] in *Wales* of the literary awakening in Scotland, the Rector had an invitation to go there for a week to address meetings on the history and literature of Wales.[36]

Thomas's Scottish article, 'Some Contemporary Scottish Writers', was published by Keidrych Rhys in the autumn of 1946.[37] In the same issue of *Wales*, Thomas's responses to a questionnaire were given prominence, above, for example, those of Vernon Watkins. Previously, in the autumn of 1945,[38] Rhys had run another piece by the poet, 'The Depopulation of the Welsh Hill Country', and this had been well received.

All three of these prose pieces show Thomas's increasing knowledge of the Welsh literature of Wales. In the relatively narrow circle of Welsh and Anglo-Welsh literati at which they were aimed, these accomplishments would not have gone unnoticed.

This is only to say that Thomas, an impressionistic memoirist, is unconcerned, and would not claim to be concerned, with the minutiae of an exact chronology. The precise dates of his first meetings with Lewis, Islwyn, Young and many other 'figures', among them Gwenallt and Waldo Williams, if they can be established at all, must await the investigative scholarship of future biographers. What does transpire, however, from the sketchy materials currently available, is that between 1943, and the publication of 'A Peasant', and the end of 1946, and the appearance of his first collection of poems, *The Stones of the Field*, R. S. Thomas established himself as a known voice within a movement, or political literary tendency, whose subsequent momentum his writings did so much to sustain.

Denied the minutiae, we must, perhaps thankfully, confine our attention to the two known quantities: those who became, loosely or otherwise, Thomas's cultural associates; and the occasional prose writings that proclaimed the same cultural association.

The cultural associates can be divided into two broad groups, while allowing that neither was exclusive of the other: the Welsh literati, and their 'Anglo-Welsh' counterparts. Immediately however a problem arises. Thomas's engagement with the literature of Wales, in whichever language, is across the board. Although certain of his contemporaries, including those writing around Welsh themes in English, sometimes command his respect, it is with Welsh-medium literature as a whole, past as well as present, that his mind takes exercise. And again, while he may, later on, write praise poems to Saunders Lewis and Gwenallt, equal or greater artistic debts are due, for instance, to Dafydd ap Gwilym in the fourteenth century, or Siôn Cent in the fifteenth. In this sense, his work, but particularly his poetry, is culturally steeped, even before account is taken of its obvious and continuous relations with English verse, and its less obvious relations, for example, with Latin and even Greek antecedents.

Here, however, considering the Manafon years, we are concerned with the ferment in Welsh, and in particular 'Anglo-Welsh', writing that took place at or around the end of the Second World War, and its specifically 'nationalist' flavour. During the nineteenth century there had been a resurgence of Welsh letters, principally (but not exclusively) through the activities of Nonconformist preachers and the revival of *eisteddfodau*. Although the literary form best beloved of the period, the novel, failed to inspire any Welsh-language talent of the highest order, a number of gifted poets – Islwyn and Ceiriog among them[39] – had emerged to reassert the traditions of Welsh verse. As importantly, with the arrival of the universities, Welsh scholarship too took root. Suddenly there was a market for serious Welsh writing, an opportunity exploited by such able scholar-editors as O. M. Edwards (1858–1920), John Morris-Jones (1864–1929) and W. J. Gruffydd (1881–1954). Welsh literature, after a long hiatus, was audibly and visibly on the move again.

Since the end of the First World War especially, there has been a continuing development and flowering of a true indigenous literature expressing itself in most if not all the recognized genres. At the same time Welsh writing in English, though bedevilled by the term 'Anglo-Welsh', has emerged as a parallel and equally significant literature.

Given that an increasing proportion of Wales's population was, from the mid-nineteenth century, raised and educated as monoglot English speakers, and that between England and Wales there has been a continuous movement of peoples, it is to be expected the Welsh should have made a distinctive contribution to English letters. Gerard Manley Hopkins, Edward Thomas and Wilfred Owen are but three outstanding examples of poets of more or less Welsh extraction. None of them, however, can readily be dubbed 'Anglo-Welsh' except by expanding any available definition of the term beyond useful application. Rather 'Anglo-Welsh' has progressively come to mean those writing in English about Welsh subject-matter from a 'Welsh' point of view.[40]

In the nineteenth century there was nobody who fitted this bill with any enduring imaginative originality. Indeed it is not until after the First World War that, the hunt for historical precedent aside, it is reasonable to speak of an 'Anglo-Welsh' literature in the sense provided; and even then the figures who appear tend not to conform to later expectations of the rubric – a hazard warning, perhaps, of the folly of applying negotiated labels. Three writers it is worth anyone's while to read – Caradoc Evans (1878–1945), Idris Davies (1905–53) and Dylan Thomas (1914–53) – have each, for different reasons, sometimes been excluded from the Anglo-Welsh circle by its critical high-priests.

Caradoc Evans was as Welsh as anyone: indeed his stories and novels are written in a style of English that sometimes consciously apes elements of Welsh syntax. But sub-Joycean verbal inventiveness, combined with a lack of prurience that for his time is both astonishing and refreshing, was used by Evans to savage the manners, personalities and hypocrisies of the Nonconformist Cardiganshire communities he grew up in. A master of coruscating caricature, his sin was to deride the Welsh more roundly than any Englishman would dare. Idris Davies, on the other hand, was too loyal to his subjects. The 'Rhymney poet' sang, in 'Gwalia Deserta' and 'The Angry Summer', of the coal valleys and the people of the coal valleys, and also of the General Strike of 1926. At one time a communist, he was, in his best work, a proletarian poet par excellence.[41] He could intellectualize, as could his fellow Rhymneyites, but preferred the idioms of the music-hall and pantomime to nail his social targets. An acute observer of one corner of Wales, his socialist disregard for more traditional Welsh themes has made him at best only an honorary member of the Anglo-Welsh 'club'.

Dylan Thomas's relationship is even more ambiguous, partly because he is so well known. Even those Welsh who profess not to like him are likely to have committed large chunks of his poetry to memory, and are apt to go dewy-eyed when accessing those chunks on their vocal screens. No serious compiler of Welsh-English anthologies would dare leave him out. But what stands against him is precisely the quality that makes him unique among poets and raconteurs: he is at once intensely lyrical and intensely entertaining. He has the sharpest ear for the hidden wit of common speech, but gives such wit an elegiac spin. *Under Milk Wood*, the most ambitious and successful of his creations, is both cruel and loving. It is a piss-take on the grand scale, but it is also caringly intimate in the way it depicts its small Welsh fishing community. It is Caradoc Evans in the role of Father Christmas. Small wonder then that responses to Dylan have been widely divergent, while those floundering to evaluate the poet have too often snatched at the straws of his personal debauchery. The drinking and the womanizing that made him famous in London and America were tailor-made to shock, as well as fascinate, his chapel-bred home readers. But the trouble with his international reputation was he deserved it. He was Welsh, but he burned to shine outside the parish of his Swansea upbringing. He had no interest in the Old Language, and he wished a pox on nationalism. At the same time he lacked, as spiritedly as anyone can lack, high seriousness. Having made his mark in the 1930s, he died young, in 1953, but for some of the new breed of Anglo-Welsh coming to fruition in the 1940s, not young enough. His offence was his blithe virtuosity.

'The only thing Welsh about Dylan,' wrote R. S. Thomas, twisting a two-edged knife, 'was that he knew his Bible.'[42]

Besides Evans, Davies and Dylan Thomas, there were other writers writing about Wales in the 1920s and 1930s; the poets Huw Menai and Vernon Watkins, for example, the novelists Jack Jones and Gwyn Jones. Some of these continued writing after the Second World War, and there continued to be new recruits to their broadly a-nationalist tradition. Their works are often saturated with *hiraeth*, but *hiraeth* accepted as a more or less poetic fact of life, and not a cause for change.

From 1936 onwards, however, the face of Anglo-Welsh letters fissured irreparably, to the extent that, in the minds of some Welsh writing in English, the very epithet became eventually one of abuse.

It was Saunders Lewis (1893–1985) who threw down the gauntlet. This remarkable, towering but sometimes unappealing man was born not in Wales, but in Wallasey, Cheshire. His family, however, was Welsh Calvinist Methodist, with roots in Anglesey, and much of his childhood was spent among the Welsh citizens of Liverpool. He was educated at the Liscard School for Boys, before studying English and French at Liverpool University. It was while at college that his interest in the land of his fathers was kindled. Like others who became ardent for Wales though, his Cymric odyssey appears to have begun with the discovery of Anglo-Irish writing (Yeats, Synge, Padraig Colum) and the Irish cause. On his own admission, the example of the French patriot novelist, propagandist and Catholic apologist Maurice Barrès also nudged him closer to a nationalist position. Later, he would speak sympathetically of Maurras and the French neo-fascist right. During the Great War he served, as an officer, with the South Wales Borderers. Wounded at Cambrai, he subsequently worked in military intelligence in Athens. When he returned to Liverpool to finish his degree, he stayed on at the university to write a thesis later published under the title *A School of Welsh*

Augustans. This showed how a prevailing and very English cultural orthodoxy had been adapted to Welsh ends by Goronwy Owen and other figures of the eighteenth century, and immediately established Lewis as a serious and committed critic of Welsh culture. At the time of its publication, 1924, he was already installed at University College Swansea, as a lecturer in the Welsh Department, and had made a speech to a group of students at the Mold Eisteddfod of 1923, advocating not only home rule for the Welsh, but also the formation of a Welsh militia – even though this would, in some quaint way, be 'non-violent'.

Thereafter Lewis, converting to a Catholicism outspoken in its repudiation of the Nonconformist ethos, divided his energies between the literary and the political. In the same year as the publication of *A School of Welsh Augustans* he helped found Y Mudiad Cymreig, 'The Welsh Movement', a body that soon amalgamated with its northern counterpart, the equally militant Byddin yr Ymreolwyr or 'Home Rule Army', to form, in 1925, the Welsh Nationalist Party, better known by its later name, Plaid Cymru. In 1926 Lewis was elected its President.

The first ten years of Plaid Cymru are notable mainly for its lack of a following. To those who knew about it it seemed little more than a collection of eccentrics who would never persuade the broad mass of Welsh to follow its ways. It did not compete with Labour, as broadly it does today, but rather opposed Labour. Indeed, Saunders Lewis, its most voluble spokesman as well as its leader, deliberately excluded mass participation from his vision of a free and independent Wales. In a 1929 paper delivered to the Celtic Congress in Glasgow he writes: 'Give her [Wales] a government and a capital, and she will in time gather an urban class which will be the basis of a new Welsh aristocracy.'[43] As though to bury all hope of significant electoral support, Lewis also advocated the de-industrialization of the south. Quite where the de-industrialized thousands – by no means all of them 'incomers' – were to live and what they were to do were questions not readily answered. Lewis held up agriculture and rural life as the backbone of his future nation, even though he was something of a townee himself, and saw the Welsh town as the natural home of its rulers. In words that unwittingly and uncannily mock some of the more idealist Welsh-cause poems of R. S. Thomas, Lewis writes:

> It was in a city that I was brought up, in cities that I have had the best experiences of my life. I prefer cities to the countryside, and city life to country life . . . Modern Welsh poets are unfair to cities . . . A sinful life, in their poems, means going to town. Conversion to religion means returning to the hills and fields. Their cities are also too melodramatic. City life is not as infectious as they describe. Nor is country life all purity. One can be as filthy in a cowshed loft as in a Paris hotel.[44]

Claiming to reject all ideologies, he proposed in their place reliance upon the family first, and then the community: a revival, in fact, of the ancient Welsh way of the commote. Nor was he an out-and-out separatist. Rather he wanted an 'independent' Wales to renegotiate its membership of the Union, as a dominion, and thus retain its ties with the monarchy; for 'Monarchy in England is better for Wales than a republic' and 'Wales's links with the English throne are centuries older than its link with the House of Commons.' Indeed, Parliament, in Lewis's view, and not the Crown, was Wales's true enemy; while the Welsh *gwerin*, or ordinary folk, approximate too closely in his conception to *Das Volk* of Nazi propaganda.

Where, one might ask, did Lewis derive his ideas? In essence, it seems, from an idiosyncratic vision of the European Middle Ages, in which kings and princes behaved decently towards their Catholic subjects. To this he added notions gleaned, but not systematized, from an eclectic reading of mainly traditionalist European authors. He was sincere, the more so as, from a Welsh nationalist point of view, the British democratic system stymied rather than encouraged specifically 'Welsh' rights. But, were it not for a most extraordinary thing that happened in 1936, Saunders Lewis might easily, in his political incarnation at least, have passed into the lesser annals of history, and with him the Welsh national party.

The extraordinary episode was a largely symbolic act of arson. In the early hours of 8 September, Saunders Lewis and two other party stalwarts, D. J. Williams and the Rev. Lewis Valentine, fire-bombed some empty huts and a stack of wood at the site of a proposed R A F bombing school at Pen-y-berth on the Llŷn Peninsula. Immediately afterwards, Lewis, Williams and Valentine gave themselves up at the nearest police station.

Ever since, as then, the 'Fire in Llŷn' has struck a chord at the heart of the 'Welsh' imagination. Its very quixoticness, in contrast to the Irish Easter Rising of 1916, could not have been better designed to express (but also promote) the frustrations of a small, proud but peace-loving nation. As 'civil resistance' it was a masterpiece. It put Welsh nationalism on the map where before it had been a joke. David had catapulted his stone, not between Goliath's eyes, but at his feet. Suddenly, from being an able academic but a political crank, Saunders Lewis was a living legend.

The Pen-y-berth Three were brought to trial, on charges of arson and malicious damage, first at the Caernarfon Assize Court, where the defendants were obliged to answer the case against them in English, and then, when the jury failed to reach a verdict, at the Old Bailey. There they were found guilty without the London jury bothering to leave the courtroom. The sentence they received however – nine months in Wormwood Scrubs – was, like the crime, a token one. Even the English judge recognized that to make martyrs out of an act that could have been construed as treasonable would have been unwise. Nevertheless, martyrs they became, in the people's eyes, the embodiment of heroic failure.

For Saunders Lewis, who saw his act of protest in Nietzschean as well as patriotic terms, the penalties were more severe. While still in prison he was dismissed from his post at Swansea University College. Coming out of prison, Lewis announced his 'retirement' from public life. Henceforward he would devote his time to writing. He had already published, in Welsh, a verse drama. He now set about creating a substantial body of work, both plays and poems, that is generally regarded as the greatest individual Welsh-language achievement of the twentieth century. He also, from time to time, continued to make personal interventions in Welsh politics. Immediately after his 'retirement' he began contributing a regular column to the patriotic weekly, *Baner ac Amserau Cymru*. His suggestion that Wales remain neutral during the conflict with Hitler attracted the attention of the censors. His pamphlet *Is There an Anglo-Welsh Litera-ture?*[45] proposed that the term be used exclusively of Welsh writers who wrote about 'Welsh' concerns. Dylan Thomas was not included. Then, in 1962, using his fame as a dramatist and poet, he delivered a radio lecture that galvanized the nation in the same way that the Pen-y-berth episode had done. *Tynged yr Iaith*, as it was called, 'The Fate of the Language', predicted the death of Welsh as a spoken tongue some time in the twenty-first century. A masterpiece of Celtic self-accusation reprimanded Lewis's audience for giving way to faint-heartedness and despair:

> The language is more important than self-government. In my opinion, if any form of self-government came to Wales before the recognition and use of the Welsh language as official language in the entire administration of local and national authorities in the Welsh-speaking parts of our country, then it would never be an official language at all, and the demise of the language would be quicker than it will be under English rule.[46]

This stirring address, delivered of course in Welsh, led directly to the founding of Cymdeithas yr Iaith Gymraeg, the Welsh Language Society, with Lewis as its honorary President. It also fuelled a nation-alist revival that during the course of the 1960s would see Plaid Cymru's first elected MPs, a spate of civil disobedience activities and also the first sustained sabotage campaigns.

Though his close reasoning often lacked commensurate logic, Lewis's analysis was and remains visibly correct. Since the majority of Welsh citizens (to coin a phrase) are not Welsh-speaking it is unlikely that they would elect or even suffer a government that insisted they become so. Ever since the Welsh Language Society has campaigned doggedly to overturn this situation. Were the society to succeed then the case for an independent Wales conducting its affairs in the Welsh medium would be irrefutable. But as Lewis also acknowledges, this is only likely to come about in the 'Welsh-speaking parts', or Welsh Wales, so that what he proposes is in fact the formal division of an already divided country.

In 1969 Lewis opposed Charles Windsor's investiture as the Prince of Wales at Caernarfon, despite his oft declared fealty to the English throne. Seven years later, however, in 1976, he resigned the honorary presidency of the Welsh Language Society. This was the result of another bizarre episode that again concerned a military site, this time at Aberporth, on the west coast. Other members of the society wanted to see off the proposed creation of a missile base. Unexpectedly Lewis came out fighting on the other side. He said a soldier's profession was an honourable calling, and that a sovereign state must always be allowed to protect itself.

The former WWI intelligence officer had resurfaced. For his political inconsistencies Lewis is not to be criticized, at least not too harshly. He was after all Welsh, and passionately so, and divided loyalty is, through no wishing of their own, the unenviable condition of many a Welsh conscience. Indeed it is the determining factor of much contemporary Welsh culture. But even in the Welsh context Saunders Lewis was something of an oddball. If his medievalism was sometimes eccentric, an ambiguity in his attitude towards Hitler challenges liberal tolerance. It is difficult, for example, to read his play *Brad* (1958), 'Betrayal', without reaching the conclusion that Lewis's only objection to Hitler is that he wasn't a Catholic. Some of Lewis's early poems are anti-semitic, although anti-semitism was more rife in parts of Wales – the coal-mining areas, for instance – than anyone is now likely to acknowledge. Nor was Lewis's disdain reserved for Jews. His long Welsh poem 'The Deluge 1939'[47] contains these lines:

> The dregs arose from the empty docks
> Across the dry ropes and rust of cranes,
> Their proletarian flood-tide crept,
> Greasily humble, to the chip shops,
> Loitered, blood about the feet of policemen,
> And spread, a lake of siliconic spit,
> Through the faceless valleys of the industry of the dole.

No amount of casuistry can excuse the vulgarly superior sentiments here expressed towards what in 1939 was a hard-pressed labour force. If Lewis succeeded, as he sometimes did, in arousing the Welsh 'nation', he also bequeathed a legacy of distrust towards some of that nation's self-appointed spokesmen. His legendary aphorism, that 'there is no future for man unless he rejoins the past', could be taken any number of ways, not all of them appealing.

Nonetheless, in the 1940s, as again in the 1960s, Lewis and his immediate coterie were more widely regarded as saints than sinners. After all, how could Welsh consciousness assert itself? History hadn't worked, nor had democracy. In the post-war reconstruction the faceless state, which was also the English state, seemed to be casting its irons ever more deeply into the flesh of Wales. While some rejoiced at the creation of a welfare society, pioneered by the likes of Aneurin Bevan and his Labour associates, or were thankful for its mercies, others adopted a more caustic and embittered view. When, they asked themselves, would it ever be right? When had it ever *been* right?

For writers of both languages, new forums appeared, and old ones were revived. In Welsh there was *Y Fflam*, 'The Flame', launched by Euros Bowen in 1946, and modelled on the pre-war *Tir Newydd*, 'New Land'. There was also *Y Faner*, or *Baner ac Amserau Cymru*, 'The Banner and Times of Wales', a paper originally started in 1859, but which had seen its fortunes rise and fall. Partly because of Saunders Lewis's regular contributions, in the mid-'40s it once again became a voice of Wales, radical and combative in tone. Then in English, there was Keidrych Rhys's *Wales*.

Rhys was a literary type with an eclectic taste and a passion for his country. Although *Wales*, first published by Rhys's own publishing company, the Druid Press in Carmarthen, in 1937, but suspended in 1940, was designed as a showcase for new and 'progressive' talent of whatever hue, Rhys's criterion was, 'though we write in English, we are rooted in Wales.'[48] Relaunched in 1943, *Wales* survived six years, before Rhys took himself off to London and an authorial career of his own. In a 'tenth anniversary' issue, published in the summer of 1947, Rhys proudly printed a list of previous contributors.[49] The roll-call included Dylan Thomas, Caradoc Evans, Glyn Jones, H. L. R. Edwards, Vernon Watkins, Sir Idries Bell, Alun Lewis, Huw Menai, Iorwerth C. Peate and Lynette Roberts, as well George Barker, Robert Graves and John Cowper Powys. But while many of these names represented the old, 'soft' school of Anglo-Welsh writing, the same issue offered pieces by the new, harder school: Vernon Watkins and Glyn Jones were still there, but so too were Emyr Humphreys, Roland Mathias, Davies Aberpennar (Pennar Davies) and R. S. Thomas. Indeed, Thomas contributed, as well as a not wholly complimentary review of poems by Mathias – he has never been shy to criticize his contemporaries – a poem called (what else?) 'Wales'; an allegorical nature poem whose meaning is wrapped up in its references to the *Mabinogion*.

But the figures who seem most to have excited R. S. Thomas's admiration during the 1940s, and for a long time after, were largely absent from the pages of *Wales* for the simple reason they wrote in Welsh. Saunders Lewis has already been mentioned. Of the older poets, T. H. Parry-Williams (1887–1975) was the acknowledged master. A Gwynedd man, Parry-Williams had taken the 1912 Eisteddfod by storm, winning both the Chair and the Crown – a feat he repeated in 1915. At the time he was still a student. He had read Welsh and Latin at Aberystwyth, graduating in 1908 and 1909. A lifelong interest in philology and linguistics had then taken him to Oxford, Freiburg and Paris. In 1914 he had returned to the Welsh Department at Aberystwyth as an assistant lecturer, but in 1919 failed to become Professor of Celtic Studies because he had spoken out against the participation of Welshmen in the Great War. Enraged, Parry-Williams returned to being a student, this time in the Faculty of Medicine. But within a year the Professorship of Welsh fell vacant, and at the age of thirty-three the most brilliant literary mind of his generation was rewarded with a promotion many thought should have been his at the age of thirty-two.

As a poet, Parry-Williams exhibits many qualities that are echoed in the work of R. S. Thomas. His mature voice was spare, intellectually detached, sometimes ungiving; but set against this was an abiding passion for Wales, and an apprehension of a mystic dimension in the landscape of Wales, particularly Eryri (Snowdonia). Even as a young man, witnessing a lunar eclipse at Oerddwr, he could write:

Mae nodau annaearoldeb yn naear y fan
('There are marks of unearthliness in the earth of the place')[50]

The two poems that won the 1912 Eisteddfod had as their subject-matter *Y Mynydd* ('The Mountain') and Geraldus Cambrensis (Gerald of Wales). Technically, Parry-Williams was equally adept at the strict metres and free verse forms, and often sought to combine the two. Indeed it may be said that he propelled Welsh prosody into the twentieth century. Like Thomas, he was a modernist who had at his command centuries of distilled craft. He was also patrician in outlook, and shares with Thomas an obsession with the lonely self and its identity.

Less patrician was David James Jones (1899–1968), better known as Gwenallt. Born a generation after Parry-Williams, Gwenallt was, unusually for anyone admired by R.S., a scion of the industrial southern valleys. His life, however, can be interpreted as a frustrated atonement for that fact. Born near Pontardawe, north of Swansea, Gwenallt grew up in a Welsh-speaking chapel family. The early death of his father, killed in an accident at a local steelworks, contributed to, and may even have set in motion, the future poet's revolt against his background. Forsaking Nonconformity, Gwenallt at first embraced communism, then, during the Great War, he became a pacifist. Twice he was sentenced to imprisonment as a conscientious objector. When the war ended he enrolled to read English and Welsh at Aberystwyth, where he later returned as a lecturer, in fact in Parry-Williams's department. He also returned to Nonconformity, as a Calvinistic Methodist, although his Christian commitment was sufficiently broad-minded to extend a tolerant hand towards Catholicism. At the same time he became a keen supporter of Plaid Cymru, and an intimate of Saunders Lewis.

Like other Welsh-language poets, Gwenallt first established his reputation at the Eisteddfod, winning the Chair in 1926. His important work, however, which includes essays and criticism – Gwenallt was a founder member of Yr Academi Gymreig, the Welsh Academy, 1959, and the first editor of its journal *Taliesin* – eschews the slightly smug aura of that forum. His poetry is prized for its real sense of difficult and contrary emotions anvilled into expression. He is haunted by whatever he has endeavoured to turn his back upon, so that, although his nationalism develops broadly in line with Lewisite imperatives, enough of the young socialist survives to make his writing complex in an interesting way. Even the phrase for which he is best known, his depiction of Wales as an 'unclean street woman' ('*putain fudr y stryd*') needs to be understood as a many-layered utterance. Bitterness however was his forte, as R. S. Thomas, in the concluding lines of his eulogy to Gwenallt, 'A Lecturer',[51] recognized with reciprocal acerbity:

> Watch him,
> As with short steps he goes.
> Not dangerous?
> He has been in gaol.

Another member of what may loosely be termed the Saunders Lewis coterie, who also gave vent to Welsh consciousness in its purgatorial aspect, was Waldo Williams (1904–71). In *Neb* we encounter him as an organizer of the first protest Thomas took part in, against the enlargement of an army base at Trawsfynydd in Meirionydd (later the site of a nuclear power station):

One day Islwyn told him of a plan to go to Trawsfynydd to prevent the military from extending their camp there. The thing was entirely secret, and the day had to be changed because someone blabbed. But finally the day did come, and in the morning the Rector set out for Traws. As he came down into Dolgellau he saw a small crowd outside a café drinking coffee. D. J. Williams was amongst them. So too were Gwynfor [Evans] and Waldo, and many another one, but short of the hundred who had promised to come. Notwithstanding this there were enough, and each took his place on the lane leading to the camp in order to close it. They succeeded well enough by exchanging places from time to time. But when Gwynfor explained how each group of four should replace the group of four in front, Waldo exclaimed [in perfect *cynghanedd*]: 'I see! After some food, the second four.'[52]

On a different occasion, or so it is told, Waldo was effectively placed under house arrest, to prevent his participation in another demonstration. To make sure he stayed put, the police turned up in a van at his cottage in Mynachlogddu (North Pembrokeshire) to remove his bicycle. As they were about to drive off Waldo called them back from his gate: 'You forgot this!' he cried out joyfully, holding up a bicycle pump. But although he was full of jests, Waldo Williams is the most strangely impressive of all the patriotic poets. Only one collection of his work was published in his lifetime, *Dail Pren*, 'Leaves of the Tree', and that not until 1956. Up until then, his poetry was known only through magazines and newspapers. Yet even in the late 1940s, among the Welsh literati, his was a name to be conjured with.

Waldo's father was a Haverfordwest schoolmaster. He was also a Baptist, a pacifist and an articulate radical. These strands passed largely undistorted to the son. Unlike many of his contemporaries and near-contemporaries, Waldo was, from an early age, morally and psychologically centred; at least, there is little evidence that he experienced those convulsions of identity which have affected other Welsh writers. Rather there was a convincing roundness to his personality that emerges in the poetry as a largesse, even immensity of soul. There was pain in his life – the childhood death of a sister, and the death of his wife after only a year of marriage, in 1943; but the pain came more from the outside than from the inside. As a pacifist he was a relentless campaigner, both in defence of his homeland in rural West Wales against the encroachments of the military, and more broadly in defence of humanity. Famously in 1950 he announced that he would withhold income tax in protest against the Korean War, which the British government supported; and in 1960 and 1961 he twice went to prison rather than contribute to the state's nuclear arsenal.

Hiroshima was as fit a subject for his verse as the despoilment of his native Preseli hillsides. His passion for Wales was matched by a belief, naive perhaps, in an essential fraternity among mankind. He was nonetheless a fervent supporter of Plaid Cymru, and stood, unsuccessfully, as a candidate in the parliamentary election of 1959. To Waldo there was no disjunction between the active and contemplative life. His poetry is valued by Welsh readers for its combination of the Romantic, the concrete and the mystic in roughly equal measures, and with almost outlandish success.

Many others besides Parry-Williams, Saunders Lewis, Gwenallt and Waldo supplied the creative milieu out of which the rector of

Manafon emerged as a figure in his own right. The poet and Eis-
teddfodwr Sir Albert Evans-Jones ('Cynan', 1895–70) should be
mentioned, as should the novelist Kate Roberts (1891–1985), and
the 'London' Welsh artist and writer David Jones (1895–1974),[53]
author of *In Parenthesis* (1937); but individual portraits, even quick
thumb-nail sketches like those above, are preferable to lists. The
point to be made – and one he would undoubtedly wish to make
himself – is that R. S. Thomas, for all that his poetry projects the
image of an anguishedly isolated man, belonged if not to a regi-
mented school then to a flow, a sea of sorts. To deny him such Welsh
antecedents and influences would be to deny him Wales itself.

This sense of a provenance becomes quite clear if, before turning
to the poetry, we cast an eye over the prose Thomas wrote at Manafon.
Critics of Thomas, while mindful of his essays and other occasional
writings, have tended to see them as being subordinate to the poems,
useful only for whatever added light they can shed on the latter. But
once we regard Thomas as a cultural operator, as well as a significant
poet, his prose pieces, some of which were written in Welsh, take
on a life of their own.

The earliest essay is entitled 'The Depopulation of the Welsh Hill
Country', and was published by Keidrych Rhys in *Wales* in 1945.[54]
Thomas's concern here is the decay and threatened elimination
of the uplands farming communities such as he had discovered in
Montgomeryshire, but his tone alternates between the ‘idyllic
and the jejune. The depopulation of the Welsh hills he com-
pares to the destruction of crofter society in Scotland. Up on the
moors,

> The imagination busies itself with the idea of some poetically-minded
> hill farmer in love with solitude, with a kitchen that might prove
> the perfect setting for a *noson lawen*.[55] But wait a moment. Turn your
> binoculars on it and what do you find? A broken chimney and gaping
> windows. The place is uninhabited and is being used as a kind of
> dilapidated *hafod*,[56] or Scotch shieling, by a neighbouring farmer,
> who lives somewhere nearer civilisation, but who is himself probably
> a mere bailiff for someone in the richer, more fertile lowlands.

And so on across the whole roof of Wales. But it is not the disrepair of the buildings that grieves the rector so much as the men who have 'been forced to abandon them, thus losing for ever their real meaning in life'.

But how can Thomas substantiate such a claim? Despite the countless ruined homesteads, he tells us, there are yet a 'considerable number' of small farms and crofts where 'the true Welsh peasantry' subsist, armed with 'ready smiles and carefree ways' – a far cry from the much grimmer portrait he will present of Iago Prytherch and his kind in the poetry. But having adopted this tack, Thomas sticks to it, because it is the tack that most usefully serves his bucolically nationalist purpose. Those who remain in the uplands 'are happy too, and have no wish to change. Happy as cuckoos the lowlanders call them with something of contempt, although one suspects a certain envy there too.' Even though such people are 'but the shadows of what their fathers were' their lives are 'more colourful and more interesting' than those of their materially more prosperous counterparts. And to support this assertion, Thomas spins out a quick tapestry of poets, musicians, *penillion*[57] singers, and men possessed of a rare personality, who will pass into local tradition as *hen gymeriadau*, 'old characters': among them one eighty-three-year-old who 'died having no English': 'A terrible condition for a Briton of the twentieth century? No, he was as merry and much more interesting than the crickets which sang to him from his hearth.' These presumably were the same characters Thomas despairs of discussing higher matters with in *Neb*.

It is all rather absurd. Without doubt, a way of life was disappearing in the Welsh uplands, and this may have been regrettable to those left behind. But why should Thomas the migrant pastor be so nostalgically concerned? The answer of course lies in the essay's ideological underpinning. With regard to the uplands, Thomas tells us, 'No one who knows this district intimately, but can feel its wayward and carefree charm, realise that here still, however faintly, beats the old heart of Wales.' Yet this is ruined by an earlier contention: 'How often has it been said that the health and wealth of a country depends upon its possession of a sturdy, flourishing peasantry?' Is such a peasantry the essence of 'Wales', or only a necessary condition?

As either sociology or anthropology, 'The Depopulation of the Welsh Hill Country' is inadequate. It is the subjectivity of its author, and his insistence upon what his reader must think, that come across as the essay's actual themes. 'Are not three-quarters of our modern ills due to the fact that we have forgotten how to live, being unable or unwilling to allow ourselves time to relax?' Thomas asks; but the question is never more than rhetorical. It is Thomas's own nostalgia that the essay elaborates. He is preaching to a readership of the converted, himself one of its newer, and rawer, recruits.

The rawness disperses however. Consciously or otherwise, Thomas soon finds his range as a cultural nationalist. The following year, 1946, the autumn issue of *Wales*[58] carried a second essay by R. S., 'Some Contemporary Scottish Writing', and also his responses to a 'Wales' questionnaire that Keidrych Rhys had sent to a number of English-writing Welsh authors. In the latter, Thomas turns on a new voice: authoritative, dismissive, a little vain and with a penchant for obiter dicta. It is as though he is already rehearsing the part of Welsh Oracle:

For whom do you write? Yeats's words come to mind:

> All day I'd looked in the face
> What I had hoped 'twould be
> To write for my own race
> And the reality.

The urge to write is instinctive in me, but there is present almost simultaneously the hope that my friends, my countrymen, those nearest to me may still sift a little gold out of what I have wrought.

What is your opinion of the relationship between Literature and Society? Yeats's gyres, Jacob and the angel, Paul's flesh and spirit, there come to mind a hundred images which seek to express two mutually dependent entities, each striving to be free, yet each reacting upon the other.

Should 'Anglo-Welsh literature' express a Welsh attitude to life and affairs, or should it merely be literature about Welsh things? 'Ye shall know them by their fruits.' In other words, let every 'Anglo-Welsh' writer be a Welshman first, a writer secondly, and leave others to feel the mountain shadow darkening upon his words, and hear the clear stream bickering through his sentences.

And again:

> To the artist . . . a sense of Welsh Nationhood should be consistent with a very definite attitude to life and affairs, namely the constant realisation that he lives in or belongs to a country of great age, that by geography and tradition has developed an individual way of life, and that his chief duty as an artist is to beautify, to purify and to enlarge that way of life. After all, why chant the praise of Helen, when Nêst remains unsung?

and adding: 'Why worry primarily about the starving people of India or China, when our own countrymen are walking the roads?'

'Some Contemporary Scottish Writing'[59] is more self-consciously judicious, or at least starts that way, as Thomas seeks to combine the two roles of literary reporter and nationalist. Inevitably his interest in Scottish writing is slanted towards the 'Scottish renaissance', and he employs a version of the 'no true Scotsman' argument;[60] anyone who is Scottish and doesn't contribute to the revival of Scottish consciousness cannot be a real Scotsman. By extension the same applies to Welshmen and Welsh writers. Inevitably his hero is Hugh MacDiarmid,[61] not only a poet of the first rank, but also as a founder of the Scottish National Party. Along the way, however, Thomas takes every opportunity to swipe as best he may at whatever doesn't take his fancy. Praising MacDiarmid for his use of the Scottish word 'laverock' (i.e. lark), he asks whether it does not 'awaken memories of what we used to call the bird before the stranger came with his superior lisp?' Commending Douglas Young's translation of Valéry's *Le Cimetière marin*, he dismisses the 'clap-trap of so-called progressive writers'. He also attacks his own compatriots, some Welsh-speakers among them: 'There are people living under the harsh crags of Cader Idris and Yr Wyddfa, or on the bare gaunt moorland of central Wales, but their verse is tame to the point of lifelessness.' What he urges in its place is 'an air of fierceness' that in turn will stimulate 'the expression of *saeva indignatio*'.

But that is only the beginning of it. Thomas's survey of Scots letters gives way to a diatribe about Welsh writing, and what he conceives to be the way forward. But there is a twofold difficulty for him. First, as a poet he had so far written only in English, and in fact always would. Therefore, like it or not, he is obliged to confront the issues bound up in the phrase 'Anglo-Welsh'. Secondly, although there were Scottish writers who wrote in the old Gaelic language, most notably Sorley Maclean, the Scottish revival consisted in refurbishing 'broad Scots', a language that, having the same parentage as English, is more or less accessible to the English ear. For the Welsh literary nationalists – Saunders Lewis primarily, but also R. S. – the problem was quite different: how to expand the remit of a language that had largely been thrust aside as a lingua franca, while at the same time preserving its high culture status.

Faced with all this, the argument Thomas develops is not especially ordered, but rather a series of possible positions, some of them overstated. The poet Adam Drinam is singled out for 'his success in conveying an unmistakably Scottish atmosphere by means of the English tongue'. Thomas immediately continues:

> I cannot yet see how we Welsh poets writing in English are to surmount the fact that much of our environment bears names which are irreducible to English, such as *bwlch, cwm, talar*,[62] and so on, but a man like Drinam shows us how to begin.
>
> For our own part the best thing we younger poets can do is to follow Saunders Lewis's advice and read more of the typical Welsh writers like Emrys ap Iwan.[63] For all we know, our movement may be a phase in the re-cymrification of Wales. What of it?

Indeed, what of it? But in a page or two, Thomas has second thoughts, as though he were still in the process of drafting a personal manifesto:

> . . . if those of us who write in English would read more widely among such men as Dafydd ap Gwilym, Tudur Aled, and Goronwy Owen, as well as paying more attention to the discipline of the strict metres, our work might begin to show some difference from that of the essentially urban-minded English poets who write for the most part in a highly sophisticated manner and with a consistently town outlook.

Then, as though suddenly surprised by the spectre of a truly ghastly hybrid, having muddied his waters once he muddies them again:

> Of course, we must be honest. The muse is not to be browbeaten into singing an accompaniment to an ideology. We have ample proof of that not only in the work of some of the London political poets, like Julian Symons, but in that of John Singer, whose book, *The Fury of the Living*, is a peculiar mixture of Whitmanesque and traditional verse, interspersed with occasional pieces of a more individual and moving quality. But if communism is not sufficient in itself to lift verse to the level of poetry, neither is nationalism, which in a way is only the communism which begins at home. We must beware of lauding work merely because it has a national flavour. Poetry can still be bad poetry for all its tang. Whatever we mean by good poetry, we are agreed that it always possesses the 'rich, authentic tone', and until we have cleared away a great deal of the rubbish in which we are as a generation bogged fast, until we have rinsed our eyes in the clear Welsh stream, and rid our ears of the continual, monotonous drone of modern propaganda, we shall continue in our aimless cacophony.

Stirring stuff, to be sure, but even in its own terms devoid of steady sense. Thomas, in his eagerness to break every mould around him, says too much in too short a space, however much, in the context of his own poetry, individual clauses and sentences have a resounding clarity.

'Some Contemporary Scottish Writing' goes on yet further. As Thomas adds in more and more of his bugbears, his emotions overcome him:

> Most British history in the English tongue is traced from the Roman period onwards, and this conception of England as the cradle of British civilisation has been gradually foisted upon the Cymric and Gaelic peoples, and until recently was rarely questioned. But now a new Don Quixote has arisen in Scotland [i.e. MacDiarmid] to break a lance with the all-pervading twentieth-century rationalism that goes hand in hand with western democracy and industrial development. Perhaps it would hearten him to know that his good servant, Sancho Panza,[64] keeps up the fight in Wales against the same enemy.

The exaggeration and conflation in these three sentences are such that they actually damage the very real arguments that can be advanced in defence of a Welsh nationalist position. Most sensible historians, even of the earlier century, however Anglo-centric, do not in fact regard the Roman invasion as the beginning of British history, nor the English as an unmixed race. How else is it that Boudicca has been a national heroine since the eighteenth century? Nor do they confine rationalism to the development of democracy and industry, or see those projects as being exclusively English. By 'most British history' Thomas means a certain sort of history taught in the lower grades of school; but he refrains from saying this.

Sticking with MacDiarmid, Thomas notes that he 'may record his recreation in *Who's Who* as anglophobia, but it is the quislings and lickspittles in his own country that are his chief enemies'. Then, calling upon Fionn MacColla's novel *And the Cock Crew*, he comments: 'The book is also valuable to us Welsh people in its portrayal of Calvinism's paralysing effect on the will of the Highlanders to active resistance.' And in case his firebrand message is not clear, on the next page he spells it out:

> It is against the English conception of Scotland, a one-sided view down to which generations of Scots have been levelled, a view fostered and supported by directors of education and the capitalist press, a Scotland of 'chortling wut', that MacDiarmid is fighting, and it is against a similar conception of Wales that we should take up arms.

Take up arms? But just how metaphoric is this? 'The reader may think,' Thomas expatiates, 'I am now confusing literary with political aims, but if we subscribe to Shelley's description of the poet as unacknowledged legislator, then it is only by upholding such an ideal in poetry that we can at long last change the people and lead them back to their essential dignity.' And again, though more perspicaciously: 'It is a formidable task this winnowing and purifying of the people, because it so nearly forms a vicious circle.'

Unwittingly perhaps, Thomas had put his finger on it. His 'formidable task' calls into question the very legitimacy of 'cultural nationalism', which, in the available typologies of nationalism, is widely considered as a prerequisite of militant nationalism. The 'winnowing and purifying' of a people is a grandiloquent phrase, but is suggestive of nothing so much as propagandizing, even brainwashing. It replaces a conception of art as that which holds a mirror up to life with something far more wilful, far more pro-active. And the irony of it is that, to prepare this move, Thomas invokes Shelley, an English socialist, and therefore, from the point of view of his particular nationalism, a double anathema. Unless, that is, one allows the improbable contention that 'nationalism' is indeed 'only the communism which begins at home'; but that can only be done by stripping 'communism' of its Marxist-Leninist understanding Thomas appears to allow a few lines earlier.

But what is interesting in these writings is not that Thomas fails to forge a consistent manifesto for himself, but that he tries. One senses all along that he wants to close on a four-wall deal: a Welsh nationalism based on the Welsh language that will expunge the Industrial Revolution and with it Nonconformity. In this he is not unlike Saunders Lewis. Like Lewis he knows this deal is unrealistic; but unlike Lewis he also finds himself partially excluded from it. He writes his poetry in English. He is also a pacifist, so that the ultimate logic of the nationalist position – 'we should take up arms'– is problematic.

Paradoxically, had Thomas succeeded in serving his muse in Welsh, then the strong possibility is he would not have gone on to write so much poetry, or poetry of such troubled power. As it was he managed only two poems in Welsh, and then conceded the day.[65] But by 1946 he had sufficient confidence in his Welsh prose to begin contributing the occasional piece to Y Fflam. He also translates into English a story, 'The Guests', by Dilys Cadwaladr, which Keidrych Rhys published in Wales in 1948.[66]

Of the Welsh essays written at Manafon, two demand attention. 'Llenyddiaeth Eingl-Cymreig', 'Anglo-Welsh Literature', appeared in Y Fflam in 1952. This shows that, despite a six-year passage, Thomas has still not resolved the issues raised in 'Some Contemporary Scottish Writing'. The very term 'Anglo-Welsh' rankles:

What is it? Literature by Welsh people about Welsh things? Literature by English people about Wales? Or literature by Welsh people about any subject at all? We have examples of all three in the work of men such as Caradoc Evans, Thomas Love Peacock and Vernon Watkins. One can, no doubt, group such writers together to make a 'school' but the sum of their contributions does not necessarily create a literature with a feel of its own to it.[67]

But where is this 'feel' to come from? Thomas now tries a critical solution. Rather than invoke the ideology of his fellow nationalists, he turns first to Matthew Arnold, then to the scholar and critic Sir Idris Bell (1879–1967). Arnold he rightly rejects on the grounds that the qualities he identifies as 'Celtic' are not in fact peculiar to Celtic literature. But Bell, Thomas thinks, is 'closer to the mark' 'when he describes the chief characteristics of Welsh literature as "a feeling for discipline; a love of clear concise and elegant phrasing; a force and precision of utterance"'. But really this is too diffuse. The objection against Arnold holds equal force against Bell. The same virtues can, for example, be extracted from the *Ars Poetica* of Horace. The only special circumstance is the 'feeling for discipline' in the sense that *cynghanedd* probably is the most complex prosodic system known to man. But even that works both ways. For the talented poet the strict metres are indeed a compelling challenge. But it can also be restricting. In lesser hands it produces no more than a species of sometimes meaningless needlepoint.

Nonetheless Thomas struggles on, half aware that creativity and iron laws do not go hand in hand: 'Perhaps it is *possible*, even in Wales, for an artist to create whatever he wants to, but is it *right*? That is what some of the English-speaking Welsh have forgotten in seeking to satisfy only the English. They have sinned against their own nation.' The commissar in Thomas wins through. He observes that the English have a 'name' for his third category of writers, and that the name is 'Regionalism':

What is this but another name for 'blood transfusion'? The ageing body of English literature will stave off death so long as new blood continues to flow into it. From where have the chief influences of English literature come over the last half-century if not from men such as James Joyce in prose, and Manley Hopkins, Edward Thomas, Wilfred Owen and Dylan Thomas in poetry – the first an Irishman, and the others all Welsh? The tragedy for the Welsh language culture is that these writers have had to write in English, indeed one must say in fairness to them that the majority of the Anglo-Welsh school write in English not by whim but by necessity. We have been deprived of our heritage.

What, one wonders, is the true purpose of any literature? But, by means of an extraordinary somersault – in effect substituting 'mainstream' for 'regionalism' – Thomas has boxed himself in and boxed in he stays: 'My view is this: since there is in Wales a mother-tongue that continues to flourish, a proper Welshman can only look on English as a means of rekindling interest in the Welsh-language culture, and of leading people back to the mother tongue.' As an individual or personal strategy, this is of course perfectly allowable. If Thomas feels that is what he wants to do, then by all means let him do it. But where he confounds the issue is by refloating the 'no true Scotsman' argument – in this case, the 'no proper Welshman' argument. And to emphasize his bias, he goes on to tell us, apparently with a perfectly straight face, that because far too many English-speaking Welsh writers have come from the 'industrial areas' they therefore 'tend . . . to give an unbalanced picture of Wales, creating the impression that it is a land of coal miners. But to me the true Wales is to be found in the country.'

Plus ça change. In an earlier Welsh essay, however, *Dau Gapel*, 'Two Chapels',[68] published in *Y Fflam*, Thomas leavens his bread, to the extent that he acknowledges the central position of Nonconformity within the Welsh matrix, although in other respects he bakes a familiar cake. Nonconformity is considered purely in a Welsh context, and Thomas's starting point is the landscape. Both the chapels he considers – Maes-yr-Onnen in Radnorshire, and Soar-y-Mynydd in Cardiganshire – are located in the deep countryside. They are characterized as the 'Chapel of the Spirit' and the 'Chapel of the Soul'. The people who built them, he suggests, are, or were, the inheritors of the earlier 'saints' who founded monastic communities in difficult places. But again, what Thomas discovers is largely in the eye of the beholder, and the weather plays its part. At Maes-yr-Onnen, with a stiff wind blowing from the east, he has a near mystic experience. He imagines the first congregation, two centuries earlier, creeping inside, their 'soft' voices and rustling of the pages of the Bible mingling with the wind.

> And almost immediately I saw, I understood. As with St John the Divine on the island of Patmos I was 'in the spirit' and I had a vision, in which I could comprehend the breadth and length and depth and height of the mystery of creation. But I won't try to put the experience into words. It would be impossible. I will simply say that I realised there was no such thing as time, no beginning and no end but that everything is a fountain welling up endlessly from immortal God.

Yet it is the 'Chapel of the Soul', Soar-y-Mynydd, that Thomas claims to prefer. The day he visits it is cold and cloudy, albeit the month is August. The 'only sounds to break the silence were the thin, complaining voice of the stream and the constant drip of moisture from the trees'. The place is deserted, but unlike Maes-yr-Onnen, well kept up. Patently Soar-y-Mynydd is still in use, and the congregation Thomas imagines is the present-day one, members of a 'scattered community' making their weekly Sunday trek across the moorlands from their 'hidden, inaccessible homes'. And contemplating this,

> I saw the soul of a special type of man, the Cymro or Welshman. For the very source of Welsh life as it is today is here in the middle of these remote moorlands in Cardiganshire. And it is in places of this sort that the soul of the true Welshman is formed.

Instead of a mystic vision, a communion with nature. Thomas experiences at Soar-y-Mynydd an intense longing, 'a longing for some small chapel like this in the Welsh hills, with its small congregation of sober down-to-earth people'.

The choice Thomas makes is indicative of his temperament at the time. Curiously, his second collection of poetry, *An Acre of Land* (1952), contains a beautifully crafted sonnet in fact called 'Maes-yr-Onnen'.[69] By invoking, for the first time in his verse, the *Mabinogion* figure Rhiannon in the concluding lines of the poem, Thomas seems here to be placing the 'Chapel of the Spirit' at the heart of his Wales:

> You cannot hear as I, incredulous, heard
> Up in the rafters, where the bell should ring,
> The wild, sweet singing of Rhiannon's birds.

In the context of the whole of Thomas's poetry, the contest between the spirit and the soul, in as far as it is a real contest, is never so easily settled. But in 1948, and in his prose, it is the political that suborns the religious. Like his other essays, 'Dau Gapel' again gives way to schematic diatribe in its conclusions.

> Speaking of denominations, I must admit that Nonconformity wins hands down. The formal ostentation of Catholicism won't do here. And the Church in Wales isn't any longer Welsh enough in spirit. But there is something else to be said. I haven't much to say to mysticism and other-worldliness; this is obvious from my choice of Soar-y-Mynydd over Maes-yr-Onnen. Nor, in my opinion, do these things appeal to the Welsh as a nation either. I am always ready to admit the value of the spirit, but how often do we hear today of the spiritual as something opposed to ideas of nationalism and so on. The truth is that a nation fighting for its survival cannot afford to change its soul for some obscure spirituality no matter now excellent that may be from the individual's point of view.

Thomas is prepared, in other words, to set aside his own religious experience, the vision of creation, for the more immediate matter of his people. Yet even there it doesn't end. For he is adamant that it is in the Welsh countryside that the Welsh soul, 'strong and deep', is and must be forged, and he ends with a predictable flourish against those communities that other Nonconformist chapels served by the thousand: 'In the towns, especially the towns in England, what else awaits you but the spiritual? But towns are not characteristic of Wales, they are evidence of foreign influence, and the sooner they disappear the better.'

And Thomas the churchman? In addition to Y Fflam, Thomas also contributed, most usually through the correspondence column, to the Church in Wales's Welsh-language weekly Y Llan. Indeed his first writing in Welsh appeared in this paper, as early as 1945.[70] In a letter printed in September 1949[71] we again find Thomas's neck sticking out as far as it will reach. On this occasion he traps his target, the Church in Wales itself, in a pincer movement: from both the nationalist and the pacifist viewpoints the Church is seen to have failed:

> Despite the two ugly wars which have gone by, there is continuous talk of another war, and considerable preparation in that direction. In the face of all this there are some preaching pacifism, some others demanding Welsh regiments, while the majority of our young people will be quietly joining the British army. Is the Church in Wales giving any consistent guidance in these circumstances? It isn't. It is accepting things as they are, as it did before and during the last war ... And things as they are smell of Englishness and Englishness is under suspicion now, because it has a bad reputation, not only in Wales, but in the world.

The English, or at any rate a majority of them, are 'contemptuous of the Welsh nation'. In this, Thomas admonishes, 'they are discourteous, if not un-Christian.' Why, he asks, is it necessary to have bilingual churches in areas that are 'wholly Welsh', simply because 'there's a rich English person living there?' If such a person wants to worship, then 'let him learn its language'.

In one respect at least, Thomas had parted company with Saunders Lewis. The medieval conception of Christendom as a single community of souls regardless of race, language and sovereignty, has little place in these sentiments. Rather we see, in the prose utterances, an early adumbration of that exclusionary coalescence of God and Wales that, in some of the poetry, may cause even the Welsh reader misgiving. Yet the same impulse, a raising of the drawbridge to seal off a moated retreat, also enabled Thomas to launch a sustained assault on what he perceives as the invasive materialism and godlessness of the twentieth century.

Throughout his career Thomas's poems have appeared in a wide variety of magazines and journals. At Manafon he continued to contribute poetry to the *Dublin Magazine*, and, until its demise, to *Wales*. He was also an early and regular contributor to *Dock Leaves*, a literary magazine set up in Pembroke Dock in 1949 under the editorship of Raymond Garlick,[72] renamed the *Anglo-Welsh Review* in 1957. But from early on R. S. sought, and found, a readership beyond the so-called 'Celtic fringe'. 'A Peasant', as we have already seen, appeared in the London-based *Life and Letters*, albeit in a specifically Welsh issue. Thereafter, in the 1940s and early 1950s, poems by Thomas were to be found in forums as diverse as *Horizon*, *Poetry* (London), *Counterpoint*, *Encounter*, the *New Statesman*, *Outposts*, *Time and Tide*, the *Listener* and *The Times Literary Supplement*. So too with his verse collections. The first, *The Stones of the Field* (1946), was published, at Thomas's own expense, by Keidrych Rhys's Druid Press in Carmarthen. The second, *An Acre of Land* (1952), was produced by the Montgomeryshire Printing Company, in nearby Newtown. The same firm also published his radio drama, *The Minister*, the following year, 1953. But in 1955 R. S. Thomas's wider arrival was marked by the appearance of *Song at the Year's Turning*, from the London house of Rupert Hart-Davis.

Song at the Year's Turning was, in effect, a Manafon retrospective. It contained, as well as *The Minister* and a handful of poems collected in book form for the first time, generous selections from both *Stones of the Field* and *An Acre of Land*. It also contained an 'Introduction' by John Betjeman. According to an interview given by Thomas in 1990,[73] his work had been introduced to Hart-Davis by the novelist James Hanley, then living at Llanfechain, and to whom *Song at the Year's Turning* is dedicated. Previously R. S. had approached a number of London editors, including T. S. Eliot at Faber's, but without success. Betjeman's midwifery must have made up for at least some of the disappointment, although the suspicion must be that the future Poet Laureate, for all the fulsomeness of his praise, failed to grasp either the true range or depth of Thomas's verse. There is also, in Betjeman's preface, not a little of that condescension of the English towards the Welsh that has so often infuriated the latter. 'Though he is essentially a local poet,' he writes, the appeal of R. S. Thomas goes beyond the Welsh border. There certainly have been local descriptive poets whose work will be fully enjoyed only by those who know the locality they describe, for instance the parson poets of the eighteenth century who wrote heroic couplets or Thomsonian blank verse in praise of hills and ruins in their own neighbouring parishes. R. S. Thomas is himself a parson, the rector of a parish in Wales. He is of Welsh origin and was born in Cardiff. He taught himself Welsh when adult and his knowledge of the language helped him to understand the remote hill people who appear so clearly in these poems.

It is to the pastoral tradition that Betjeman confines his appreciation of R. S. Reaching reflexively for Samuel Lewis's 1840 topographical dictionary of Wales, and its entry under 'Manafon', the English poet observes that 'R. S. Thomas breathes the wind and the wild flowers into this estate agent's language.' But, after an unfocused digression on the impact of Calvinist Methodism on the Montgomeryshire community (again derived from Lewis) – 'A feeling for Dissent in R. S. Thomas's poetry gives it a peculiar Welshness,' he says lamely – and an acknowledgement of the influence of W. B. Yeats, Betjeman comes good at the close: 'This retiring poet had no wish for an introduction to be written to his poems, but his publisher believed that a "name" was needed to help sell the book. The "name" which has the honour to introduce this fine poet to a wider public will be forgotten long before that of R. S. Thomas.'

But it is not simply that Betjeman limits Thomas to the pastoral; it is that his sense of the pastoral is itself too narrow. For the time this was surprising, even for someone as conspicuously unwilling to intellectualize, or indulge in intellectual faddism, as Betjeman. A critic so much in vogue that he was neither easily nor lightly to be ignored was the poet William Empson. Although Empson's *Seven Types of Ambiguity* (1930) remains his unsurpassed critical achievement, *Some Versions of Pastoral* (1935), for all the eccentricity of its brilliance, was also a turning point in English studies. In it, Empson expanded the purview of 'pastoral' far beyond its normative connotation of a self-contained genre descriptive of the countryside and its inhabitants. Rather he showed that the constituents of pastoral are apt to break in, or break out, at the most unexpected places. His method, however, is demonstrative rather than exegetical. Instead of presenting his findings as a laboriously maintained argument, he offers a series of essays, each an excursion into what he considered a key element of his theme. Thus, inter alia, we are given 'Proletarian Literature'; 'Double Plots: Heroic and Pastoral in the Main Plot and Sub-Plot'; 'They That Have Power: Twist of Heroic Pastoral Ideas in Shakespeare into an Ironical Acceptance of Aristocracy'; 'The Beggar's Opera: Mock Pastoral as the Cult of Independence'; even 'Alice in Wonderland: The Child as Swain'. Pastoral, in other words, is not so much a branch of literature as a river that waters its plains.

But Empson also uses his enlarged understanding of what may be at stake in 'pastoral' to re-stretch prima facie members of the traditional genre into newly perceived configurations: Gray's Elegy, for example, or Marvell's Garden. 'Good writing,' he proposes at the very outset of his inquiry, 'is not done unless there are serious forces at work; and it is not permanent unless it works for readers with opinions different from the author's.'[74] Thus. 'The essential trick of old pastoral,' he writes, 'which was felt to imply a beautiful relation between rich and poor, was to make simple people express strong feelings (felt as the most universal subject, something fundamentally true about everybody) in learned and fashionable language (so that you wrote about the best subject in the best way). From seeing two sorts of people combined like this you thought better of both; the best parts of both were used.'[75] And again:

> The feeling that life is essentially inadequate to the human spirit, and yet that a good life must avoid saying so, is naturally at home with most versions of pastoral; in pastoral you take a limited life and pretend it is the full and normal one, and the suggestion that one must do this with all life, because the normal is itself limited, is easily put into the trick though not necessary to its power. Conversely any expression of the idea that all life is limited may be regarded as only a trick of pastoral, intended to hold all our attention and sympathy for some limited life, though again this is not necessary to it either on grounds of truth or beauty; in fact the suggestion of pastoral may be only a protection for the idea which must at last be taken alone.[76]

Leading to: 'This indeed is one of the assumptions about pastoral, that you can say everything about complex people by a complete consideration of simple people.'[77]

If we recall 'A Peasant', the first outing of Iago Prytherch in Thomas's poetry, these propositions have the resonance of timpani. Whether in fact Thomas was familiar with Empson's essay in the 1940s, either at first or second hand, is not known, and is perhaps immaterial. What matters is an uncanny affinity between two quite disparate figures, and two quite disparate minds, at a level that is at once subterranean and conceptual. It is as though, having absorbed Empson's critique, Thomas responds with a counter-critique, a counter-pastoral of his own; but in so doing vindicates Empson's central assumption that 'serious forces' make a final mockery of the genre approach.

In fact many, if not most, of the poems included in Thomas's first three collections have to do with a particular Welsh landscape and its inhabitants. But Thomas's use of those inhabitants is anything but consoling. In this way he both voices and explodes the 'trick' of pastoral described by Empson. For one thing, he does not claim ever fully to 'know' such inhabitants. There is an opaqueness about them he cannot finally penetrate. For another, far from enabling the poet to come to terms with his own discretionary existence, Thomas's peasantry induce an acute discomfort. And this state of mind and emotion is replicated in his responses towards other existential manifestations that are equally important to him, but equally elusive: Wales and God. Further, because his contemplation of each of the three subject-matters, or orders of being, induces a roughly equivalent agitation, the three become integrated, as though, in all the world, there were a single source of vexation: in Empson's gloss, the essential inadequacy of life.

This is reflected even in the title of the first collection, *The Stones of the Field*, taken from the Book of Job: 'For thou shalt be in league with the stones of the field.'[78] Job, it will be remembered, was stripped of great earthly riches by God in order to test his faith. In a series of dialogues with his friends, Job reveals that his faith is indeed tested: he rails against his tormentor, but in so doing displays his own vanity. 'Art thou the first man that was born?' Eliphaz asks him, 'or wast thou made before the hills?'[79] And again: 'Are the consolations of God small with thee? is there any secret thing with thee?'[80] Only when Job acknowledges God's simple force majeure are his lands and his chattels restored. But there is no firm promise of a more lasting salvation, so that the Book of Job remains memorably at odds with later Christian thought. Job's lament, summarized in the words, 'For we are but of yesterday, and know nothing because our days upon earth are a shadow',[81] goes unparried. At best, 'the ear trieth words, as the mouth trieth meat.'[82]

Thomas never expressly identifies himself with Job, but a sense of personal trial, of being cast into a wilderness, informs several of the poems in *The Stones of the Field*, notably 'A Priest to His People':[83]

Men of the hills, wantoners, men of Wales,
With your sheep and your pigs and your ponies, your sweaty females,
How I have hated you for your irreverence, your scorn even
Of the refinements of art and the mysteries of the Church,
I whose invective would spurt like a flame of fire
To be quenched always in the coldness of your stare,

The address here is declamatory, as Yeats is often declamatory, and the tone almost infinitely bitter. Already though the core ingredients of Thomas's mental universe have been introduced: the peasantry, Wales and, via the 'mysteries of the Church', God. And the problem for Thomas is that they are, at first sight, antithetical. Something must give, and what gives is the poet-priest's own implied identity as the keeper of the mysteries of the Church, and with it the mysteries themselves. Why should, he asks, his congregation come to him for 'crumbs', as though they were sparrows, when in fact their hands 'dabble in the world's blood'? And the resolution, presented in the poem's third section, is as much an admission of personal defeat:

I have taxed your ignorance of rhyme and sonnet,
Your want of deference to the painter's skill.
But I know, as I listen, that your speech has in it
The source of all poetry, clear as a rill
Bubbling from your lips; and what brushwork could equal
The artistry of your dwelling on the bare hill?

Yet there seems something palpably incomplete about this surrender. For one thing the verse is elaborately formal, and remains so to the close. Rhyme, and also alliteration, increases as the poem unfolds. For another, there is no suggestion on the poet's part that he is ready to abandon his other role as priest. He remains the arbiter of reality in both guises. What begins as a harangue develops as the accretion of sorrow. Yet set against this is the deft impress of William Blake:

> What immortal hand or eye
> Could frame thy fearful symmetry?[84]

What immortal hand/what brushwork; could equal/could frame; symmetry/artistry. The ghosting is too adjacent to be accidental, even though the metrics are divergent. The unspecified mysteries of the Church are rendered redundant by the irreducibly more manifest mystery of life on the bare hill – just as it is the tiger that commands Blake's surrender. Similarly, the poet's art is superseded. God, Wales and the peasantry are reconciled, seemingly at the cost of Thomas's own exclusion. Yet, in a very real way, it is the poet's art that engineers this reconciliation, so that he too is part of it after all, and not just in the presumptuous manner at first indicated. Dauntingly, Thomas adds an eight-line coda to 'A Priest to His People', the immediate effect of which is almost to disown the carefully wrought rapprochement that precedes it. The people will forgive the priest his 'initial hatred' and 'intolerance', but only in a spirit of indifference. They will continue to 'unwind' their days in the landscape's 'crude tapestry', as they will continue to 'affront' and yet 'compel' the poet-priest's 'gaze'. In a sense therefore the achieved resolution is irrelevant. Nothing in fact is changed, nothing has really been affected by whatever Thomas does or says, or can be so affected. All takes place beneath 'the jealous heavens'. Whatever accommodations men make between themselves, or fail to make, is mere contrivance compared to the actual grounding of their existence.

The coda, if indeed it is a coda, leads the reader to re-examine the whole poem. As is so often the case with R S, a great deal more is happening than the eye may at first detect. The deliberate if unsignalled invocation of Blake provides both a clue to and a warning of the complexity of the poet's thought processes. Thomas's verse needs to be read, and re-read, far more carefully than its not infrequently strident, even over-confident surfaces suggest; and even then there is no getting rid of an apprehension that not all the ore will have been extracted. It is not just the case that he can change a poem's direction in a few lines, or few words even: he can in fact be pursuing a wholly different direction to the one ostensibly indicated.

The first poem of *The Stones of the Field*, 'Out of the Hills',[85] introduces us at once to the essential Thomasian landscape, and the essential Thomasian peasant figure, but in a particular way. He might as well be Iago Prytherch, although, at this preliminary stage, Thomas refrains from naming him. Instead he imbues him with a deliberate stateliness, worthy of a hero-to-be:

> Dreams clustering thick on his sallow skull,
> Dark as curls, he comes, ambling with his cattle
> From the starved pastures.

The curtain rises slowly, ponderously even, on the Welsh hills. The lines are very nearly over-written. But instead of presenting a scene for the reader to inspect, the reader is confronted by a slow but implacable advance. Nor, despite the grandiloquence, is there anything remotely sentimental about this. As the peasant comes towards our camera, he brings with him starved pastures, the weight of the sky, the lash of the wind's sharpness, clouds of cattle breath. There is summer sweetness too, but only in a remembered state.

He is coming towards us, but he is also coming down to a town. We are not trespassing on his territory so much as he is trespassing on ours:

> The shadow of the mountain dwindles; his scaly eye
> Sloughs its cold care and glitters. The day is his
> To dabble a finger in, and, merry as crickets,
> A chorus of coins sings in his tattered pockets.
> Shall we follow him down, witness his swift undoing
> In the indifferent streets; the sudden disintegration
> Of his soul's hardness, traditional discipline
> Of flint and frost thawing in ludicrous showers

Of maudlin laughter; the limpid runnels of speech
Sullied and slurred, as the beer-glass chimes the hours?
No, wait for him here. At midnight he will return,
Threading the tunnel that contains the dawn
Of all his fears. Be then his fingerpost
Homeward. The earth is patient; he is not lost.

One by one, Thomas piles up the reversals. The landscape, 'his scaly eye', the abrupt intrusion of merriness, the disintegration of the soul's hardness, the 'thawing' of flint and frost. We are almost persuaded to cry, It cannot be! But as in a Greek drama, the 'action' takes place off-stage. The reader is prohibited from entering the tavern. We hear, but do not see, the maudlin laughter, the slurred speech. We become indeed the chorus itself, with the poet voicing our thoughts. And so the suspended catharsis. The figure will return. The earth guarantees it. He is not lost. But not lost to what? To the earth? To us, his self-appointed minders? Or not lost in a more general, soteriological way? In which case the earth is the source of salvation; and by implication those of us who are not governed by its bleakly strenuous regimen are the ones who will be lost.

All this challenges the conventional assumptions of pastoral, particularly as they were developed by the Augustan poets of the eighteenth century. Thomas contrives not to make us feel better about ourselves, but to feel worse. Indeed, to feel good about ourselves, in the context he provides, would be banal. So then, what is his purpose? To provoke us?

Certainly Thomas himself is provoked. Again and again in *Stones of the Field*, and also in *An Acre of Land*, he returns to his obdurate hill farmer, in a seizure of double-confrontation. Thus, in 'Affinity',[86] we are once more presented with the lone figure in a field. But so that he may be more, Thomas gives him less:

Gaitered with mud, lost in his own breath,
Without joy, without sorrow.
Without children, without wife,
Stumbling insensitively from furrow to furrow,
A vague somnambulist; but hold your tears,
For his name also is written in the Book of Life.

238

Indeed, it is not Thomas who is Job, in the first instance, but his archetypal peasant, reduced to the barest essential. But if Thomas plays the role of God in this respect, by making him so, then he scarcely does so with an easy conscience. Immediately he chastises himself, and chastises us:

> Ransack your brainbox, pull out your drawers
> That rot in your heart's dust, and what have you to give
> To enrich his spirit or the way he lives?

The 'Affinity' granted in the title of this poem is at once minimal and profound, bitter and generous:

> From the standpoint of education or caste or creed
> Is there anything to show that your essential need
> Is less than his, who has the world for church,
> And stands bare-headed in the woods' wide porch
> Morning and evening to hear God's choir
> Scatter their praises? Don't be taken in
> By stinking garments or an aimless grin;
> He also is human, and the same small star,
> That lights you homeward, has inflamed his mind
> With the old hunger, born of his kind.

Priest and labourer are differentiated as much by their respective and mutually defined failings as by their separate paths towards redemption. Thus each is stripped naked in the other's presence, until only a rump humanity remains. The 'He also is human' could as well be 'I also am human'. In his flurry of self-accusation, flagellating himself with words and thoughts, Thomas insists that he too should partake of the identity of Job.

But what of 'the old hunger, born of his kind'? Thomas's peasant is not rooted in just any old earth, but in a particular earth. What else should the 'old hunger' be but *hiraeth* in its strongest expression? Such at any rate becomes apparent in the second Iago Prytherch poem, called 'Iago Prytherch'.[87] Once Thomas's peasant is provided with a Welsh name, a greater intimacy, even a warmth, becomes possible:

Ah, Iago, my friend, whom the ignorant people thought
The last of your kind, . . .

The circle is redrawn. We are still outside it, but Thomas moves
halfway within. He can empathize with Prytherch in a way withheld
from the non-Welsh.

Ah, Iago, my friend, whom the ignorant people thought
The last of your kind, since all the wealth you brought
From the age of gold was the yellow dust on your shoes,
Spilled by the meadow flowers, if you should choose
To wrest your barns from the wind and the weather's claws,
And break the hold on the moss on roof and gable;
If you can till your fields and stand to see
The world go by, a foolish tapestry
Scrawled by the times, and lead your mares to stable,
And dream your dream, and after the earth's laws
Order your life and faith, then you shall be
The first man of the new community,

Suddenly the landscape, and the figure within it, is irradiated by the
light of a millennium. The hill farmer and his observer are also newly
fused in a potentially productive relationship. The means to achieve
the 'new community' lie in Iago's hand, but the poet is there to offer
him encouragement.

Yet there is also something mocking about 'Iago Prytherch' as
though the bitterness that informs Thomas's previous poems, apparently absent here, had somehow to be retained. The pivotal words
are 'if' and 'dreams'. Just as 'A Priest to His People' invokes Blake,
so 'Iago Prytherch' invokes the far more unlikely person of Rudyard
Kipling:

If you can dream – and not make dreams your master;
  If you can think – and not make thoughts your aim;
If you can meet with Triumph and Disaster . . .
If you can fill the unforgiving minute
  With sixty seconds' worth of distance run,
Yours is the Earth and everything that's in it,
  And – which is more – you'll be a Man, my son![88]

The hills depopulate, 'Wales' continues to evaporate; what can the poet do but commiserate? Hence the wicked irony of calling upon the most 'English' of all poets.

An Acre of Land contains a number of peasant poems – 'Death of a Peasant', for example, 'Cynddylan on a Tractor', 'The Mixen' and 'The Labourer' – and the encounter with Iago Prytherch is continued in 'The Gap in the Hedge'. Indeed, the starting point of his second collection is much the same as it was for the first – a view of 'The Welsh Hill Country'[89] – only now the landscape is acutely distanced:

> Too far for you to see
> The fluke and the foot-rot and the fat maggot
> Gnawing the skin from the small bones,
> The sheep are grazing at Bwlch-y-Fedwen,
> Arranged romantically in the usual manner
> On a bleak background of bold stone.

So too, in the poem's third and final stanza, is that landscape's habitually solitary occupant;

> Too far, too far to see
> The set of his eyes and the slow phthisis
> Wasting his frame under the ripped coat,
> There's a man still farming at Ty'n-y-Fawnog,
> Contributing grimly to the accepted pattern,
> The embryo music dead in his throat.

But Thomas's second collection significantly expands the scope of the poet's handling of Welsh themes and Welsh issues. The embryo music is a metaphor for a much wider stasis, that of an entire, stillborn culture in fact. In particular, he begins taking a more detailed notice of his nation's history, as well as sometimes focusing attention on more overtly contemporary issues. Often he combines the two, as in 'The Old Language',[90] via Wordsworth's sonnet 'England! the time is come when thou shouldst wean . . .' an almost Miltonic elegy:

England, what have you done to make the speech
My fathers used a stranger to my lips,
An offence to the ear, a shackle on the tongue
That would fit new thoughts to an abiding tune?
Answer me now. The workshop where they wrought
Stands idle, and thick dust covers their tools.
The blue metal of streams, the copper and gold
Seams in the wood are all unquarried; the leaves'
Intricate filigree fails, and who shall renew
Its brisk pattern? When spring wakens the hearts
Of the young children to sing, what song shall be theirs?

Yet not all is lost. What *An Acre of Land* (the title is taken from a line by the sixteenth-century Welsh poet Siôn Tudur) also strongly manifests is R. S. Thomas's excellence, even genius, as an observer of the natural world. Typically, his descriptions of nature are synaesthetic; that is, as a way of manipulating metaphor, he substitutes one sensory or descriptive order for another. But the nature he uncovers is invariably Welsh in character, and there is a strong sense throughout his work that so long as that survives, then Wales itself cannot entirely vanish:

Listen, listen! Where the river fastens
The trees together with a blue thread,
I hear the ousel of Cilgwri telling
the mournful story of the long dead.

Above the clatter of the broken water
The song is caught in the bare boughs;
The very air is veined with darkness, hearken!
The brown owl wakens in the woods now.

The owl, the ousel, and the toad carousing
In Cors Fochno of the old laws –
I hear them yet, but in what thicket cowers
Gwernabwy's eagle with the sharp claws?

Here, in the poem 'Wales',[91] Thomas incorporates the 'fable of the oldest animals', from 'Culhwch and Olwen' in the *Mabinogion*. The relative age of each animal is deduced by asking it the whereabouts of Mabon ab Modron. The suggestion Thomas makes is that if we concentrate our ears sharply enough, then the past may yet be recovered. Yet concentrating the ears also involves familiarizing ourselves with the ancient literature of Wales, so that the poem also contains a hidden plea on behalf of the language. In 'The Tree', subtitled 'Owain Glyn Dŵr Speaks',[92] Thomas appeals, at some length, to what has become the most romantic episode in Welsh history, at least in its anti-English conception. At the same time he asserts the centrality of the figure of the poet in his country's affairs. But his appeal, while depending upon an idealized version of the Welsh rebel, is also caustic. Again, a primary concern is with the old language, *yr hen iaith*. Glyn Dŵr's soliloquy – arguably the finest of Thomas's relatively few narrative poems – begins with an acknowledgement of the influence over him of one of the poets at his court:

> Gruffudd Llwyd put it into my head
> The strange thought, singing of the dead
> In *awdl* and *cywydd* to the harp,
> As though he plucked with each string
> The taut fibres of my being.

The court itself, at Sycharth, is re-created from a praise poem written to Glyn Dŵr by Iolo Goch, although since 'Red' Iolo in his younger days also wrote a praise poem to Edward III, he may be the intended target for the prince's admission that

> I had equated the glib bards
> With flattery and the expected phrase,
> Tedious concomitants of power.

At any rate it is the less famous Gruffudd Llwyd[93], steadfast in his loyalty to the great princes of the past, who shakes Glyn Dŵr out of his complacency.

Little by little the poem's central metaphor takes shape. The mystery of where and when Glyn Dŵr died enables Thomas to advance the poetic notion that he didn't die at all, but became instead part of a tree; and it is as a tree that the poet has the prince retell the story of his campaign against the English, which was also a campaign to establish the Welsh nation. From the seed implanted in his thoughts by Gruffudd Llwyd the rebellion grows, the 'far tribes' rallying to its 'green/Banner'. Briefly the golden age returns, and with it – always the highest seal of Welshness at Thomas's disposal – the birds of Rhiannon, nesting in the branches of the restored nation. But as the tree in nature is deciduous, so the span of Glyn Dŵr's uprising is limited. Autumn comes, the 'obnoxious' east wind blows (invariably a metaphor for English oppression), and the leaves fall, albeit in a 'gold shower' around its base.

Now it is still winter, and Glyn Dŵr is trapped by and inside the tree's roots. And yet:

> . . . he who stands in the light above
> And sets his ear to the scarred bole
> Shall hear me tell from the deep tomb
> How sorrow may bud the tree with tears,
> But only his blood can make it bloom.

The commemoration of Glyn Dŵr is a stock theme among Welsh poets, regardless of which language they write in. To be a Welsh poet and not to write a Glyn Dŵr poem is the exception. What lifts Thomas's poem above the common ruck is the persistence with which he exploits the image of the tree, enabling him to locate the decline and hoped-for resurgence of Wales within a seemingly immutable cycle. Yet, like Lenin, when the Russian revolutionary proposes that the immutable laws of history can sometimes do with a helping hand in the form of a vanguard, so Thomas, here the uncompromising patriot, issues a call to arms; or at least puts one firmly in the mouth of the past.

There is also the neat concluding irony. Only the blood of one standing 'in the light above' can bring the tree to bloom. In a Wales occupied by the English, the person standing by the tree could be of either race. In either case, however, only his blood, as sacrifice or by way of revenge, will make amends.

In neither case though is there a sense of the priest wringing his hands in despair at the prospect of blood shed. In other poems too from *An Acre of Land*, the cultural nationalist crosses the line. 'Welsh

Landscape', as we have already seen, is apophrastic invective designed to arouse a sleeping giant. 'Welsh History'[94] similarly berates as it extols:

> We were a people taut for war: the hills
> Were no harder, the thin grass
> Clothed them more warmly than the coarse
> Shirts our small bones.
> We fought, and were always in retreat,
> Like snow thawing upon the slopes
> Of Mynydd Mawr; and yet the stranger
> Never found our ultimate stand
> In the thick woods, declaiming verse
> To the sharp prompting of the harp.

For fifteen lines Thomas rehearses the chronicle of Welsh setbacks and calamities. But as he reaches the present, he comes full circle with the past. 'Welsh History' concludes with the 'prophetic' lines already given above (see p. 192):

> We were a people, and are so yet,
> When we have finished quarrelling for crumbs
> Under the table, or gnawing the bones
> Of a dead culture, we will arise
> And greet each other in a new dawn.

As printed in *Song at the Year's Turning*, however, the last line is cryptically amended to

> we will arise
> Armed, but not in the old way.

This could mean almost anything, and in the *Collected Poems* the original reading is restored. Even so, a certain ambiguity is perpetrated. Will the 'new dawn' come after the Welsh have reasserted themselves militarily, or will it be the beginning of that reassertion? Conceivably Thomas had something entirely different in mind, but in the context of the rest of the poem it is difficult to think what.

But even in the course of *An Acre of Land* Thomas's political passion ebbs. The book closes with gentle, tender words addressed to Iago Prytherch, as Thomas imagines himself standing beside 'my friend' in time of 'mild weather'. For a moment 'Memories', rather bizarrely excluded from the *Collected Poems*, threatens to redeliver the warlike rage of 'Welsh History' and 'Welsh Landscape', but instead turns off down a more enchantingly reposeful lane:

> I will sing
> The land's praises, making articulate
> Your strong feelings, your thoughts of no date,
> Your secret learning, innocent of books.
> Do you remember the shoals of wheat, the look
> Of the prawned barley, and the hissing swarm
> Of winged oats busy about the warm
> Stalks? Or the music of the taut scythe
> Breaking in regular waves upon the lithe
> Limbs of grass? Do you recall the days
> Of the young spring with lambs mocking the snow
> That was patched with green and gold in the bare fields?
> Or the autumn nights with Sirius loud as a bird
> In the wood's darkness?

Thomas is not often given to simple nostalgia, bucolic or otherwise. Their music apart, what enriches these lines is the position Thomas finds himself in. Gruffudd Llwyd and Iolo Goch sang to Owain Glyndŵr. Thomas sings to his hill farmer. In one sense this expresses the demotion of the bard in Welsh society. In another, it promotes the common man – call him an ordinary Cymro if you must – to the rank of prince.

The Minister[95] is Thomas's longest verse piece, and his most ambitious; in fact his only genuinely 'long' poem. It was written, and broadcast, as a radio play for BBC Wales, in a series of such dramas brought about by the producer Aneirin Talfan Davies. Other such 'radio odes', as they have been collectively called, were written by, among others, Huw Menai, Raymond Garlick, Glyn Jones, Gwyn Williams, Sally Roberts Jones, Leslie Norris, Anthony Conran, Roland Mathias, Harri

Webb and John Tripp.[96] The most famous Anglo-Welsh radio ode of all, *Under Milk Wood*, was not part of the series, although inevitably it left its mark on many of them. *The Minister*, however, escaped its influence, although had it been written exactly as it is after the first production of *Under Milk Wood*, and not before, then interestingly the verdict might have swung the other way. R. S. Thomas's use of a 'narrator' and other 'voices' derives instead from the medieval morality play, and possibly the early dramatic work of T. S. Eliot, particularly *Murder in the Cathedral*. There is also a resonance with the later 'church parables' of the composer Benjamin Britten. There is no actual dialogue as such, no exchange of views; only a statement of them.

The plot is disarmingly simple. A Nonconformist minister, the Reverend Elias Morgan BA, arrives to take up his post at a chapel in the hills – 'religion's outpost'. He has reckoned, however, without the manners and mores of the community he has come to serve. Eventually he dies of disillusion, a sickness of heart that finds echoes in some of R. S. Thomas's earlier hill country poems. *The Minister* is and isn't autobiographical. It isn't autobiographical in that it deals with Nonconformity. But it is autobiographical in that it patently draws upon Thomas's personal experiences as a rural priest. At least one of the characters, Job Davies, appears elsewhere in Thomas's poetry. The sweetness and warmth extended to Iago Prytherch in 'Memories', however, is altogether lacking, though *The Minister* is not without occasional humour. Rather Thomas uses the sectarian shift implicit in the drama's title to unbosom himself of some of his sharpest criticisms, and also his sharpest insights, concerning the hill farming community.

Ministers are not appointed over, but are selected by the congregation, which also provides for their upkeep. While in some circles this has been seen as a curiously democratic procedure, Thomas views matters rather differently. The villain of his piece, in as far as there is a villain, is Job Davies, a better-off farmer, as well as a deacon. His method for choosing a minister is the same as his method for choosing a horse. In the chapel vestry Davies employs the 'logic of the Smithfield', rather than acknowledge that 'even a pastor/ Is a man first and a minister after.' Physical strength is one of the qualities he looks for in the new man; another is marital eligibility. The choice falls on Elias Morgan, wearing a black coat and fresh out of college, but ignorant of the natural world: a bigot in fact, but nonetheless one who can find himself troubled by the singing of a thrush in a cypress bush close to the manse, suggesting 'a tune John Calvin never heard.'

At first the community is pleased with the new pastor, and expresses its appreciation with customary gifts: eggs, bacon, cheese. They are even ready to listen to his hellfire sermons, though for the wrong reasons:

> It was sex, sex, sex and money, money,
> God's mistake and the devil's creation,
> That took the mind of the congregation
> On long journeys into the hills
> Of a strange land, where sin was the honey
> Bright as sunlight in death's hive.

They have an appetite for the stories contained within the 'Black Book', without understanding them as 'parables'. Nonetheless, one night Elias Morgan can boast that, with the *hwyl* upon him, there might have been a 'revival', if only 'the organ had kept in time'. But little by little the honeymoon wears off. The community settles into studied disregard if not for the new minister, then for his mission. When Morgan opens a Bible class, no one attends except 'Mali, who was not right in the head', and who wants only to flirt with him. Soon enough, as St Francis once preached to the birds, the Reverend Elias Morgan finds himself preaching to flies and spiders.

Morgan absents himself for a month's holiday, and returns with renewed determination. But his hopes are quickly dashed. A broken window and a dead bird foretell what is in store for him. Now too he learns what is really going on around him. The dispersed hill-top families, far from being potentially upright and God-fearing, are riddled with immorality. In particular Job Davies is discovered to be a sinner. His wife being old, he has seduced a young girl, Buddug. Their eyes first meet precisely in the chapel, during one of Morgan's services. But Davies is also, in effect, Morgan's paymaster, and warns him not to meddle. Thus the minister finds himself

> a man ordained for ever
> To pick his way along the grass-strewn wall
> Dividing tact from truth.

Time and the seasons pass; weddings come, funerals go; and the Minister can effect neither a lasting nor a temporary change. In the end his heart sickens, and he dies.

About Morgan's death there is neither shock nor surprise. The radio drama is more an elegy than a tragedy. The individual players are not quite caricatures, but nor do they break loose from their stereotypes. Morgan the Calvinistic Methodist represents the ideology of Welsh Nonconformity, and it is as an ideologue that the 'Narrator' observes him. The action takes place at some unspecified time in the 'darkness of the vanished years': presumably though between the wars, since at one point politicians arrive in their 'cars'. But it is also overly dominated by the Narrator, whose voice assumes a blend of frigid superiority and lofty gall.

At the end the Narrator comes belatedly to the Minister's defence:

> Is there no passion in Wales? There is none
> Except in the wracked hearts of men like Morgan,
> Condemned to wither and starve in the cramped cell
> Of thought their fathers made them.
> Protestantism — the adroit castrator
> Of art; the bitter negation
> Of song and dance and the heart's innocent joy —
> You have botched our flesh and left us only the soul's
> Terrible impotence in a warm world.

In the context of the whole drama however this is an extraordinary eruption. It is the poet himself speaking, ex cathedra. Its Yeatsian rhetoric is at odds with an otherwise well-sustained mimicry. During the course of *The Minister* Thomas has unexpectedly revealed a talent for satire; but at this moment such talent is almost wilfully put to one side. Nothing in the drama itself embodies 'the heart's innocent joy', the 'song' and the 'dance'. Therefore the poet removes the reader or the listener outside and beyond the action, into an area of unsecured cultural and sociological speculation.

The poet's personal concerns surface in another respect. Through the Narrator he indicates that Morgan's primary failing is not his inability to relate humanly to the needs and the foibles of his flock, but his unwillingness to listen

> to the hills'
> Music calling to the hushed
> Music within.

It is not immediately apparent how, had Morgan managed to listen to such music, this would have helped him deal with the likes of Job Davies. The insinuation is though that by adapting to the tempo of the seasons he could have identified Davies and his kind as creatures of the natural cycle.

At a pinch, this might have saved Morgan; but it does not, on this occasion, save Thomas. Early on in the drama the Narrator speaks of Wales as God's 'peculiar home' – a theme that will assume near Gargantuan proportions in the poet's later work. Yet the Wales that confronts him in *The Minister* is antithetical to his naturalistic ideal. How then can it be God's peculiar home?

Thomas's suspicion of Nonconformity, on this showing, is not in doubt. Yet at the same time his own religiousness obliges him to acknowledge a kinship of sorts with Nonconformity and its practitioners. Having grown up in Wales, he cannot disregard what from the late eighteenth century had been the main current of Welsh religious, and also social, life. In *The Minister* he seems to acknowledge that he too has been stained by the Protestant ethos: it is otherwise difficult to explain the unambiguous passion of the Narrator's closing outburst. If Morgan is bereft of the heart's innocent joy, then so too must be the poet who writes about him thus.

In a way this is an example of Thomas's well-advertised 'honesty': he does not baulk at the implications of being Welsh. Indeed, he goes looking for them; and it is perhaps no accident that the Welsh priest-poet's longest single work should embody his responses to Nonconformity. But by the same token the poet finds himself, not for the first time, entangled among severe ambivalences.

*   *   *

Between them, *The Stones of the Field* and *An Acre of Land* contain 68 poems. Of these, 44 survive in *Song at the Year's Turning*, with another 19 previously uncollected poems added. If we add to these twenty or so poems that have remained uncollected, then Thomas's output, over a twelve-year period, was a shade over a hundred poems. Given that in the great majority of cases his separate verses fit easily on to a single page, this is by no means a prodigious output, and does not compare with the volume of poetry written subsequently. Even so, my survey of the poems written at Manafon, as given above, does R. S. Thomas less than full justice. His earlier work is broader than I have suggested. Both the first two volumes, for instance, contain occasional pieces dedicated to specific figures.

The most significant of these, though not the most successful, is 'Memories of Yeats whilst Travelling to Holyhead,'[97] from *The Stones of the Field*. Thomas strains just a little too hard, and in terms too reminiscent of his subject's own rhetoric:

> Who could have guessed the futility even of praising
> Mountain and marsh and the delicate, flickering tree
> To one long impervious and cold to the outward scene,
> Heedless of nature's baubles, lost in the amazing
> And labyrinth paths of his own impenetrable mind?

Yet, however awkwardly, Thomas openly acknowledges what is perhaps his principal poetic debt outside the Welsh language. In more ways than one Yeats was his model. On the expressive level he was a Celtic poet using the English language to forge, with supreme confidence, a poetry that was decidedly Irish in flavour, just as Thomas's poetry is decidedly Welsh in flavour. Again, both poets willingly create and frequently use a sometimes high-minded first person to bind their poems together. But as well as that, Yeats provides Thomas with an example of a poetry that is successful in terms of an off-centre cultural nationalism. Yeats's problem vis-à-vis political Irish nationalism was that he did not share its provenance. His background was conservative Anglo-Irish protestant. Only by going back in time, and revivifying ancient Irish legend, could he establish a common ground with men about whose purposes he was in any case sceptical. And so with Thomas. As an Anglican he does not belong with the majority of Welsh, nor do his anti-urban, anti-industrial, anti-Labour attitudes gain him fellowship among the people of the south. Again, growing up as a monoglot English-speaker, he is separated from those who would otherwise be his natural allies. Like Yeats as an Irishman, he has to work hard to create a viable 'Welsh' identity. Learning the language was the principal solution; but Thomas's exploitation of Welsh history and his adoption of a fiercely anti-English stance contributed to his strategy.

Other poems in *The Stones of the Field* I have overlooked are 'On a Portrait of Joseph Hone by Augustus John',[98] and 'The Airy Tomb'.[99] The first is interesting because it sets a precedent for work R. S. was to do much later on: poems and series of poems that stand as idiosyncratic commentaries on works of art. The second, an unusually long 'peasant' piece, is clearly Wordsworthian in character, if not in message, and points to another influence which, on a more submerged level, was to assume increasing importance in Thomas's work.

In *An Acre of Land* there is the praise poem to 'Alun Lewis', and another to 'Saint Antony', both omitted from the *Collected Poems*. The latter especially reminds us of Thomas's intensely private and inward spiritual vexations, which were to become the major theme of his later poetry:

> Saint Antony on the sand saw shapes rising,
> Formed by the wind, sinuous, lewd
> As snakes dancing; their bitter poison
> Entered the soul through his pale eyes.
>
> Sleep came; the dances were renewed
> Upon the retina, the lids not proof
> Against the orgy of the spheres.
> Night long he ranged the Bacchanalian dark,
> Himself the prey, the hunter and the wood.

But if Thomas's future energies were to be increasingly absorbed by such mystics and other overtly 'religious' figures, it would be completely wrong to draw hard and fast lines between different categories in his work, say between the spiritual and the secular. All Thomas's themes are interrelated. No subject-matter is ever entirely abandoned, just as no subject-matter is ever entirely unprefigured in what goes before. Thus many of his hill-farmer pieces can also be read as spiritual exercises, for example 'Priest and Peasant',[100] from *Song at the Year's Turning*. Here Thomas addresses Davies, whom he regards as 'ill in mind', having 'laid waste' his potential for the appreciation of 'delight' and 'beauty':

> And so you work
> In the wet fields and suffer pain
> And loneliness as a tree takes
> The night's darkness, the day's rain;
> While I watch you, and pray for you,
> And so increase my small store
> Of credit in the bank of God,
> Who sees you suffer and me pray
> And touches you with the sun's ray,
> That heals not, yet blinds my eyes
> And seals my lips as Job's were sealed
> Imperiously in the old days.

Davies is a version of St Antony just as St Antony is a version of Davies, and R. S. Thomas is a version of both:

> To one kneeling down no word came,
> Only the wind's song, saddening the lips
> Of the grave saints, rigid in glass;
> Or the dry whisper of unseen wings,
> Bats not angels, in the high roof.
>
> Was he balked by silence? He kneeled long,
> And saw love in a dark crown
> Of thorns blazing, a winter tree
> Golden with fruit of a man's body.
>   ('In a Country Church')[101]

Even the relatively small number of 'new' poems added to *Song at the Year's Turning* show Thomas working on all his familiar fronts. 'A Welshman to any Tourist'[102] offers an apology for Wales, while drawing on the legend that King Arthur and his court lie sleeping in a hidden cave:

> He and his knights are the bright ore
> That seams our history,
> But shame has kept them late in bed.

There is a 'Lament for Prytherch',[103] and a portrait of another rural type in 'The Poacher'.[104] 'Pisces'[105] is a not untypical bitter-sweet little nature poem. But perhaps the two most significant additions are the title poem, and the last poem of all, 'No Through Road'.[106] Both are poems of departure, written at the very end of Thomas's sojourn at Manafon. 'Song at the Year's Turning'[107] is the more difficult, an evocation of sorrow, and an empty autumn:

> Shelley dreamed it. Now the dream decays.
> The props crumble. The familiar ways
> Are stale with tears trodden underfoot.
> The heart's flower withers at the root.
> Bury it then, in history's sterile dust.
> The slow years shall tame your tawny lust.

The specific reference is to Shelley's 'Autumn: a Dirge', which closes with the lines:

> Ye, follow the bier
> Of the dead cold Year,
> And make her grave green with tear on tear,

And make her grave green with tear on tear,

> Winter rots you: who is there to blame?
> The new grass shall purge you in its flame.

But it is hard to extrapolate the 'dream' from 'Autumn: a Dirge', which is somewhat slight. Perhaps something else is meant, for instance Shelley's 'Hymn to Intellectual Beauty'. Thomas's poem strives to incorporate as much as any poem can incorporate in eighteen lines. The middle stanza reads:

> Love deceived him; what is there to say
> The mind brought you by a better way
> To this despair? Lost in the world's wood
> You cannot stanch the bright menstrual blood.
> The earth sickens; under naked boughs
> The frost comes to barb your broken vows.

Love here is both God's love, and common mortal, even animal, love. But is Thomas talking about Shelley, or himself? 'Song at the Year's Turning' is not only a dirge, but a powerful intellectual, and also Romantic, riddle. It is about a way of seeing things that is without hope, not least because it sees itself that way.

There is nothing riddling about 'No Through Road', however, though again the subject-matter is a poet and his work. Here Thomas offers a personal statement, which is also a lament. He has, he tells us,

> failed after many seasons
> To bring truth to birth,
> And nature's simple equations
> In the mind's precincts do not apply.

Where shall he turn to next? he asks, though there cannot be an answer; for, after winter, which will repeat itself, the prospect of 'green places' is only 'the old lie'.

He leaves Manafon for the western reaches of Wales. But the precincts of the mind accompany him. Behind him, a hundred or so poems. In front of him, another nine hundred; his monument in fact to 'truth's' inaccessibility.

IV

THE DRAGON APPARENT

It became my delight to rouse him to these outbursts for I was the poet in the presence of his theme. Once when I was defending an Irish politician who had made a great outcry because he was treated as a common felon, by showing that he did it for the cause's sake, he said, 'There are things that a man must not do to save a nation.' He would speak a sentence like that in ignorance of its passionate value, and would forget it the moment after.

W. B. YEATS, on John O'Leary,
in *Autobiographies* (1926)

IN WALES, the Second World War was not followed by the same sense of disillusionment as had come in the wake of 1918; at least, not immediately. During hostilities Saunders Lewis and other Plaid Cymru leaders had argued Wales's right to remain neutral. Indeed, a couple of dozen party members were given custodial sentences for refusing service on political, not religious grounds. This, and Lewis's dissenting comments in *Y Faner*, it was later revealed, attracted the attention of the Abwehr. In Berlin it was seriously considered whether there might not exist in Wales a possible seed-bed of quislings.[1] There is, however, no evidence that any definite approach was made by German agents, to Lewis or anybody else. Rather Plaid Cymru's neutralist stance, although reinforced by the nonconformist or 'Independent' pacifism of some of its members, was adopted chiefly as a means of emphasizing a separate Welsh identity. As Lewis himself put it, 'The only proof that the Welsh nation exists is that there are some who act as if it does exist';[2] and in fact many among Plaid Cymru's still slender following did enlist.

There were other groups opposed to the war as well, notably the Christian pacifist Cymdeithas Heddychwyr Cymru. But in general it was difficult to construe the fight against Hitler simply in terms of a power struggle between great powers. As the scale of Nazi atrocities became apparent, there was a widespread sense of relief that 'good' had triumphed over 'evil', whatever the means adopted to achieve that victory. It was also the case that less than half the number of Welsh soldiers killed in the First World War died in its successor: 15,000 as against 30,000.[3] Conversely, although the number of civilian casualties was far higher, the calamitous air-raids on Swansea and other cities of the south had promoted a sense of shared purpose with the rest of Britain. Against a common enemy everyone was in the same boat. But more than these considerations, for a decade or so after 1945 Wales appeared especially to benefit from post-war reconstruction programmes, engineered, initially, by a Labour government a majority of the Welsh electorate had voted for. The pre-war malaise of double digit unemployment was seen off, replaced by nationalized industries and a welfare system that worked. An immediate period of post-war austerity gradually gave way to real and historically unparalleled mass prosperity.

In time, the Welsh economy offered a greater diversity of employment opportunities, and a greater diversity of life-styles, than ever before. 'Pluralist' was the new spin put upon the fragmentation of society. As Britain struggled, sometimes painfully, to adapt to a reduced role in the world, 'little Englander' values were replicated west of Offa's Dyke. The Conservative Prime Minister Harold Macmillan's 1957 assertion that 'You've never had it so good',[4] essentially a plea to abandon old imperial dreams in favour of self-embourgoisement, applied as much to the citizens of Cardiff, Swansea and Carmarthen as it did to those of London, Manchester and Norwich. Middle class this aspiration may have been, but being middle class was perceived as a realistic ideal for everyone. Henceforward in Wales, as in England, the mainstream political temperature was increasingly subject to the relative success, or failure, of the consumer revolution.

Wales was indeed transformed. For a while, the old heavy industries of coal and steel, now under state supervision, were revived. In the long run, coal would all but vanish, as oil, diesel and nuclear power became the preferred fuels of manufacture and transport, and as Margaret Thatcher's government took revenge on a workforce that had twice brought Britain to a standstill. For the mining communities of the valleys the demise of coal spelled disaster, but the south was spared the worst ravages of industrial decay as new businesses and technologies took root. After the war, mass automotive manufacture arrived in force. Indeed, 'industrialized Wales', far from contracting, spread. In the 1960s Milford Haven became Britain's largest oil port and refining centre, while in far-off Anglesey Rio Tinto Zinc, in 1970, established its aluminium processing plant. Also on Anglesey was Wales's second nuclear power station, at Yr

Wylfa; the first having been built at Trawsfynydd at the end of the 1950s.

On a smaller scale, industrial and trading estates sprang up across the land, and tourism also became a major business. Before the war there had been a handful of seaside resorts: Aberystwyth, Barmouth, Llandudno, Tenby, as well as the spa towns of Llandrindod Wells and Builth Wells. After the war, many new areas were opened up to a broader cross-section of local and English holiday-makers. All around the coast, and sometimes inland, caravan sites became an established feature of the Welsh landscape. Small towns and villages that had once been isolated became targets of attention precisely because of their seclusion. Effective efforts were made to preserve and restore the great Norman and Plantagenet castles; while in the mountains, dozens of pony-trekking stations and camping sites set up their stalls.

The greatest changes occurred in the countryside. Matching the inflow of tourists was an outflow of manpower. Partly because of the need to help feed Britain between 1939 and 1945, but also thanks to the Agriculture Act of 1947, farming in Wales was profoundly altered. With the provision of subsidies, what had once been an often precarious way of life became more obviously commercialized. Simultaneously an old labour-intensive industry was mechanized. The tractor became the norm, not the exception. Between the census years of 1951 and 1971 the recorded number of farm labourers dwindled from 33,385 to 11,275. During the same period the number of farms roughly halved as their size doubled. It was more efficient, more profitable, to work more land with fewer men. The small-holder and tenant farmer were pushed out by kulak types, some of them Englishmen seeking an alternative existence to life in the city, but unable to abandon their acumen for accountancy.

R. S. Thomas was perfectly correct therefore to refer to the 'depopulation' of the Welsh hill country in his 1945 essay. It was depopulating, yet in productive terms it was also serving its economic purpose better. But the interior Welsh landscape also exhibited other symptoms of centralized state planning. The armed forces, which in 1945 effectively controlled 10 per cent of Wales, developed a number of bases and training camps. These included a firing practice range at

Castlemartin in South Pembrokeshire, later used by a Panzer tank division on the grounds that nowhere in West Germany was sufficiently under-populated. To provide Liverpool, Birmingham and other English cities with water, artificial lakes or reservoirs were created in remote mountain valleys. The best-known, and most notorious, of these, for reasons to follow, was at Tryweryn. Often within sight of such creations, new forests were planted, in an extensive afforestation programme. Mainly these were of a Canadian conifer, later adjudged to be ecologically unsound, since they displaced the natural habitats of important flora and fauna. But at the time they were visible expressions of what centralized government, in the shape of the Forestry Commission, could achieve. Even the intractable Welsh uplands could be Whitehalled.

In as far as these policies, these transformations, were contemplated by their instigators in a specifically 'Welsh' context – and mainly they weren't – the attitude of post-1945 governments was, and has continued to be, in the broadest historical terms, ameliorationist towards Wales. That is to say, far from excluding Wales from a newly designed Britain, planners have treated the Principality as an integral and equal part of the union, so that any observable difference in its material fabric compared to England's is more likely to be one of degree than of kind. At the same time 'concessions' have been made to Welsh identity, enabling Wales to retain and expand its sense of nationhood. But however such concessions came about, whether by protest or by parliamentary manoeuvre, a measure of bifurcation on the part of government is evident, exposing a contradiction that lies at the very heart of the notion of a centralized or bureaucratic democracy. As it happens, Britain is not as centralized in its state machinery as it could be, and has grown rather less so since the 1950s; nor is it at the forefront of democratic practice. Successive regimes have declined, for example, to adopt the principle of proportional representation. Yet the dilution of these contradictory elements within the prevailing compact tends to exacerbate matters, not resolve them.

The spate of mainly Labour Acts of Parliament establishing a command economy and the welfare state, thus guaranteeing that every part of Britain partake of the mixed capitalist-socialist polity prevalent among all western states, was followed by a number of measures specific to Wales. Some of these were enacted by Labour governments, others by Conservative administrations. The thirty-six Welsh seats in the House of Commons were a small but sometimes necessary prize to be gained in election contests where the margins of victory or defeat were unpredictable and not infrequently narrow.

The earliest creation was the Council for Wales and Monmouthshire in 1948. This consultative body could advise on policy, but was powerless to determine any of its own. A Ministry for Welsh Affairs was set up inside the Home Office by Winston Churchill's government in 1951, but again this was little more than window dressing. The same was not true, however, of the Welsh Office, finally put in place by Labour in 1964, with James Griffiths as the first Secretary of State for Wales.

Griffiths, a leading parliamentarian of his generation, had for many years fought a running battle with his fellow Welshman Aneurin Bevan. Despite his upbringing, Bevan, architect of the National Health Service, was a state corporatist. He held no truck at all with any argument in favour of any kind of devolution. Like Neil Kinnock in the 1980s he held that a centrally operated socialism was the only panacea for most if not all life's ills. Both also recognized that without the increment of its safe Welsh and Scottish constituencies the chances of Labour winning an election were severely reduced. Griffiths on the other hand belonged to the less centrist wing of the party, and remained more loyal to his 'roots'. In the early 1950s he was prominent in a 'Parliament for Wales' campaign, a cross-bench movement that, like the vast majority of cross-bench causes, got precisely nowhere. And it was largely due to Griffiths's pressure that the Welsh Office, when it opened, had real administrative responsibility: at first only for local government, planning, roads and housing; but later for health, agriculture and education.

At the time the Welsh Office was intended as a sop to Welsh sentiments, although some nationalists waxed indignant at the very idea of a sop of any kind being offered to Wales by anyone. In Griffiths's hands though, and in those of subsequent Welsh-born Welsh Secretaries, the illusion that Wales had something governmental it could call its own was more or less sustained. The trouble came in the 1990s when the ruling Tory Party, with scant Welsh talent to draw upon on its side of the Commons, appointed John Redwood as Secretary of State. At a time of recession and particularly high unemployment, the unfortunate right-winger, who preferred to sleep in England rather than in Cardiff (officially designated the capital of Wales in 1955), was quickly dubbed 'The Governor-General', even 'District Officer to the Cambrian Tribes'.

By then Westminster had made its biggest ever concession to Celtic pride. On 1 March 1979, St David's Day, parallel referenda were held in Wales and Scotland to determine whether or not these countries should acquire elective assemblies of their own. This was done under the auspices of a critically weakened Labour government that needed the handful of Plaid Cymru and SNP votes in the House of Commons to survive. It was not, however, a genuinely democratic exercise. The proposed assemblies were minimalist in the powers that would be granted them. In both cases too the rule was imposed that even such limited devolution would come about only if a minimum of 40 per cent of the total electorate voted in favour.

The government, having enacted the necessary legislation for the referenda to take place, argued against a devolutionist outcome. In this campaign they were joined by the Conservative and Liberal parties. Only Labour's Welsh MPs took up the challenge, and even then not all of them. Neil Kinnock was among those who argued a firmly unionist line. Indeed, of those parties that had seats in the Commons, only Plaid Cymru and the Scottish National Party supported devolution.

The outcome was not unexpected. Although in Scotland voters narrowly decided in favour of a Scottish assembly, the 40 per cent rule negated the popular verdict. In Wales, the same rule was irrelevant. Only 58 per cent of the electorate turned out, less than in most general elections, and of these only one in four voted for an assembly.

For Welsh nationalists this was a ghastly blow. Their nation had voted overwhelmingly to retain the constitutional status quo. But worse than that, a fearsome apathy had been revealed. Close to half the electorate were clearly uninterested, one way or the other, in what could have been the most decisive day for Wales in modern times. Instead, fifteen hundred years of history appeared to have gone up in smoke.

Thus at least the outcome according to the numbers game. That it was not surprising was partly due to the fact that many of the electorate were non-Welsh-speaking, and that among these a significant proportion were 'incomers', i.e. those born outside Wales, but who for one reason or another had settled there. Yet the referendum, far from decisively healing an old and festering wound, only rubbed salt in it. If 956,330 votes had been cast against devolution, 243,048 were in favour. This latter figure must have accounted for a good number of those who could still speak Welsh: according to 1971 census figures a mere 20.9 per cent of a population of 2,656,000, children included.

The whole affair was a sham. It defined Wales simply in terms of a geographic boundary. For those inside that boundary who had other ways of defining their Welshness, for example by ancestry and tongue and culture, to be told that they belonged to a minority only reminded them of what they already knew. But within their own families, their own communities, their own tongue, their own culture, they were not a minority. They were a people the same as any other people, so why shouldn't they have equivalent rights? Why instead did they have to kowtow to a peculiar democracy's arbitrary dictation of what a majority was, and what a minority wasn't?

Within the year the first English-owned holiday cottages had been torched: a campaign that, on and off, has continued to the present day, without the arrest of any of its perpetrators. Most nationalists, however, have dissociated themselves from the targeting of private property. Their quarrel is not with individual English, but with the modus vivendi an essentially English state has imposed upon them; and in any case, of all 'minority' nationalisms the Welsh is (as yet) the least disposed towards violence. It inhabits a different mentality from say, its Basque, Palestinian, Tamil or Chechen counterparts.

Not that the centralizing corporatist state has had everything its own way. From the mid-1950s onwards a distinctively Welsh voice, sometimes accompanied by calculatedly provocative actions, made itself heard beyond the confines of community and print. That this was so reflected not only a cultural shift inside the Principality, but a transformation of outlooks in Britain and the West in general. The material prosperity that attended the success of post-war economic reconstruction induced less defensive, more questioning attitudes. As much greater numbers of young people attended college and university, so colleges and universities fostered a much greater array of independent thought and ideology. In the 1960s, with the Vietnamese and other 'anti-imperialist' struggles never far from public consciousness, this exploded into an unprecedented and radical youth movement, characterized by an at times wilful disregard for authority, or what was called the 'Establishment'.

In this context, it is instructive to observe the developing fortunes of Plaid Cymru. Under Saunders Lewis's presidency it had never been much more than a token party. During the first thirty years of its existence its few thousand adherents seldom made any impression on the ballot box. It never even came close to winning a seat, either locally or nationally. The biggest cause of rejoicing was a saved deposit. In the 1950 general election, seven Plaid Cymru candidates collected a total of 17,000 votes between them, barely sufficient to have won one seat. What Plaid Cymru lacked was any coherent political framework. Its ideology, as far as it had one, was Christian, conservative, even elitist. It had more to say about the past than the future. Its leaders tended to be academics, writers and Nonconformist ministers: men of great individuality, great Welshness, but lacking pragmatism.

A new direction was signalled by a breakaway group from the 'Parliament for Wales' campaign of 1949–56. This was the Welsh Republican Movement. As well as being anti-royalist, it was avowedly socialist. Some of its supporters were also Plaid Cymru members. By the mid-1960s Plaid Cymru had followed down the same road. It presented the Welsh electorate with a genuinely left-radical face that offered to compete with Labour as much as it challenged the Tory and greatly declined Liberal parties. Correspondingly, Plaid Cymru enjoyed its first victories at the polling stations. Gwynfor Evans, party president since 1945, created political consternation by winning the parliamentary seat of Carmarthen in a 1966 by-election.

Although he subsequently lost Carmarthen in 1970, a precedent had been set. In the February 1974 election, Plaid Cymru candidates Dafydd Wigley and Dafydd Elis Thomas triumphed in Caernarfon and Meirionnydd. Both men held on to these gains in the October election, when Gwynfor Evans also recaptured Carmarthen.

All three seats belonged to 'Welsh' Wales: the western and north-western parts. Later on Anglesey and Ceredigion would be added to their number. But if their distribution emphasized the mainly rural complexion of a viable Welsh nationalism, lesser victories made the point that Plaid Cymru had emerged as a party that could address the whole of Wales in its geographic expression. In 1976, the party gained control of the Merthyr Tydfil borough council, in the very heart of the old industrial south. In other local government constituencies too, in traditional Labour strongholds, Plaid Cymru regularly demonstrated its capacity to confound expectations.

The national party, however, was only one aspect of a burgeoning Welsh identity. Its electoral successes tended to follow in the wake of other events rather than trigger them. The 1936 'Fire in Llŷn', when Saunders Lewis, D. J. Williams and the Rev. Lewis Valentine set fire to the RAF huts at Pen-y-berth, had shown just how deeply some Welsh could feel about the 'land of their fathers'. From the 1950s onwards the flooding of several remote valleys to create reservoirs to supply distant conurbations in England evoked similar responses. The most notorious of these was at Tryweryn, a valley near Bala. Enabled by a parliamentary bill of 1957, Tryweryn had been acquired by the Corporation of Liverpool. Included in the drowning was the village of Capel Celyn, home of the first Sunday School in Wales. Despite the fact that virtually every MP representing a Welsh constituency had opposed the bill, it became law. The sense of outrage spread throughout Wales, suggesting that however much the country's various communities lived apart from each other, there was a potential for national focus. Not only was a traditional heartland threatened, but there was no discernible gain for Wales itself, economic or otherwise.

The opening of the reservoir in 1965 was attended by demonstrations and a good deal of hostile comment in the Welsh press. Prior to that, some on-site transformers had been sabotaged. Whitehall, however, dismissed this and the subsequent protests as so much hot air that, given time, would disperse. But then, over the following twelve months, other installations at Tryweryn and at sites elsewhere were attacked with gelignite. Suddenly there were new forces on the scene, calling themselves 'The Free Wales Army' and 'Mudiad Amddiffyn Cymru' – 'Movement for the Defence of Wales'. Soon uniformed members of the former regularly began appearing in public, along with recruiting posters.

Meanwhile, three years earlier, Saunders Lewis had delivered his catalytic radio lecture '*Tynged yr Iaith*', out of which was born the most effective of all manifestations of Welsh 'dissidence': Cymdeithas yr Iaith Gymraeg, or Welsh Language Society.

The society's objective was to secure the acceptance and use of the Welsh language in official and public forums. It was not 'anti-English' as such, although individually the feelings of many of its predominantly student members – their ground leader was Dafydd Iwan, a popular singer most readily characterized as a Cymric Bob Dylan – often ran that way. Its relationship with Plaid Cymru was ambiguous. There was considerable cross-membership, but the two bodies maintained their separate identities. In a sense the society was a pressure group on the party, forcing it into more militant, and more left-wing, positions. Equally though the society was a spawning ground for future party activists.

In his address Lewis had commended a Llanelli mining family called the Beasleys. Acting of their own accord, the Beasleys had requested that their rate-demands be made in Welsh, not English. Naturally the local authority refused, and naturally the Beasleys declined to pay. Over a period of eight years they were brought to court twelve times; and three times the bailiffs came to their house to remove their belongings. But at the end of the day the bloody-minded Beasleys won their point. Llanelli Council sent them a bilingual bill.

This strategy of civil resistance Cymdeithas yr Iaith Gymraeg adopted as its own. Its members regularly played havoc with public bodies precisely on the language question. No Welsh, no payment. But it was not just financial transactions that were affected. The first of the society's many public, and well publicized, disruptions was a protest organized on the outskirts of Aberystwyth in February 1963.

Above St Michael's Theological College, Llandaff.

Below From the College register at Bangor.

373			
	Name of Student in full	*Thomas, Leslie* Evan	*Thomas, Ronald* Stuart
	Date of Birth	June 25th 1906	March 29th 1913.
	Last School and Name of Headmaster or other person from whom Testimonials are presented	Coleg Harlech, Harlech B. B. Thomas Esq M.A.	Holyhead County School E. Derry Evans. Esq. M.A.
	Parent or Guardian (if any) — Name in full and Profession	Evan Thomas — Photographer	Thomas Hubert Thomas, — Marine Shore Officer
	Parent or Guardian (if any) — Residence	3. Albert Terrace, Rogerstone Mon	"Kimla" Garth Road. Holyhead
	Date of Entry	Oct 1932	Oct. 1932.
	Terms in which registered	Aut. 1932. Spn. 1933. Sum. 1933. Aut. 1933. Spn. 1934. Sum. 1934. Aut. 1934. Spn. 1935. Sum. 1935. Aut. 1935. Spn. 1936. Sum. 1936. Aut. 1936. Spn. 1937. Sum. 1937.	Aut. 1932. Spn. 1933. Sum. 1933. Aut. 1933. Spn. 1934. Sum. 1934. Aut. 1934. Spn. 1935. Sum. 1935.
	Scholarships, Exhibitions or Prizes held		
	Examinations passed, or distinctions won	B.A. 1935. 1st class Honours German. B.A. 3rd class Div I Honours in Philosophy 1936.	B.A 1935. 2nd class Div I Honours Latin.

Making his mark: *Above* the tennis team of St Michael's College, Llandaff, Trinity 1936, R. S. Thomas standing third from the left, behind the warden, E. W. Williamson. *Below* the poet's initials in the belfry at Manafon.

Right R. S. Thomas officiates at the wedding of Hazel and Michael Boulton at Manafon in 1966.

Below left St Michael's, Manafon.

Below right The Rectory at Manafon.

Above The Penyberth Three, from the left, Lewis Valentine, Saunders Lewis and D. J. Williams.

Left Cayo Evans leading an FWA demonstration in Aberystwyth.

Right The Vicarage at Eglwysfach.

Above St Michael's, Eglwysfach.

Right The interior of St Michael's at Eglwysfach, as redecorated by the poet.

Above The disused church in upper Aberdaron. *Below* The churchyard at St Hywyn's.

Above Ynys Enlli (Bardsey Island) seen from the end of the Llŷn Peninsula.

Right Sarn-y-Rhiw, R. S. Thomas's retirement cottage.

A member had been charged by the police for carrying his girlfriend on the cross-bar of his bicycle. The young man, Gareth Miles, refused to appear in court until a summons was issued in Welsh. When the court declined, the society came out in force, staging a sit-in on the public highway at Trefechan Bridge.

Similar episodes, aimed at tax offices, post offices, libraries and colleges, led to a spate of imprisonments. They also led to the concessionary Welsh Language Act of 1967. But like the British government's other concessions, this too was constructed on a half loaf basis. The act legislated the 'equal validity' of the Welsh language in Wales. It did not, however, legislate in favour of bilingualism. If someone wanted an official form in Welsh, then they were entitled to it. But the act did not oblige any organization to initiate bilingual communications.

The dog had been thrown a bone, but there was no real meat on it. As a result Cymdeithas yr Iaith Gymraeg redoubled its efforts. The protests and the demonstrations went on (and still go on). Then, in 1969, the society launched its road-sign campaign. Where road signs had not been made bilingual, the English was either blackwashed or whitewashed over. The intention was not to get rid of the English names for Welsh places, for example Swansea for Abertawe, even less to endanger motorists' lives: it was quite simply to gain acknowledgement of the Welsh way of saying things inside Wales.

However, 1969 was an uncommon year. On 1 July Charles Windsor was invested Prince of Wales by his mother Queen Elizabeth II of England. The pageant took place in the precincts of Caernarfon Castle: one of the more impressive strongholds built by Edward I in his thirteenth-century subjugation of Wales. World media attention focused on Wales as never before and never since. But so also did the attention of the security services. The age of international terrorism, which could only survive on publicity, had already begun. But the immediate enemy was within. In the months leading up to the Investiture the Free Wales Army had been especially busy. So too had the Special Branch. The FWA's leaders, increasing their exposure, had been rounded up and put on trial at the Assize Court in Swansea. By a spectacularly inept piece of timing, on the very day that 'Charlie the Greek' received his crown, three FWA men were sent down.

Or was it so inept? The English establishment perhaps was determined to stamp its whole authority on that day of days. And in this the media largely colluded. A short while before midnight on 30 June two 'Welsh extremists', as such men were labelled, in a scene redolent of Conrad's *Secret Agent*, inadvertently blew themselves up with gelignite in the small Denbighshire town of Abergele.

Alwyn Jones and George Taylor, both members of the Mudiad Amddiffyn Cymru, were the first, and in fact the only, individuals to die as a consequence of 'terrorism' in Wales. Their deaths did not, however, make the main headlines of most British newspapers: those were reserved for the Investiture itself. Whether their bomb was intended to kill or maim any of the royal party is unknown. It seems unlikely. On the same night another bomb exploded at a postal sorting office in Cardiff. As with every previous device, care had apparently been taken to avoid actually hurting anybody. Was the Abergele bomb the intended exception? Probably it wasn't. More likely its purpose was to cause disruption; to make a statement.

There were no other deaths connected with the extremist campaigns of the 1960s, but there were two cases of serious injury. In September 1968 an airman lost an eye and a finger in a bomb blast at an RAF station outside Pembrey, on the southern coast. Then, four days after the Investiture, on 5 July 1969, a small boy was maimed when he stumbled into a workshop in Caernarfon and accidentally detonated another device. For the most part, however, bombs laid by the Free Wales Army, Mudiad Amddiffyn Cymru and other related groups were timed to go off in the dead of night, thus minimizing the risk of human fatality. When they failed to detonate, someone usually rang the police to give a hazard warning. Mostly too the devices were planted in remote rural places, to disrupt water supplies to England, although on at least five occasions the bombers selected targets in Cardiff: a tax office in March 1966; the 'Temple of Peace and Health' in November 1967; the Welsh Office in May 1968; a police station in April 1969; and, the night before the Investiture, the postal sorting office.

Compared to the activities of the IRA all this was small beer. Indeed about the Free Wales Army there was something intrinsically whimsical. As one of its more colourful leaders, Cayo Evans, put it: 'To be honest, I think that any folk museum would have been pleased to acquire some of our arms.'[5] Of necessity, the 'Army' was organized in 'columns', without a central committee: not just for 'security' reasons, but also because there were inherent difficulties in getting men from Gwynedd, say, to follow orders issued anywhere other than in Gwynedd. The 'uniforms' were impromptu. The 'green jackets' were bought in local market places, then dyed. Unwittingly, Milletts was clothing a revolution. Forage caps were also acquired commercially, before having the FWA's insignia stitched on: the 'White Eagle of Eryri', and the legend *Fe Godwn Ni Eto* – 'We Shall Rise Again'. Transport was more of a problem. Such cars as the extremists owned tended to break down in mid-mission. Dilapidated vehicles, loaded up with small quantities of gelignite, would be hauled out of ditches by kindly but unsuspecting farmers in remote valleys in the dead of night. Sometimes cadres were required to hitch a ride to wherever they were going. On one occasion at least an operative discovered he had accepted a lift from a detective. The explosives themselves though presented less of a problem. With Wales's multitude of moribund collieries and slate quarries, 'friends' could usually be found to palm a few sticks of something potent the Free Army's way. As for timing mechanisms, the DIY guerillas used either ordinary alarm clocks, wiring the minute and hour hands, or switches removed from public lamposts.

'Cayo' Evans (first name Julian), a Carmarthenshire man, headed the 'West Wales' column. His father had been a senior civil servant in India, and Cayo was educated privately in England, at Millfield Public School. His first and abiding love was horses. He gained some notoriety by riding a white stallion into the saloon bar of various inns and pubs. At Millfield, he fell under the spell of his language master, a Polish exile named Yanick Helczman. Helczman's specialities were a fervent patriotism, an equally fervent anti-communism, and a deep regard for the Church. But just as important to the formation of Evans's outlook was his National Service posting to Malaya during the Emergency, or 'anti-bandit' war. There he discovered that, despite Helczman's finest imprecations, the communists did have a thing or two to teach. 'Towards the end of my military service one fact became indelibly imprinted on my mind. That being how easy it was for small numbers of determined insurgents to tie up many thousands of regular troops, and almost paralyse the normal governing and administration of vast areas of country.'[6]

If Malaya, then why not Wales? When he returned home, Cayo's blood was up and running:

> I had never been interested in the culture-vulture nationalist playing dirges on a lofty harp in a draughty pavilion with his patriotism safely submerged in history, and his day to day life spent in the ivory towers of some educational establishment. Equally I disliked the left-wing politics of the trade union officials, replete with plastic macs and duodenal ulcers. Cloth cap and peppermint-sucking politicians would never restore freedom to Wales. What was needed was to combine the latent power of the really die-hard nationalists into a single force, dedicated to gaining independence for our country. But before they could be combined it was necessary to seek them out as individuals.[7]

Thus began a ten-year career of cut-price insurgency. In Malaya Cayo had encountered Irish Republican sympathizers who not only inspired his own love of country, but now provided him with IRA contacts across the Irish Sea. Duly, Cayo and some of his followers attended the fiftieth anniversary celebrations of the 1916 Uprising in Dublin. Duly too the FWA received the occasional consignment of rusty weapons. The IRA, however, being professional in these matters, preferred to keep Cayo Evans and his kind at arm's length. They recognized that conditions in Wales were not the same as they were in the Six Counties; nor were the Welsh extremists sufficiently ruthless in the pursuit of their objectives.

Indeed, for Cayo, unwilling to resort to the bullet, the difficulty always was finding anyone to take him seriously, except in a negative way. In 1966 Plaid Cymru, at a conference held in Dolgellau, dissociated itself from the FWA and other militant groups. The following year, in a bid for publicity, but attired in jackboots, a band of FWA and Patriotic Front members travelled to a London television studio. David Frost wasted no time making them appear not dangerous so much as farcical. As luck would have it, David Coslett, one of the better known extremists after Cayo Evans, was wearing a black eye-patch that day. 'Ah, you must be Dai Dayan,' Frost quipped.

Even the prison sentence Cayo Evans collected on the day of the Investiture – fifteen months – was unbecoming a local Che Guevara. A more telling punishment was meted out in 1970 to John Jenkins, effectively leader of the Mudiad Amddiffyn Cymru, proven to have been responsible for some of the Cardiff bombings. Jenkins got ten years. His activities were more definably treasonous than Cayo's, and he could not be so easily dismissed as a *Boy's Own* revolutionary. By virtue of being a sergeant in the British Army, albeit a storekeeper with the Dental Corps, Jenkins had broken his oath to the Crown. He was also a lot more hard-headed than his stallion-riding compatriot. In *To Dream of Freedom*, a narrative of FWA and MAC personalities and operations written by Roy Clews, and at one stage referred to the Director of Public Prosecutions, Jenkins sets out his philosophy in stark terms:

In Wales we could not call upon that most constant of revolutionary aims, the foreign power whose mass media is at the rebels' disposal, like the Irish can call upon the Americans, or the Cypriots call upon the Greeks, and obtain as a bonus technical aid and assistance. We had none of these things. Our base was here in Wales. We couldn't, for example, call upon 12 million Welsh-Americans and they'd be up in arms. They wouldn't, they assimilate too easily, their bread is too well buttered . . . So the only way we could get personally to the mass of Welsh people was to involve them in conflict. The only way to involve them in conflict is to have a soldier beating their door down with a rifle butt, and the only way you'll get that, is carefully planned violence . . . That is, you initiate something that will bring retribution, and the retribution will fall indiscriminately. It happened in Cyprus where from a friendly village there would come a shot as the troops were passing. No one knows who pulled the trigger, so the whole village is searched and perhaps manhandled. In 24 hours that once friendly village is full of enemies. You see the psychology of people is to hate the end result, not what initially caused it . . . That is the classic pattern for rousing an apathetic population, and gradually it could have come about like that here in Wales.[8]

But neither the state nor the people were so easily gulled. Welsh respectability, nurtured over two centuries of God-fearing noncon-formity, and reinforced by pacifist beliefs that had their origin in a much older religious practice, turned its back on John Jenkins, Cayo Evans and their ilk. Violence of any kind, even the relatively mild violence of disrupted water supplies, was not the way.

One reason for the extremists' failure was their inability to furnish nationalist aspirations with a pragmatic ideology. Of several manifes-tos designed to set the tinder alight, we may take as representative *The ABC of the Welsh Revolution*, by Derrick Hearne. Published in 1982 by the same Talybont house (Y Lolfa) that produced Roy Clews's *To Dream of Freedom* – sensibly perhaps both books had washable rain-proof covers – this attempted to provide a contempor-ary equivalent of Bukharin and Preobrazhensky's *ABC of Communism* (1919). Hearne's message was anything but Marxist however. Some Marxist terms are used – 'alienation', for instance – but the message is trenchantly anti-communist. Less trenchant are Hearne's criticisms of fascism, 'a creed written off as mere opportunism, without serious intellectual foundations'. A rapprochement is adumbrated, effected through a rejection of representative democracy:

> When the Welsh are once again a free people, the form and style of the English parliament will be of no relevance as a pattern of our development. Our own circumstances are so different, and the times and conditions under which people's rule will operate in Wales are so novel and fraught with danger that the manner of the English parliament is of no more consequence than the *Estates-General* of France. Effective people's rule is dependent upon local democracy, civic and industrial, and in these matters Wales will have to set its own precedents. It is on these concerns that nationalists should now be focussing their attention. Parliament is part of a dying order.[9]

Hearne proposes instead a version of 'guided democracy' based on syndicalist workers' councils that would do away with the need for trades unions. Also outlawed from Hearne's republic is freedom of the press. Instead, and with an ominous lack of clarity, there should be censorship:

> The prime role of communication is to draw the community together, to educate it in the possible options open to it, and to give each individual the absolute emotional certainty that, within the limits of what is possible in Wales, it is all up to him ... Entertainment is within a national context, but distraction has no place whatsoever in the new revolutionary order.[10]

Hearne's real obsession, however, is messianic. The polity he recommends is probably closer in texture to Islamic fundamentalism than to anything that replaced the Weimar Republic. Although his polemic is obscured by a welter of bogus economics, at regular intervals the clouds part. 'Strange to relate,' he writes in an attack on communism, 'ordinary human being[s] need both God and a nation. However many betrayals of Christian principles may have taken place in history, it is a fact that whenever God's law is overthrown, freedom, truth, justice, tolerance and kindness soon fly out of the window.'[11] And again,

> A nation is the creation of God ... The fact that any majority do not at this point in time accept the duties of nationality is of no consequence. God's law is not a matter of majorities but of absolutes. The techniques of persuasion have not changed since the trial of Christ. The people of Jerusalem welcomed Jesus riding upon an ass in triumph into the holy city on Sunday, but they asked Pilate for Barabas in place of the King of the Jews on Friday. A few cheer-leaders placed strategically in a crowd by a skilful and determined enemy can always sway a mob.[12]

In Hearne's republic, such elements of democracy as survive will be guided by divine authority, presumably as interpreted by the regime's enlightened elders.

A less chiliastic picture of Welsh nationalism is to be found in *The Welsh Extremist*,[13] by Ned Thomas: in the overtly polemical literature the one abiding classic. At the time of its publication, 1971, Thomas was a lecturer at University College of Wales, Aberystwyth. Hitherto a varied career in journalism and broadcasting had taken him to, among other destinations, Moscow, as a teacher on a British Council exchange programme. He was well versed in many nationalisms of different hues, and this, together with a distinctly Orwellian mindset, gave him a purchase on the Welsh problem not all his compatriots share. He was also, on his own admission, a non-believer. He looks at Wales both passionately, as a Welshman, and dispassionately, with a nose for cant. The title of his essay is in part ironic: he is not especially concerned with either revolutionary practice or incendiary techniques. Rather, concentrating his inquiry on Welsh language and Welsh culture, he advances the proposition that 'extremism' is an entirely natural consequence of a real predicament. It is, he argues, the very existence of an indigenous literature, and its practitioners, that disables the lazy view of Wales as being simply another 'development area':

> The attraction of the best literature in Welsh is not merely that it identifies with our life: it holds up the ideal of a civilised and humane society, which is an ideal for people in other places. Because of its small size, the Welsh language community feels in extreme form the mindless destruction that is carried out everywhere in the name of economic logic.[14]

'The issue,' Ned Thomas states, 'is whether a small community, with its own language and culture and values, its literary and intellectual traditions, its way of seeing the world, its own way of being human, can go on existing in these islands.'

Wales as a geographic expression is excluded. Ned Thomas does not seek to prescribe a new order applicable to every person west of Offa's Dyke. He is a realist. Yet even in defining a smaller culture, he is aware of the fallacy of drawing hard and fast boundaries. 'The Welsh language community,' he writes, 'like every other national community, is a series of overlapping groups, and some of those overlap with the non-Welsh-speaking Welsh.'[15] For example, within Plaid Cymru, there are some who deplore the direct action of the

Welsh Language Society, and others who approve it. His business is not to legitimate one course of action, one political agenda, at the expense of all others, but rather to reveal the underlying causes of any specifically 'Welsh' politics, and thereby engage his English reader's sympathy.

If Ned Thomas wins his reader over, it is because he is constantly ready to make common-sense concessions. 'No Welsh issue can be a major conflict in Britain,' he submits, 'because only 2½ million people are involved.' He also acknowledges that Welsh nationalism, in as far as it is capable of description, is bound to strike those who encounter it as a 'curious blend' of pacifism, internationalism, co-operative socialism and Christianity. Not all these ingredients are to his own liking. But that is not the point. The thing exists, and the thing concerns his fellow human beings. It is humiliating, he reminds us eloquently, for 'an educated Welshman' to have to spend so much of his time and energy 'fighting for what should be unquestioned rights'.[16] The language campaign is not in itself an enjoyable pursuit. Rather, 'People must be given enough power to negotiate with other groups and to set their own priorities.'[17]

'Extremism' turns out, therefore, in the Welsh context, to be innately defensive. 'The Welsh speaker has to assert his identity, because this identity will otherwise not be respected.'[18] It is not the campaign on behalf of the Welsh language but the historic campaign against it that is the more extremist, precisely because it overlooks, and by overlooking overrules, humanity's defining characteristic:

> A different language does not assert one's total difference from other groups of the human race, but it registers the degree of difference that in fact exists; it is from the recognition of this that all worthwhile efforts at understanding between groups must start.[19]

If the language cannot be, or is not to be, preserved, then what else is there?

Ned Thomas acknowledges that, 'in present-day Wales', maintaining the Welsh language requires, at the least, 'a positive act of will.'[20] The odds against survival are stacked up high. Television, advertising, the press, education and 'the whole commercial side of life', the vast quotidian run of things, are carried out in English. Small wonder then that there should be 'the growing realisation, as among the young everywhere, of a connection between all the elements of social structure, that you cannot be a cultural nationalist only.' Nonetheless, cultural nationalism remains for Ned Thomas the sine qua non. Without it, without the expressions of Welsh culture recorded in the Welsh language, without the actuality of Welsh culture, every other argument would lose its force.

The Welsh Extremist becomes a series of essays, a series of homages, paid to contemporary Welsh authors: Gwenallt and Kate Roberts and D. J. Williams, as well as Saunders Lewis. But crucially Ned Thomas does not restrict himself to what might still be considered by some readers as the enclave of Welsh literature. Such an enclave, he suggests, does not in fact exist. Rather,

> The English-speaking and Welsh-speaking Welsh are not two quite separate language groups who happen to be rubbing shoulders, like English and French-speakers in Quebec Province; they are one group that has suffered a split in its consciousness, and this produces a curious emotional ambivalence which can be exploited for conflict but which is also the hope for cultural and political solidarity.[21]

Suddenly, some of the contradictions seemingly inherent in the 'Anglo-Welsh' movement are resolved. It is not an absurdity after all for a Welshman writing in English to mourn a language he doesn't speak, or doesn't write. What he is in fact mourning is a consciousness he hasn't altogether lost. And because he retains a part of such consciousness, it stands to reason that the sense of loss should be greater, not less.

Ned Thomas specifically recommends his namesake R. S. in this respect. 'In the recent poetry of R. S. Thomas,' he writes, 'one catches the note of desperation and resistance that is hardly to be distinguished from a great deal of what is being written in Welsh.'[22] And again: 'The note of desperation and of protest rings true as a style in English, and it is true to the Welsh language culture in which he lives his life.'

But what of the many hundreds of thousands of English-speaking

Welsh people who do not participate in the desperation and resistance and protest? Ned Thomas is too honest to ignore them. Nor, as an Orwellian socialist, can he dismiss them as a 'rabble', as Saunders Lewis and Derrick Hearne do. Yet to *explain* them, he resorts to avenues of thought that struggle to convince. One such is the old, Marxisant spectre of 'alienation', or as Ned Thomas calls it, 'passive alienation'. 'The Welsh identity', he writes.

> is dearer to me precisely because it lacks the strain of militarism and imperialism which is there in the British identity. I should make it clear that I am not exonerating Welshmen from having participated in British imperialism. It is merely that when they did so they did so as Britishers, not as Welshmen. The Welsh language was not part of that imperialism, and as a Welsh speaker in his own country the Welshman was himself the victim of a kind of imperialism.[23]

Elsewhere in *The Welsh Extremist* Ned Thomas argues that the Welsh identity has been corrupted by imported bureaucracies and con-sumerisms. Like R. S., he has something to say about the dehumaniz-ing aspects of the 'machine'. But if we take these arguments seriously – and there is no reason why we shouldn't – then we are led to a romantic, almost Jungian view of humankind. We must accept that there is something there to be alienated and dehumanized in the first place. That consciousness is not, as some contemporary imagery encourages us to believe, a neutral, value-free framework into which stray animal passions and purely arbitrary cultural markers (including whatever language it is we happen to use) are introduced.

In his chapter on Kate Roberts, Ned Thomas asserts:

> Always the outlines of the scenery are deep in the Welsh consciousness as if scored in thick paint on canvas. But one only knows this quality of depth through reading, in history and literature, about the past, feeling it as it has been left by those who have lived Welsh history within that landscape.[24]

And it is this theme, this avenue, that is developed in the concluding chapter of *The Welsh Extremist*. Ned Thomas offers us a series of interlocking pronouncements:

One can, of course, *deny* one's Welshness, and numbers of educated Welshmen have done this, particularly in the older generation, at great psychological cost to themselves.[25]

One of the great values of the Welsh language is that in a world where social controls are built into the individual through the pattern of work and leisure ... it preserves an area of inner freedom, of conscious alienation from the system.[26]

We may not be all politically radicalized, but we are all very easily capable of it.[27]

The image of Wales as a garden, a vineyard, a landscape shaped and humanized by the care of generations is one that recurs in our literature. The wind is always there, usually with its religious meaning of something cleansing, blowing away the props of our complacency.[28]

Even if such utterances do express a truth, we are entitled to ask whether such truth is necessary or contingent. The feeling that the Welsh landscape, or any other landscape come to that, is there in our consciousness to be dug out by our reading upon such subject-matter is largely tautologous. The reading itself must play a part in the creation, or re-creation, of that landscape.

The same sort of criticism may be levelled against each of his other assertions. But to take Ned Thomas to task for failing to be ultra-sceptical is to miss the broader argument of *The Welsh Extremist*. It is not finally an essay about politics, but an essay about a literature, and the centrality of that literature to human dignity. Or rather, it *is* about politics, but only if it is allowed that human dignity should be a goal, and not the occasional by-product, of the political process.

What is exposed is the uncertain character of dignity itself. Is it an innate quality, which is suppressed at our peril? Or is it merely added on, as circumstance allows?

The same question may be rephrased in religious terms. Is divine grace an illusion we create for ourselves, a mere chimera? Or is it something outside human imagining, outside time even?

I return to R. S. Thomas.

*　　　*　　　*

In the autumn of 1954 Thomas's search for a 'Welsh parish' in which to serve as priest took him and his family from Manafon to Eglwysfach, just south of the boundary between Ceridigion (Cardiganshire) and Meirionnydd, and a few miles north of Aberystwyth. Thirteen years later, in May 1967, aged fifty-three, he moved again, to Aberdaron, a seaside parish almost at the end of the remote and magical Llŷn Peninsula, at the extreme north-west of the Welsh mainland. There he remained as rector until his retirement in 1978. He continued living on Pen Llŷn another fifteen years, in a 'four-hundred year old' cottage on the Plas-yn-Rhiw estate. Then, in 1994, following the death of his wife Elsi in 1991, and a brief sojourn outside Prestatyn, he removed to Anglesey, taking up residence on a wind-blasted hillside not far from his native Holyhead.

Thus the simple, seemingly uneventful outline of the second half of the priest's life, leavened only by a handful of mainly bird-watching expeditions abroad, in Norway, Spain, Denmark, Greece and Alaska: in Crockford's, a career barely distinguishable from those of the mass of other Welsh clergymen who never rise to high office within the Church. During the same period, however, Thomas emerged as an undoubted heavyweight not just on the 'Anglo-Welsh' literary scene, but also within the highest echelon of English poetry. At the same time, in as far as he presented a face to a diffuse public, he became known for his irascibility. He became both a cultural force and an idiosyncratic cultural icon.

Given the strongly patriotic and anti-English flavouring of a very large number of the poems R. S. wrote at Manafon and subsequently at Eglwysfach, and the equally entrenched views contained in his early prose essays, there was the possibility that Thomas would also emerge, during the 1960s, when the profile of Welsh nationalism was greatly enhanced, as a politically active figure. And so, in a tangential way, he did. He supported the Welsh Language Society, and sometimes turned out for its protests. He also added his support to Adfer, a Bangor-based splinter group of the Cymdeithas yr Iaith Gymraeg set up by Emyr Llewelyn in 1971. As its name suggests – the Welsh word means 'to restore' – Adfer campaigned for the restitution of monolingualism in those parts of Wales that were still definably Welsh. In particular it advocated property laws that would make it impossible for outsiders to buy their way into Welsh Wales, and recommended expeditory community action. Since the influx of outsiders was pushing up property values in many rural areas, to the extent that younger local residents were often priced (or prized) out of home ownership, not surprisingly this movement gained a significant following. Student adherents of Adfer were also conspicuously involved in the disturbances at Bangor University in 1978–9.

Thomas, as has already been said, participated in these. On other occasions too he has voiced stridently nationalist opinions in public arenas. At the event organized to celebrate his eightieth birthday at the Sherman Theatre in Cardiff, a woman in the audience quizzed Thomas whether 'you mean that anybody born in Wales who does not speak Welsh is not Welsh?' Thomas replied, 'That's right!'[29] Rather more controversially, in 1990 he appeared on the platform of a meeting of the diehard Cyfamodwyr y Gymru Rydd, the Covenanters of a Free Wales. At that meeting he has been quoted as saying: 'I deplore killing, but what is the life of one English person compared to the destruction of a nation?'[30] Indeed, when the opportunity has presented itself, R. S. has never been shy to express uncompromising opinions, echoing statements made in his poetry, which is also, of course, another kind of public forum.

In the 1980s too, R. S. antagonized Welsh respectability by refusing to condemn outright the activities of Meibion Glyndŵr. 'The Sons of Glyndŵr', secretive successors to the Free Wales Army and Mudiad Amddiffyn Cymru, were behind the arson attacks on English-owned holiday cottages. Their tactics created a real possibility that sooner or later fatalities would occur. Asked specifically about Meibion Glyndŵr and the 'limits of direct action' in an interview conducted by Ned Thomas and John Barnie for the magazine *Planet*, R. S. gave consideration to his reply:

> As you know I have always been careful to preface any remarks I make in the context of Welsh opposition with the reminder that I have been a priest of the Church, that my interpretation of the Gospel is pacifist and although a case can be made for the use of force in the condition which Cymru now finds herself in, I am not prepared

to incite others to do what I am not prepared to do myself. The ability of most of the general public to think clearly has been eroded by various means. Many people lost their heads completely over my remarks about Meibion Glyndŵr. What I said in answer to a loaded question was that I admired their courage and was glad that the Welsh spirit was not totally subdued. We know that if they are caught they will be given massive sentences. They know it, too. Therefore it takes courage on their part to risk it.[31]

Yet even this sits precariously on the fence. As in so many of his poems, the perspective shifts and shifts again. But if Thomas has continued to tolerate nationalism in some of its more vehement manifestations, it would be misleading to label him an extremist in the sense that Cayo Evans or John Jenkins were extremists. His capers have all been with the tongue, not with gelignite. His remark to the Covenanters exactly catches one of the tensions in his thought; and Thomas's quality as a writer greatly depends on his readiness to display whatever tensions in fact exist amid his speculations, regardless of whether those speculations are voluntary or involuntary. The notion of violence on behalf of a troubled nation one belongs to and loves is a genuine *point d'appui*. One feels he would like to countenance violence, but in fact is constitutionally incapable of doing so. Significantly, living in Llŷn, as well as supporting Adfer, he also joined the Pwllheli branch of the Campaign for Nuclear Disarmament (CND): a movement that strongly appealed to his pacifism, as well as his antipathy towards modern technologies (though not apparently the technology of the modern printing press).

A determined advocate, anxious to stick Thomas with the charge of militancy, might reasonably ask: Where in fact does poetry end and action begin? In the prevailing typology of nationalism, the break between its cultural and political phases is less clear-cut than it used to be.[32] A literature that constantly celebrates, for example, the insurgence of Owain Glyndŵr, to which body of work Thomas has contributed manifoldly, is in itself a kind of praxis. The 1916 Easter Uprising in Dublin did not occur in a verbal or imaginative vacuum.

By the same token, were such an advocate to raise a case against R. S., one would have to ask: in whose pay is he advocating anyway?

The resort to collective violence, or violence perpetrated in the name of a collectivity, seldom is a simple issue of right and wrong. If it were, there would not be so much of it. In the 'case' against R. S. Thomas, however, it is important to sift the defendant's own testimony. In *Neb*, Thomas has written specifically about the nationalist ferment of the post-war period:

> The sixties were also a time when the political situation deteriorated and some of the young Welsh started using more direct action against English oppression. Men like Emyr Llewelyn were treated in a pretty loathsome way by the police, and the poet from Eglwysfach responded by writing more patriotic verses. Naturally he was accused of narrowness by English critics. This was the time of his most bitter poems against the English. But he did not take direct action. Instead he remembered the advice of Saunders Lewis, when he said that not much action should be expected from a writer, because it is through his work that he could influence others.[33]

No matter that 'direct action' is not clearly defined, here Thomas precisely asserts its consanguinity with cultural nationalism. But what is also noteworthy is the readiness with which he adopts Lewis's proferred 'advice'. The 1960s were, after all, also a period which witnessed the presence of many creative faces at the barricades. In Britain the most famous instance was the arrest and imprisonment of the philosopher Bertrand Russell. Nor is the phenomenon historically limited. Among poets too, there have been many active patriots and dissidents: Adam Mickiewicz in Poland, for example; the Italian Gabriele D'Annunzio; Hugh Macdiarmid in Scotland and Saunders Lewis himself in Wales; even the Bosnian Serb Radovan Karadzic. Indeed there is no prima facie evidence to suggest a necessary antinomy between creativity and action.

The cynic's rebuff to this might be: Thomas wasn't prepared to chance his arm in circumstances that threatened his personal liberty. But a better understanding is reached if we look at what sort of poet, and for that matter what sort of man, Thomas is. Further on in *Neb*, commenting upon his preference for the outdoor world to scholarly or even literary company, he writes:

No-one can avoid learned company without a loss to himself. At the same time it is necessary to remember the difference between scholars and creative people. It is easy to spend a day over a lyric, yet fail at the end of it. In the same space of time a student or a scholar will have read an entire book and perhaps, have memorized it as well. Typically though the creative mind has a poor memory. That is, it easily forgets things that are on the surface of life; but unknown to him, other things sink into the subconscious, to form there a matrix or pool he can draw upon sometime in the future. In this way do many of the successful poems come into being.[34]

This is not offered as a pretext for avoiding action. It is said in a different context entirely. Nor is it necessary to test the validity of what Thomas says about creativity against the testimony and experience of other poets. Its value is as regards what it tells us about Thomas. And there is no reason to suspect that what he tells us about himself here is fabricated. Elsewhere too, in several places, he insists that the essential conditions for his ability to function as a poet are solitude, time and silence.

But solitude, time and silence are also the soil of inwardness. At least, if the tree is to be judged by its fruit, this is almost spectacularly true of Thomas, as any reading of his work must confirm. The question of the relationships between patriotism and activism, and between militancy and pacifism, can partly be resolved therefore by having a regard for the particulars of the poet's creative personality, which must also in some measure be a reflection of his character as a man. Some choices are simply not available to him, however much, as an artist and a Welshman, he may entertain them in his mind or heart. Other factors are also involved, including Thomas's religious vocation, and the social status he appears sometimes to aspire to. In Wales too, the convergence of the nationalist and the peacenik in one person is virtually a stereotype. But critically, in Thomas's case, the relationships in question, and the tensions they imply, become internalized to an uncommon degree.

The move to Eglwysfach, on the A487 between Aberystwyth and Machynlleth, proved a mixed blessing for R. S. He could perform at least some of his churchwork in Welsh, and the small 'roadside' village's proximity to the sea partially satisfied his yearning for the environment of his Anglesey childhood. He also found himself living closer to 'Welsh' Wales than at any time since his student days at Bangor. The old language was still spoken in many of the surrounding villages and towns, particularly to the south in Cardiganshire. He no longer had to travel long distances to practise his Welsh. At Aberystwyth, less than half an hour away by car, not only was there the National Library of Wales, but also the University College – the foremost centre for the promotion of Welsh studies. Yet about Eglwysfach itself Thomas had miscalculated. His new parish, territorially much smaller than Manafon, contained an unhealthy proportion of what he regarded as the worst sort of Englishmen: 'retired tea planters' and 'ex-army officers'.[35] Moreover, there was a preparatory school whose boys dutifully filed into St Mary's Church every Sunday morning, and for whom the poet had to tailor his sermons.

Thomas had been angling for a Welsh-speaking parish for some while. Eglwysfach was adventitious. In 1953 he learned that a bird observatory was opening on Ynys Enlli, Bardsey Island, a holy place off the nethermost tip of Llŷn. In time, Thomas's involvement with Bardsey, and more especially the Bardsey Island Trust, established in 1979, and separate from the 'Bardsey Bird and Field Observatory', would grow. For now, he enrolled as a 'Friend' of the Observatory, made his first visit to the island, and called on its Hon. Secretary, William Condry. Condry, a Birmingham-born naturalist, and for many years the *Guardian*'s nature correspondent, lived at Eglwysfach, near Aberdyfi. Sharing Thomas's concern for the preservation of the Welsh countryside, when he learned that his vicar was shortly to retire he wrote to the rector of Manafon suggesting he apply for the post. As chance would have it, the then Bishop of St David's, in whose diocese Eglwysfach lay, was William Havard, formerly the Bishop of St Asaph. Thomas wrote immediately to Havard, and Havard replied as immediately that the job was his.

The Thomases took up residence in October 1954. The move caused some inconvenience to Elsi Thomas, who was halfway through completing a commissioned mural for the nurses' dining hall at the Orthopaedic Hospital at Gobowen. But as R. S. puts it in his

'Autobiographical Essay', 'she coped in her usual competent way.'[36] For the first six months it rained continuously, but this did not detract from the poet's appreciation of his new habitat:

> Eglwysfach was in an attractive part of rural Wales. It was a main road village, some five miles from the sea as the crow flies, with the river Dyfi going by it. Hill country rose steeply behind the road, and frothing brooks ran down the valleys to the narrow plains between sea and mountain. It was an area that was Welsh in appearance, with the hills of Meirionnydd rising in the north and an occasional sighting of Cader Idris from the high ground. After a storm, if the wind dropped, the sound of the sea was to be heard to the west. But better than that, once a day the tide came up the river with smells of the sea on its foam.[37]

However, R. S. is quick to identify the fly in the ointment. What he didn't know before moving to Eglwysfach was 'how weak the Welsh were'. In the parish were 'many big houses', and these belonged to 'English' owners, 'despite the Welsh names of almost all of them'.[38] Worse, apart from the outlying farming community, those Welsh resident in the village were all 'maids and gardeners' in the employ either of such houses, or of the preparatory school. 'And even amongst the village folk there was considerable intermarriage with the English from places like Herefordshire.'[39]

For this there was a literary precedent of sorts – two, if one includes the poet's own marriage. In 1819 the satirical novelist and Londoner Thomas Love Peacock, staying in the area, met, fell in love with and married Jane Gryffyth, the daughter of the then vicar of Eglwysfach, and gallantly described by Peacock's friend Shelley as a 'White Snowdonian antelope'.[40] Peacock subsequently published, in 1829, *The Misfortunes of Elphin*, a Ceredigion extravaganza based on legends pertaining to Taliesin and other figures from the remote Cymric past. Like many of his other novels, *The Misfortunes of Elphin* contained several songs and ballads, some of them based on early Celtic verses, including the famous 'War-Song of Dinas Vawr':

> The mountain sheep are sweeter,
> But the valley sheep are fatter;

We therefore deemed it meeter
To carry off the latter.

The marriage, however, was not a conspicuous success. Translated from her native soil and lumbered with a bookish husband, Jane Gryffyth sickened.

It is possible, though improbable, that R. S. has Peacock in mind when, in both *Neb* and the 'Autobiographical Essay', he tells us that the society he encountered at Eglwysfach would have made a good subject-matter for a light novel; by inference, no grist to a serious poet's mill. There were, he found, two 'factions' in the village, reflecting the interests of the two major landowners, Lewis Pugh and Hubert Mappin:

> And in the middle of all this was the Vicar, like a coconut for shying at if they decided to treat him so. At Manafon he had had enough of filth. But now, looking back, he could see that the farmers there had more excuse for their coarse attitudes. They had little education and little experience of the wider world. But here in Eglwysfach there was a layer of people who had had both, and who were therefore less able to plead ignorance. The Vicar gradually learned of the old weaknesses of man: snobbery, for example, or envy, or avarice. But he also realised the challenge before him. Faced by a more sophisticated congregation there was a need to plan his sermons carefully, to deal with the new situation. He could not continue to talk about nature all the time, but tried instead to confront some of the problems of the day and the human mind.[41]

Yet, as he proceeds immediately to tell us, he also adhered to a pattern of life that had become established at Manafon: study in the morning, country walks in the afternoon, and 'visiting his flock by evening'. The new priest, as much as he could, kept himself to himself. Raymond Garlick, a visitor to the Vicarage, has recounted how a conversation with R. S. was interrupted by the telephone ringing. After a brief exchange, the humorist in Thomas expressed the view that life would be much simpler if the people in his parish could so arrange matters that they were born, married and buried all on the same day each month, leaving all the other days free.[42]

As the narrative of *Neb* unfolds, one senses a premature hardening of the arteries. Even the allurements of Aberystwyth prove short-lived:

> Shortly after he settled there, a professor from Cambridge came to lecture on Chekhov, and the Vicar went there expecting a feast. But alas! For an entire hour the lecturer didn't once raise his head from his little book, the driest lecture the Vicar ever heard. His enthusiasm for attending lectures vanished. And he didn't much enjoy the library either. The books were there of course, but he soon realised he was not a scholar willing to spend hours in that great dry place, when the glorious day called him outside.[43]

There was more pleasure, he insists, watching the plentiful birdlife on and around the Dyfi estuary. That way he could 'forget about the little problems of the parish'. But not entirely. In a page or two he returns to his assault:

> One cannot escape entirely. People's words and ideas murmur away in the mind, and he had enough of these from the English of Eglwys-fach. There is no-one like the English. And such a blessing to the rest of the world! 'It would be good to hear someone other than an Englishman say that,' would be his reply. But his was a voice in the wilderness, apart from Gwydol Owen's at the Post Office. When Churchill died many of the English thought the Vicar at fault for not offering prayers in the church. When Kennedy was killed some of these self-important people came to the church wearing black, to show their kinship. And when there was a fashionable wedding or funeral, they came in clothes hired from Moss Bros![44]

As Thomas puts it in *The Echoes Return Slow*, 'When the English colonize a parish, a vicar's is chaplain's work.'[45] There, the poet's dislike for his non-Welsh parishioners is not softened by the passage of years, but turns to loathing:

> There are sins rural and sins social. Does a god discriminate? Education is the refinement of evil. The priest is required to make his way along glass-sown walls. It is easier to divide a parish than to

unite it, except on Sundays. The smell of the farmyard was replaced by the smell of the decayed conscience.[46]

While across the page, in the verse counterpart:

> And this one with his starched lip,
> his medals, his meanness;
> his ability to live cheap off dear things.
>
> And his china-eyed children
> with their crêpe-de-Chine hair,
> product of a chill nursery,
>
> borrowing nastiness from
> each other, growing harder and thinner
> on the day's diet of yawns and smirks.
>
> His wife and his friends' wives,
> reputations congealing about their mouths'
> cutlery after the prandial remarks.[47]

According to these portraits Eglwysfach was clearly, for Thomas, a village of the damned. A part of the problem was that the military types ensconced there were used to regarding a priest as a subordinate. Thomas is 'reminded . . . that journeying is not necessarily in the right direction'.[48] Hence the cutlery in his own mouth. The sources of such rancour are not hard to locate: they all reside within Thomas's personality, poetic or otherwise. There is the frustrated patriotism, the feeling that to be Welsh is to be pulverized, that one's territory has been irredeemably taken over; there is the man's obvious unsociability, given vent here as unbridled misanthropy; but as well as these there is a religious intractability, Thomas as Isaiah or Jeremiah reborn, not just Myrddin. The ungodly are not ungodly by degree, but are absolutely ungodly. No distinction is drawn between mere foible and mortal error; only a deep fury that the world is not as it should or could be.

Inevitably much of the poetry written at Eglwysfach is a poetry of affliction. Again and again Thomas presents the reader with statements of personal suffering. What makes such poetry important, however, apart from its obvious acuteness of expression, is the determination of its author to persevere under the tutelage of an oppressive muse. There is a sense of continuous descent, of a going round in Dantean circles, and also of a praeternatural exhaustion. Thomas, treadmilling through his forties, is old before his time. Some of his lines might well have been written by Yeats at a much greater age. There is also a similar awareness of the poet qua poet, brooding over a people and a landscape, that only compounds the bleak futility of much of what he beholds and describes. Yet set against this is a counterpoint of sorts. If the descent is an unavoidable consequence of the conditions of the poet's life, it is also a quest for whatever redemption may exist. In an unspiritual world, traces of spirit are clung to with grim determination.

Such traces however are located mainly, if not exclusively, in the past. Or rather in two related pasts: the historic past of Wales, and Thomas's own more recent past in Manafon. Very few of the poems bear an ostensible relationship to Eglwysfach. By a cruel irony, the *hiraeth* that took R. S. westwards across the mountains towards the sea generates a mordant nostalgia for what is left behind in his wake. At regular intervals Iago Prytherch is taken out, dusted down and forced into dialogue.

Excluding the retrospective *Song at the Year's Turning*, between 1954 and 1967 four collections of verse are published: *Poetry for Supper* (1958); *Tares* (1961); *The Bread of Truth* (1963); and *Pietà* (1966). Between these is an unusual measure of similarity. Each contains between thirty and forty poems, and each is between forty and fifty pages in length. The covers too, designed by Elsi Thomas, are uniformly austere; while inside the covers are commensurate assortments of poems on variegated but increasingly predictable themes: poems about members of the hill-farm communities Thomas has left behind; poems offering statements about Wales; poems about being a priest; poems about nature and God; poems about being a poet. Each volume complies with a common format. The differences between them are to be detected only by detailed inspection. The reader must become a Thomas-watcher. The excitement is not in any dizzying formal experiment or departure, but within the minute exactions the poet makes within what appear to be static parameters.

That said, the very first poem of these four books, 'Border Blues',[49] in seven sections, and superficially indebted to T. S. Eliot's 'The Waste Land', does offer a fresh stylistic direction. Of all Thomas's Welsh elegies, it is the most tantalizing, the most teasing. There is a deliberate ease of rhythm, a real bluesiness, that, if proof were wanting, demonstrates Thomas's actual prosodic versatility:

> I was going up the road and Beuno beside me
> Talking in Latin and old Welsh,
> When a volley of voices struck us; I turned,
> But Beuno had vanished . . .

Beuno here is the sixth-century Celtic saint who fled Powys to escape the Saxon invaders. The subjective voice is and isn't Thomas himself: for much of 'Border Blues', the identity assumed is that of a younger man of the hills, the confused inheritor of a confused heritage. Here, as Beuno disappears,

> in his place
> There stood the ladies from the council houses:
> Blue eyes and Birmingham yellow
> Hair, and the ritual murder of vowels.

The last clause though, 'the ritual murder of vowels', seems out of place. It belongs to another poem, another sortie. Quite apart from its mocking racism, its rhythm is at odds with the gentler stresses of the surrounding lines. Yet the poet is the first to acknowledge this. 'Border Blues' continues:

> Excuse me, I said. I have an appointment
> On the high moors; it is the first of May
> And I must go the way of my fathers

It is as though he neither wants to be dragged into the quarrel between races, nor to engage in building bridges. He turns his back on the Birmingham ladies, but he also turns his back on any meaningful encounter with them. The question of language remains central to the poem, just as it is central to a great number of verses written at Eglwysfach. Welsh words and lines from Welsh songs are woven into the text as Thomas evokes a series of Border ghosts, Glyndŵr among them. But any militancy is subdued, controlled, carefully weighed.

> As I was saying, I don't hold with war
> Myself, but when you join your unit
> Send me some of your brass buttons
> And I'll have a shot at the old hare
> In the top meadow, for the black cow
> Is a pint short each morning now.

Paragraph by paragraph the poem's issues and concerns slide about with deceptive facility. What in fact is being said in the lines above is that the economy of cattle is of equal or greater importance than the economy of nations. But the sense of this is wrapped up in an apparently carefree drift of consciousness that purports to allow for anything and everything. Yet the poem does climax in a manner that, while honouring the whole poem's style, is specific enough.

> Despite our speech we are not English,
> And our wit is sharp as an axe yet,
> Finding the bone beneath the skin
> And the soft marrow in the bone.

This sudden juxtaposition of opposites, the brittle hardness of bone, the yielding marrow, encapsulates the plight not just of the Welsh, but nearly every small beleaguered people. It explains at once their aggression, and how they have been reduced by their own want of aggression. 'We are not English', Thomas continues, and then quotes the old Welsh song 'Y delyn aur', the golden harp: 'Ni bydd diwedd/ Byth ar sŵn y delyn aur.' There is no end to the sound of the golden harp, nor to its enchantment.

Something of the insouciance of 'Border Blues' is recaptured in the poem that opens The Bread of Truth, 'A Line from St David's':[50]

> I ramble; what I wanted to say
> Was that the day has a blue lining
> Partly of sky, partly of sea;

The two poems though are untypical. One reason they work as well as they do is because they are set off by the surrounding prosodic field. They offer Thomas-watchers an unexpected glimpse of their quarry at bay. In the main the poet prefers the far more taut, and far more combative, constructs on which his early fame rests. Capable of great elegance, at this stage he chooses still to crack his consonants, then await their echo in the silences of the soul. Thus in a celebrated poem towards the end of *Pietà*, 'In Church',[51] a self-portrait of Thomas at prayer after the departure of his congregation, we are given:

> The bats resume
> Their business. The uneasiness of the pews
> Ceases. There is no other sound
> In the darkness but the sound of a man
> Breathing, testing his faith
> On emptiness, nailing his questions
> One by one to an untenanted cross.

The questions are also nailed by the clipped consonants of these lines, and their pouncing breaks. But the succession of consonants that drives home the conclusion is accompanied by a contradictory sibilance: resume, uneasiness, sound, darkness, sound (again), testing, emptiness, questions. And finally, of course, the word 'cross' itself, combining, as it were, the two countervailing musical tendencies. The man prays, but there is no knowing the outcome. The untenanted cross is compounded equally of bone and marrow, of resistance and grace.

'In Church', echoing the volume's title-poem, 'Pietà',[52] is sometimes regarded as the point of exit from Thomas's 'early' Welsh subject-matter poetry into his later 'religious' poetry. The 'untenanted cross' is beheld as a marvellously compact image for the great issues of faith and doubt that consume many of the older poet's energies. And so it is. But 'In Church' may just as well be seen as a summation of all that goes before. In it, R.S. finally assumes unto himself the extreme isolation that he has hitherto repeatedly witnessed, with some detachment, among his hardened hill-farmer types.

This at least would explain the almost supplicatory attitude

towards Iago Prytherch that is developed by Thomas in the earlier
Eglwysfach volumes. Once again, I think, it must be conceded that
Iago Prytherch is not the poet's alter ego, as some critics have suggested, but is a real entity forcing its attention upon Thomas from
without. Prytherch and the other farm characters, Evans for example,
or Job Davies, and their many unnamed companions, do not merely
represent an aspect of Wales under threat, they *are* such an aspect.
To assume otherwise is to indulge in academic caprice. Yet that said,
it certainly is the case that at Eglwysfach, removed from Manafon
and the specific moorlands above Manafon, Thomas must trade on
the memory of Prytherch, and not his corporeal actuality.

So much is vouchsafed in the first of the Iago Prytherch poems
to emanate from Eglwysfach, 'Temptation of a Poet',[53] in *Poetry for
Supper* placed immediately after 'Border Blues':

> The temptation is to go back,
> To make tryst with the pale ghost
> Of an earlier self, to summon
> To the mind's hearth, as I would now,
> You, Prytherch, there to renew
> The lost poetry of our talk
> Over the embers of that world
> We built together; not built either,
> But found lingering on the farm
> As sun lingers about the corn
> That in the stackyard makes its own light.

The earlier self is Thomas's, in his Manafon incarnation. A few pages
later, in 'Green Categories',[54] the difference between Thomas and his
interlocutor could hardly be expressed more starkly, or for that matter
more sneeringly: 'You never heard of Kant, did you, Prytherch?' This
momentarily resurrects the original shock to the poet's 'refined,/But
affected' sensibility when the two first met, except that now Thomas
projects himself as a reader of philosophy, rather than an aesthete.
Yet the purpose of 'Green Categories' is to suggest, not altogether
plausibly, a theoretical coming-together of two exceedingly disparate
figures:

> Yet at night together
> In your small garden, fenced from the wild moor's
> Constant aggression, you could have been at one,
> Sharing your faith over a star's blue fire.

Too much, however, depends upon the poem's title. 'Categories' leads us to Kant's 'categorical imperatives', while 'green' recommends the world of nature. Kant, the suggestion is, would by the necessity of his own logic have found himself in league with Prytherch, just as he would have found himself in league with 'Wales'. As has often been said, the 'garden' is of peculiar importance in Welsh (as in other) poetry. It represents the allowable limits of man's exploitation of nature to his own ends. It is a moral state, and by locating both Kant and Prytherch within it Thomas seeks to reconcile what he clearly feels are contrary forces within his own make-up. But the fact that he can only do this by resorting to a type of bathos shows the extent to which the poet's consciousness is riven.

In *Tares*, Prytherch is introduced immediately, in the opening poem, 'The Dark Well'.[55] However others may see him, Thomas again asserts Prytherch's moral integrity:

> To me you are Prytherch, the man
> Who more than all directed my slow
> Charity where there was need.

Just as Prytherch shares his empty moors with Thomas, so Thomas shares his pastoral vocation with Prytherch. But as well as that, he credits Prytherch, as the title suggests, with providing a voice for his poetry:

> whose heart, fuller than mine
> Of gulped tears, is the dark well
> From which to draw, drop after drop,
> The terrible poetry of his kind.

In 'Servant',[56] from *The Bread of Truth*, R. S. takes his indebtedness one step further. He plays on the conventional conceit of role reversal between master and servant. Thomas acknowledges Prytherch's service to him in the sense of opening his eyes to the 'land's story', and 'proving' it to him in bone and blood. But this 'truth', Thomas says, venturing his own superiority, is incomplete:

> Is not the evolving print of the sky
> To be read, too; the mineral
> Of the mind worked? Is not truth choice,
> With a clear eye and a free hand,
> From life's bounty?

But as the dialectic swings one way, so it must swing back, and it is Prytherch's superiority that the poem finally celebrates:

> Not choice for you,
> But seed sown upon the thin
> Soil of a heart, not rich, not fertile,
> Yet capable of the one crop,
> Which is the bread of truth that I break.

The inferences of that last image are heady, even dangerous. The bread that a priest breaks is Christ's body. But if Christ is equated with the Welsh peasantry, Thomas also draws upon the duality of Christ as perfect servant and perfect master. In his perfection as a servant Prytherch commands both priest and poet.

It is in 'Absolution',[57] from the earlier volume *Poetry for Supper*, that the role reversal between Thomas and Prytherch reaches its apogee. Here, it is the peasant who performs the role of the priest. Thomas approaches him as a sinner, asking him whether he can 'forgive'

> One who strafed you with his thin scorn
> From the cheap gallery of his mind?

Forgiveness is granted, by the 'slow lifting' of Prytherch's hand, but there is no 'welcome'. Any expressions of camaraderie between the two, suggested in other poems, is, after this, mere sentimentality. Thomas as supplicant is effectively cast out. He is denied what apparently he seeks, which is fellowship with Prytherch. The 'Absolution' is only partial. And by a reciprocal gesture, in *Pietà*, Thomas begins distancing, or redistancing, himself. In 'For the Record'[58] and

'Aside'[59] Iago Prytherch is returned to the fields much as Thomas originally discovered him, a noble savage in an impoverished landscape; while in 'The Face'[60] the poet concedes his own usage. When he closes his eyes, the bare hill and the man ploughing it spring instantly to mind:

> He is never absent, but like a slave
> Answers to the mind's bidding,
> Endlessly ploughing, as though autumn
> Were the one season he knew.

Yet we can only speculate that this is Prytherch, for in the poem itself he is not named.

Thomas's infatuation with Prytherch is similar to a lover's. The relationship, while it lasts, transforms the poet-lover's perspectives. He strives to see the world through his loved one's eyes. And when the relationship finishes, he emerges a wiser but sadder being. His own perspectives are restored to him, but in a subtly altered condition.

In the case of Prytherch, however, the relationship is only one aspect of a much stronger and more abiding partnership: that between Thomas and Wales itself. All four Eglwysfach volumes are packed full of poems that explore the whole gamut of love and hate – too many to analyse or even list here. Many have rightly become the stuff of 'Anglo-Welsh' anthologies. Some, like 'Welcome'[61] and 'Strangers',[62] expend their energies deploring the English – the rival lover. Others – 'Rhodri',[63] for instance, or 'Those Others'[64] – berate the Welsh themselves for their failure to keep faith. The language issue is never far beneath the surface, and sometimes rises violently through it, as in 'Welsh',[65] where Thomas recalls Gwenallt:

> I want the town even,
> The open door
> Framing a slut,
> So she can speak Welsh
> And bear children

> To accuse the womb
> That bore me.

Such utterances, whether or not, as here, they are dramatized through a borrowed persona – Thomas is good at 'voices' – have it within them to cause offence in divers quarters. Were it not for the gentler side of Thomas's longing for Wales, the marrow, the temptation would be to dismiss him as a fanatic. But the gentler side does break through, as in, quite memorably, the sonnet 'The View from the Window':[66]

> Like a painting it is set before one,
> But less brittle, ageless; these colours
> Are renewed daily with variations
> Of light and distance that no painter
> Achieves or suggests. Then there is movement,
> Change, as slowly the cloud bruises
> Are healed by sunlight, or snow caps
> A black mood; but gold at evening
> To cheer the heart.

Thus far it is just the beauty of the landscape that is extolled. And Wales *is* beautiful to the human eye. But the glory of the sonnet is in its almost irresistible implication of how such beauty comes about:

> All through history
> That great brush has not rested,
> Nor the paint dried; yet what eye,
> Looking coolly, or, as we now,
> Through the tears' lenses, ever saw
> This work and it was not finished?

Thomas does not spell it out, but the hand of God is at work. What is being done to the Welsh landscape, as attested in a poem such as 'Afforestation',[67] therefore is sacrilege.

In the same breath, Thomas manages to provide statements about the desecration of his country, and about a personal faith. But what adds power to his elbow is precisely the whole poetic context of 'The View from the Window'. The sonnet, with its carefully controlled assertions, stands wondrously by itself, but it also gains strength from the poems around it: for example, the single phrase 'the tears' lenses' is both an ophthalmologically charged description, and a marker for Wales's desuetude. The poem becomes, even, another version of the Celtic battle cry.

But then that is a feature of R. S., not just in the four Eglwysfach volumes, but throughout his work. His poems have an astonishing capacity to gather meaning and momentum from their companions, as sometimes they can also rub up against each other. It was a trick learned from other poets, most notably W. B. Yeats; and like Yeats, Thomas is adept at creating tranches of metaphor and image that endure not only from one page to another, but across volumes. But in the Welshman's hands, the trick very nearly becomes a comprehensive poetics.

The same is less true, say, of John Donne or Thomas Hardy or Philip Larkin or Thom Gunn: all poets whose output, like Thomas's, is characterized by multiple brevity and concision. Thomas is an inordinately fine craftsman, but he is not in the end simply the occasion's artificer. Partly perhaps the difference is down to a version of Celtic gestalt. Every poem he writes, whatever its immediate subject-matter, emanates from a consciousness that cannot relinquish any of its deeds, any of its creations. The individual statement is vacuous except as it relates to a totality so prodigious that its very birth is fraught with impossibility. Yet each statement contributes to and sustains that totality. Hence the fragmentation; hence the splintering of the mother-lode into a thousand inter-coded messages. Hence, too, for the outsider, the unobtainable allure of the artistry.

It becomes progressively awkward even to attempt to sort Thomas's poems into categories. Taxonomy fails the Thomas-watcher. The best one can do is observe, and take note of, changing emphases, changing weather conditions. In the four Eglwysfach volumes, one such current-shift is a deepening concern with the poetic medium itself. This too though is part and parcel of the holy horror Thomas endures at the necessity of having to declaim in a non-Celtic tongue. In the title poem 'Poetry for Supper',[68] the poet eavesdrops on two other poets discussing their craft in a tavern. The one argues in favour of the validity of sudden inspiration, the other of the 'long toil' that 'goes into the poem's making'. Neither has a monopoly on truth, just as both are aspects of Thomas himself. And then of course there is the 'Epitaph', placed at the end of the same volume:

> The poem in the rock and
> The poem in the mind
> Are not one.
> It was in dying
> I tried to make them so.

The obvious resonance here is with the epitaph Yeats wrote for himself at the closure of his late poem 'Under Ben Bulben':[69]

> Cast a cold eye
> On life, on death.
> Horseman, pass by!

While it might be thought that, aged just forty-five, R. S. was jumping the gun somewhat, there is a subtle dissonance. The point of Yeats's epitaph is: life's turmoil is over, so let it be. By contrast, Thomas seems to be saying, life's turmoil, though equally divided between two polarities, is not adequately resolved by death.

In 'Poetry for Supper' there is no conclusion to the poets' debate, which is also one between mind and rock. He leaves them as he finds them, quarrelling. Yet he adds a coda:

> So two old poets,
> Hunched at their beer in the low haze
> Of an inn parlour, while the talk ran
> Noisily by them, glib with prose.

Here it is the tail that wags the dog. It isn't said, but it can be imagined which language the glib prose is delivered in. But more than that, there is the sense of the two poets dissipating their energies and talent; getting pissed even, for the sake of professional conviviality. Whereas what they should be doing . . .

Thomas takes both his vocations, poet and priest, with the utmost seriousness – his three vocations, if we add in being a Welshman. Each involves its own tensions, its own discipline, its own remorse.

Combined, they threaten personal extinction. The way out? In 'This To Do',[70] from the final Eglwysfach volume, *Pietà*, Thomas tells us he must

> overdraw on my balance
> Of air, and breaking the surface
> Of water go down into the green
> Darkness to search for the door
> To myself in dumbness and blindness
> And uproar of sacred blood
> At the eardrums.

The way forward, to adapt T. S. Eliot's phrase, is not the way back, but the way down. The sea in Thomas presents two opposing realities: a mirror that reflects nature in its tranquil, ordered state, the heavens even, all the generosity of God's creation; and a 'window' through which the horrors and the turmoil of the same creation can be viewed.

R. S. is cast, or casts himself, through the latter. He expects to find 'no signposts' there, nor any light

> but the pale
> Phosphorous, where the slow corpses
> Swag.

Nevertheless

> I must go down with the poor
> Purse of my body and buy courage,
> Paying for it with the coins of my breath.

Thomas promises not only to describe a descent into the underworld, but to undertake it. While this confers upon him a modernist status, it also attaches him to Celtic and Orphic traditions, rather than the Homeric.

Thomas's descent into the chambers of the sea, at once a literary project and a personal quest, provides the setting for much of the poetry written subsequently, in Llŷn. One aspect that marks it off from the Homeric tradition is its overall unstructuredness. There is no epic involved, but rather a constant chiselling away at surfaces and textures encountered. Thomas does not return from purgatory with a tale to tell, but sends us mixed messages from it. What he achieves is a latterday version of romantic agony mediated by Christian remorse. Part of its attraction, however, is its relative detachment. Thomas retains an ability to re-enter the over-world reflected in the sea's mirror. Harmony may be hard won, but counterpoint is endemic. The journeying undertaken is a form of superior penance. There is something voluntary about it. It becomes progressively intellectual. We admire him for plumbing the depths more than we are engaged by the idea of a particular individual's unavoidable torment. Only when he writes, laconically as ever, about age and the process of ageing, and also of his wife, are we permitted a strangled glimpse of the warmth that others might more obtrusively insist resides at the human core. He does what has to be done on our behalf, within the context of culturally determined parameters.

In this, Thomas ascends to the universality his detractors would deny him. Yet the man himself does not appear, either at Eglwysfach or in Aberdaron, to endure outward misfortune of an unconscionable kind. He is beneficed, he has a living, he is not subjected to an intolerable restriction of his ordinary rights. No attempt is made to induce his silence. Nobody tells him what to write, or what not to write. He partakes, if you like, of the pax of middle-class Britannia, however much he would prefer the pax of a more traditionally ordered Cambria. The oppression of the English falls egregiously short of the oppression of Beijing. Except where pornography is involved, Special Branch doesn't meddle much with literature, even on the Celtic fringes.

At Eglwysfach, by no means everything is bleak. In particular, Thomas is himself able partially to colonize an aspect of British, even English, cultural life. He becomes a poet recognized above the common run. He is up there with Ted Hughes, he challenges Wystan Auden. He appears at poetry readings up and down the land, dressed casually, often in black, and nearly always sporting a red tie, and fishing his work out of a hiker's rucksack. Each collection that he publishes adds to his burgeoning reputation. Even adverse comment affirms his stature.

In 1955, following the enthusiastic reception of *Song at the Year's Turning*, he wins the Heinemann Award. In 1962, alongside Lawrence Durrell and Elizabeth Jennings, a selection of his poems is published in the first volume of the Penguin Modern Poets, an immensely influential as well as commercially successful series. In 1964 the Royal Society for Literature gives him the Queen's Gold Medal for Poetry. Later, in 1978, he will win the Cholmondeley Award; and when he is nominated for the 1996 Nobel Prize for Literature, the Arts Council of England adds its support.

Thomas's acceptance of the Queen's Medal has raised as many eyebrows as the offer of it. In 1990, he told *Planet*:

> I would not now accept the medal. Indeed, this interview is a concession as a result of my relationship with *Planet*. I no longer give interviews in English or accept invitations to go and read my poems in England. Eglwysfach was a very Anglicized village which I, in part, accepted, although I did start a Welsh Society there in an effort to redress the balance. In his letter to me on the occasion John Masefield spoke of the medal as 'a thing of great beauty' so I was hoodwinked to some extent. I would not describe what came through the post in such terms.[71]

He added: 'The medal had not been awarded for some years, but such was the indignation at my being given it, that it became almost an annual event to mollify the geniuses that had been slighted.' Nonetheless, in 1995, with the Nobel Laureateship nomination in the offing, R. S. began giving rather a lot of interviews in English.

This is one of the 'contradictions' in Thomas's character; contradiction in this case being a euphemism for perceived hypocrisy. A part of the post-war 'Anglo-Welsh' movement's ideology was to censure some pre-war Anglo-Welsh authors, notably Dylan Thomas, for being London-centred. In practical terms this seems not to have troubled R. S., the great bulk of whose poetry has indeed appeared on the lists of well-known English houses: Hart-Davis, Macmillan, Chatto & Windus, MacGibbon, J. M. Dent, and latterly the Newcastle-based Bloodaxe Books.

About such inconsistency any number of glib excuses could be offered. 'Hoodwinked' is perhaps an example. For a while in Wales there simply were no publishing houses that had anything like the market clout of their Saxon counterparts; although the steady emergence of the Gomer Press (Gwasg Gomer), founded in Llandysul in 1892, as well as, more recently, Seren, the imprint of Poetry Wales Press, has to some extent eroded this imbalance. Again, for a Welsh patriot, it may have been more important to disseminate one's message as widely as possible, especially among the English. But in the case of R. S. Thomas, the reality is as ever more complicated. To have insisted that his poetry only be published in Wales would have given Welsh publishing a much-needed fillip. But this would have involved Thomas in an equal hypocrisy. However 'Welsh' his themes are, and however wholesome the nourishment, technical or otherwise, he has derived from his reading of Welsh classics, he is equally and inescapably rooted as a poet in English verse. If he has pursued his poetic career within an English setting, it is also where it belongs.

This becomes apparent not just from the poetry itself, highly steeped in selected traditions of English prosody, and 'aware' of such contemporaries as Ted Hughes, William Carlos Williams and (especially) Wallace Stevens, but also if we look at the prose productions of the Eglwysfach years. There is a steady movement away from the somewhat shrill, self-consciously nationalist prose of the Manafon period towards the acceptance of a new role for himself, that of qualified literary purveyor. An exception is 'The Qualities of Christmas', a short essay published in a briefly relaunched *Wales* in 1959.[72] Here, in what is probably an adapted sermon, and certainly the most sermon-like of all Thomas's writings, in a small church way, the poet argues for a rural understanding of the Nativity. 'The very word Christ,' he says, discarding Jesus or Jesu, 'has that thin, crisp sound so suggestive of frost and snow and the small sheets of ice that crack and splinter under our feet, even as the Host is broken in the priest's fingers.' Bethlehem may indeed have been a town, but it was only a little town, and all around it lay the country. 'This was the glory of the early towns. "The dark satanic mills" had not arrived.' And so, Thomas adjudicates, it should be 'here and now. Despite our many towns and cities, we are a country folk at heart.'

Appearing in *Wales*, there was no need for Thomas to belabour the point: Welsh Wales and Christianity are naturally centred in each other. Yet even so, the piece ends with a quotation from Thomas Hardy.

Much of the prose written between 1954 and 1967 is precisely concerned with literary subject-matters. In the London periodicals, particularly the *Listener*, but also, more surprisingly, the *New States-man*, Thomas contributes occasional book reviews, usually on Anglo-Welsh compilations. He also takes on editorial work: *The Batsford Book of Country Verse* in 1961; a *Selected Poems of Edward Thomas* in 1964 and *A Choice of George Herbert's Verse* in 1967, both for Faber & Faber. For the same publisher he will later furnish *A Choice of Wordsworth's Verse*, in 1971. But while Thomas's introductions to these, and the selection of poems made in each case, reflect his known sympathies, a more provocative compilation was *The Penguin Book of Religious Verse* (1963), displaying a familiarity with the whole sweep of English poetry. It included the work of such un-Thomasian poets as Byron and Swinburne. But more significant are the organization of Thomas's selection, into five sections called 'God', 'Self', 'Nothing', 'It' and 'All'; and Thomas's prefatory comments. These tell us much about his own poetics, not least his growing conviction of the intimacy of the relationship between poetry and religion. Taking his cue from Coleridge, whose dictum that the true antithesis of poetry is not prose but science becomes one of the mainstays of Thomas's own artistic creed, R. S. writes:

> The nearest we approach to God ... is as creative beings. The poet, by echoing the primary imagination, recreates. Through his work he forces those who read him to do the same, thus bringing them nearer the primary imagination themselves, and so, in a way, nearer to the actual being of God as displayed in action. So Coleridge in the thirteenth Chapter of his *Biographia Literaria*. Now the power of the imagination is a unifying power, hence the force of metaphor, and the poet is the supreme manipulator of metaphor. This would dispose of the idea of him as a minor craftsman among many. The world needs the unifying power of imagination. The two things which give it best are poetry and religion. Science destroys as it gives.[73]

These words are as close to a personal manifesto as Thomas comes. At their heart is not just a belief in the divine, but also in the poet's special status in relation to it. Later, when pressed by interviewers about the 'contradiction' between being a poet and a priest, his answer is ready-made. The gospels themselves are a type of poetry, the ultimate in metaphor.[74] Here, in his 'Introduction' to the Penguin volume, he prepares the ground:

> The need for revelation at all suggests an ultimate reality beyond human attainment, the *mysterium tremendum et fascinans*. And here, surely, is common ground between religion and poetry. But there is the question of the mystic. To him the *Deus Absconditus* is immediate; to the poet He is mediated. The mystic fails to mediate God adequately insofar as he is not a poet. The poet, with possibly less immediacy of apprehension, shows his spiritual concern and his spiritual nature through the medium of language, the supreme symbol. The presentation of religious experience in the most inspired language is poetry. This is not a definition of poetry, but a description of how the communication of religious experience best operates.[75]

These are heady claims, fraught with hubris, to which not all poets, some good ones among them, would subscribe in an uninebriated state. Yet if Thomas begs too many questions, for example the 'need for revelation' – as much the product of poetry and religion as their stimulant – he locates 'religious verse', and with it himself, within a tradition that embraces, inter alia, Vaughan, Herbert, Milton, Blake, Hopkins, Edward Thomas and T.S. Eliot – though the last-named is curiously absent from the Penguin compilation.

Crucially, however, Thomas insists on the inherent validity of such a tradition. As an editor he does not stand aside and describe it as an objective phenomenon that may or may not have some correspondence to 'truth'. Nor does he view, as some of his contemporaries have done, the historic religiosity of poetry as a kind of impasse. Rather, and most tellingly as regards his own development, he regards religious verse as the logical pinnacle of all verse. But more than that, seen in this light, such poetry can never be merely an expressive means to some or other end. Rather it is part and parcel of the very fabric of life, its 'tremendous and intriguing' mystery.

Poetry then is an inherently serious occupation, more serious, if 'serious' has any meaning at all, than any other. It is the conduit between God and Man. No distinction is made between poetry that is 'about' religious subjects, and poetry that is (in Thomas's terms) creatively religious (or divinely creative). In two further prose writings of the Eglwysfach period, Thomas explores this creed. In 'Words and the Poet',[76] originally delivered as the W. D. Thomas Memorial Lecture at University College Swansea in November 1963, and subsequently published as a pamphlet by the University of Wales Press, he takes us on a guided tour of the basics of his craft. The tone adopted, before an academic audience, is diffident to begin with, but ironically measured at the end. He declares himself to be 'almost entirely ignorant' of the 'comparatively new subjects of linguistics and semantics'. Therefore he must 'fall back . . . on the components of language', i.e. words, because words are the 'materials' the poet uses. But having laid his stall out modestly, what he has to say about words is something of a tour de force. Drawing on the precepts and examples of other poets as diverse as Lewis Carroll, Edith Sitwell, 'A. E.', Philip Sidney and Mallarmé, he shows us that not only does he have a highly principled notion of what poetry is or should be about, but once again that in poetry he is incomparably well read. It isn't just that he knows his stuff, but he knows it exactly.

He discusses meaning and nonsense, assonance and dissonance, rhyme, half-rhyme and delayed rhyme, consonants and vowels, metaphor and persona – almost everything one could think of from the point of view of a poet actually wrestling with a half-born poem or a half-born stanza or a half-born line. Yet aside from words, their choice and their use, there is the question of a poet's subject-matter. Here, as the address progresses, Thomas offers an array of statements about his own work, his own stance. There can be no such thing, he hints, as a 'pure poet':

A pure poet is one who, presumably, lives for his art, interested in the interior world of words and thought, rather than in the everyday world of noise and pain and evil. I think, when I examine my own position, that I have never been a pure poet in that way. To make a poetic artefact out of words has never been, or rarely ever been my first aim or satisfaction. There is always lurking in the back of my poetry a kind of moralistic or propagandist intention.[77]

The two things, he goes on, that appeal most strongly to his imagination are 'Wales and nature, especially as the latter manifests itself as the background to a way of life'. And because he believes in the 'profound and lasting value' of both ideas, he is 'prepared to preach this sermon in verse'.

Thus, albeit in an incidental way, Thomas reaffirms the connection between poetry and religion. His poems are a species of sermon. Now, though, he adds another 'recurring ideal', that of simplicity: 'At times there comes the desire to write with great precision and clarity, words so simple and moving that they bring tears to the eyes, or, if you like, as Wordsworth said, are "too deep for tears".'[78] This quest for 'miraculous simplicity', as he calls it, must involve all art's resources. But the question of subject-matter remains. Gone are the days, Thomas laments, when an 'eye for nature and a flair for describing it were the normal appurtenances of a poet'. And even where the eye and the flair can still be found, where is the audience for them? 'The common environment of the majority is an urban-industrial one. The potential audience of a poet is one of town dwellers, who are mostly out of touch, if not out of sympathy, with nature. Their contact with it is modified by the machine.'[79] Could it be, though, that the boot is on the other foot? Is not such a poet out of touch? Thomas believes not. The poet 'who chooses to write about an agricultural environment' is not necessarily 'insular, escapist or even provincial'. He concedes that in theory a new poetry could be fashioned out of the new words and the new terms engendered by the urban industrial setting. But then he asks, as an intended coup de grâce, 'Where are the poems?'

Much of this is special pleading. An outstanding example of a poet who does not always rely upon either rural imagery or rural context is W. H. Auden. But it is special pleading to a high moral purpose. Something like the full Thomasian equation is set in place. The syllogism runs: Poetry is a divine pursuit; real poetry belongs to a particular way of life found only in the country; therefore that way of life is divinely sanctioned.

Secondly, there is 'A Frame for Poetry', a short essay that appeared in *The Times Literary Supplement* in March 1966,[80] Here Thomas directly confronts several issues arising out of the relations between poetry and Christianity, including the personally irksome contemporary 'misunderstanding' that the 'two professions of priest and poet are so divorced in the public eye as to be quite beyond the possibility of symbiosis'. By committing himself to the outmoded baggage of Christian symbol and Christian metaphor, so the argument runs, the poet stifles whatever latent creativity he may possess. But Thomas stands this argument on its head:

> So far as we can tell, there are no works of poetry being produced today that are of comparable stature with those of Chaucer, Spenser, Shakespeare or Milton. Whether these writers themselves were avowedly Christian or not, they wrote within a Christian framework. Is there a relation between the decline of Christianity in Britain and in the decline in works of high poetry?

As Thomas extrapolates this view he makes it a little more subtle than this bald rhetoric suggests. He draws a distinction, for instance, between 'Christianity' and 'Christian dogma'. He also, predictably, introduces 'science' as a factor in poetry's undoing. Set against a 'waning Christianity' is a 'waxing secularism'. But his thesis, as presented in the *TLS*, is still too broad-brushed. The notion of a 'high poetry' has become almost infinitely problematic. The very term is a matter of convention and consensus, and Shakespeare is too dangerous a poet to sit quietly on the Christian podium. To abide by it, as Thomas does, is to introduce a circularity. For him, a high poetry that is not also a religious poetry is inconceivable. But he also says, apropos of Herbert and other conspicuously Christian poets, that they 'refreshed themselves daily in the very doctrines and disciplines which are supposed by the critics to have such deadening effect'. This too can be taken as a personal statement, and is widely validated in Thomas's own poetry.

One can say then that at Eglwysfach Thomas consolidated the literary niche his published collections of verse had carved out for him. But to the poet himself, it was anything but a niche, just as 'nature' was infinitely more than something he wrote poetry about in the tranquillity of his vicarage study. Both were integral aspects of his world, *the* world, as were his feelings for Wales and his vocation as a priest. An obvious statement to make maybe, but a necessary one, given that even in Wales the majority of people these days avoid church and chapel, do not read let alone write poetry, and have only a day-tripper or at best weekend relationship with the land.

Thomas was different. In particular he became a devoted bird-watcher. One of the two principal landowners at Eglwysfach, Hubert Mappin, turned out to be not such a bad egg after all. In Thomas's own words, Mappin was 'a wealthy and generous man who was also an ardent churchman'.[81] His many-acred estate, Ynyshir, 'Long Island', stretched to a salt-marsh on the banks of the Dyfi, and Mappin gladly allowed the vicar to wander over it at will. Its chief attraction for Thomas, apart from the respite it gave him from 'the little problems of the parish',[82] was its abundant birdlife. At the same time, Thomas's friendship with the naturalist Bill Condry grew, to the extent that in April 1966 the two of them set off, in Thomas's Mini estate, for a bird-watching excursion in southern Spain.

This adventure is described both by R. S., in *Neb*, and by Condry, in his 1995 autobiography *Wildlife, My Life*. Condry recalls:

R. S. Thomas and I exchanged the moist green hills of Wales for what, in all but a name, was a piece of the Sahara. We had been drawn to the Cota Donana, near Seville, by Guy Mountfort's *Portrait of a Wilderness* which had described irresistibly the wildlife-rich region of estuary marches, cork-oak woods and far-spreading mountainous sand-dunes. Mountfort, we found, had not exaggerated. The marshes were lively with pratincoles, stilts, squacco herons, night herons and various terns. Mixed colonies of grey herons, cattle egrets, little egrets, spoonbills and storks crowded some of the trees with their nests. Flamingos were distant passing pink clouds. Kites, both black and red, circled overhead, ready to drive and snatch at anything edible. Far away above the woodlands we saw a magnificent pair of imperial eagles. Great spotted cuckoos chattered everywhere in the thickets, and we never got used to the colourfulness of hoopoes, rollers, orioles, bee-eaters and azure-winged magpies. Unfamiliar warblers sang from every bush; and the tiny, fan-tailed cisticola, lisping his feeble notes high in the air, was a real touch of Africa.[83]

From hot, mosquito-infested Cota Donana they made for the cooler heights of Ronda, where another ornithological banquet awaited them. Thomas's account is more detailed, and, as one would expect, more idiosyncratic. It was not his first trip abroad – the previous year he had gone to Denmark, partly to bird-watch, and partly to discover what he could about Søren Kierkegaard; but there is still a naive quality to the poet's descriptions. Crossing the Pyrenees, they came to Burgos, then journeyed south.

> Ahead waiting for them was Andalucia, a mountainous region of white cottages that showed a Moorish influence. They were greatly tempted to drink from the frothing streams that came from the mountains to the villages, but R. S. insisted their canteens were filled by someone trustworthy, and tablets dropped into them for fear of fever. The beauty of some of the villages was deceptive, Grazalema particularly so. But before reaching it they were warned not to touch the local cheese because it contained goat's milk.[84]

Throughout the journey they camped in open fields. After a week in Cota Donana it was time to turn back homewards. By mutual agreement the two naturalists had decided to 'give culture a skip'. Thus they avoided 'the Prado, the cathedrals, the monasteries and the architecture of such places as Granada'. But Thomas had no regrets. 'That's what he was like,' he tells us. Given the choice between the countryside and anything else, the countryside always came first. But it wasn't only the wildlife that drew him in Spain. In a fine semi-rhymed sonnet, 'Burgos',[85] from his 1968 collection *Not That He Brought Flowers*, Thomas describes the land around the Spanish town:

> The day dawned fiercely
> On the parched land, on the fields to the east
> Of the city, bitter with sage
> And thistle.

The unsparing dryness of the scene provokes the unsparing dryness of Thomas's poetic personality. One can almost feel the rustle in his soul as he identifies with another peasantry:

> Lonely bells called
> From the villages; no one answered
> Them but the sad priests, fingering
> Their beads, praying for the lost people
> Of the soil.

But who are the 'lost people'? Are they among those who died during the Spanish Civil War? In which case, one must ask, on which side? For Burgos at one point was the seat of General Franco's Nationalist Government. Prior to that, at the close of the Middle Ages, it had been the capital city of Castille, so perhaps Thomas mourns the passing of an especially Christianized feudal order. More probably the description is less specific. The 'lost' people of the soil may not after all be dead, but lost in the sense of being lost either to civilization, or, like some of Thomas's unruly Manafon labourers, lost to God. Certainly this is suggested in the closing lines:

> In the air an eagle
> Circled, shadowless as the God
> Who made that country and drinks its blood.

In Spain, of course, the Catholic church allied itself with Franco, so what at one point seems like an unwelcome political avowal is balanced out. But while 'Burgos' evokes a particular Spanish landscape, and with it a particular history, it is also a poem about Wales, in that Thomas responds to what he sees as though it were a version of what he adumbrates so often elsewhere. We may, for example, recall 'The Lost', written a quarter of a century later (see above, pp. 77–8) and perhaps the poet's outstanding expression of minoritism:

> If we follow our conscience
> it leads us nowhere but to gaol.

In Spain too, the Basques and the Catalans are threatened peoples, with threatened languages. The eagle circling above may be an emblem of God, but it is also an imperial insignia. Wittingly or otherwise, Thomas in Spain is not quite the innocent abroad we may suppose from his prose descriptions.

Back in Eglwysfach, he was soon confronted by a more immediate death: that of his friend Hubert Mappin. What would happen to the Ynyshir estate? There were no children, only Mappin's wife Patricia, who had served as a churchwarden. The exact sequence of events is unclear, but between them Thomas and Condry had already persuaded Mappin that Ynyshir should be declared 'a sanctuary with no permission for shooting over it'.[86] The next step was to covenant Ynyshir to the National Trust, to prevent its future exploitation, say as a caravan site, under a different ownership. Not that Mappin needed much persuasion: a quiet, diffident man, he was himself a nature-lover. Towards the end of his life he was known around Eglwysfach not just as the master of Ynyshir Hall, but also for his beehives. Events, however, almost overtook all three of them. Mappin's condition suddenly deteriorated. It was clear he could die any day.

In the event, Mappin signed the covenants either two or three days before his demise. The whole thing, from a first contact with the National Trust office at Llandeilo, had been arranged inside the space of a week,[87] with R. S. Thomas as a chief instigator. The essential negotiations were carried out between Thomas, Patricia Mappin and the National Trust Land Agent, Huw Griffith. The deed itself was witnessed by Bill Condry. After Mappin's death, Patricia Mappin endeavoured to give Ynyshir to the Trust in lieu of death duties, but H. M. Treasury declined to co-operate. In 1969, however, the Royal Society for the Protection of Birds stepped in and purchased the estate from Mrs Mappin, so that today R S P B Ynyshir is, as its original owner intended it should be, a permanent and valued sanctuary. Only Ynyshir Hall, now run as a distinctively upmarket hotel, has remained in private hands.

In this outcome the intervention of Thomas and Condry was critical. Under Condry's tutelage, Thomas also became an active member of the Kite Committee, a body set up by Condry and others for the protection and propagation of the endangered red kite, a bird most commonly associated, in Britain, with areas inland from the West Wales coast. These affiliations, together with his involvement with the Bardsey Island trust societies, and also his membership of the Pwllheli CND Committee, show the extent of Thomas's environmental concern. Passages from both *Neb* and Condry's autobiography further reveal the practical aspect of the same commitment: Thomas rescuing a bird here, persuading a farmer to record bird sightings there. Yet the same associativeness also tells us other things about the poet. Many of his colleagues-in-conservation were either English or heavily 'anglicized': Condry and Mappin, for instance, or the Chairman of the Kite Committee, Capt. H. R. H. Vaughan RN. Another contradiction? Thomas himself was not unaware of it, but what was he to do?

> There was an interesting history to the protection of the kite in Wales. From being a common bird in England in the middle ages, it had fled to the inaccessible hills of Wales, and by the beginning of the century were reduced to three or four pairs. Early in the century a few English people started taking an interest in them. Some farmers and shepherds in Cardiganshire remembered these people by name. By the time the protection committee had been formed their number had increased slightly but they were still endangered. But most of the members of the Committee were English, with Captain Vaughan ex-fleet its head. Very often when speaking to farmers it was difficult to get them to understand what you were on about until you used the English word kite. Neither was it an uncommon experience to hear a farmer deny that they were in his area, and a kite flying overhead as he spoke![88]

In this instance, the survival of a species overrode every other concern perhaps. Yet there was another aspect to some of Thomas's new acquaintance, exemplified in the case of Hubert Mappin. Whatever else he was, Mappin was a local grandee, *crachach* even, and it was not just his land that Thomas regularly visited.

In Llŷn, a similar relationship developed with the celebrated Keating sisters.[89] These three, Honora, Eileen and Lorna, daughters of a successful Nottingham architect, were authentically eccentric. In 1914 the youngest of them, Honora, a Slade-trained artist, visited

Aberdaron on holiday. After the war she returned with her sisters, and between them, in 1938, they acquired Plas-yn-Rhiw, a dilapidated late Elizabethan or early Jacobean mansion sited, as its name suggests, on a hillside. According to legend the estate had been continuously occupied by one family, the Lewises, from the tenth century until 1874, when the last Lewis died in America. The hillside was to the east of Aberdaron, and overlooked Porth Neigwl – Hell's Mouth. Plas-yn-Rhiw itself had for a long time been used as a farmhouse, but during the course of the nineteenth century had reverted to being a 'gentleman's residence'. When the Keatings took possession, however, the house had stood empty for twenty years and was falling apart.

The Keatings decided to devote the remainder of their lives to restoring the buildings and creating a garden around them. To do this they agreed, in 1949, to hand Plas-yn-Rhiw over to the National Trust, in return for some much needed grants. By 1966, when the eldest of them, Eileen, died aged eighty, some 380 acres of land had been recovered and restored, and the house had already become a popular tourist attraction. Yet the Keatings' activities in Llŷn were not restricted to Plas-yn-Rhiw. They supported the Council for the Preservation of Rural Wales, energetically recruited new members for the National Trust, and in 1958 organized a petition against the siting of a nuclear power station at Edern. That the same station was eventually built instead at Trawsfynydd was due in no small measure to their determined campaigning.

Honora died in 1976, while Lorna survived until 1981. All three sisters are buried, along with their mother, in the churchyard at nearby Llanfaelrhys. None of them was ever married. The sisters also shared a certain belligerence of character, often arousing local prejudice by their relentless efforts against, for example, litter and illegal caravan sites. There, however, the similarities ended. A key component of their story is the way in which their labours were divided according to character. Honora, a natural spokeswoman, handled public relations; Eileen attended to business matters, while Lorna supervised domestic arrangements.[90] Between them they put paid to two myths: first, that siblings cannot combine harmoniously in a common enterprise; secondly, that a small group of women are incapable of providing the whole gamut of skills necessary to sustain an enterprise.

At Bill Condry's urging, the Thomases called on the Keatings in August 1954, during an excursion to Bardsey Island. According to *Neb*, they were given a warm welcome by the three sisters, and stayed with them overnight. This 'established a relationship that developed over the years into a friendship'[91] – a state of affairs confirmed by several letters housed among the Keating papers in the Public Record Office at Caernarfon. Thereafter, while they were still at Eglwysfach, the Thomases often took holidays at Plas-yn-Rhiw, staying at Fron Deg, one of several renovated cottages within the estate's boundaries. Even after the move to Aberdaron, R. S. and Elsi frequently repaired to Fron Deg for its peace and quiet.

Knowing the Thomases' liking for the cottage, Honora and Lorna Keating offered it to them as a gift for their 'retirement'. Fron Deg was too small, however, and R. S. regretfully declined the Keatings' generosity. The next thing, he was offered a tenancy, to last for the duration of his and his son Gwydion's lifetimes, of the larger Sarn-y-Rhiw cottage, also known as Sarn-y-Plas, where the Thomases had sometimes stayed. Gratefully R. S. accepted, and, when the time arrived, in 1978, he adopted Sarn-y-Rhiw, which most fittingly also overlooked Hell's Mouth, as his retirement home.[92]

In fact, between 1972 and 1978 Thomas had been rector of Rhiw with Llanfaelrhys, as well as being being vicar of Aberdaron with Bodferin from 1967. In an era of dwindling congregations and fewer ordinations it was usual for one priest to minister to more than one parish. Aberdaron, however, was Thomas's principal responsibility, and between 1967 and 1978 he resided at its Vicarage, a large house in the upper part of the two-tiered village. Close by was an ugly nineteenth-century church, built at the instigation of Pen Llŷn's largest landowner, Lord Newborough, whose family also owned Ynys Enlli. The historic church, St Hywyn's, was in lower Aberdaron, so close to the shore that in bad weather a preacher could make himself heard only with the greatest difficulty. Whether because of this, or in spite of it, Aberdaron's small number of Anglicans preferred the latter, so that today the upper church is used only as a place of burial.

It was a choice anyone would make. St Hywyn's, sometimes called 'the cathedral of Aberdaron', is not merely old, with parts of it dating from the twelfth century: it is one of the special churches of Wales, erected on a site second only to Bardsey itself in local holiness. In R. S. Thomas's own words, 'God's acre – not in the sea, but by the sea.'[93] The stone chamber of its double-naved interior, lit by large plain-glazed altar windows, is strangely airy. Hywyn himself was a saint of the Celtic church, a follower of St Cadfan, and probably the first abbot of the monastic community on Bardsey Island. This was at the end of the fifth or beginning of the sixth century, before the second 'conversion' of Britain by Rome. As the western Roman empire entered the terminal stages of its collapse, throughout its far corners Christians established small settlements for the purposes of prayer and witness, and hoped-for survival. This monastic movement, which had its origins in Egypt and in Palestine, was initially one of retreat; but in time its bases became centres for Christian revival. Hence the 'Celtic Church' in Wales, independent of Rome, and having a diversity of loci.

Almost certainly some monks had set up on Bardsey before the arrival of Cadfan. It was Cadfan though, an Armorican, who, with the help of the then Prince of Llŷn, Einion Frenin, established the religious house that later became known as St Mary's. He came by boat from Brittany with a group of monks, one of whom, Hywyn, set up his own oratory at Aberdaron. But the connection between Bardsey and Aberdaron, with just a short stretch of water between them, remained close.

No trace of the original wooden structure remains, although two recently discovered Celtic tombstones, dating from around 650, are now kept inside St Hywyn's. Over the succeeding centuries Aberdaron became an important centre of religious study and instruction, one of the 'mother churches' of Wales in fact. The Welsh word for this was *clas*, meaning a religious community that followed no particular monastic rule, but was gathered under the leadership of an elected head, or 'abbot'. The Normans, wherever they could, endeavoured to suppress *clasau*, but because of its remoteness the *clas* at Aberdaron survived longer than most, well into the Middle Ages. In addition, the church itself was a sanctuary protected by the Laws of Hywel Dda. Famously, in 1115, Gruffudd ap Rhys ap Tewdwr, prince of the southern kingdom of Deheubarth, took advantage of this privilege while fleeing the attentions of Henry I of England.

By the time of the Reformation, however, although the original single-nave stone church had been enlarged to twice that size, Aberdaron had lost its collegiate status. Thereafter it suffered the same fate as many other Welsh churches. It struggled to survive financially, and, falling into the gift of St John's College, Cambridge, in 1624, became the victim of absenteeism. Tithes due to the church went unpaid, and then came the competitive tide of Nonconformity. Few if any of the St John's men spoke Welsh, and in any case they were never there. By the end of the eighteenth century St Hywyn's was a church in name only, its fabric sadly deteriorated.

Some time around 1840 St Hywyn's was abandoned as a place of worship. A part of the church had been closed off for use as a school; rather than enter through the imposing Norman archway of the main door, pupils came in through an empty window. So close to the sea, the church was sinking into the soft, sandy ground. Only if a costly sea-wall were built could St Hywyn's be saved. It was partly because of this that the new church was raised on the firmer soil up the hill. But when the new church opened, the people of Aberdaron realized what they were losing, and the requisite efforts to rescue and restore St Hywyn's began. The essential work was done by 1868, although it was not until 1906 that St Hywyn's re-opened its doors to worshippers.

For R. S., the attractions of Aberdaron were obvious. Nearby Plas-yn-Rhiw and Bardsey Island were places already familiar to Thomas, and important to him. Pen Llŷn, the far end of the Llŷn Peninsula, the headland culminating in Mynydd Mawr, Big Mountain, was still predominantly Welsh-speaking, its landscape sparse yet eerily beautiful: 'A bough of land between sea and sky, with the clouds for apple-blossom, white by day, pink towards evening.'[94] But above all perhaps there was the sea, in close proximity all around, and the views of Anglesey and Holyhead, Môn and Caergybi, from the northern shores of Llŷn and many higher points inland.

As soon as the living fell vacant, in 1965, Thomas was interested; but for as long as Hubert Mappin was alive R. S. felt it inappropriate to abandon Eglwysfach. Eighteen months later, however, Aberdaron was still without a vicar, and R. S. gained the benefice he had set his mind and heart on. At the time he was only fifty-three, yet from his published comments about moving to Aberdaron, it is clear he took with him an older man's attitude. 'He had reached the destination of his own personal pilgrimage,' he tells us in *Neb*.[95] And again, in *The Echoes Return Slow*: 'This was where he had crawled out, far as he could go, repeating the pilgrimages of the saints. Had he like John Synge come "towards nightfall upon a race passionate and simple like his heart?"'[96]

Far more than Eglwysfach or even Manafon, Aberdaron and its environs satisfied Thomas's emotional and mental needs. In the very remoteness of Pen Llŷn there was a proximity to the ultimate truths and values the poet sought. If the landscape, suspended between sea and sky, seemed precarious, it also contained, as Thomas had perhaps already discovered, some of the oldest rocks in Europe: the pre-Cambrian outcrops of Braich-y-Pwll, in the shadow of Mynydd Mawr. Throwing his own shadow against them, Thomas could test his faith and his intellect against the manifest paradoxes before him:

> My shadow
> sunning itself on this stone
> remembers the lava. Zeus looked down
> on a brave world, but there was
> no love there; the architecture
> of their temples was less permanent
> than those waves.

Plato and Aristotle, the poem 'Pre-Cambrian'[97] continues, 'furrowed the calmness/ of their foreheads' in their search for truth; yet in so doing contributed to the science that eventually produced 'the bomb'. Then, looking out across the waters, Thomas invokes the further paradox of his double-aspected sea:

> I am charmed here
> by the serenity of the reflections

in the sea's mirror. It is a window
as well. What I need
now is a faith to enable me to out-stare
the grinning faces of the inmates of its asylum,
the failed experiments God put away.

The rapid transition from mirror to window immediately obliges the reader to reconsider the apparent straightforwardness of 'charmed'. The poet remains charmed by the beauty of what he sees, but he is also charmed in another way. A spell has been put on him, perhaps by the sheer scale of the time-spans involved at Braich-y-Pwll. As poet, he is, or at least becomes, a Prospero figure. Yet simultaneously he is like one of those charmed by Prospero. He lacks the key that will enable him to 'outstare' the monstrosities around him. Unless he finds that key, or faith, then he is no more than one of them.

The word 'experiments' is of particular significance. A feature of the poetry Thomas writes at Aberdaron is its resort to scientific vocabulary and scientific metaphor. In 'Pre-Cambrian', it is not creation Thomas beholds so much as a laboratory, God's laboratory, in which mistakes are made and acknowledged. Yet Thomas too is a worker in that laboratory, observing the same experiments, measuring them, and making his notes. What he lacks, or seems to lack, however, is the laboratory manual. Only by working backwards through the experiments, and conducting some of his own, can he hope to reconstitute it.

'Pre-Cambrian' appeared in the 1978 collection *Frequencies*. Three years before he published another collection in fact called *Laboratories of the Spirit*. It can be taken as read therefore that Thomas's concern with the concept of experimentation is no passing indulgence. Rather it is a recognition of one of the central procedures of western rationality. Being central, Thomas is obliged to take it seriously, even if his core position is 'anti-science'. Thus Pen Llŷn becomes his own laboratory, providing, in its remoteness and isolation, at least some of the required 'laboratory conditions'. Into a clinically secure environment Thomas can introduce the objects of his inquiry, and play around with them to see what they offer, and what they are made of.

Yet, for all that the juxtaposition of a man and his shadow on the pre-Cambrian rocks inevitably induces perceptions of human insignificance, of true *neb*-ness, the poet-experimenter's own persona cannot be discarded at the laboratory's door. Other poems written about Llŷn — and there are many of them — flesh out and round out the vicar of Aberdaron's responses to his geographic journeying's supposed end-place. There is for example 'The Moon in Lleyn',[98] from *Laboratories of the Spirit* itself, in which Christian imagery and a residual *hiraeth* combine to produce a very different kind of speculation to the scientific.

> The last quarter of the moon
> of Jesus gives way
> to the dark; the serpent
> digests the egg.

The poet once again is priest, kneeling now in a different church, St Hywyn's,

> that is full only
> of the silent congregation
> of shadows and the sea's
> sound.

He has brought his vestments with him, into the laboratory of the spirit. His meditation, centred on the operations of time, is of the eternal kind; but it is also self-consciously as a poet that he speaks:

> it is easy to believe
> Yeats was right. Just as though
> choirs had not sung, shells
> have swallowed them; the tide laps
> at the Bible; the bell fetches
> no people to the brittle miracle
> of the bread.

Thomas is conducting another experiment here, he is playing with time, but only in a manner traditional to poets. The conceit of choirs swallowed by shells is soon followed by an equally elaborate, and equally effective, conceit that takes on the very stones around him:

> The sand is waiting
> for the running back of the grains
> in the wall into its blond
> glass.

And there is a third, concealed conceit, of course. The 'grains' echo the 'bread' and its 'brittle' miracle. Bread, as distinct from the communion wafer, is not usually brittle, nor is it quite right to speak of stones that are composed of grains. Yet the scriptural charge of 'The Moon in Lleyn', and the knowledge that St Hywyn's actually is sinking into the sand, resolves these difficulties, using them to uncanny advantage. But, as though tired of such clever contrivance, Thomas immediately confronts us with the stark statement:

> Religion is over, and
> what will emerge from the body
> of the new moon, no one
> can say.

He pulls the rug away from underneath him, so to speak. If there was any doubt about it before, it now becomes clear that the reference to Yeats can only be a reference to Yeats's apocalyptic poem 'The Second Coming':[99]

> Surely some revelation is at hand;
> Surely the Second Coming is at hand.
> The Second Coming! Hardly are those words out
> When a vast image out of *Spiritus Mundi*
> Troubles my sight: somewhere in sands of the desert
> A shape with lion body and the head of a man,
> A gaze blank and pitiless as the sun,
> Is moving its slow thighs, while all about it
> Reel shadows of the indignant desert birds.
> The darkness drops again; but now I know
> That twenty centuries of stony sleep
> Were vexed to nightmare by a rocking cradle,

And what rough beast, its hour come round at last,
Slouches toward Bethlehem to be born?

Thomas, however, is ambivalent in a way that Yeats is not. What looks like an expression of final despair on the part of the priest is also an extraordinary affirmation. The new moon, simply as new moon, reinforces the uncertainties of the immediate and godless future. But the new moon is also, or may also be, still the old 'moon/ of Jesus', in Yeats's phrase 'come round' again. That we are unsure contributes to the uncertainty; but even so Thomas preserves the one small grain of hope.

To emphasize this ambiguity, Thomas breaks the poem here, in mid-line – by the mid-1970s a well-tried prosodic manoeuvre of his. In the shorter second half of 'The Moon in Lleyn' Thomas pursues his meditation, which is also a species of prayer, from a different angle. A voice in his ear asks:

>   Why so fast,
> mortal? These very seas
> are baptised. The parish
> has a saint's name time cannot
> unfrock.

'Mortal' extends the ambiguity, but in a different register. The word at once rams home man's puniness, but, as a form of address, implies that he is being watched over, perhaps caringly; confirmed by the notion of the sea's baptism. Again, in time's inability to 'unfrock' the saint's name, Thomas strongly suggests the mystic's belief that time itself is contained by a greater reality.

'The Moon in Lleyn' concludes with an invocation of Pen Llŷn's character as a place of pilgrimage. The situation today is not unlike the situation in the fifth and sixth centuries:

>   In cities that
> have outgrown their promise people
> are becoming pilgrims
> again, if not to this place,
> then to the recreation of it
> in their own spirits.

'You must remain kneeling,' Thomas tells himself. Even as the moon
makes its way

> through the earth's
> cumbersome shadow, prayer, too,
> has its phases.

Thus, in compelling fashion, Thomas makes good his claim, expressed
previously in the *TLS*, that poets can still refresh themselves in the
doctrines and disciplines of Christianity; even if the refreshment
offered by his working of them is at best tentative.

Thomas's narrow aperture on such matters as faith and hope is
endemic to all his later poetry, and not just the product of his
responses to Llŷn. Even so, a poem like 'Retirement'[100] from the
1986 collection *Experimenting with an Amen* — another 'scientific' title
— does make a specific suture between theme and place:

> I must try to content
> myself with the perception
> that love and truth have
>
> no wings, but are resident
> like me here, practising
> their sub-song quietly in the face
> of the bitterest of winters.

Although 'Retirement' in its entirety also makes rich use of both
the bough imagery of Llŷn and the sea's mirror—window dichotomy,
'bitterest of winters' is not sufficiently explained internally, other
than by the sense of 'retirement' inevitably heralding the drawing
to a close of life. Possibly though, almost certainly in fact, Thomas
has another closure on his mind. Within two years of arriving at
Aberdaron it was discovered that his wife Elsi had a life-threatening
illness. Nowhere in his writings does Thomas specify the condition,
but the symptoms he describes suggests a lymphoma of the
stomach.[101] One of the more drawn-out types of cancer, lymphoma
of the stomach also induces progressive deterioration of the eyesight,
as well as weight loss: for an artist such as Mildred E. Eldridge, a
double suffering.

Thomas's concern with human pain, constantly evinced in his

Aberdaron poetry, and a naturally pessimistic sensibility, can only have been deepened by this experience. Its true emotional cost to the poet will only be accounted, if at all, by his future biographers. Yet alongside this, Thomas retained in his poetry, as well as an intermittent capacity for religious surrender, his companion grief for Wales. 'Drowning',[102] from *Welsh Airs* (1984), is another poem about Aberdaron and Pen Llŷn:

> They were irreplaceable and forgettable,
> inhabitants of the parish and speakers
> of the Welsh tongue. I looked on and
> there was one less and one less and one less.
>
> They were not of the soil, but contributed
> to it in dying, a manure not
> to be referred to as such

Not, one has to say, an example of Thomas at his most subtle, tasteless even, but for all that a potent reminder of an abiding truth, as well as a record of how even the furthest reaches of Gwynedd were giving way to change:

> I ministered uneasily among them until
> what had been gaps in the straggling hedgerow
> of the nation widened to reveal the emptiness
> that was inside, where echoes haunted and thin ghosts.
>
> A rare place, but one identifiable
> with other places where on as deep a sea
> men have clung to the last spurs of their language
> and gone down with it, unremembered but uncomplaining.

Like other pilgrims, Thomas came to Pen Llŷn with baggage he was unwilling or unable to abandon.

'Drowning' is an elegy for the Welsh language, but it is not vituperative in the way so many of his earlier poems on the same theme are. And indeed, the longer Thomas lives in Llŷn, the less inclined he becomes to expend his energies lacerating either the English or his fellow Welsh. The inwardness, already apparent in a number of poems written at Manafon and Eglwysfach, emerges as the new hallmark. By a curious irony, however, with the waxing of Thomas's fame as a poet, the anecdotal, two-dimensional figure familiar to the public is born. His reputation as a difficult, obdurate, even eccentric individual balloons.

Some of this had to do with serious critical and political responses to his work. English reviewers could be expected to take offence at Thomas's importunately Anglophobic sentiments. The marvel of it is perhaps that many did not. But in Wales too there were voices of mistrust. An early, stinging attack was made by Dafydd Elis Thomas, soon to be Plaid Cymru MP for Meirionnydd Nant Conwy, in the Anglo-Welsh magazine *Poetry Wales* in 1972.[103] The politician, also a lecturer at Coleg Harlech, accused R. S. of living in the past, of shackling the idea of Wales to a history that was at best dubious, of exhibiting 'middle-class contempt' for the working classes of the industrial south-east, and of generally projecting Wales as 'an image of death'. Being Welsh should not, in Dafydd Elis Thomas's opinion, be a 'cause for depression', as he found to be the case in many of R. S. Thomas's poems.

In this particular instance, the critic was floating his own boat. As in the rest of the world, so in Wales: warfare is positional. Dafydd Elis Thomas was very much on the new left of the Welsh national party, which wanted to disengage Plaid Cymru from its Saunders Lewis-style mooring and find for it a mass following. Indeed, if a foreword he later wrote endorsing Gareth Miles and Robert Griffiths's incendiary pamphlet, *Socialism for the Welsh People*, is anything to go by, Dafydd Elis Thomas was close to being an orthodox Marxist. Yet in the same issue of *Poetry Wales* the Anglo-Welsh poet Leslie Norris writes:

Large areas of human generosity and tenderness are missing from Thomas's universe. His world is one in which the dead die alone, the neighbours – they are never *friends* – turning 'heartless away from the stale smell/ Of death.' There is no love, for the farmer is 'stripped of love/ And thought and grace by the land's hardness' and where he has 'been hurled with hot haste into manhood' and marriage without love. Sometimes, as in 'The Airy Tomb', even those dubious comforts are denied. One would never know that the hill men are quick of wit and speech, tender and passionate as any other men, loyal and tolerant and helpful friends. Not all, of course, and not always, but they are human. And what of their humour? Who would guess from these poems that Iago [Prytherch] could be guilty of hilarity? Last year I arrived at Saron, just after the hunt had gone through, and learned that John, one of the shepherds, had fallen in the river in his excitement. Even as we spoke he emerged, dry and clean, from his cottage. He wore an unaccustomed suit. 'A bit cold for swimming, John,' I said. 'Good God!' he replied, 'Has that news got up to England already?' But Thomas in all his work has never suggested that such a retort could be fashioned beneath the torn cap John usually wears.[104]

Many years later, in the same forum, another poet, Nigel Jenkins, berates Thomas for being 'the defeatist priest of Llŷn who must sometimes have looked down his long nose of a northern peninsula and despaired at the decadent conviviality . . . of the crowded urban south':[105] a charge that has frequently been levelled not just at R. S., but also at Saunders Lewis, as well as Gwenallt. While it is hard to resist the impression that a lesser poet is having a go at someone who dominates his craft, it is noticeable that the more devoted of Thomas's academic admirers, while extolling his art in innumerable essays and reviews, either disregard Thomas's political incarnation, or treat that side of him with kid gloves.

Such reservations about Thomas fed into and were reinforced by media representations of the poet as a withdrawn and perversely opinionated character. R. S. has only rarely consented to be interviewed by the press, but when he has there is a predictable sameness about the outcome. As early as 1964 Benedict Nightingale, filing for the *Guardian*, set the standard:

Over the telephone the Rev. R. S. Thomas is markedly cool in his agreement to be interviewed. In person a tall, imposing figure of about 50, he is courteous but aloof. 'I'm not a talker,' he says. 'I don't really like to talk. I don't mix with people.' He has refused to reply to letters from hopeful interviewers; he once sent back a literary questionnaire unanswered to the editor of a famous magazine; he describes the experience of addressing poetry enthusiasts as 'utter misery'.[106]

Somehow, though, Nightingale penetrated the defence. At Eglwys-fach he found a man 'proud' to be a Celt, and 'sympathetic' to Welsh nationalists. 'The trouble is,' R. S. tells him, 'that the Welsh welcome newcomers; perhaps they are too open-handed.'

A decade later, Byron Rogers makes the trek to Aberdaron, for the *Daily Telegraph* magazine.[107] Rogers is, like nearly every would-be interviewer of Thomas, sold on the poetry and therefore nominally 'sympathetic', but even so his attempt at a more intimate portrait slides quickly into gothic caricature with a dash of necromancy:

> The house is cold, even austere. Cold pastels, pale waxed wood, the white skulls of sheep and dogs laid on an old oak chest, Miss Eldridge's fantasies in ink. In one of the drawing rooms are the feathers and bodies of dead birds which both Thomases pick up, and preserve. In one of the poems he writes about 'the strict palate', 'the simple house'. After a half-hour of trying to be Heathcliff I asked if we might have the second bar of the fire. Thomas smiled, which is to say his lips curved suddenly downwards. 'My wife always said that people would freeze in our house.'

The journalist in Rogers overcomes the cold. It is the poetry-lover in him that is frozen out. He is on to a good story and he knows it. Quickly he discovers (quite wrongly, in fact) that R. S. has no friends. '"I had one or two in Bangor, but we didn't keep in touch after. I haven't got any now. What is a friend? Someone whom you see often? I can't afford to go 60 or 70 miles in a car to say 'How Do' . . . Don't say that, I'll have people coming to see me."' But of course there is a reason for all this. There has to be:

> It is not the reserve, or coldness, in the man, though he is both reserved and cold. It is just the distance between you. The questions are answered politely, but the way a tired man would answer a child. There is no reason for the question, no value in it being answered, but the child has asked it so a reply will come. 'Journalism is such an unreal world, don't you think? All they want to know is what

kinds of socks he wears. Or they'll say, "Ah, he made a good jab there." People are like that.'

The effect is quite amazing. The sense of the man's separation even from himself is such that you begin to think of the whole proceedings as fantasy; after all, why should one have come all this way to talk to a clergyman in late middle age at the end of Wales?

Why indeed? The trick is of course in that use of the word 'you'. Not I, Byron Rogers, begin to think that the whole proceedings are a fantasy, but you, anyone, everyone. Not a visitor with a particular personality on a particular day, whom the poet may or may not have regretted inviting, but Fleet Street in person, the great and objective true lens on the world. Thomas's aspersion upon journalism as 'an unreal world' must be swiftly squashed. And better still, what if the interviewer can get Thomas to poke a bit of fun at himself? Thomas obliges. 'We get eight months of winter here', he tells Rogers. '*There was almost pride in his voice.*' Finally:

He got up. At 60 he seems as athletic as men half his age. Then he said something which I only remembered long after. It could not have been a slip of the tongue: Thomas is too careful with words for that. 'Let's have some lunch.' He paused at his bookcase, his face away from me. 'You can answer the rest of your questions after.' He is a private man.

Or a public Sphinx? Journalism very largely does depend on cliché and commonplace, which are anathema to any remotely good poet. Twenty years later Rogers revisits his quarry, now living on Anglesey, this time for the *Sunday Telegraph*.[108] The famously unforgiving raptor of Llŷn cannot be all that unforgiving. But nothing much has changed. Rogers recycles a great deal of his earlier interview, in particular the passage about the electric bar fire. And still he cannot really believe in what he is doing. He begins complimenting Thomas on his poem 'A Marriage', but stops in mid-sentence, 'struck by the unreality of interviewing a lyric poet. You can compliment a model on her appearance, a politician on his rhetoric, but words trail away when you find yourself confronted with a man who has set down such an intimate moment in verse.' But then Rogers must still cope with the legendary reticence. 'Say Mr Hyde had been an athlete: Dr Jekyll might have talked similarly of his achievements, with a weary and distant interest. It is hard to come to terms with this.' Hence perhaps the insinuation of monstrosity. But if Rogers wants to rumble Thomas, Thomas has already rumbled Rogers.

Aged 82, and retired from a parish so remote that it took the church 15 years to replace him, Thomas has latterly emerged as a public figure on account of his opposition to English holiday homes in Wales. This has delighted the English Press ('The cantankerous clergyman', 'The fiery poet-priest') and even more its photographers. A gaunt, grim figure appears, taken against the sky, and in one photograph in particular, crouched in the half-door of the 17th-century cottage where until recently he was a tenant of the National Trust, he looks like an ogre out of a Rupert Bear book.

So I was nervous about meeting him again. 'The chap in those photographs looked off his rocker,' I said.

'When they decide you are an ogre, they find the right photograph,' said R. S. Thomas.

But, along with everything else, R. S. has a widely un-celebrated sense of humour. Asked by the *Oldie* in August 1993 to answer some questions for its 'Death File', he picked them off with ease:

My ideal way to go . . .
    Saving a young life.[109]
My life expectancy . . .
    I never expected anything. Why start now?
My last words . . .
    You again!
My method of disposal . . .
    Thrown to the critics, and may it choke them.
My funeral arrangements . . .
    Since the composers and liturgiologists have done their worst, there's nothing left to arrange.
My special effects . . .
    A cortège of women priests in gaiters.
Memorial service . . .
    To parody Herbert Spencer, it will be better for people to ask:

Why hasn't this man a memorial service than why he has one?
Who would you like to meet on the other side? . . .
Not the ones I directed there.

Elsewhere in the press we find such headlines as 'English vicar faces Welsh language dragon',[110] 'The harsh high priest of our national culture',[111] 'Poet at odds with the universe'[112] or, as we have already seen, 'Biographers: they can go to hell'.[113] Fortunately, not all interviews with Thomas are two-dimensional. When the questions asked are considered, then so too are the replies. These, though, are to be found in the literary journals, not in the newspapers: a reminder of the folly of trying to turn what is not news into news.[114]

But what of Thomas's own account of himself, unassisted by media men and media women? *Neb*, published in 1984, was written five years after his retirement, and sixteen years after settling in Llŷn. Despite this passage of time, he has less to say about Aberdaron and its environs than about either Manafon or Eglwysfach. The experience of hope followed by disillusionment that afflicted him in his previous parishes is repeated, but in a lesser way. Having arrived within hail of where he was born, and close to the sea and a distinctive community of Welsh speakers, Thomas declares that his *hiraeth* is finally assuaged. 'Thus for the first time in his life R. S. was from now on in a parish where he could use the language with almost everyone, every day.'[115] He continues to 'chew over' the problems of Eglwysfach, particularly the enlarged egos of his wealthier parishioners there, but he has no nostalgia for the place. Realizing too that Aberdaron is likely to be his last ministry, and looking back on his clerical career, he again finds no cause for regret. Being 'fastidious' people, R. S. and his wife ask themselves 'many times' whether it mightn't have been better to leave the countryside 'in order to avail themselves of the artistic advantages available in the main centres'. But, although this is at odds with statements made elsewhere that as regards high preferment Thomas was overlooked, he knows the answer 'almost before asking':

If he had to choose between a majestic cathedral and a small country church, he would choose the latter every time. As for the cathedrals with their ostentation and their war banners and the organ booming sufficient to wreck the roof – well, they smelled of the nationalism and militarism of England. As far as he was concerned the English were mostly people who continued to dote upon such things. But it was the plain, unassuming little things that appealed to him. That was what stirred him in Manafon to write of the cottager in his small fields. That's why he wrote articles in magazines like *Y Fflam* praising places of worship like Soar-y-Mynydd and Maes-yr-Onnen.[116]

At Aberdaron these requirements were amply fulfilled. In his congregation was no resident *crachach* type asking him to pray for the military. As country churches go, St Hywyn's was a jewel, and the surrounding landscape was pitted with reminders of the Celtic heritage. More, Pen Llŷn was a staging post for many different species of birds in the spring and autumn migrations. Above all though, because 'he found himself in an entirely Welsh community, he didn't see the need to emphasize his Welshness any more, but could accept it as entirely natural. Welsh was the language of the majority of the inhabitants and there was no question that it should not be spoken in their homes and at their meetings.'[117]

But there was the other side to Aberdaron. In the summer months it is a small seaside resort popular with tourists, especially those from the industrial cities of Lancashire. Indeed, during the season, the whole of Llŷn becomes something of a holiday camp. Outside the nearest town, Pwllheli, was a Butlin's, and everywhere caravan and camping sites. There were, in addition to the owners of a more or less plentiful supply of holiday cottages, a growing number of 'in-comers', English who wanted to retire there, or enjoy an alternative lifestyle. And if this were not enough, some of the high ground was despoiled by radar installations, and at all times of the year the sky was liable to be rent by jets exercising out of RAF Valley, across the sound in Anglesey.

Thomas is more graphic:

By the summer the promontory was full of strangers, with Aberdaron chock-full, the English licking their ice-creams or standing in a queue

to buy newspapers to stick their heads in. Mynydd Mawr was opposite
Holy Island and not far from Capel Mair and its well. The views
were miraculous, but the most common sight was of cars in rows
and the motorists with their heads in their papers swallowing the
petty news of the material world. And overhead the Air Force would
rehearse noisily almost every day to impress them. It became obvious
to R. S. that there was tension here. On the one hand there was the
eternal view of the heather and the rocks and the sea, but above and
everywhere else was evidence that the twentieth century demanded
attention to the extent of destroying all that was left of the Middle
Ages.[118]

But there was a more personal tension as well. What 'became known
about him' in Aberdaron, he says, was the fact that he had to write
his poetry in English. This was a contradiction he could neither conceal
nor run away from. Rather he admits it fully, and also admits how it
further prejudiced his attitude towards in-comers and holiday-makers:

> Living in a traditional Welsh area like Llŷn, speaking the language
> every day, and yet expressing himself in a foreign language! That was
> his view of that language as it lay on the lips of the visitors. Very
> quietly, he cursed their language. But the longer he stayed in the
> area, the more danger he saw to Welsh. It was this that made him
> into a greater patriot than ever before, if not in his literary work.[119]

Thomas tells us about 'an Englishwoman' who approaches him one
day after matins. 'I'm sorry we didn't pray for the Queen,' she says.
'Lady, be thankful that you had a service in a foreign language at
all', he realizes he should have said, but is not quick enough off the
mark.

In fact some of Thomas's most virulent nationalist poetry, contained in *What is a Welshman?* and published by Christopher Davies
at Llandybie in 1974, was written during the first few years at
Aberdaron; but it remains the case that thereafter, although Wales
is always present in his poetry, Thomas redirects his attention. It
may also be said that as regards such problems as he encountered in
his new parish, he largely turned his back upon them. In a revealing
passage he writes:

Aberdaron had been without a vicar for a year; therefore the people were glad to have even someone like R. S. Neither did he make a secret of the fact that he had more or less come there to retire. It is necessary to be clear about this matter. In every parish that he served R. S. carried out his work as diligently as he could. He was neither a popular nor a first-rate preacher, but he visited his parishioners regularly, especially the sick ... Despite this, R. S. so arranged his time that he had quite a bit of freedom. He studied in the morning, feeling that at that hour a priest should be found in his room.[120]

As he tells us elsewhere though,[121] study meant reading literature and serious works of theology and philosophy, and laying such books aside if a poem germinated in his head.

For Thomas, the advantage of a country parish was precisely that it gave him the 'peace and quiet' necessary to a poet. Yet out of that same peace and quiet, so strongly related to the surrounding landscape, emerged his distinctive philosophy of life. Something like the last third of *Neb*, his autobiography, is given over to an extended airing of his assumptions, his attitudes and his beliefs. He continues to recall episodes in his life, but uses them only to illustrate, or explain, what at heart is a moral tract, part harangue and part confession of Christian piety. Thomas's focus though is eclectic. His thoughts do not move in a particularly orderly fashion, but are addressed to topics that well up spontaneously. If there is a unifying theme, it is the poet's willingness to deprecate himself as much as he is eager to deprecate others.

Thus, a typical paragraph runs:

And consider church services. How many people knew how to worship, as they kneeled and closed their eyes and offered themselves to God? There was a mark of dissent on too many of them. Despite his respect for many Nonconformist ministers, R. S. noticed their rather bold attitude toward the Deity. When they prayed, too often it was as though they thought God was eavesdropping outside the door. And the music! God help us! How many church congregations can sing? How many organists can master their instrument? Talk of strife among singers: it was rampant in Manafon. That was one of the things that made him go to Eglwysfach. Patricia Mappin was able to play the organ and choose classical pieces to perform before the start of the services. But even then, R. S. was not fond of hymns, third-rate verses set to similar tunes. He much preferred chanting in the style of monks, but he was not himself such a good musician as to teach such singing to the congregation. That was another of the deficiencies of the training he had received at theological college.[122]

In the succeeding paragraph he discusses the 'tension' between religion and poetry, and his belief, shocking to some of his congregation, that what is written in the Gospels is metaphoric. And then, since he is on the subject of his own theology, he treats his reader to his thoughts on the relations between Christianity and the countryside. This in turn leads to a passage that is purely descriptive of the glories of the Welsh landscape.

But the long finishing straight of *Neb* is not merely or even primarily garrulous, despite its surface appearance of being that way. It is rather a determined attempt to come to terms with the different strands of Thomas's outlook, and of the poet's personality. If the strands seem too closely woven together, then that is because that is how Thomas, in his ideal self, would like things to be. Such an ideal self, however, which is not so much Thomas's personal self as a self in the abstract, is dependent upon an ideal way of life, an ideal society. It is in these circumstances that everything knits, or would knit together. And it is because such a society does not exist, has indeed been destroyed in Thomas's opinion by a whole gamut of forces characteristic of the industrial revolution, that the self is necessarily damaged, is living outside its proper remit, and is condemned to being a *neb*, or nobody.

The broad-brush rejection of modernity is scarcely unique. The desire to return to a bygone, apparently better mode of existence is itself a characteristic of the nineteenth and twentieth centuries. We need only think of Thoreau's *Walden*, or William Morris and Kelmscott, or, less appetizingly, Hitler's appeal to the forest in German mythology, or Oswald Mosley's vision of a recreated Tudor England. The concept of 'alienation', propounded by Marx and Freud among others, but also having its roots in the Babylonian Captivity and other biblical episodes, informs many contemporary social and personal philosophies. Ironically, many of the English in-comers berated by Thomas share his longing for a traditional land-based lifestyle. What is significant about *Neb* is the particular colourings Thomas gives to what might almost be described as the modern ur-myth par excellence. The lost society he hankers after is specifically Welsh, and specifically Christian.

But the poet takes things a furlong further than that. Recognizing that the pulpit is no place for polemics, he nonetheless writes that, given a Welsh congregation – and at Aberdaron, such congregations seldom numbered more than half a dozen souls – then he 'saw the need' to remind them 'of who they were and to urge them to be proud of their nation'. In this context,

> A very dear verse indeed to him was that from the Book of Deuteronomy, the seventh verse from the seventh chapter: 'The LORD did not set his love upon you, nor choose you, because ye were more in number than any people; for *ye were* the fewest of all people.' A very heartening message to a little nation like Wales, but on the whole his words doubtless fell on pretty stony ground.[123]

This though is not quite as straightforward as it may seem. In providing a translation of this passage I have substituted the English of the King James Bible for the Welsh of Bishop Morgan: '*Nid am eich bod yn lluosocach na'r holl bobloedd yr hoffodd yr Arglwydd chwi, ac y'ch dewisodd; oherwydd yr oeddych chwi yn an-amlaf o'r holl bobloedd.*' In both cases, however, the verse ends not with a period but with a colon. The eighth verse completes the sentence. In the Authorized Version: 'But because the LORD loved you, and because he would keep the oath which he had sworn unto your fathers, hath the Lord brought you out with a mighty hand, and redeemed you out of the house of bondmen, from the hand of Pharaoh king of Egypt.' In other words, the size of Israel, great or small, has nothing to do with it. God is fulfilling a covenant. Thomas, however, by truncating this sentence, makes it seem the other way. This he is able to do because the Welsh word *oherwydd* (in Bishop Morgan, '*o'herwydd*') can mean both 'for' and 'because'. But even in the Welsh Bible the sense exactly parallels that of the English. In Morgan, verse 8 of Deutoronomy 7 begins; 'Ond o'herwydd', which can only be translated as 'But because'.

In their own right, these two verses from Deuteronomy are problematic. They are one of many occasions where the Old Testament promotes the credentials of Israel as being the chosen people of God. For any people to insist that they are specially favoured by the divine is dangerous: whether among Jews, Christians or Moslems, it leads to bigotry and racial suprematism. Here, Thomas doesn't quite go as far as to say the Welsh are a chosen people, but an echo of it is certainly there in his handling of Deuteronomy, just as is the distant hint of a comparison between England and Egypt. For why else would R. S. have been especially drawn to this area of the Bible?

At any rate, in *Neb*, consideration of Deuteronomy 7.vii leads into an unusually sustained diatribe about the use of the English and Welsh languages in Wales, and in Llŷn in particular. Even when the people speak the latter, they will tend to use the former in their everyday business transactions, in shops and post offices and so forth. Contemplating this, his eyes opened by Cymdeithas yr Iaith Gymraeg, Thomas speaks of 'the split in the Welshman's soul'.[124] In his own case he describes a tussle he has had at Aberdaron with the Church authorities. After some pressure from Welsh language campaigners, it was agreed that church registers could be bilingual, but with the proviso that English should come first, with Welsh as an optional second. Thomas protested, writing letters to the Public Registrar. Eventually the issue was raised at a meeting with his rural dean. The rural dean, however, insisted 'that the matter should not be taken forward'.

Whether Thomas considered resigning over this issue is not stated. 'When the sickness of the Welsh is discovered,' he comments bitterly instead, 'they lose their temper. Worse than the enmity of the English towards the foreign language in their midst is the enmity of so many Welsh-speaking Welsh to their mother tongue when it becomes an essential.'[125] And again: 'If there were plans afoot to strike the English yoke from our shoulders, it would be the Welsh themselves who would be amongst the first to betray them to the authorities.'

To the outsider such strongly expressed feelings may appear overstated and dramatic. A word such as 'yoke', historically applied to the Normans, surely has no place in today's broadly liberal democratic society? But to the Welsh nationalist, or patriot, or whatever else he chooses to call himself, the situation is quite obviously different, and for Thomas impossible:

> The tragedy of the matter is that the only way to win freedom is to fight for it. That is the lesson of history. Although R. S. was a pacifist, as a priest should be, he knew of no example to the contrary, with the exception of India. And to this day it is the people who have used force who have made the deepest impression on their oppressors. How many government leaders in Africa and India today haven't spent time in English prisons before succeeding in throwing off the yoke of their oppressors?[126]

Then, in what seems a casuistical leap, R. S. swivels his eye towards the natural world, where again his pacifism is affronted. 'Whoever has seen a peregrine falcon descending like a thunderbolt on its prey is sure to have felt some thrill, that makes him feel humble enough. These are the masters of the natural world. One of the eternal rules of that world is that life has to die for life. If there is another way in this world, God did not see fit to follow it.'[127]

In the closing pages of *Neb*, all Thomas's preoccupations continuously intermesh. The God-given land of Wales is corroded not only by the English and their tongue, but also by all the appurtenances of modern material culture. 'Land of pylons and wires, land of television masts and police poles, land of new roads escaping to the sea is Wales today.'[128] All that remains for the priest is prayer, for the poet the birds. But even these become fused, so that scanning the sea for a rare bird and waiting patiently for some sign from God become a single activity.

That sign, when it comes, is as likely to be a shift in the weather as anything else. 'People disappoint one, but Wales is never unfaithful. She is always there in all her immaculate virginity, despite the atrocious things we do to her.'[129] If paradise does not resemble the Welsh landscape, its moors and its streams and its mountains, illuminated alike by sun and rain, then Thomas has no desire to go there. On earth though, he must remain perplexed: by life's pain; by man's refusal to restrain his venality; by the operation of 'secondary causes'; and by God's apparent complicity in the wreckage.

Yet it is to God that Thomas finally turns. 'The possibility of judgement is clear on the horizon', he writes:[130]

> By living in a four hundred year old cottage, and thinking about the cottage's families over the centuries, he imagined he saw their faces watching him from the stones in the walls. By hearing the eternal sound of the waves breaking on the beach at Porth Neigwl, or responding joyfully to the dance of sunlight through his room, and then turning on his radio and hearing another example of the foolishness or bestiality of man – all this causes R. S. to brood on thoughts that are, as Wordsworth said, too deep for tears. What is appropriate to man any more but to repeat, day after day: *Miserere me, Domine?*[131]

A finely blended admonitory vision? Or a mish-mash of anger, superstition and prejudice? Aspects of Thomas's sermon in *Neb* are certainly vulnerable to scrutiny in their detail. His insistence on the primacy of the Welsh language as irreplaceable consciousness, for example, sits uncomfortably with his theological and poetic characterization of language, *all* language, as metaphoric mediation. But to push such criticisms would be to miss the wood for the trees. Thomas is not concerned to construct a philosophically watertight argument. His purpose is more inherently human than that. He wants to show us the whole garment of his life in Wales and in the Church, including its lining; and he is prepared to tell us where that garment hangs uncomfortably on his frame.

Between Thomas the media creation and Thomas the ruminating individual there is a considerable gap. Is there any way of reconciling the two? What lies in between? Having visited Holyhead, Bangor, Cardiff and Manafon, I continued my physical pursuit of R. S. But if like Byron Rogers there were moments when I found myself involved in something akin to fantasy, this was not because of the poet's presence. Rather it was because of his absence.

Driving up from my home in Dyfed, and passing through Aberystwyth, I descended upon Eglwysfach. Thomas's description of it was perfectly correct. Eglwysfach is a roadside parish, easy to miss, the road skirting steeply banked hills to the right, the flatlands of the

Dyfi estuary to the left. The scenery was unexpectedly rich, but I was aware that here too was an arena of bald sheep-runs, though set at a greater distance than at Manafon. Since it was lunchtime when I arrived, I looked for a pub, but saw none. St Mary's was there, and the vicarage, two grim chapels and a few small houses and bungalows, but nowhere to drink. Taking my heart in my hand therefore, I turned up a lane that led to the Ynyshir Country House Hotel.

Since I had to start somewhere, Hubert Mappin's erstwhile Georgian residence was as good a place as any. Both as a country house and a hotel Ynyshir had much to commend it, not least its present owners: Bob and Joan Reen. Bob was an artist, born like Dylan Thomas in Cwmdonkin, Swansea. His large and daring canvases were hung in the lounge and the dining room and entrance hall. It was his wife who seemed to run the establishment. Both were welcoming. When I mentioned my reasons for being in Eglwysfach though I noticed a quick glance between them.

'He was not the most popular of men, by all accounts,' Mrs Reen said. 'I wasn't here at the time, but the stories about him are not especially flattering. Have you seen what he did to the church?'

'Not yet. What did he do to the church?'

'He painted everything black. If you want to go inside you'll have to get the keys from Ivy Hughes, the churchwarden.'

'And the present vicar'?

'There isn't one. Or rather he's also the vicar of Borth, where he lives. I imagine that's because nobody's gone inside the church there with a tin of black paint. The vicarage here is for sale, if you're interested.'

Purchasing R. S. Thomas's former residence, I thought, would be a little too obsequious. So instead I asked, 'Does R. S. ever come back?'

'Occasionally. Very occasionally. He was here a few weeks ago, as a matter of fact. In the dining room, with one of the professors from Aberystwyth. Walford Davies, I think. Having some very good wine. But then we only have good wines here. Would you like to see the list?'

'Thank you, but it's a little early in the day.'

'Did you know that Ynyshir once belonged to Queen Victoria?'

'I had no idea.'

'Ah. I'll get you a brochure.'

Joan Reen left me to a plate of sandwiches. After lunch she pointed me in the direction of Ivy Hughes, who lived in one of the modern bungalows I'd already passed. I knocked on her door. A woman on the threshold of age appeared. It occurred to me that it was not impossible she had been a warden when Thomas was vicar.

'I'm doing some research on R. S. Thomas,' I said, asking for the keys. 'I was wondering . . .'

'But you won't find any trace of *him* at the church.'

'I'm told he painted everything black.'

'Not everything. Just the pitch pine pews. And some mosaics on the floor. Here. Go and see for yourself.'

I walked back along the road to St Mary's. There was a particularly fine lych-gate, a well-kept graveyard and the usual guard of yews. Inside, the church *was* unnecessarily austere, despite attempts to brighten it up with hanging baskets of flowers. It was true, I noticed: the pews were black, as was the area of floor in front of the altar. An otherwise simple interior was weighed down like a coal-barge. It was an old church, restored, like so many in Wales, during the nineteenth century. Also hanging from the ceiling was a heavy iron candelabra, called a corona, that I knew from *Neb* Thomas had commissioned from the English blacksmith Allan Knight. This too was black. But the thing that most caught my attention was the panel of stained glass to the right of the altar. This depicted St George.

That must have slain R. S., every time he didn't look at it. Myself, I looked inside the visitor's book. Nothing related to R. S., although there was an entry that spoke of the 'great poet' Thomas Owen who had been 'priest in this church'. As far as I know there is no even mildly commendable Welsh poet of that name, so perhaps someone had failed to do their homework.

Mrs Hughes was right. The black paint apart, there was no trace of R. S. at St Mary's Eglwysfach. Nor was there any sign of him in the village. If this were Laugharne, I thought, there'd be a statue of him by now, and tourist shops selling his books and tapes and other souvenirs. But this wasn't Laugharne, and R. S. isn't a commodity like Dylan.

Perhaps it will come one day. Perhaps the coaches will stop at Eglwysfach – at Manafon too – and disgorge hungry culture vultures who can than be taken to the RSPB sanctuary. But it hasn't started yet.

I returned the keys to Ivy Hughes. Perhaps I had caught her at an inconvenient moment earlier. She was more communicative now.

'Did you see the pews?'

'Yes, indeed I did.'

'Aren't they awful?'

'Pretty.'

'That wasn't all he did. You may not have noticed, but there's a hole in the wall near the organ. There used to be a memorial tablet there, but *he* had it removed. That cost him an argument with Mrs Mappin. Mr Thomas stripped the place bare within weeks of arriving. There was a fine red altar cloth, for example, which he sold at a jumble sale, though the money of course went into parish funds. To purchase the black paint, I expect.'

'What about the stained glass windows?'

'Oh, the windows.' Ivy Hughes smiled girlishly. 'I'm afraid there wasn't much he could do about those. The Bishop would have been straight round.'

'What was the problem, do you think?'

'I don't know. Some people are just made like that. It had quite a lot to do with the Welsh thing, I suppose. I'm English, as you must have guessed. But my husband was local. He spoke more Welsh than the vicar, but that didn't stop Mr Thomas. My husband was in the post office shop one day, buying some postal orders, when he was rounded upon. "Why don't you ask for those things in Welsh?" Mr Thomas demanded. Well, my husband gave the answer everyone gave. "For the same reason," he said, "that you don't write poems in Welsh." That shut him up.'

'When was that, do you remember?' I wanted to know whether this had been before or after the launch of the Welsh Language Society. Pedantic of me, but the problem with having a history degree is that a regard for chronology keeps butting in. But Ivy Hughes couldn't help me with that one.

'It was about thirty years ago,' she said. 'Beyond that I couldn't be precise.'

It was a version of the standard R. S. anecdote, usually told to indicate a personality for whom the world is never right.

I didn't accomplish much else in Eglwysfach that day, other than a walk round the bird sanctuary. There weren't many birds about either; nor was Bill Condry at home when, crossing the salt marsh, I found his farmhouse. It can all wait for another time, I told myself as I drove back home. A fortnight later though, heading northwards again along the unsurpassable West Wales coastal road, I drove straight through Eglwysfach. Ianto Owens was with me, wearing a leather jacket. This was for my own protection. We were on our way to Gwynedd and the Llŷn Peninsula. Owens had said:

'I'm not letting you go up there on your own, boy. They'll bloody murder you when they hear your accent.'

'What's wrong with my accent?'

'Don't you know, boy? It's English. Dead English. I don't mind it myself, I've always said I dislike more Welsh persons than I do *Saeson*, but then I've met more Welsh haven't I? But up there it's different. Gogs, we call them in the south. And you should hear their accents! Very nasal it is, and they gobble like turkeys.'

When we came to Eglwysfach, I slowed the car and said:

'Shall we stop here or what?'

'What's the pub like?'

'There isn't one.'

'Then drive on, boy.'

We stopped at other places though. Machynlleth, for instance, with its Victorian gothic space-rocket of a clock tower, and beforehand in Cardigan, which I liked inordinately. We also detoured to Harlech. From there I caught my first sight of Llŷn, which indeed stretched out between sea and sky like the bough of a tree. Or God's finger? 'Who can deny God's finger!' R. S. once reproved an interviewer.[132] But it was not God that impressed me so much as the gentleness of so many of the Welsh towns we passed through. Small places going nowhere, but possessed of an aura of community. Perhaps, I thought, that's why Welsh nationalism has lagged behind its fellows: community before nation, friends and family before brigades. Nationalist revolutions belong to big cities, and such big cities as Wales has are all in the anglophone south.

From Machynlleth, up into the mountains, the long, steep climb towards and past Cader Idris. Now this was God's country. The eight-mile glaciated canyon, sheep sticking to its vast green sides like dollops of chewing-gum. And the self at the wheel, minuscule, watching the lake at Tal-y-llyn grow smaller and ever more dazzling in the mirror.

Then Dolgellau, the detour to Harlech, via Barmouth, now almost a ghost resort, the marshes of Traeth Bach, and around to the narrow toll road that took us to Porthmadog. Everything now is more built up, and because it is May, Porthmadog is already aswarm with visitors. Fifteen-ton coaches jammed in old windy streets. But after Porthmadog, where Llŷn begins, the congestion eases, and then it is Criccieth, with its castle overhanging the sea, and Pwllheli, and then there are no more towns, just the bending road and telegraph poles and signs off to small resorts, Nefyn to the north and Abersoch to the south, and rising in the far distance the spectre of Mynydd Mawr.

And the last bay, more than a semi-circle, was Aberdaron, which we came down upon like a small aircraft angling for a beach-side strip. A tiny gaggle of white houses clustered around a small bridge over the river Daron, which is no more than a stream, and St Hywyn's, half-submerged by grassed dunes, like a wise head drowning, exactly as it was supposed to be.

Beyond the bridge was a little piazza with a shop and the old post office and two hotels: the Ship Inn and the obviously more expensive Tŷ Newydd. We tried the Ship first, but they had no rooms available, so we checked in across the street. The receptionist there, an American girl called Caitlin who was studying at Bangor, told me, when I enquired, that Thomas was famous in Pen Llŷn for annoying everybody by driving his white mini as slowly as he could and refusing to let anyone overtake him.

'He is quite old, you know. Old people drive like that.'

'Not him. He does it intentionally. He thinks people shouldn't have cars.'

My room at the Tŷ Newydd was on the top floor and had an unobstructed view of the bay: a great bowl of water, with its two Seagull islands arranged like boulders in a Japanese rock garden, and thin, unbroken waves, a mile or more long, lapping the shore metronomically.

It was late afternoon. 'This is heaven,' I said when Owens knocked at my door.

'I won't know about that until I've had a drink. You coming for a pint?'

'Is the bar open?'

'Not here. It's too respectable. At the Ship. I've made some enquiries and there's no pub, but the Ship is where the locals hang out. If you want to find out about R.S. that's your best bet.'

I'd been thinking about poking my nose into St Hywyn's, but Owens as usual was irresistible.

'Just watch what you say, boy, that's all. I don't know these people yet.'

We repaired to the Ship. The long bar there was already filling up. Probably this had something to do with the barmaid, an especially fine-looking woman called Sue.

'Where are you from?' I asked.

'Manchester. I'm one of the dreaded lergies around here. But then a lot of us are. I came with my husband a few years ago. We bought a croft.'

'Problems?'

'Not really. The people are mainly very nice as it happens.'

'Does the name R.S. Thomas mean anything to you?'

'Oh *him*!'

'You know him?'

'Who doesn't? Mainly from the rear though. The rear of his car that is. Blocking up the lane. Why do you ask?'

I explained to Sue my mission in life. She said:

'The good thing is he moved away a year or two ago. Gone off to Holyhead I think. He had a genius for making himself unpopular round here, at least among us English-speakers. He used to be vicar, but was retired by the time we came. He had a reputation for being keen on birds though. You can't imagine what happened. One afternoon I found a gannet on the beach. Poor thing's wing was broken. Well I knew where Mr Thomas was living, up in Rhiw. So I put the gannet in a box and took it to him. Was he interested? As soon as I opened my mouth he asked me where I was from and how long had I lived here and when was I leaving? I told him I'd only come because of the bird. Oh, there's nothing I can do about that, he said. I thought it was all very offensive of him and said so to his face. Not that it made the slightest difference.'

'And the gannet?'

'The gannet I ended up taking to a sanctuary in Anglesey. It was well cared for and survived.'

'I like this place,' Owens broke in, 'I like this place very much. Shall we have another?'

We had another, then we had supper. When we returned to the bar at the Ship, Sue had gone, replaced by an older barmaid called Ivy. Ivy was also from Manchester, and was even more outspoken in her opinions about Thomas. When I mentioned his name she cackled.

'I could never make that one out,' she said. 'I was here when he first moved in. I'd heard there was a new vicar coming, and I'm a churchgoer myself. Or I was until then. The first time I saw him was outside on the bridge. "Morning, Vicar!" I said to him, wanting him to feel at home in his new parish. But he just turned his head and looked the other way, like so. I was very upset at the time, although afterwards people told me he usually did that when people greeted him in English. But was that the proper way for a man of God to treat his flock?'

'Perhaps he was busy thinking up some poetry.'

'I dare say he was. But it's no way to treat people. That was his attitude, you see. There's also the thing about his car. Where he lives in Rhiw is a cottage off the main road. What he used to do was go to the shops, then stop his car in the middle of the road and take his bags out one by one. Nobody could get past, but bugger everyone was his notion.'

'What else?'

'Oh loads and loads. Like the time he went to Pwllheli and took part in a march wearing a balaclava, just like the IRA. And him a priest! It's not right. I tell you, there's a black spot in that man's head, a very black spot indeed.'

It was my turn to laugh. If R. S. was wearing a balaclava, how did anyone know it was him? That story I doubted. But I could tell Ivy wasn't out to impress me. She actually did bear a grudge against the man. And I knew from Thomas's own reminiscences that he was quite capable of deliberately snubbing people.[133]

'Terrific, isn't it?' said Owens. 'You could write your whole book here if you wanted to.'

'I'd like it to be a little bit more than a compendium of bar talk.'

'Why, for God's sake? Bars are where people are known, to the bottom of their tankards. That's why people with something to hide keep out of them. Like your Ronnie-head-in-air. Are we having another?'

We had another, then another. Ivy got busy in other directions as well, but she was helpful in pointing out customers who might have a thing or two to tell about Thomas. Some of them did, and some of them didn't. Mainly it was confirmation of R. S.'s reverse banditry on the roads. The real locals though, those who spoke Welsh, were the more reticent. Not that they were unfriendly, far from it, just more reticent. There was one Cymro though, Alwyn Hughes, a biology teacher, who took more than a passing interest in my enquiries. He was a quiet, shrewd man, in his early fifties. He would like to talk to me, he said, writing down his telephone number, but now was not the time. He was with friends.

By then the bar was steaming full. At some point I lost Owens, or rather Owens, my self-appointed bodyguard, had lost me. When I found him in the press he was having a rather dodgy conversation with three men wearing ties.

'Ah there you are, boy. I was just telling these gentlemen I don't like small businessmen.'

The gentlemen in question were of course small businessmen, and Owens was well on his way to being tanked.

'Nice to meet you,' I said, before turning to Ianto: 'I think we'd better be going, otherwise the bar at the Tŷ Newydd will be closed.'

'What's wrong with here?'

'Nothing, but they'll chuck us out at eleven. Then we'll be high and dry.'

Owens understood. 'Oh okay then, but I still don't like small businessmen.'

The bar in the hotel had already shut, but the owner, a likeable Irish woman called Breda, said we could sit out in a lounge with a drink. For a while she joined us. But if I thought the Celtic bond would induce Breda to say some good things about R. S. I was mistaken. She had married an Englishman, and this he couldn't forgive her for. 'So you see when a television company came to Aberdaron and wanted to take a shot overlooking the church from the verandah outside with R. S. Thomas standing in the foreground they had to use a stand-in. R. S. simply refused to set foot inside the place.'

'What kind of man is he?' Owens said after she had gone. 'What kind of man is he?'

'Not a small businessman, that's for sure,' I said.

'Doesn't he understand, we Welsh are just not like that? Has he ever got pissed, I wonder.'

But I had, and Owens had. As Breda could not be found to replenish our glasses bed was the only option. But all night I listened to the long thin waves of Aberdaron being plucked like harp strings by the shore.

Next morning I looked around St Hywyn's, both inside and out. Inside had not been painted black, although I noticed a replica of Allan Knight's Eglwysfach corona hanging from the rafters. That could only have been Thomas's doing. Some of Thomas's books were on sale, along with monographs about Bardsey Island, but it was still light years away from Laugharne. I made a note of the new vicar's phone number, then looked at the graveyard. Many of the headstones bore Welsh inscriptions, some *englynion* among them, but the one that took my imagination was in English, in memory of a young sailor drowned in a 'melancholy shipwreck'.

It was Stephen Spender who described a cemetery as the 'heavy page of death'. Here, at Aberdaron, the graveyard was more like a piece of loose parchment half dipped in water. God's peace was in the bay. With the possible exception of Mwnt, I could think of nowhere else in Wales I'd rather be buried.

Owens meanwhile had been walking on the beach. For no particular reason he had woken up unusually restless. When he returned we set off for Mynydd Mawr and Braich-y-Pwll, the extreme tip of Llŷn. The pre-Cambrians failed to move me though. Whether rocks are a thousand years old or a hundred thousand times that age doesn't make a lot of difference to a non-geologist. A rock is a rock is a rock, and in Wales there are a lot of them, particularly the part where I live. But the view from the summit of Mynydd Mawr was something else. Far down below were fields cut into the same narrow strips as seven hundred years ago, in feudal times. And out to sea was Bardsey, Ynys Enlli. In the May morning mist, in the great seamless pale blue vault of sky and water, it seemed like an anchored whale.

'You know,' said Owens, 'twenty thousand saints are supposed to be buried on Bardsey. Twenty thousand holy men.'

I gazed at it, and wondered about the language thing. There are places in Wales that are unlike anywhere else on earth in their subtle, changeable beauty. It is indeed very easy to imagine, once the idea has been proposed, that the divine is present there. But why then the anger about words? Was it because language is part of the mystique of a place? Japan for example would simply not be Japan without its language; or so it must strike the traveller, when he sees the hieroglyphics hanging out on paper bolsters in front of every shop, and hears the people playing on the throat's abacus. And the same surely is true about any 'foreign' country: it is the language that makes it foreign, that gives it an aura.

Here, at the end of Llŷn, the mystique was certainly in place. But where was the language? I wondered therefore about Thomas, to whom for so long Welsh was a strange tongue. Could it be that, having fallen for the mystique of the Welsh landscape at its best, he had unconsciously made the connection between mystique and language? That his attitude in this matter was not so much of the man inside desperate to survive, but the man outside determined to protect and cherish a compelling otherness? Was it in fact primarily a question of aesthetics with him?

But this was idle speculation, or worse; and certainly had nothing to do with the very real threat to Welsh Wales. In any case, Owens was still fretting. He had his pipe out now.

'You want to get back to Dyfed, don't you?'

'I'm sorry, boy, but you're right. It's beautiful up here in Llŷn, but I don't belong somehow.'

Too many small businessmen, or not enough?

'It doesn't matter. Really. I'll come again by myself.'

We went back to Aberdaron and loaded up the car. Before leaving, however, Owens wanted to post his wife a card. I waited for him as he went across the bridge, to a makeshift post office there. When after a few minutes he didn't return, I went looking for him. I found him in conversation with one of the men I had met the night before, Alwyn Hughes.

I wouldn't swear to it, but it was as if he had been waiting for us. This quiet, unassuming man wanted to get something off his chest. 'We're talking about R. S. . . .' he said, when I came up.

A little of it came out. Hughes considered himself to be as Welsh as any man alive. Also, his three children spoke Welsh. He had taught them himself, and made sure they were taught Welsh at school.

'But R. S. never did that with his child. Not that I don't admire R. S. for learning the language himself. I do. But he didn't go that extra mile, did he? And while the Welsh he does speak is very good, or became very good after he'd been in Aberdaron for a while, it is also very proper, classical Welsh. What we call "perfect" Welsh, in fact. But not colloquial at all. Now I never made a fuss about it myself. I never had much time for the Welsh Language Society and all those people. I just got on with speaking the language, and seeing to it that my children did as well. But then along comes the Reverend Thomas, who writes his poetry in English, but who didn't grow up in Llŷn, and starts telling everybody in that stand-offish manner of his what they should do.'

Then Alwyn Hughes laughed, a dry, sincere laugh.

'You must think we've all got bees in our bonnet round here. I wish you could have met my father, Jack Hughes. He knew R. S. much better than I. Though they had their spats as well. I'll tell you, my father and R. S. were standing over there on the bridge one day when the Pwllheli bus came in. An ancient yellow double-decker. It was virtually empty, so R. S. says, What a wicked waste, why doesn't the bus company get something smaller, a mini-bus for instance? To which my father replied, Yes, vicar, and why don't they get you a mini-church while they're about it, since that's usually empty as well?'

On that note we left, though I knew I would see Hughes again. In the car Owens was full of admiration for him.

'Perhaps you didn't notice, but we were talking in Welsh when you appeared. But knowing you're English, he immediately switched language. That's how it always was in the south as well. Common courtesy I think it's called.'

'Everyone starts from a different position, I suppose.'

'Christ, don't they just! Perhaps God will inform us one day which one's the right position.'

'Some people think he's already done that. But that's just another position.'

'The hell he has, boy, the hell he has!'

I returned to Aberdaron in July. Meanwhile an extraordinary story began circulating about R. S. He had remarried. The woman in question was described variously as being English, Irish and American. It seemed improbable, but the rumours persisted. Not bad for an octogenarian, eh? And of course, this was why he had abandoned the cottage in Rhiw. To be with his beloved. But where were they? Some thought they had eloped to Clwyd, others to Anglesey or even Alaska. It all sounded unlikely, though I know the old can act with even greater abandon than the young: they have less to lose. And in any case, what business was it of mine? Or put another way, what exactly was my interest in this man? What was the nature of my inquiry? Sometimes I wondered. It had begun with Wales, and had moved on to Thomas, as a poet of Wales. Now, in an attempt to understand both, I was being tempted to trespass on his privacy, which I had never intended. If I asked questions about these rumours I felt oddly guilty. I was casting myself in the role of a snoop. And if

I didn't? If I didn't, there was always that old saw about Shakespeare's laundry list, and its implications. Only in this case the implications went beyond mere noseyness. I defy anyone who has read his poem 'A Marriage' to put it entirely out of their mind:

> We met
> under a shower
> of bird-notes.
> Fifty years passed,
> love's moment
> in a world in
> servitude to time.

If R. S. really had remarried, then it seemed a quite enormous betrayal had been committed: not just against the memory of Mildred E. Eldridge, but also against the sincerity of his art. For I could not imagine a deeper expression of a profound emotion than is contained in those lines.

As before, I arrived in Pen Llŷn at the end of the afternoon. How would I make out on my own, without Owens for company and 'protection'? This time there was a room at the Ship Inn, overlooking St Hywyn's, with a segment of sea thrown in for good measure. I had to bend my head for these views however. Swifts had nested in the eaves outside my windows, caking the upper panes with faeces.

Downstairs was a woman behind the bar I hadn't met before: Carys, whose brother Gareth Roberts was the National Trust's warden for Llŷn. He would, she assured me, be pleased to have a chat. She gave me his number. Already, I felt, I was making progress. I went for a pre-prandial stroll around Aberdaron. Nothing had changed. There was a balminess about the place I thought never could change. Somewhere out of time that those like myself, trapped in time, are sometimes free to visit.

I stopped at a knick-knack store and put my by now habitual question to the man serving behind the counter. 'I've been here seventy-seven years,' he replied, 'which is a great deal longer than Mr Thomas was, and I'm still here, which he isn't. If you want to know what sort of man he was I'd say to you he was independent. Make of that what you will.'

Yes, nothing had changed. Anxious to see its Irish proprietor again, I dined at the Tŷ Newydd. Thus do men of letters spread their favours evenly. As luck would have it Breda's brother Seamus was there as well. Seamus looked my age, but claimed to be sixty. He was, like so many southerners, an expansive and beguiling talker. Tonight his theme was neo-militarism in the contemporary world, and he covered more ground than Alexander the Great. He spoke though without venom, only with wit and grace and charm. We sat at a table on the hotel's verandah staring across a completely tranquil bay. Why, I naively asked myself, couldn't all Celts be so? Nor was it alcohol that rendered Seamus so affable. He was a teetotaller.

By night, my room at the Ship filled with the sea's natural lullaby as my room at the Tŷ Newydd had done. Only now did it strike me:

> We met
> > under a shower
> of bird-notes.

The cadence of the sea-shore, the push and drag of the tide: the essential mechanism of so much of Thomas's later verse, as though indeed the poetry were reaped from the fields of the deep.

And then it was Sunday, and an unusual intention of going to church. After breakfasting at the Ship I walked over to St Hywyn's, to find out the time of the service. I had already made an appointment to see the vicar, Christopher Armstrong, that afternoon at his home in Llangwnnadl, where he was also the incumbent. Again, the exigency of the contemporary church having to fill several posts with one priest. At that hour, however, St Hywyn's was deserted, save for the organist practising upcoming hymns on a rusty harmonium parked behind the pews.

The organist's name was Mary Roberts, though no relation of Carys and Gareth: a round, gentle, infinitely polite woman who expressed no surprise at all when I sidled up with my inevitable enquiry. No, she was never organist during the Rev. Thomas's time. That honour had belonged to Miss Lloyd, but there was no point in my talking to Miss Lloyd because Miss Lloyd was not a well person these days. But she, Mary Roberts, knew about R. S. of course. Every-body in Aberdaron knew about everybody who had ever been in Aberdaron. What did she think of him? Now *there* was a question. What *did* she think about him? He was a good man, she would have to say that, though she could not deny a certain awkwardness of manner.

'Did you attend his services?'

'Of course. I always did.'

'What were his sermons like?'

'Oh his sermons!' Mary Roberts beams. 'His sermons were the same whether they were in Welsh or English. The language was always the finest, and what he said was to the point. Short and strong were his sermons.'

The organist smiles again, then, like her harmonium, sighs.

'A good man was R. S., but . . . *Lle bo camp bydd rhemp.*'

'*Lle bu camp bu* what?'

'*Bydd rhemp.* A saying we have. Where there is excellence there is excess. Here, I will write it down for you.'

Where there is excellence there is excess! *Rhemp* is the problem word, a word admitting no exact translation. Excess, disorder, pecu-liarity: a number of English equivalents exist, but none of them quite fits. Mary Roberts though expressed some of her own personal-ity when she chose the milder option. Someone more anglicized might have quoted Dryden:

> Great Wits are sure to Madness near allied,
> And thin Partitions do their Bounds divide.[134]

*   *   *

The service was at eleven. I went back to my room to change into a suit. At ten to eleven the bell began ringing. Through the swift-enriched window I saw the extraordinary sight of a sexton pulling on a rope. He was exactly like something out of *Peter Grimes*: bearded, stocky, weathered, and wearing long boots. The rope itself ran up the Norman wall, to a simple stone bell-cote. Two older women, dressed in shawls, were making their way towards the Norman doorway.

I hastened to join them. There were perhaps twenty in the congregation. A couple of tourists perhaps, but no more than that. The service was bilingual. That is to say, although it followed the Book of Common Prayer, it did so in both tongues. This arrangement extended to the singing of hymns and the susurration of a psalm. In the responses, there was a syllabic fit, but nothing more. The result? Since neither Welsh speakers nor English speakers predominated, dismal to the ear. But then that is another economy the Church in Wales has had to make: by trying to satisfy two congregations simultaneously, it threatens to drive both away. And the chapels are emptying even faster.

Mary Roberts read the lesson from her seat at the harmonium. My immediate interest, however, was directed at the Revd Christopher Armstrong, R. S. Thomas's eventual successor at Aberdaron, after a fifteen-year interval during which St Hywyn's was untenanted. I knew from a newspaper article that Armstrong was Anglo-Scottish, and although he had undertaken to learn Welsh, he had not, on his appointment, been spared the poet's ire. 'The English stand up for their language,' Thomas was reported as saying; 'if we cannot stand up for ours this is what happens.'[135] Yet the first thing that struck me was how physically alike the new vicar was to the old. A tall, lean man, though his face was not quite as unyielding as R. S.'s. He had, however, in the two years since his appointment, made good progress with his Welsh.

Armstrong delivered his sermon from the sanctum. He spoke, in English, about Bardsey, Ynys Enlli. He had just returned from leading a retreat there. He began with the proposition that Christ was a workaholic. 'But we don't all have to be workaholics to enter the kingdom.' The people who attended the retreat were all sorts. There was, for example, the woman – 'I can't help mentioning her' – who came with five bathing suits in her very large portmanteau. But there was also a company man suffering 'chronic' ME who insisted on stumbling around the island picking up litter. 'We must each find for ourselves a way of scratching the pig's back . . . so to speak.'

My mind begins to wander, as it always does in church. During marriage ceremonies, for instance, or funeral services. But then it is mesmerized. The vicar is in full rig. Behind him, across the screen of the large plain glass altar window, dance two butterflies. Had I believed in God, I would have known his presence then, whatever was being said or sung. Beauty is the unsuspected snare.

The sermon ends. The altar-rail is closed by the sexton figure, who shuffles. I watch as, in two shifts, the congregation kneels on one side, with the vicar on the other, dispensing wafer and wine, flesh and blood. Old people mainly, older than the vicar himself, yet submitting themselves to him like children.

To the outsider, the ritual enactment of a time-honoured custom, the length and breadth of its meaning partially occluded; although what I can grasp is the extraordinary elevation of the person of the officiating priest.

If the Reverend Armstrong harbours any grudge against R. S. for what were unwelcoming comments in the press he keeps it to himself. In the afternoon I visit him at his Llangwnnadl home: not a traditional rectory, but a compact newly built concrete job, more appropriate perhaps for an upwardly mobile junior executive than a seasoned priest. And Armstrong is a seasoned priest. Originally ordained into the Roman Catholic church, he transferred his allegiance to Anglicanism in the 1960s, gaining a ministry in the Episcopal Church of Scotland. The posts he has held include, as well as parish ministries in England, five years as Director of Westcott House in Cambridge, an advanced theological college. Because he is now vicar of Aberdaron he is closely associated with Bardsey Island, where he leads retreats three or four times a year. These, he says, are 'very much bring your own tea-bag experiences'. In his role as leader, however, he often takes with him some of R. S. Thomas's more overtly religious poems. They are, he says, excellent texts for focusing meditation and discussion, the more so as they concentrate precisely on those areas of doubt which beset the contemporary Christian.

'But you will want to know about the parish and its composition, and what kind of priest Thomas was. There is a story that the day he retired R. S. made a bonfire in his garden and threw his cassock on the flames. I don't know how apocryphal that is, although I do know Thomas wanted to stay on at the vicarage in Aberdaron on a part-time basis, but the Bishop wouldn't allow it.[136] There was some anger there I think. But I also know that subsequently he must have applied for and got a licence to preach, which one needs after retirement, because he sometimes took services in Llanfaelrhys. As a priest, he was what we call a Prayer Book man. That is, he adhered to the prescribed rituals. Beyond that it's hard to say. He was neither bells-and-smells, nor a north-ender. Neither very high nor very low. He was certainly conscientious as a country priest however. Aberdaron is an exceptionally large parish geographically, but no farm was too remote for him to visit.'

'Provided the farmer spoke Welsh?'

'Yes, there was that to it as well, though of course around here all the farmers do. Very roughly, the parish divides up 60 per cent Welsh, 40 per cent English. R. S. did I think have a special regard for the former. The local council by the way is solidly Welsh, and conducts its business in that language. There is I suppose some tension between some of those living in and around the village, and some of those living further out, towards Mynydd Mawr for instance. One learns to appreciate that the farming community is still very close-knit, and there is certainly a virtue in that. Also, one has to say, there is a strong chapel tradition here. That is, when somebody wants to marry they go to a minister because that is what their fathers and mothers did. In the Anglican congregation there is only a small but very precious group of Welsh speakers. We do our best to look after them.'

And so the conversation proceeded. My impression was Armstrong wanted to preserve clerical solidarity. On the matter of Bardsey for instance he was not particularly forthcoming. Although the Bird and Field Observatory, created in 1953, had flourished, because the island was privately owned, by the Newborough family, there had always been the possibility that Bardsey would one day be commercially exploited. In 1975 Bardsey was acquired by Michael Pearson, later Lord Cowdray. By 1977, it was again on the market. In order to protect the island's natural and spiritual heritage the Bardsey Island Trust was formed and an appeal launched in order to raise the £103,000 purchase price. Patrons included the Archbishop of Wales, the Marchioness of Anglesey, Plaid Cymru's MPs and such distin-

guished naturalists as Sir Peter Scott and R. M. Lockley. The Appeal
Fund itself was under the presidency of Wynford Vaughan-Thomas,
and the chairmanship of Susan Cowdy. By 1979 the necessary funds
had been raised, and Ynys Enlli was 'saved'. Later, in 1986, Bardsey
was declared a National Nature Reserve.

But the Bardsey Island Trust was the grand overseer body. Subordi-
nated to it was the Bardsey Island Trust Council. According to the
rubric this was 'set up to represent the various interests in the island.
Members will serve as individuals, not as formal representatives of
other organisations.'[137] And the first chairman of the council, established in 1978, was none other than R. S. Thomas.

Thomas, however, resigned in March 1979. Why? 'I'm not at all
sure why,' Armstrong tells me. 'I know very soon after the island
passed into the Trust's hands it befell R. S. to welcome Prince Charles
there. But that wasn't it. I think it was something to do with
accepting a grant from the Nature Conservancy Council, which he
regarded as English money and therefore polluted in some way. But
you would have to ask others.'

Later in the day I do just that. Gareth Roberts, the National Trust
warden not just for Pen Llŷn but for the whole pensinsula, occupies
a house on a hill to the immediate west of Aberdaron. He is local,
his family Methodist. Growing up on a farm nearby he expected to
become a farmer himself. He understands the land and its requirements exactly. He also understands the different communities that
live there.

'You want to know about the in-comers? Up until 1980 Llŷn was
a sort of retirement park for the English. This was to the benefit of
local businesses. But in the decade following 1980, the first ten
years of Mrs Thatcher, the pattern changed. Younger people started
arriving from England, people who had sold up, who had a hundred
thousand in their pockets. In the get-rich-quick society either they
had made money on property deals, or they had received generous
redundancy payments. At first their intention was to drop out, but
after a while they found they had got their sums wrong and had to
find work again. Some started new businesses. The net effect of this
was to take trade away from those born and established here. These
younger ones also had children, monoglot English speakers of course.

As a result the balance in our schools was changed. The language of the playgrounds became English. But since then things have changed again. The recession of the early nineties reversed the trend. Those families that have stayed, and the few new ones that arrive, are happy for their kids to learn Welsh, so that the playgrounds are reverting to Welsh.

'Language is not the only issue though. I don't want to be dogmatic, but there was a difference between the two communities. Self-evidently those who came to Llŷn to settle here had abandoned their own communities in England. I don't want to impute anything to their motives, I can imagine anyone wanting to live in Llŷn, but it was not the same as being born and bred in the area. What I mean is they were not always so careful about their image. But for the Welsh, for those with long connections to an area, image matters. By that I mean it matters whether you get on or not. There is pressure from the community to succeed, whether that be as a farmer or at college or whatever. That pressure is not easily avoided. It is a very Welsh thing, I think, but all the same you noticed the same pressure didn't affect some of the in-comers in quite the same way.'

'And R.S.?'

'R.S. was neither the one thing nor the other. He was a kind of in-comer himself, but he preferred to speak Welsh and resented the English as much as anyone. He could rant and rave about that, but he was also a person of contrasts. You know about Plas-yn-Rhiw and the Keating sisters? They were English of course, but Mr Thomas had no problem accepting their hospitality. I think though his wife had something to do with that. She was a striking figure in her own right. I would say she was middle class, but very unmodernized. As for R.S., well he's buggered off to Holyhead, with another English lady. The cottage is used by his son Gwydion. You should go and have a look at it: someone has inscribed the words "Cartref R.S. Thomas" on the gate. In Wales that is an enormous compliment. Speak to his neighbours there, Ieuan and Megan Williams. They have a small dairy farm lower down the hill.

'But don't get the wrong impression about R.S. Most of us remember him as someone who cared passionately for the environment. He was famous for bird-watching. You could see him standing with his binoculars for hours, sometimes in the middle of a road. In that mood he wouldn't give anyone the time of day. He left people alone and expected to be left alone in return. Unless, that is, he wanted some brambles cutting or his well cleared out. Because the Plas-yn-Rhiw estate now belongs to the National Trust, that was my responsibility. If he wanted some brambles cutting or his well cleared out then he could be very communicable. But I don't mean that in a snide way. It's just how things are, with him, and with others. It was the same with the CND. Mr Thomas was an active member of the Pwllheli branch, for which I admired him. Sometimes it was difficult though. I remember him taking a petition round once. He knocked on every door. He entered into long debates with people. But he had an ability to block out what he didn't care about. If his mind was made up about something, no argument could change it. He could lose an argument, but still retain his position.'

'What about Bardsey Island? Why did he resign from the Council?'

'I can tell you about that. There were two things. Buying the island was one thing, restoring and maintaining it another. A lot more money was needed, around £200,000 I think. In the end, the Nature Conservancy Council came to the rescue. R.S. thought the money should be refused because it was English. He wanted Welsh people to be more involved than sometimes they are in preserving their environment. But there was also the matter of siting a beacon for yachts and other pleasure craft at the end of the island. This was a Chatham House affair. R.S. thought this would only encourage more tourism in the area, which he was against. So quite quickly he resigned. The beacon went up, but was blown away by a storm and hasn't been replaced.'

I had arranged to meet Alwyn Hughes in the bar of the Ship the following evening. In the morning I drove over to Pwllheli, to nose round a couple of bookshops. On my way back I called in at two places: Plas-yn-Rhiw and Plas Glyn-y-Weddw, at Llanbedrog.

Plas Glyn-y-Weddw is one of the oddities of Llŷn. Neo-gothic, it was built in 1856 as a dower house for Lady Elizabeth Jones-Parry, the widow of Sir Love Jones-Parry. Sir Love was upper gentry, the owner of the Madryn estate, also in Llŷn, and a sponsor of the efforts to create a Welsh colony in Patagonia earlier in the century. From the outside, Glyn-y-Weddw is a glum building, but this only adds to the surprise of its magnificent if a little film-settish hallway, which seems to occupy most of the interior. Off this atrium and its double staircase lead a series of fair-sized but less than baronial rooms.

Today Plas Glyn-y-Weddw is run as an art gallery – *oriel*, in Welsh – by its present owners, the painter Gwyneth Tomos and her husband Dafydd ap Tomos. My reason for visiting it was that the Tomoses had mounted an exhibition of paintings inspired by individual poems of R.S. Thomas. Mainly they were by Welsh artists, and mainly it would have been hard to guess their connection. All manner of modernist styles were represented, although if I had to identify a common theme then that would have been a pervasive and angry melancholy. Three of the nineteen works reproduced in the catalogue were responses to the poem 'Welsh Landscape':[138] a fact of some sociological significance perhaps, given that no other poem inspired more than one canvas. But by far the most interesting *objet* was a pencil portrait of R.S. done by his wife in 1978. In this, the poet's habitually implacable countenance is softened. The famously craggy features are refined by an Italian touch. The lips are hair-clip thin, but the eyes are melliferous with sorrow.

And so to Plas-yn-Rhiw. It didn't take long to find Sarn-y-Plas, the four-hundred-year-old cottage overlooking Hell's Mouth, although it is set back from and above the narrow road, nestling in a scoop in the wooded hillside. I recognized it at once from photographs, although there was no sign of the words 'Cartref R.S. Thomas' (Home of R.S. Thomas). Either his son or someone else had removed them. I hesitated, however, to approach within more than a few feet of the gate. The absolute mortification if R.S. were there, paying a call on his Gwydion or whatever.

I turned instead down the hill. Within a hundred paces I came to a cramped dairy farm. Megan Williams was at home: an old woman, but sweet as she is hospitable. She invites me at once into her parlour. And it is a parlour. Her chair is set beside a coal-burning stove where I could imagine her receiving visitors all day long. Not a wealthy farmhouse, but welcoming; although the Williamses can

scarcely be that impoverished, since they own a field across the way
that is now a holiday site for campers and caravanners. As we talk,
various of these 'guests' come in and out, either just to say hello or
to purchase a pint of milk.

Megan's voice is small, and has that slight lilt to it decades of
music-hall and cinema and radio have conditioned the English ear
to expect of the Welsh. To catch every word I must lean forward,
so that my unannounced intrusion immediately becomes an intimate
encounter. 'Oh, so Mr Thomas it is that interests you. Mr Thomas,
indeed!' One can almost sense her setting a timer. Now here's chat
that will be a good hour. And she's away. To begin with she tells
me what so many others have told me, that R. S. is a naturally aloof
man fixated on bird-watching. This, Megan Williams assures me,
he did twice a day, once at dawn, and once in the afternoon. But he
was a good neighbour. 'Never any trouble, and always he would buy
his milk from us, though eggs he bought elsewhere, further up the
hill. And dropped in he did quite often, for a chat by the fire. But
if anyone else came by, and looked to sit down, then he was away,
faster than a racing car.'

'And Mrs Thomas?'

Megan Williams's eyes quicken, but in a generous way.

'Oh, Mrs Tho-mas. You want to know about her as well do you?
She was very fine, very fine, though she didn't visit like Mr Tho-mas.
She was never very well. So sad that was. They took her away eventually, to the hospital in Caernarfon. And Mr Tho-mas he was not well
too for a time, he had to have a hernia operation, so he should never
have done what he did. He had to go up to London, and when he
came back he collected his wife in Caernarfon and brought her back
here all by himself. He carried her up the steps to his cottage, when
he shouldn't have been lifting so much as an apple. He didn't ask
for any help. But it was always like that between them, and a few
days later of course she died.

'I don't think he wanted anyone in the world to be with him
then. The funeral was very private, just one or two people from away.
Relations of his, we thought, or relations of hers. But then there was
this other lady. She hung around a bit, and a few weeks later she
came back, and then a third time she came back. And it was not

long after that Mr Tho-mas left us. The garden he said had become too much for him.'

Megan Williams gives me a knowing look, then continues:

'So his son Gwydion has the cottage now, as his holiday home. There was a time father and son did not get on at all. That had to do with a woman as well, a friend of Gwydion's. A young thing covered in bangles, who came down with him from London. Mr Thomas could not approve of her at all. But it was all years ago. We used to say to Mr Thomas, let the boy follow his own life, let him find happiness as it comes. But he wouldn't listen to us. Now we would say the same thing to him, if it is true what I hear that he is married again. If it makes him happy, then all well and good. But it is sad he has left us.'

Again, the little knowing look, almost sly. Old Megan Williams is so open with me I have to wonder whether in fact I am being taken in in some way. Her family she tells me is chapel. Therefore, given her age, one would expect a certain censoriousness. Yet she seems not to want to censure anybody. 'We are all God's children,' she tells me, apropos Thomas's alleged reserve. 'But he was funny about people, and that's one thing I couldn't understand about him. He could pick and choose. But we are all God's children.' Is her forgivingness for real, or is it a vehicle for saying things she thinks one should know?

I had not meant to pry this far. Yet my pursuit of R. S. enables me to interact with different segments of a Welsh community in a manner that might otherwise have been impossible. What I learn about the community in question, however, is that the man comes first, the poet second. For whom then does he write?

I walk back up the road to where my car is parked, beyond Sarn-y-Rhiw. Megan Williams has told me there is no one in the cottage at the moment. My camera is lying on the driver's seat, ready and waiting. Just one photograph perhaps? I stare down into Porth Neigwl, Hell's Mouth, looking for a sign. There is none. But I remember an ugly occasion in London once. Coming out of a friend's house late one night I saw some press photographers swarming outside a doorway. The doorway belonged to Anthony Armstrong-Jones, Princess Margaret's former husband. Armstrong-Jones was expected home any minute. He was coming out of hospital where he had had an eye operation. The last thing he needed was a dozen flash-guns exploding in his face. Nonetheless the photographers were waiting. When I tried remonstrating with them I was told what I could do with myself.

Surely though this was different? There was no physical hazard involved. It was a building I wanted a picture of, not an unwilling individual. Must one not be at least a little bold in one's profession?

Wondering just what profession it was I belonged to, I picked up the camera and strolled with exaggerated nonchalance towards Sarn-y-Rhiw. Then I darted up the steps. The gate, however, was locked. There was a thick chain around it.

I stared at the padlock. For a moment it seemed a sort of metaphor for R. S. The cunning Dragon of Llŷn had rebuffed me again. Dutifully I poked my lens through the bars of the gate, clicked the shutter twice, and climbed down to the road.

There were magpies in the hedgerows, and a quarrel of rooks. Wales is a very large aviary.

In Aberdaron the sun still had a long way to fall. I decided therefore to drive on to Mynydd Mawr, for another look at Bardsey. One day I would cross over to the island, but not this week. Tomorrow I had to leave again. Ynys Enlli when I saw it was still brushed with haze, still lying like an anchored whale, only now both haze and whale were golden. I sat for an hour, hoping to spot chough. When the evening breeze picked up I got into my vehicle. A few minutes later, as I crossed a cattle-grid, there was a noise like a collapsing xylophone. The rear of my exhaust had separated from my chassis.

Soon another vehicle appeared and some people from Conwy stopped and gave me some string to tie the exhaust up. First though I had to let the thing cool, otherwise the string would burn through. As I waited I saw a man emerge from a farmhouse a hundred yards or so away.

'*Noswaith dda*,' I said.

'*Noswaith dda*,' the farmer repeated, staring at the string in my hand. 'But you're not Welsh, are you?'

I shook my head. 'Alas not,' I said.

'*Dim* problem. If an Englishman speaks two words of Welsh that's enough for me. Here, you'll need this.'

The farmer produced a penknife, but before I could take it he was down on his back, fixing my car for me.

'It won't hold,' he said. 'What I'll do is remove the exhaust for you and put it in your boot. Your engine will be noisy like a bullock, but it'll get you to the garage at Rhoshirwaun.'

'Thank you. Do you smoke?'

The farmer took a cigarette. I asked whether . . .

'Yes, I remember the Reverend Thomas. Myself I'm chapel, but the children always went down to the church at Christmas. He seemed a good sort really. He even persuaded me once to sign a petition. To do with something nuclear I think it was.'

As I drove off the farmer stood in the road waving until I was out of sight.

The people from Conwy were also staying at the Ship, so the session that evening got off to an early start. At nine thirty Alwyn Hughes came in. For an hour or so we sat by ourselves in a quiet room. Hughes added a few things to what he had previously told me about R. S. He was not, he said, a recruiting priest. He didn't proselytize, nor did he go chasing after lost sheep. He visited his parishioners once, and thereafter it was up to them whether or not they came to St Hywyn's. Nor did he judge people by whether or not they attended his church. If he was made welcome in a house he would often drop by to chat.

'He came to our house quite often. As I told you before, he and my father knew each other well. They both enjoyed a debate. I listened in quite a lot. Sometimes I sensed R. S. wanted an argument, so he would say something provocative, something against the grain, to get things going. When I was older, and studying biology at college, I joined in. Most of the arguments I had with him were about evolution. It became something of a favourite topic. He would never concede the logical and empirical bases of what Darwin said, however often I tried to explain them to him. There's quite a lot of science in his poetry, but it has to be looked at carefully. It was his birds I think. Birds for Thomas were God designed and God made, and that was the end of it. He didn't mind so much about other species, but no way were birds to be made subject to the Darwinian laws.'

'It would be wonderful of course if he was right.'

'Would it?' Hughes looks at me sharply, digesting my suggestion. 'I'm not so sure about that. I've seen what birds can do. But then that was R. S. for you. What he held on to he held on to. When his mind was made up . . . I should tell you another story. Perhaps you've heard it before. He didn't have a television set. The haunted fishtank was another anathema. But on Saturday afternoons if there was a rugby match, and Wales was playing, he would go to someone's house and watch the thing. Until one Saturday, when a referee's decision went against us. I expect it was an England match. Thomas didn't like it, and that was the last time he ever watched rugby on telly.'

Hughes paused, then said pointedly: 'I think that must have been around the same time we fell out.'

'Fell out? What about?'

'That was to do with television too. Some people came to Aberdaron and made a film. R. S. appeared in it and said the people here were semi-educated. There's a newspaper article I should have brought with me. Perhaps I'll drop it off for you in the morning.'

I tried pressing Hughes about this, but he was reluctant to say more. I sensed divided loyalties. He had told me things that perhaps he shouldn't have told an outsider like myself. Yet at the same time there was something gnawing at him, some or other grievance that wanted to get out.

Furious interiors again? I let it drop. Hughes had after all opened up for me, he was a good man, and I didn't want to preclude the possibility of his remembering the newspaper article in the morning. In any case it was not far off eleven, when the main bar would close, and he was with some other men.

The Conwy people were still drinking. Alwyn Hughes introduced me to his friends. We all went on drinking. I'm a little hazy what happened thereafter. Because hotel residents and their 'guests' could go on drinking after hours, a few of us piled into a smaller lounge. Among this group was a fisherman, Emlyn by name. Emlyn fished directly below Sarn-y-Plas in Porth Neigwl. R. S. would tease him about how much income tax he paid. But then he saw R. S. with a film crew one day, and called out: 'You getting a fee, Vicar?' The vicar laughed. Then the talk turned to other matters, and it was past three when I got to my room. For the last hour or so there was only myself, Emlyn and another called Alan Jones. I heard later, though, that at least a dozen Aberdaron men had sat up all night drinking with me. Word had got round quickly. Unwittingly I had provided an alibi to those who wanted to skip their domestic curfew. God knows what they were up to, but they should have joined us anyway.

At breakfast a brown envelope was waiting on my plate. Alwyn Hughes had not forgotten. Inside was a cutting from the *Caernarfon and Denbigh Herald*, hand-dated July 1984. This was a letter written to the newspaper by Hughes:

Sir,

I wish to comment on the HTV programme on Aberdaron broadcast last Thursday – a programme which took Aberdaron as an example of what it claimed was the destruction of Welsh culture and language by the influx of tourism and English residents.

This programme seemed more of an excuse for giving the personal and uncharitable views of the Anglo-Welsh poet, the Rev. R. S. Thomas.

The Rev. Thomas criticised the local people for adapting their village and its life to benefit from tourism. Did he not hold English services in Aberdaron church every Sunday morning during his time as vicar of the community?

He admitted disliking English settlers even more than second-home owners (who make less impact on the community). 'Love thy neighbour' provided he is locally born and Welsh seems to be his interpretation of the scriptures.

According to the Rev. Thomas, we the people left in Aberdaron are 'semi-educated' with no concern for our birthright which we are willing to sell for a mess of tourists.

Let me state my credentials which are typically those of most people in the Aberdaron area. I am a Welshman, the son of Welsh-speaking parents, brought up Welsh-speaking, married to a Welsh-speaking woman, with children for whom Welsh is their first language. The Rev. Thomas's credentials compare very poorly with these.

What are his contributions to the Welsh way of life and the Welsh language? Incidentally, the local children today speak a much improved Welsh to what we were taught thirty years ago, thanks to the policy of Gwynedd Education Committee and the primary school teachers. Could the Rev. Thomas not have uttered a word of praise and encouragement to those little English girls who, after only a few months in our school, both read and speak the Welsh language?

We the unintelligent, ill-educated, locally born people of Aberdaron by some strange workings in our dulled minds know that the assault on Welsh culture and language began centuries ago, was fostered by the wealthy, the 'well educated', the men of power and the snobbish intellectuals, but was resisted most fiercely by the small farming and fishing communities like Aberdaron.

We also know that the change in our way of life seems to be the only means by which we can remain in Aberdaron. We know, but it seems to have escaped the notice of the Rev. Thomas, that there has been a universal change in small communities and not just those in Wales, part of much wider issues the programme chose to ignore. Take away tourism and you will remove even more local Welsh people from Llŷn.

The Rev. Thomas should learn that we are a proud people and do not take kindly to the aloof contempt of outsiders. His views and interests might receive more consideration if they were expressed with kindness, understanding and good humour, and then together we might discuss any problems we might have.

Perhaps the Rev. Thomas should spend his latter years, not castigating us of Aberdaron but moving with missionary zeal amongst the Welsh in England, inspiring them to return to their native land.

Yours etc., A. Hughes

And Christ said: 'Think not that I come to send peace on earth: I come not to send peace but a sword' (Matthew 10:34). Looked at dispassionately, however, this letter shows that the respective

positions of its author and R. S. Thomas are not irreparably far removed from each other. The question of civility apart, the substantive
separation is that between pragmatism and idealism, with the
poet, as one might expect, defending the latter. Both are committed to the preservation of Welsh Wales. Yet it is just when there
is common cause, but disagreement about ends, that real acrimony
arises.

Even as an idealist, however, Thomas is, to the English reader,
idiosyncratic; though not to the Welsh reader versed in Welsh
classics. The foremost of all Welsh poets, Dafydd ap Gwilym, found
his greatest inspiration in his rejection by the women (real or imagin-
ary) he courted, just as eight hundred years before Aneirin was
'inspired' by the defeat at Cattraeth. Similarly Thomas depends upon
the idea of Wales as a lost nation, just as he depends upon the idea
of a God beyond his reach. It is only when all is not lost that all
becomes lost. And, of course, vice versa.

I left Aberdaron hoping always to return. On my way out of Llŷn I
had one further call to make. The National Trust's administrator of
the Plas-yn-Rhiw estate, Madeleine Dick, to whom I had introduced
myself the previous day, recommended that I contact Mary Allan,
an archivist working on the Keating sisters' papers lodged at Caernarfon. In the event I lunched with Mary and her husband Ian Allan,
an architectural historian, at a hotel outside Abersoch. Mary had
already prepared meticulous notes for me on letters exchanged
between the Keatings and the Thomases, beginning in the late 1950s.
Both had vivid memories of R. S. But it was Ian's characterization
that most stuck in the mind. 'He seemed not to care about his
image,' he said. 'Sometimes you would see him striding along the
middle of a street in Pwllheli, oblivious of everything around him,
including the motor cars. If one didn't know better one might have
mistaken him for a Fabian, the way he was dressed.' Ian, I should
record, was in a blazer and a crisp yellow shirt. But at the end of
the meal he added: 'His withdrawal from Llŷn was a noticeable and
actual loss. When someone like that leaves, a part of the landscape
goes with them. There is one mountain less.'

Thus far the weather had been all sun. But now, in Eryri and around Cader Idris, there were deafening cloudbursts. If my repaired exhaust had fallen off again, I would not have heard. Like the rain, the landscape I passed through was driven. On a tight bend a gaunt chapel welled up, then disappeared, its greyness a depressed echo among depressed greens. But by Aberystwyth the world was again well lit. An evening sun blazed over the Celtic Sea. I stayed overnight there, in the house of an old friend, the academic economist Karel Williams. Karel was away teaching in Manchester, but his wife Gwenda put me up just the same. When I asked about her husband, she told me he had started re-reading the Bible. Karel's father was formerly rector of Llanelli, but Karel himself, or at least the Karel I know, is a confirmed aetheist.

'He hasn't . . . ?' I began.

'Oh no. Nothing like that. But Karel finds the Bible an excellent source for pertinent quotations to put in his lectures. It's the Welsh thing with us, I suppose. We make a profession of returning to our roots.'

Three months later, with autumn already upon the land, I made my visit to Holyhead. But if my tracking of Thomas wasn't strictly in sequence, according to the chronology of his career, there was good enough reason for this. If Anglesey was where Thomas's life journey had begun, it was also where he had now gone to earth. The 'Demon of Hell's Mouth', to use one of several not entirely unaffectionate epithets I'd heard applied to the poet, had, after vacating Llŷn, finally removed to Llanfairynghornwy, a village inland from Carmel Head in the north-west, the most rugged part of Môn.

In the interim I had discovered what I take to be the facts about R. S. Thomas's 'second marriage'. There was no marriage at all. He was indeed sharing a house with the woman in question, an Anglo-Canadian, but it was a matter of two elderly people taking care of each other. The woman was in fact herself married, but her husband was in a home, in a persistent vegetative state. The couple had been known to the Thomases for many years, and the arrangement was one of mutually supportive friendship.

From Caergybi it was a half-hour drive to Llanfairynghornwy. It was not an easy place to find, nor was it entirely clear where the village began. I drove down into a wooded valley and saw a small secluded church, but very little else. Such houses as there were were set back from the road, and the place appeared deserted. I drove on, passing a shop of sorts, which was closed, until, at the end of an increasingly narrow lane, I came to a farm. The gentleman farmer, Robert Jones, was busy among his pigs. He was not aware that any poet had moved into the area, but gladly said I could walk across his land to a place on the cliffs where, according to my map, there were the ruins of a monastery.

The ruins, when I came to them, were more like those of another farm than a religious house. But the view was good. There was the sea and a wide windswept valley with a silvered stream running through, and ancient stone walls, and the sun flickering over it as clouds thick and thin sped across a huge sky. A place that for no exactly definable reason could only have been in seaboard Wales.

But to spend one's whole life there? From an outer into an inner field a train of Farmer Jones's bullocks were dawdling back towards the farm buildings. With the wind beginning to bite I joined their rear. Robert Jones himself was still tending his pigs when I reached the head of the slow-moving bovine queue. He looked up briefly, asked if I had found what I wanted to see, then apologized that he couldn't pause to talk. 'For months on end,' he said, 'I never get a single moment to myself.'

In the lane again I had to pull in to let a van pass. On the off-chance I asked the driver if he knew where R. S. Thomas lived. To my surprise he was able to give me precise directions. He indicated a hill rising above Llanfairynghornwy, back past the church. A few minutes later I was standing on one of the highest points of Anglesey. There was another fine vista, a three-way panorama. To my left was the sea, to the right, as I turned my head, the faintly visible peaks of Eryri. But straight ahead, beside Cemlyn Bay, was an unmistakable blot on the landscape: Wylfa atomic power station.

That Thomas should finally have arrived to be confronted by *that* every time he looked out of his window was, in one aspect, a joke of gargantuan proportions. Surely he could have found somewhere remote and beautiful and Welsh that did not contain a nuclear installation? Or was Wylfa the symbol of a grisly masochism?

I thought of St Aelred of Rievaulx, just one of many ascetic monks in the Middle Ages who inflicted pain on themselves in order to maintain the alertness of their minds towards God. In the contemporary reckoning, self-chastisement is invariably explained as a psychological, not an objective, necessity. Where there is no God, the need to offer him our souls may still be felt, but is not sustained.

Thomas's world is different again. In it he endeavours to reconstitute the objectivity of God and therefore of life itself. It is the vanishing of this he holds responsible for the decadent state he finds the actual world to be in. Of that decadent state, Wylfa is as good a metaphor as any. That it should be there is, in another aspect . . . a blot on the landscape. Also within view was the building where Thomas and his friend Betty now lived. What was I trying to establish? His singularity? His eccentricity? His perversity even? Each of these terms could be applied, and at the same time none of them. That part of my investigation was over, even though I still had a quiverful of leads to follow. What more could I hope to learn about the man that might be useful? Why bother to reconfirm what was already established? Over the course of a year's research I had collected any number of stories and anecdotes. Some I have left out. The story of R S arriving at a cathedral to read some of his poems at a service, and stomping off in a huff when he discovered a modern version of the Bible would be used. Or the story of a fellow priest who dined with Thomas at Eglwysfach, and broke a stony silence at the table by commenting how much he liked the poetry of George Herbert and John Donne, only to be told nobody could like both Herbert *and* Donne. To which should be added less overtly entertaining accounts of the poet, given me by those whose claim to know him is well founded: that R.S. is in fact, for all his reserve, a man of humour and generosity; that, when he is in the mood, he is an excellent conversationalist; that he is capable, for example, of an extraordinary rapport with children.

How much was true, and how much false? How much tittle-tattle, and how much justified resentment? How much is the perception of R.S. filtered through smeared lenses? Thomas's public image, and his image as a priest in the communities he was paid to serve, is largely unenviable. There are things about him, his legendary inconsistencies, that stick in the craw. Yet what are these compared to what he has written? A true poet exists inside and outside society. His perceived persona, part social, part cultural, is necessarily hybrid.

V

FURIOUS INTERIORS

If no-one asks me, I know. If someone asks, I do not know.
St Augustine, *Confessions*, Book 11

Pand englynion ac odlau
Yw'r hymnau a'r segwensiau?
A chywyddau i Dduw lwyd
Yw sallwyr Dafydd Broffwyd.

DAFYDD AP GWILYM[1]

IN JANUARY 1975, in an interview broadcast by the BBC's Radio 3, R. S. Thomas told listeners that whereas he 'used to propagandise on behalf of the Welsh identity' he had 'now wrung that dishcloth dry'.[2] This however was a momentary lapse on the poet's part. The dishcloth remains moist to this day, even if from around the time of the interview Thomas's poetic output did ostensibly veer towards other subject-matter. To his credit Thomas has in fact never ceased to propagandize on behalf of a Welsh identity, albeit in a manner suggestive of a minority-within-a-minority opinion.

Attention has already been directed at the sentiments contained in *Neb*, the Welsh-language autobiography published by Thomas in 1985. But although *Neb* remains Thomas's most ambitious prose work, in terms of scope as well as length, it does not stand alone. *Blwyddyn yn Llŷn* (1990), 'A Year in Llŷn', though scarcely more than a booklet, can be seen as *Neb*'s companion piece. Written as a journal, and divided into twelve chapters accounting for the twelve months, *Blwyddyn yn Llŷn* is a gentler production. To the accompaniment of Elsi Thomas's line drawings, Thomas records with a naturalist's precision the seasonal changes and variations in and around Aberdaron and Rhiw. The rich bird-life, indigenous as well as migratory, is his particular concern. Yet the text, in a manner already familiar from the autobiographical writings, is frequently disturbed by the poet's usual prejudices and obsessions. Thus, among many other personal details, he tells us how he has stopped attending church because of the introduction of modern litanies; how in the summer months he avoids walking by the sea because of the profusion of English-speaking visitors; how if addressed by such a visitor he will tell them he doesn't speak English; or how he dreams he is back in Manafon, and the relief he feels on waking to find he isn't.

Age is another preoccupation. Until he was sixty, we learn, Thomas could hear the cries bats make, but not thereafter. In a memorable passage he writes how, lying in the heather at Braich-y-Pwll, and watching dragonflies go by 'like old bicycles', he momentarily forgets that he is no longer a boy. But such lyricism is as often counter-manded by outbursts against the *Sais*, and his perennial complaint against even Welsh-speaking tradespeople for their inadequate com-mand of their native tongue and their eagerness to pander to the 'foreign' customer. It distresses him when a shopkeeper fails to under-stand his request for a *gwagr*, knowing only the word 'sieve', or anglicized 'sife'. Nonetheless, the book itself, which has much to say about the relations between poetry and place, quotes English along-side Welsh verse classics.

A less beguiling publication is *ABC Neb*, published in 1995, after Thomas's removal to Llanfairynghornwy in Anglesey. Twenty short essays, with titles such as 'Bangor', 'Caer' (fort), 'Eglwys' (church) and 'Ynys' (island), bid farewell to any attempt at self-discipline. In one of them, 'Wfft', R. S. takes hold of a relatively mild Welsh expletive – 'Pfft!' in English perhaps – then proceeds to apply it:

> Perhaps the best-known example of this word is associated with the number nine: 'nine *wfft* to him', another way of showing contempt for something or someone, or of pretending that one is not afraid . . . May I take this opportunity, then, of expressing my own aversions? . . . Here they are. Nine *wfft* to the hypocrisy of the English I have already referred to. No-one has suffered more for their trickery than we Welsh . . . Nine *wfft* to the Anglo-Welsh and all those who have swallowed the British bait or who have chosen openly to take the British side . . . Nine *wfft* to those who have plenty of money to buy an expensive car, to run two of them, to own two or three television sets, and who take costly holidays abroad but allow Welsh causes and the Welsh press to wither. Nine *wfft* to those people who have petty excuses for not attending important meetings and rallies, knowing quite well what effect their absence and lack of support will have. Nine *wfft* to the Welsh who neglect nature and the superb scenery of their country by leaving the task of their care in the hands of English who enjoy and appreciate them.[3]

So far so good, perhaps. But a few more *wfft* and R. S. loses his way entirely:

Nine *wfft* to those who renege on their word. It is not easy to keep a promise at all times. Therefore it should not be made lightly and thoughtlessly. But, after making a promise, it should be kept to the extent of one's strength, especially if one promises something to a child, because a child has a long memory, and after becoming an adult remembers the promise that was not fulfilled. This brings me to the question of divorce, alas so common amongst us nowadays. Whatever happens before the law – whether in a place of worship or at a registry office – it is the vow to be faithful that is fundamental, and neither church nor chapel can but put their blessing upon it. And because so many take advantage of the concept of a selfish, materialist society to break their vows, and so cause suffering and distress to little children, nine *wfft* to them as well. I am almost inclined to say that these are the worst of all. But there is one left, the most important of all I think, and that is I myself. Therefore because of my frequent failures and cowardice and hypocrisy, I will end by saying: nine *wfft* to me too.[4]

It is just this sort of diatribe, opinionated and admitting of no reply, that, among the thinking Welsh particularly, besmirches the cause Thomas is at such pain to promote. If that is how things are to be in the Republic of Gwynedd, should anyone be blamed for choosing a cultural alternative? And who in any case is Thomas to deny them the right of choice?

This is a real dilemma, because integral to Thomas's standpoint, as expressed in other prose writings, is the idea that, under siege, only intransigence can save the Welsh language and Welsh culture. On the level playing-field of Christian-liberal ethics the weaker force must inevitably yield. Whether intransigence is more or less likely to bring about the desired result is a matter of judgement, but there can be no doubting either the sincerity or the depth of the poet's feelings.

Thomas's most sustained critique of the Welsh language problem is contained in his essay *Cymru or Wales?* (1992).[5] Indeed, the coherence of this pamphlet is such that it forces the conclusion that the seemingly haphazard structure of much of Thomas's Welsh prose can only be deliberate artistry. Dismissing the inconsistency of the essay's being written in English as 'the publisher's requirement', Thomas goes straight to the heart of the matter, disarming a powerful counter-argument as he does so:

> We are familiar in life with the tyranny of 'either or'. There are certain combative people who try to corner us by asking: 'Which is it, yes or no; black or white?' It can also be the ploy of simplistic persons. 'Come on,' they urge, 'it must be one or the other'; whereas more astute people realise how many shades of grey there can be between black and white. Nevertheless, I chose my title because I cannot in this context see a third or fourth condition. Cymru or Wales; there is nothing between, although this century has seen the growth of a literary movement known loosely as Anglo-Welsh.[6]

But whereas Anglo-Welsh literature, as Thomas would be the first to acknowledge, necessarily survives, even flourishes, by taking in two different sets of washing, Welsh as a spoken language and living culture cannot hope to do the same, say within a bilingual framework. It will simply be swamped by English, as the language of government and historic dominion, as the language of an innately rich and varied culture of its own, and as the language of commerce.

Here the poet is fully cognizant of the realities of modern life, and of the modern media. He knows that any business enterprise outside Wales, regardless of whether its product is soap powder or television drama, is unlikely to package its goods in a minority language when members of that minority are content to be addressed in the dominant English tongue. And because the resources of English and international organizations are invariably greater than their Welsh counterparts, it is inevitable that in any circumstance where Welsh competes with English, English will prevail.

Under present conditions then, it is commerce more than government that is likely to dictate the future. In this respect Whitehall and Parliament's concessions apropos bilingualism are too little too late. The side-by-side competition they invite, between the two languages, is no competition at all. Despite the successes of Welsh campaign groups, despite the existence of Welsh-language radio and television stations, despite the mandatory teaching of Welsh in secondary education, despite even the existence of some Welsh-medium schools and colleges, Welsh as a living tongue must be doomed so long as English runs beside it.

With these descriptive propositions it is hard to disagree. Thomas fleshes them out with both the broad historic background of conquest and subjugation, and with specific instances of contemporary ethnic and linguistic disadvantage. Nor does he detract from the inherent strengths of the English language per se. It is, he writes, 'indubitably a language of immense flexibility':

> Having borrowed and adapted over seven centuries or more from many other languages, chiefly Latin and Greek, England has evolved a medium which is the envy of the world, is that of the most powerful nation of modern times [i.e. the USA] and is . . . uniquely fitted for the functioning of a modern scientific state.[7]

But if this is so, then why not simply bow to the inevitable, when the inevitable has so much to offer?

Thomas's answer to this is twofold. First of all, Welsh culture, particularly as it is expressed in Welsh literature, is too precious to lose. It is a thing of value in itself by virtue of being a culture. In addition, the same culture, as perceived by R.S., contains the seeds of moral redemption. The defence of the Welsh tongue is not merely a defence of the few against the many: it is also a resistance to a morally bankrupt order that Thomas sees as part and parcel of the anglicization of Wales. The 'so much to offer' turns out to be not only too little, but wholly undesirable.

Thomas's project therefore concerns far more than the colour and shape of sounds issuing from men's mouths. The history of Wales from the Edwardine conquest and 1536 Act of Union is, in his opinion, one of unmitigated decline, and this decline has been perpetrated in English. Not only have Welsh customs and the laws of Hywel Dda vanished, but in their place has been substituted a system of constraints, leading to the wrecking of the physical fabric of the Welsh countryside by the whole paraphernalia of an alien industrial and technological society.

Whether or not we agree with the reasonableness of these

embellishments of Thomas's initial analysis – and 'reasonableness' is always liable to be construed as one aspect of the Anglo-Saxon usurpation – we must recognize their visionary flavour. Predictably, as *Cymru or Wales?* draws towards its conclusion, it also draws towards God. What makes Wales so important to Thomas is precisely its residual moral destiny:

> It is because all the things which make for the Welsh identity, her mountains and light and skies and rivers and the speech which has christened them were made by God that she is sacred to us. Nations are part of the coat of many colours, which life wears, and as each nation is absorbed by another, so the coat becomes drabber and less given to praise. And as God made Wales, so she has made us, and we must love her as a son his mother or a bridegroom his bride.[8]

The inchoate ramblings of the 'Wfft' section of *ABC Neb* are here pulled together. It may even be that Thomas's self-recriminations there, of his own 'hypocrisy' and 'failures', are explained by the injunction of the son to love his mother. What Thomas means by Cymru, and by his rejection of things English, is the restitution of 'religious' society, in which individual, family and social interactions are governed by, and redeemed by, a single seamless ethos.

In a sense, Thomas's exhortation to 'love' Wales is risible. It implies a history that in its simplicity never was. It also threatens a dangerous conjunction of the religious and the patriotic – a pathology that as we have already seen besets other Welsh nationalisms. But crucially the poet identifies the mechanism whereby his utopian society of the past has been degraded: the absorption of one nation by another, giving rise, in time, to ever larger conglomerates of peoples, of which 'Britain', seen from a Cymric perspective, must be the outstanding example. What he prefers is Schumacher's notion of small as beautiful: a civilization whose members can be honest with one another, and honest with themselves.

The price paid for such an ideal society is its adherence to a fixed and immutable code. Where God's word is law, democratically determined change has no place. Conversely such a society denies the primacy of trade and commerce among life's concerns. The downside of democracy is that it turns everyone into consumers. In as far as 'freedom' is equated with freedom of choice in the marketplace, there is good reason to regard such freedom as suspect.

Two other prose pieces written in Llŷn augment Thomas's vision of Wales. The first of these is *The Mountains* (1968),[9] a rhapsodic invocation of the peaks of Eryri (Snowdonia), and required reading for anyone attempting to scale them. A large part of its interest is the insight it gives into Thomas's sensibility, his so-called 'nature-mysticism', and his absolute need to find himself alone in barren places, beyond the 'human stain':

> And so to the summit. Five minutes later all is forgotten. The sun is warm, the air golden. The blood courses vigorously through the veins. What are death, danger? This is the top of the world and this is I; there is nothing else, no living being. There are no sheep here to run off with sharply intaken breath, like silk tearing. There are no birds, flowers. There is an immense silence, broken only by the wind, coming and going among the piled rocks and stones. This is what it is to be God.

Stretched out below him he finds 'the summer pastures of the Celtic people', while to 'live near mountains is to be in touch with Eden, with lost childhood'.

Such indeed is the power of the mountains, and the spell they cast, that for once Thomas exhibits no compulsion to propagandize on behalf of Welsh Wales: a mountain is its own message. Quite different is *Abercuawg*,[10] originally given as an address, in Welsh, to the National Eisteddfod in 1976. In bardic lore, 'Abercuawg' is equivalent to Cockaigne or Shangri-la, a 'town or place', as Thomas says, 'where the cuckoos sing'. In Welsh literature its first mention is in the *Canu Llywarch Hen*: '*Yn Abercuawc yt ganant gogeu.*'[11] A lame man, bitter because he cannot fight for his prince, nonetheless claims that he can hear a cuckoo singing in Abercuawg. This lends fine irony to R. S. Thomas's assertion that 'as a Welshman I see no meaning to my life if there is no such place as Abercuawg', for Thomas too, by virtue of his priestly pacifism, is prevented from bearing arms. By a further irony, Abercuawg does in fact exist, or at least its site does: Aberdulas, at the confluence of the Dulas and Dyfi rivers, outside Machynlleth, and only a few miles north-east of Eglwysfach. But when Thomas goes there, to see for himself, he cannot find it. There is only the name, and an ugly, modernized landscape:

> Whatever Abercuawg might be, it is a place of trees and fields and flowers and bright unpolluted streams, where the cuckoos continue to sing. For such a place I am ready to make sacrifices, maybe even to die. But what of a place overcrowded with people, that has endless streets of modern, characterless houses, each with its garage and television aerial, a place from where the trees and the birds and the flowers have fled before the yearly extension of concrete and tarmacadam, where the people do the same kind of soul-less, monotonous work to provide for still more of their kind?

Yet to say that Abercuawg does not exist, Thomas tells us shortly, 'is rather like those people who allege that there is no resurrection of the dead'. They may be right, but who can live with such a truth, such a lie? It is not just beauty that resides in the eye of the beholder, but ultimate reality as well. R. S. quotes William Blake:

> 'What,' it will be questioned, 'when the sun rises, do you not see a round disc of fire somewhat like a guinea?' 'Oh no, no, I see an innumerable company of the heavenly crying: Holy Holy Holy is the Lord God Almighty.'[12]

What is at stake is not simply the spoliation of the Welsh landscape, but also the loss of the kingdom of the mind, and the imagination divinely informed.

With the help of Henri Bergson, Plato and St Augustine the gulf between the lastingly ideal and immediate reality, between what a word ('Abercuawg') means in its essence and the meaning it borrows from immediate circumstances, is opened up and explored by Thomas in philosophical terms. Yet, in his address to an Eisteddfod audience, it is to the Bible that the poet returns:

> Were not our chapels and most of our churches built as monuments to our corrupt taste and degenerate values? And did not the lazy ones among us say: There's nothing you can do about it? And the erring

ones: We must move with the times? But a few, the true remnant
of Israel, the salt of the Welsh earth, the people who are punished
for speaking thus – they said: No, this is not Abercuawg. We must
have something better than this.

The *hwyl* is upon him. Unless the compromise of bilingualism is
rejected, the true Abercuawg will remain inaccessible. Or rather, it
will be signposted in English above the Welsh.

Although *Abercuawg* has been translated into English, in a manner
presumably sanctioned by R. S. Thomas, to read it in either language,
without actually being Welsh, is like eavesdropping. One hears what
one is not supposed to hear, as though one had stolen from the
cavalry encampment to place an ear against the skins of a Sioux tent.
Overheard are the innermost deliberations of the elders. Or as Thomas
concluded a review of Dee Brown's *Bury My Heart at Wounded Knee*:[13]
'Rise up, you Welsh, demand leaders of your own choosing to govern
you in your country, to help you make a future in keeping with your
own best traditions, before it is too late.'

Abercuawg is paralleled by a 1975 poem of the same title, collected
in *Frequencies* (1978). As verse, 'Abercuawg'[14] is less than satisfactory.
Too many of its references are oblique, and Thomas tries to say too
much in contrary directions. It is not that some palpable emotions
are inadequately expressed, rather that they are too well expressed
to lie adjacent:

> An absence is how we become surer
> of what we want. Abercuawg
> is not here now, but there. And
> there is the indefinable point,
> the incarnation of a concept,
> the moment at which a little
> becomes a lot. I have listened
> to the word 'Branwen' and pictured
> the horses and the soil red
> with their blood, and the trouble
> in Ireland, and have opened

my eyes on a child, sticky
with sweets and snivel.

The snivel and the seeker after time belong to separate sensibilities. Unusually, the poet's focus is unproductively disjunctive. 'Abercuawg' doesn't enable dialogue within itself; rather it endeavours to confine W. B. Yeats and T. S. Eliot together in a too-small space, and the result is uncomfortably raw. Even the line breaks, the studied enjambement, begin to creak.

This in Thomas is rare. One of his acknowledged virtues as a poet is his ability to manipulate vocabulary, idea and image in such a way that the unalert reader is quickly led into thickets from which there is no obvious escape. Yet the very rawness of 'Abercuawg', heady as much of the poem may seem, is revealing. The same sort of tension, or clash of sensibilities, that, carefully handled, could 'make' a poem of the stature of 'A Peasant' (see above, pp. 183ff) here has the power to wreck another. The tension therefore is nothing if not real. It is what the poem is 'about', of course, but even so insufficient care has been taken to harness the tension's energy.

'Branwen' is a Welsh girl's name. It is also the name of one of the heroines of the *Mabinogion*. She is married to Matholwch, the King of Ireland. Her happiness ends, however, when her half-brother Efnisien sparks off a war between the Welsh and the Irish by mutilating some of the latter's horses. Until rescued by her brother Brân she is condemned to work in her husband's kitchen.

The story of Branwen is deftly worked into Thomas's polemical point, which is that any female today called Branwen is unlikely to bear any resemblance to the figure of Welsh folklore. In this sense Branwen's demotion to a 'child/ sticky with sweets and snivel' is a clever ghosting of the original Branwen's demotion to scullery-maid. The 'trouble/ in Ireland' is also clever. Not only does it supply an exact reference to the *Mabinogion*, but it also conjures up the contemporary Irish conflict in both its phases; the IRA in the 1970s, and the Irish 'troubles' of the early twentieth century. In fact, and not uncharacteristically, R. S. Thomas packs a substantial amount into less than seven short lines. There are layers and layers. But the same is not true of the surrounding lines. There the abstractions are of a different order altogether. They are of a philosophical, not an allusional, kind, so that the difference between modalities, between sensibilities, is widened, not narrowed.

What is lacking, in this particular poem, but also I would suggest throughout Thomas's poetry, is a ready-to-hand all-purpose cement, or bonding agent. As a contrast one could pick nearly any later poem of Yeats. Here, since its themes roughly accord with those of 'Abercuawg', 'The Curse of Cromwell':[15]

You ask what I have found, and far and wide I go:
Nothing but Cromwell's house and Cromwell's murderous crew,
The lovers and the dancers are beaten into the clay,
And the tall men and the swordsmen and the horsemen,
             where are they?
And there is an old beggar wandering in his pride –
His fathers served their fathers before Christ was crucified.
          O what of that, O what of that,
          What is there left to say?

All neighbourly content and easy talk are gone,
But there's no good complaining, for money's rant is on.
He that's mounting up must on his neighbour mount,
And we and all the Muses are things of no account.
They have schooling of their own, but I pass their schooling by,
What can they know that we know that know the time to die?
          O what of that, O what of that,
          What is there left to say?

But there's another knowledge that my heart destroys,
As the fox in the old fable destroyed the Spartan boy's,
Because it proves that things both can and cannot be;
That the swordsmen and the ladies can still keep company,
Can pay the poet for a verse and hear the fiddle sound,
That I am still their servant though all are underground.
          O what of that, O what of that,
          What is there left to say?

I came on a great house in the middle of the night,
Its open lighted doorway and its windows all alight,
And all my friends were there and made me welcome too;
But I woke in an old ruin that the winds howled through;

And when I pay attention I must out and walk
Among the dogs and horses that understand my talk.
O what of that, O what of that,
What is there left to say?

Between these lines of Yeats, and those from 'Abercuawg', are many parallels. Not only do both poets lament the destruction of their respective nations, but each also places himself, qua poet, within the frame, and very nearly at the centre, of proceedings. Again, both Yeats ('things both can and cannot be') and Thomas ('a seeker in time') look, or affect to look, outside the ordinary conditions of time to overcome their dismay. Yet Yeats's lines are all of a piece in a way Thomas's are not.

Why is this so? The obvious answer is because Yeats sustains his rhetoric at a steady pitch, and because he does so within the pale of an orthodox prosody. His lines rhyme and scan and do all the other things that verse is traditionally meant to do. Apart from being a great poem, 'The Curse of Cromwell' is also a well-made poem. But there is perhaps more to it than that, and the clue is the refrain:

O what of that, O what of that,
What is there left to say?

This is a musical device. 'The Curse of Cromwell' is a type of rondo. There is a tune to which the poem returns at precise intervals. This suggests a dance of some sort; and indeed the more we look at 'The Curse of Cromwell' the more we realize that all its constituent elements are held together as in a dance.

In Yeats the dance is not only a supreme metaphor, it is also the ground of his philosophy, of his outlook on life. Through it, he can reconcile all irreconcilables. Within the dance everything, including the poet himself, is equidistanced. And it is this correspondence between the idea of the dance, its abstraction as an intellectual tool, and its prosodic realization, as verse, that gives Yeats an all-purpose cement.

Thomas is not so fortunate. He eschews the theatrical, and anything to do with the theatrical. The dance for Thomas would be too easy a solution, and not just because his vastly esteemed predecessor and mentor was the latest to discover it. Before Yeats, Robert Burns perhaps was the premier exponent of the dance. But Thomas's mind works in a different way. To get anywhere at all, one feels, he must work excessively hard. There is no example of the use of refrain in his entire output. Rather his poetry tends to be extracted from and shaped by the friction between ideas. Everything else is superfluous, and everything else therefore is discarded. The music is correspondingly thinner, but also correspondingly more acute. He does not set a poem in motion; rather the act of composition sets him in motion. Therefore in Thomas there is a certain unpredictability; dramatic moment as opposed to theatrical presentation or the Yeatsian pageant.

This cuts Thomas off from any kind of gaiety. Of all Celtic poets, and perhaps of all English-language poets too, he is the most Stoic in temperament. In the onslaught between men and gods serendipity of any kind is banished. Instead Thomas walks a tightrope that he may fall off at any moment. To retain his balance every movement, every word, every syllable must distribute its weight exactly.

Such at least is manifest in the development of Thomas's prosody, the manner in which he writes his poetry. In this respect R.S. is a modernist in a way Yeats isn't. Cutting the stacked deck of his poems at more or less regular intervals we encounter what seems to be a progressive reluctance to rely upon any of the traditional main supports of English verse. Even in the early collections the iambic metre, the stanza and the full rhyme are sparingly deployed. In their place he substitutes the lesser structural elements of internal rhyme, delayed rhyme, half-rhyme, assonance and enjambement, using these, rather than set metres, to sculpt a poem:

> Rhodri Theophilus Owen,
> Nothing Welsh but the name;
> He moves in a landscape of dust
> That is surer than the smell
> Of breweries. What are the moors
> To him? Shadows of boredom
> In the mind's corners. He has six shirts
> For the week-end and a pocketful
> Of notes. Don't mention roots
> To Rhodri; his address

Is greater than the population
Of Dolfor, many times
Greater, and in that house
There are three Owens, none with a taste
For the homeland with its pints
Of rain water.

Until it is looked at closely, this paragraph from 'Rhodri',[16] from the 1966 collection *Pietà*, appears as free verse. There are no full end-rhymes, and the stress pattern is irregular. The number of syllables in each line also varies. What apparently holds it together is the steadiness of its voice, the drained cadences of the poet's obvious distaste for his ostensible subject. Yet stylistically everything is happening. Whether or not they are voiced in the reading of the poem, the line breaks and the caesurae in the midst of each rocking see-saw line create a stern rhythmic matrix that is reinforced by steady alliteration: 'Nothing . . . name', for example, or 'breweries . . . boredom', or 'times . . . taste'. More subtle still are fainter echoes between words: does 'Owen' rhyme with 'name'? is the 'l' of 'Theophilus', 'landscape' and 'smell' also assonantal, or merely accidental? Then too there is the deliberately repetitive phrasing: 'landscape of dust', 'shadows of boredom', 'pocketful of notes', 'population of Dolfor', 'taste for the homeland', 'pints of rain water': a rhythmic inlay that courses down the spine of the paragraph, and which contrapuntally sets off the pomposity of the opening 'Rhodri Theophilus Owen'. It is, in fact, a kind of Celtic cross.

The verse then is not nearly so 'free', not nearly so dependent upon the poem's descriptive vigour, as at first sight appears. What Thomas does is reconstitute English prosody from its lesser elements, using particularly those features that are also emphasized in Welsh prosody. But what he does not attempt is an English equivalent of *cynghanedd*. Rather he refracts both prosodies through a single lens, producing an original blend or 'mix' on the page's screen. 'Rhodri' though is only one example. The eye alone, if it flicks through the *Collected Poems*, will notice considerable variation in the way Thomas's poems are laid out. Particular features are lines broken to begin a new 'paragraph', stanzas that are stanzas in appearance only, and the use of double, even triple indentation, as for example in 'A Country',[17] from *Experimenting with an Amen* (1986):

> It is nowhere,
>   and I am familiar
> with it as one is
> with a song.
>   I know its background
>   the terraces
> of cloud that are the hanging gardens
>   of the imagination.

As one reads these lines to oneself off the page, it is the contrast between the extreme enervation of the heard voice and the daring, even provocative, 'experimentalism' of their arrangement that creates a 'poetic' sensation. Yet, if one listened to the same lines without reference to the print, could one begin to visualize them as they are written? Almost certainly not. Again, in some of the later poetry, either on or off the page, it is difficult to recognize any formal poetic principle other than the organization of words into lines. 'S. K.', from *No Truce with the Furies* (1995), where 'S. K.' is Søren Kierkegaard, contains the following:

> Is this the price genius
> must pay, that from an emphasis
> on the subjective only
> soliloquy remains? . . .

'An emphasis on the subjective only' is, some poets would argue, despite its thin sibilance, too cerebral, too desiccated to belong in any poem. Here, it is difficult to see what Thomas achieves beyond the bare inscription of a reflection that, however valuable in itself, elsewhere, might have furnished the subject-matter of a whole poem, to be fleshed out in image and metaphor.

But for Thomas, the baldly inscriptive is an allowable manoeuvre in so far as it forms part of an overall poetic quest: to establish the nature of poetry itself. Certainly, from the example of his own verses, such regularities as end-rhyme, metre and fixed stress do not provide an answer. Only by throwing away one 'crutch' after another can Thomas hope to arrive at a conclusion. Prosodically, he hones and he hones. Famously, in his poem 'Reservoirs'[18] (from *Not That He Brought Flowers*, 1968), he speaks of 'the poem's/Harsher conditions.' These conditions preclude the dance routines of Yeats, to whom Thomas is in so many other respects indebted.

This is not to express or even imply a preference. Thomas and Yeats are two different poets pursuing greatly different visions, for all the Celtic ground common between them. Indeed, the deliberate disdain Thomas increasingly entertains for anything that is remotely orotund presents him with opportunities that are not available to his Anglo-Irish counterpart. Yet for all that R. S. pursues the well-spring of poetry with the utmost severity, from time to time he shows us how eclectic his quest is. *No Truce with the Furies* concludes with two 'virtuoso' pieces wholly uncharacteristic of Thomas's prosody at any stage of its development. The first, 'Play', is skittish in the manner of John Skelton:

> Jocosity
> through verbosity
> can lead to animosity.

The second, 'Anybody's Alphabet', begins

> All art is anonymous.
> Listen: *Ai ee, ai ee*,
> the unaspirated sound
> out of a cave in anticipation
> of human anguish, aftermath
> of the alibis of God.

This is maintained for twenty-six stanzas, each as closely worked, and each exploring a theme already familiar to the reader from Thomas's previous work.

When *No Truce with the Furies* was published, Thomas was already into his eighties. Of all his individual collections it is the most technically varied, and probably the most thematically varied as well. It is also his longest. If for a moment he lays aside his modernist mask, it is to remind us, in the matter of prosody at least, he knows the business inside out.

Little by little the scope and extent of Thomas's achievement is gaining acknowledgement in the literary world at large. To give but one example, in February 1996 the Nobel Laureate Ōe Kenzaburo told the *Nippon Keizai Shimbun*, Tokyo's equivalent of the *Financial Times* or *Wall Street Journal*, that he was planning to study R. S. Thomas, as well as Spinoza and some 'scholarly' authors, in the year ahead.[19] Thomas, he said, was not as yet well known in Japan, but to Mr Ōe his appeal was in 'helping him think about man's place in the universe', and find 'peace' in his own life. For Thomas's critics and commentators, however, peace, or at any rate respite, is a rare circumstance. The older the poet grows, the more productive he becomes. Between settling at Aberdaron in 1967, and his retirement to Rhiw in 1978, Thomas published seven collections of poetry, including *Not That He Brought Flowers*, *H'm* and *Laboratories of the Spirit*. Since then another ten have followed, among them *Later Poems*, *Experimenting with an Amen*, *The Echoes Return Slow*, *Counterpoint*, *Mass for Hard Times* and *No Truce with the Furies*. In every one of these and other published volumes are many individual poems of great distinction. Indeed, Thomas's poetic powers sometimes appear to increase, not diminish with age. Equally daunting, as Thomas focuses his poetry ever more acutely on the relations between humankind and the divine, between himself and God, he threatens to delay his reader indefinitely. Such is his instinct for ambiguity and paradox, such is the deft complexity of his metaphor and imagery, that it not infrequently becomes difficult to know when to leave a poem, if at all. Moreover, once a poem is left, then returned to, it can disconcertingly re-engage the reader as though it were something new.

This of course is true of all good poetry, as it is of all good art. It is even what makes poetry and art good, the touchstone of the thing. Anything else is mere design. The reader or the viewer is abstracted from their usual daily routine, the diarized time continuum, so that to re-enter that routine involves a measure of regret, sometimes despair. We are caught between two worlds, two timescales, each with its own allure and pressing engagements. In the case of someone like Thomas, however, what makes the wrench more painful is precisely an explored thematics of time's hidden otherness. Routine, quotidian time is progressively characterized as an altogether unwelcome environment, a decadent order brought about by modernity's crass materialism.

This emerges not only in Thomas's overtly 'religious' poetry, but also, and perhaps more markedly, in his Welsh subject-matter poetry. Although Aberdaron provided the poet with a solidly Welsh-speaking community in which he could for the first time minister and live, it is in Aberdaron that he publishes his most harshly patriotic pieces, of the sort so sharply criticized by Dafydd Elis Thomas in *Poetry Wales* in 1972. *Not That He Brought Flowers*, published in 1968 and written for the most part at Eglwysfach, contained, as well as 'The Small Window' (see above, p. 16), two regularly anthologized poems, 'Reservoirs'[20] and 'Welcome to Wales'.[21] In 'Reservoirs' Thomas takes issue with the flooding of Welsh valleys, as at Tryweryn and elsewhere, to provide water for the English. Yet it is for the supposedly pusillanimous Welsh, who allow such things to happen, that he reserves his special contempt:

> Where can I go, then, from the smell
> Of decay, from the putrefying of a dead
> Nation? I have walked the shore
> For an hour and seen the English
> Scavenging among the remains
> Of our culture, covering the sand
> Like the tide and, with the roughness
> Of the tide, elbowing our language
> Into the grave we have dug for it.

Environmental ruin and linguistic spoliation are conflated. The grave is the reservoir, containing, among other items of Welshness, the village of Capel Celyn. But the question, where can he go?, is unanswered. In 'Welcome to Wales', the same theme of entombment is pursued:

> Come to Wales
> To be buried; the undertaker

Will arrange it for you. We have
The sites and a long line
Of clients going back
To the first milkman who watered
His honour.

Again, the prime suspect in the crime against the nation is the enemy
within, those who offer the outsider the 'lowest' terms, and

Dirt cheap, a place where
It is lovely to lie.

But if Dafydd Elis Thomas hoped his rebuke would silence R. S. he
was gravely mistaken. In 1974 Christopher Davies, a small publishing house in Llandebie, produced *What is a Welshman?*, the entire
contents of which were intended perhaps to show that the vicar's
bile was as plentiful as ever. In 'To Pay For His Keep',[22] where
'Keep' is a pun on a Norman fort, Thomas tackles Prince Charles's
Investiture at Caernarfon Castle in 1969. Predictably though it is
the Welsh, not the heir apparent, who bear the brunt of the poet's
opprobrium. Indeed, Charles is presented as an innocent:

So this was the way
to the throne! He looked round
at the perspiring ranks
of ageing respectables:
police, tradesmen, councillors,
rigid with imagined
loyalty; and beyond them at
the town with its mean streets and
pavements filthy with
dog shit.

The real sting here is not the proximity of canine excrement, but
the loyalty which can only be 'imagined'. The fealty of Wales's
quislings, R. S. implies, is faked not because it is pretended, but
because those who give it are no longer capable of a real commitment,
of meaningful emotion. By contrast, Charles retains an integrity of
sorts:

> He permitted
> himself a small smile,
> sipping at it in the mind's
> coolness.

Wrapped up in his own destiny, as the Welsh are no longer wrapped up in theirs, the newly anointed Prince of Wales

> never noticed,
> because of the dust raised
> by the prayers of the fagged
> clergy, that far hill
> in the sun with the long line
> of its trees climbing
> it like a procession
> of young people, young as himself.

Here the religious enters, not just in the image of a 'fagged clergy', but also in the image of the 'far hill', Calvary outside Jerusalem. And there is the loud echo of St Mark 8:24, where the Evangelist writes of the blind man healed by Christ at Bethsaida: 'And he looked up, and said, I see men as trees, walking.' Provocatively, Thomas mixes vulgar abuse with the contrivance of allusion. The 'trees' too strike a deeper note: for trees are rooted in the soil, like the best of Thomas's *Cymro* from Iago Prytherch onwards. Now though it is not the ancient peasant who is extolled, but rather the young, those joining Cymdeithas yr Iaith Gymraeg for example, or others who might have been responsible for the detonation of an explosive device on a hill outside Caernarfon on the same day.

So what is it that R. S. wants? From the same volume comes the ultimately sardonic 'He Agrees with Henry Ford'.[23] In the present climate, even the bedrocks of Welsh culture begin to look tawdry:

> Llywelyn? Old hat.
> Glyndŵr? A con man.
> Iolo licking his arse
> for a doublet, for his next
> meal.

Regarded as so much bunk by so many Welshmen, Wales's history deserves to be confined to the

> safety of the dry
> libraries. Honours forbid
> that they should start their nonsense.

And then there is 'It Hurts Him to Think', with its reference to 'my mother's/infected milk' (see above, p. 23). Even a critic as knowledgeable about Thomas, and as well disposed towards him, as Professor M. Wynn Thomas of Swansea University cannot forbear to comment upon the 'sour venom' of such verses.[24] What may be more disturbing to readers of these poems, however, is their possible enjoyment of them. With their deliberate appeal to our less 'cultured' instincts they are a kind of political pornography, and therefore once again question the pacifist's attitude towards extreme, even violent action. *What is a Welshman?*, far from being the regrettable and hence forgettable outpouring of Thomas in a certain mood, has within its pages the power to incite.

Thereafter, however, the poet's aspersions on his fellow countrymen are cast more lightly, and more irregularly. In their place, when he does write directly about Wales, it is more usually out of *hiraeth* for its culture and its history and its people. Wales comes to mean for him an area of the mind rather than of the map or of the media, in which strange transformations and epiphanies may occur. With the exception of *Counterpoint*, a wholly religious and unusually unified collection, Thomas's equivalent perhaps of a 'theme album', no volume of poetry that he publishes is without its poems of Wales. But the tone of these – and there are a great many of them – is progressively less importunate.

We may take, as one example, 'That Place', from *Laboratories of the Spirit*, one of several poems about Ynys Enlli (Bardsey Island). Since it is not reproduced in the *Collected Poems*, I give the whole text:

> I served on a dozen committees;
> talked hard, said little, shared the applause
> at the end. Picking over
> the remains later, we agreed power
> was not ours, launched our invective
> against others, the anonymous wielders

of such. Life became small, grey,
the smell of interiors. Occasions
on which clean air entered our nostrils
off swept seas were instances
we sought to recapture. One particular
time after a harsh morning
of rain, the clouds lifted, the wind
fell; there was a resurrection
of nature, and we there to emerge
with it into the anointed
air. I wanted to say to you: 'We
will remember this.' But tenses
were out of place on that green
island, ringed with the rain's
bow, that we had found and would spend
the rest of our lives looking for.

The opening lines here almost certainly refer to R. S. Thomas's involvement with the Bardsey Island Trust Committee. The voice he initially assumes, however, is not quite his own. It is more consciously that of a man of the world. At ease, slightly bored by everything, unaware perhaps of a hunger inside. The invective, such as it is, is muted. But as the poem moves in its matter-of-fact way, in a series of easily accountable steps, towards its startling and dramatic conclusion, Thomas casts himself in a different role. He ceases to be one among several committee members, and becomes instead the leader of a retreat. At the same time, he allows his poem to be directed by another, the 'death-bed' poem of the twelfth-century Meilyr Brydydd:

May I be at home awaiting the summons
In a fold with the moving sea near it,
A desert it is of unfading honour
With a bosom of brine about its graves,
Fair Mary's isle, pure island of the pure
The heir of resurrection, it is good to be in it.
Christ of the foretold cross knows me, will keep me
From the pains of hell, the place of exile.
The Creator who created me, will meet me
In the fair parish of Enlli faithful.[25]

The two poems, separated by more than eight hundred years, coalesce. Yet, with the exception of 'resurrection', Thomas avoids transferring any of Meilyr Brydydd's specifically Christian terminology. Instead he plays upon notions of temporal and physical displacement. 'Tenses' are out of place. What is 'found' remains to be discovered. Thereby hell is brought forward, so that not to be on Bardsey is to be in hell. And yet in two ways, redemption is suggested. The 'rest of our lives' does not necessarily imply the search will be fruitless. Rather it may be that the moment of innocence will be recovered at the end of life, on the death-bed, no less. Secondly, because tenses do not apply, once experienced, the moment is never in fact lost.

This response to a Welsh holy place, later condensed into the eight sparse lines of 'Island' from *No Truce with the Furies*, is of a different order entirely from the bilious recriminations that clog *What is a Welshman?* One might almost say it belongs on a different planet. It is also a response to nature, to an island 'ringed with the rain's bow', as Thomas so cleverly adapts Meilyr Brydydd's 'bosom of brine'. And it is in nature, located in Wales, that a 'resurrection', and hence salvation, is promised.

'That Place' is explicit enough in this regard, however delicately downplayed its movement and diction. In very many other of Thomas's later poems the same coming together of the three orders, the Welsh, the natural and the divine, is effected; as indeed the same conflation is worked in the earlier 'Llanrhaeadr ym Mochnant' (see above, p. 134). There, Bishop Morgan supplied a specific focus, as he does again in 'R. I. P', in *Mass for Hard Times*. But to get the full measure of what for Thomas is clearly a real and abiding trinity, we should look at his treatment of another figure, Ann Griffiths.

Ann Griffiths (1776–1805) is one of the more remarkable phenomena of Welsh literary and religious history.[26] She stands alongside Pantycelyn (William Williams)[27] as the Welsh hymnodist par excellence. Her verses have lifted chapel congregations, and chapel-based choral societies, for close on two hundred years. They have also captured the attention and admiration of generations of Christian writers and scholars, many of them outside the Nonconformist tradition with which she is associated. It is commonplace to regard her as a mystic. Yet Ann Griffiths was neither well educated nor long-lived, and her reputation depends upon some thirty hymns only, and the survival of eight of her letters.

She was born in Montgomeryshire, in a house still called Dolwar Fach between Llanfihangel-yng-Ngwynfa and Dolanog, on the edge of the Berwyn hills, not far in fact from Manafon. Her father John Thomas was a prosperous farmer, and a devout Anglican. In her youth, his daughter hankered after such society as there was in the vicinity. She was known to enjoy dancing, a little too much perhaps, and was frequently to be seen in nearby Llanfyllin. It was at Llanfyllin, however, in 1796, two years after the death of her mother, that Ann 'converted' to Methodism, during a revivalist sermon preached by the Independent minister Benjamin Jones. In this she followed the example already set by her older brother John. Subsequently other members of the family, including the father, also converted, and by 1804 Dolwar Fach was registered as a place of Methodist worship. She joined the Fellowship at Pontrobert in 1797, by which time she was already making a monthly trek to Bala, to attend 'Communion Sundays' led by Thomas Charles,[28] a leading Calvinist whose ideas and style of preaching made a profound impression on the young woman's mind.

Precisely when and how Ann began composing her hymns is uncertain. Although she could read and write, none of her hymns was written down by her. Rather they were transcribed after her death from the memory of her maid, Ruth Evans, by a fellow Methodist, John Hughes. Hughes was Ann's immediate Methodist mentor, and it is in his hand that seven of the eight surviving letters are copied. During her last years her behaviour was often erratic. She would go into trances, and admitted to 'visitations'. Sent into the potato shed to collect potatoes she might be found hours later in a trance. Yet, perhaps because as a young woman in a rural society she had no option, she did conform to what was expected of her in at least one important respect. In 1804 she married Thomas Griffiths, a Methodist 'elder', and it was after giving birth to their child that Ann died, aged twenty-nine.

The composition of verses – songs and ballads and carols – was customary among many Welsh rural families. Ironically, one of the charges levelled against Nonconformity in the nineteenth century was that it killed off a vibrant folk culture. But although Ann would have been familiar with a variety of metres and verse forms from an early age, the hymns that she 'wrote' bear little relation to folksong. They are entirely religious, centred on the figure of Christ crucified, but also, in keeping with the style of Calvinistic Methodism, unifying Old and New Testament imagery. Indeed, the hymns of Ann Griffiths exhibit, as well as an extraordinary emotional fervour, a critical knowledge of the Bible; and it is this combination of intellect and devotion that, in the eyes of the 'experts', constitutes their greatness.

In a sense, it is peculiar that R. S. Thomas should express what is obviously a high regard for Ann Griffiths in the two poems he has written about her: 'Ann Griffith',[29] from *Laboratories of the Spirit* (1975), and 'Fugue for Ann Griffiths',[30] from *Welsh Airs* (1987). The poet has often expressed his dissatisfaction with the effect Nonconformity has had upon Wales other than its underwriting the survival of the Welsh tongue; and he has also attested his dislike of hymns in general. During the late eighteenth century, however, Methodism was still, even if aberrantly, a movement within the Welsh Anglican church, and there are in any case Protestant currents in Thomas's own thought. Again, as already suggested, Ann Griffiths's hymns have it within them to transcend denominational division, while their force depends upon a compactness of imaging that could only appeal to the later poet.

The preference for the singular 'Ann Griffith' in the first of the two poems was not an error on Thomas's part: rather it was a hankering after the Welsh form of an anglicized name. Indeed it is Ann's very Welshness that explains at least part of her appeal:

> I have seen you dance
> for the bridegrooms that were not
> to be, while I waited for you
> under the ripening boughs of
> the myrtle,

God says to Ann:

> These people know me
> only in the thin hymns of
> the mind, in the arid sermons
> and prayers. I am the live God,
> nailed fast to the old tree
> of a nation by its unreal
> tears. I thirst, I thirst
> for the spring water . . .

As well as a portrait of Ann Griffiths, these few lines are also a
mental portrait of Thomas himself. Nearly all his major concerns
and obsessions are present, although he also takes care to work in
several allusions to Ann's own work, most notably in 'the ripening
boughs of the myrtle'. On one occasion the young woman felt God's
presence in a myrtle tree near her home, and this she worked into
the opening line of one of her best-known verses:

> *Wele'n sefyll rhwng y myrtwydd*
> (Behold standing among the myrtles)[31]

In Thomas's rendition, the myrtle boughs play against the 'thin
hymns of the mind' and the 'arid sermons and prayers'. To a degree
here he is condemning the ossification of the Church in eighteenth-
century Wales, but he is also issuing a wider condemnation against
the spiritual inertia of all organized religion. By contrast God thirsts
for the 'spring water', to be found in abundance, literally as well as
metaphorically, in the Welsh landscape.

At the same time Thomas romanticizes his subject. While the
injunction to 'Play me . . . on the white keys of your body' acknowledges the sexual aspect of divine ecstasy, 'the bridegrooms that were
not to be', referring to Ann's dancing days, effects a compromise;
joyfully or otherwise, Ann was to know carnal relations with the
mortal man she married. Again, 'the poor girl from the village' is
misleading: Ann had a maid, without whom we would probably not
have such hymns of hers as have survived. But Thomas, one feels,
wants to connect Ann Griffiths, subliminally or otherwise, to the
hill farming communities his poetry so long revered.

There is also the curiosity of the final lines. The 'spring water' resides not only in the Welsh landscape, but also in Ann's heart. It is therefore a double metaphor. Its second meaning is the Welsh language. Drawn up from the human well, it is turned into wine, on Ann's 'unkissed' lips (so that the white keys of her body are perhaps her teeth): clearly a version of the Eucharist. But the blasphemy latent in the comparison of Christ's blood with the *hen iaith* is spared by the power of the conceit: the proof of the imagined transubstantiation is in the hymns themselves, composed to Christ's glory.

The 'Fugue for Ann Griffiths', one of Thomas's longest, most ambitious and also most compelling poems, refines and develops these themes. The allusiveness of its ten prosodically varied sections is endless. Thomas also plays upon two time differentials: the gap between then and now, the late eighteenth or early nineteenth century and the present, and the gap between temporal time and eternal time, time outside time. And these gaps, or differences, can be travelled in either direction:

> In which period
>   do you get lost?
> The roads lead
>   under a twentieth century
> sky to the peace
>   of the nineteenth. There it is,
> as she left it,
>   too small to be chrysalis
> of that clenched soul.

The 'peace' of the nineteenth century may make us wonder to begin with: Ann's adult life, such as it was, was contained by the Napoleonic wars. But unlike the later world wars, the earlier European furore left Wales largely untouched. Immediately, therefore, in these opening lines, the matter of Wales is pushed to the fore. In the second section too, Thomas clings doggedly to his reading of history:

> To put it differently
> yet the same, listen,
> friend:
>   A nineteenth century
>   calm;

403

that is, a countryside
not fenced in
by cables and pylons
but open to thought to blow in
from as near as may be
to the truth.

Dolanog, in other words, is a version of Abercuawg, far away, but, allowing for the intercession of eternal time, as close as close can be. And it is the intercession of eternal time that waylays Ann Griffiths, and deconstructs conventional notions about the past:

When
you are young . . . But
there was One
with his eye on her;
she saw him stand
under the branches.
History insists
on a marriage, but the husband was as cuckolded
as Joseph.

'Cuckolded' here seems too strong, too emphatic, until, looking at Ann Griffiths's letters, we find her writing to John Hughes: 'I have had very many disappointments in myself without a break. I have lately been particularly far gone in spiritual whoredom from the Lord.'[32] A part of the persuasiveness of Nonconformity, its double-take if you like, was its robust ability to condemn prurience in its own terms. Similarly Thomas, drawing on that aspect of his broader cultural inheritance, is never shy to use explicit language.

In the ensuing section of 'Fugue for Ann Griffiths', however, R. S. diverts our attention away from the grey area of a woman mystic's sexuality back to the matter of language itself, that is, the Welsh language. The dust that has settled on it is

blown away in great gusts
week by week in chapel after chapel.

Then, in the fourth section, some of it a reworking of his earlier poem, Thomas introduces the idea of a voyage:

Is there a scholarship that grows
naturally as the lichen? How
did she, a daughter of the land, come
by her learning? You have seen
her face, figure-head of a ship
outward bound? But she was not
alone: a trinity of persons
saw to it she kept on course
like one apprenticed since early
days to the difficulty of navigation
in rough seas. She described her turbulence
to her confessor, who was the more
astonished at the fathoms
of anguish over which she had
attained the calmness of her harbours.

The sea-imagery, it might be supposed, is an intrusion of Thomas's own fantasy life, until it is appreciated how often the 'sea' occurs in Ann Griffiths's own hymns, or poems. The 'fathoms', on the other hand, is an imposition, derived from Kierkegaard, sometimes regarded as the apostle of philosophical protestantism. But set against this is Ann's 'confessor', usually a Catholic figure, though in this case presumably her Methodist companion John Hughes. By such descriptive uses, therefore, Thomas manages to assert Griffiths's doctrinal inclusivity, her religious universality, even though the 'trinity of persons' ties her down to a specific nexus of doctrines, again evident in the hymns.

'There are other pilgrimages/to make beside Jerusalem, Rome;' the fifth section begins: at first sight another attempt to situate Ann Griffiths within a Catholic understanding, but in fact a fugue-like repetition of the 'broad-church' gloss at the end of the fourth. Such tolerance, however, begins to dissipate in the sixth section, as Thomas draws out, or returns to, the Welsh theme. His starting point is the Napoleonic wars, but also, following a lead given in a lecture by Saunders Lewis, the two world wars:

Hostilities were other peoples'.
Though a prisoner of the Lord
she was taken without fighting.

That was in the peace before
the wars that were to end
war. If there was a campaign

for her countrymen, it was one
against sin. Musically
they were conscripted to proclaim

Sunday after Sunday the year
round they were on God's side. England
meanwhile detected its enemies

from afar. These made friends
out in the fields because
of its halo with the ancestral scarecrow.

The last stanza is cryptic: to what does 'its' refer? Surely not England? Yet the stab at England is unequivocal. While the Welsh are rounded up by Ann's hymns to be put in the serried pews of God's army, the English are 'meanwhile' up to something entirely different. In the eighth section too, again drawing upon some remarks made by Saunders Lewis, Thomas limits the final generosity of Griffiths's visions:

What was sin
but the felix culpa enabling
a daughter of the soil to move
in divine circles? This was before
the bomb, before the annihilation
of six million Jews. It appears now
the confession of a child before
an upholstered knee; her achievement
the sensitising of the Welsh
conscience to the English rebuke.

A lot of business is transacted in these lines. The 'felix culpa' in particular needs explaining. In Ann Griffiths's writings, one of the problems she wrestles with is the notion that God defiles his own purity by descending among men in the form of Christ. The 'felix culpa' may simultaneously mean Ann's 'whoredom' before the Lord, and the Lord's reciprocal gesture towards her. In either case the fault is felicitous. The bomb and the Jewish holocaust indicate a greater, later loss of innocence than that experienced in Eden. But then the poem twists again. While the image of the child 'before an upholstered knee' is (as far as I'm aware) an image entirely of Thomas's own devising, and a very beautiful image at that – the 'upholstered knee' suggests the hem of God's skirt – the introduction of the 'English rebuke' returns the poem, not without bathos, to the political. The 'rebuke' is not specified, but could be the 'Welsh Not' hung around the necks of Welsh school-children from the mid-nineteenth century onwards. Yet to introduce this alongside, or almost alongside, allusions to Hiroshima and the holocaust will, to many readers, seem like an absence of perspective.

Thomas's point would be: linguacide is a form of genocide. 'The Fugue for Ann Griffiths' is a deeply political as well as a profoundly religious poem. This is so even in the tenth and closing section, where the word 'survival' must mean, according to the poem's 'fugal' imperatives, the survival of Wales as well as the survival of the human race:

> She listened to him.
> We listen to her.
> She was in time
> chosen. We but infer
> from the union of time
> with space the possibility
> of survival. She who was born
> first must be overtaken
> by our tomorrow.
> So with wings pinned
> and fuel rationed,
> let us put on speed
> to remain still
> through the dark hours
> in which prayer gathers
> on the brow like dew,
> where at dawn the footprints
> of one who invisibly
> but so close passed
> discover a direction.

The 'invisibly but so close' takes the reader back to the myrtle tree, back to God's waiting for Ann Griffiths, his eye steady upon her. It is the last but also the initial paradox out of which the section's other paradoxes are generated, not least the possibility of inferring survival from the 'union of time with space': for many the very thing that militates against survival. But the understanding Thomas begs is that the union of time and space, if it is to happen at all, must happen within some other arrangement; and so hope is justified by that which seems to preclude it.

The religious concern of both the Ann Griffiths poems is patent. What is slightly less obvious is the extent to which the poet's faith is secured by Ann Griffiths's specifically Welsh provenance. Both are also patriotic poems. Ann Griffiths is co-opted into the gallery of Thomas's national heroes. She is not, as she could so easily be, seen as a mystic who happened to be born in Wales, and who happened to speak Welsh. Rather her Welshness is intrinsic to the feast she furnishes. Nor is it considered that she might be anything other than divinely inspired. Thomas has no time for, say, a psychological appreciation of Ann Griffiths. No attempt is made to view her, as she can be viewed, as a gifted but unstable human being whose instability, in the manner of such things, took the form of an express-ive reworking of what, culturally, lay most readily about her. Rather her relationship with God is uncontested.

Therefore, one must add, in Thomas's scheme of things, the exist-ence of God himself is uncontested. Or put another way, Ann Grif-fiths as a suture between Wales and God confirms Thomas's own religiousness. The two poems are nothing if not affirmative. But just how strong a hand 'Wales' plays in this compact can be assessed only by focusing on the poet's own faith, as Thomas himself does quite unsparingly in his later work. There, it will be found, faith and the affirmation of faith are far harder won. Indeed, considered as a religious poet, Thomas is the polar opposite of Ann Griffiths. He does not assert basic tenets gloriously anew, but rather inhabits a spiritual minimalism. This, however, opens a way in for the contem-porary reader whose attitude may be agnostic, even atheist, and whose knowledge of the scriptures and theology is restricted.

*　　　*　　　*

The normative and the peculiar are strange bedfellows; yet which of us is not their offspring? We live our lives as given, yet a moment's reflection suggests an essential oddity to existence.

Religion, like poetry, is a structured response to that oddity. In all parts of the world gods have been worshipped and cosmogonies honoured by peoples perplexed by a mystery perceived to lie at the heart of things. As a priest and a poet, particularly such an amalgam living and writing in an era when 'faith' has declined drastically, it is almost inevitable that R. S. Thomas should be especially concerned with that mystery. Yet religion itself is a complex manifestation. It divides down a number of parallel fault lines: between the super-stitious and the speculative, between the personal and the impersonal, between the demotic and the arcane, between the social and the theological, between the institutional and the theological, between indeed the normative and the peculiar.

Considered as a religious poet, Thomas too is disjunctive. Very broadly, he operates within a tradition of Christian meditation and Christian witness. He is not, however, an organization man. Much of the ritual paraphernalia of his church is either excluded from his poetry, or treated with detachment. Nor does he have much time for the 'communion of saints', a key element of Catholic and Anglo-Catholic faith. Other aspects of Christian doctrine he abides by, in particular the Crucifixion and the celebration of the eucharist (communion). The Cross and the breaking of bread are persistently potent metaphors. He also explores Christianity's central creation myth – Adam and Eve – with an intensity and perseverance perhaps unique among English-language poets. More or less too he keeps to an anthropomorphic understanding of God: that is, as perceived by Thomas, God is a person with whom dialogue is nominally possible.

In this regard prayer is all-important: not the ritualized saying or chanting of prescribed formulae, but a contemplative offering up of the self. It is through such prayer, and only through such prayer, that the form of the dialogue with God may be established. Yet an aspect of Thomas's prayer, of his very spirituality even, is astringently intellectual. While he often seems to go along with the received notion that 'doubt' is an indispensable stepping stone to faith, it is the doubts he encounters along the way of his quest for the divine, generated by a tirelessly questioning mindset, that more often appear to motivate his verse. There *are* epiphanal passages, moments when Thomas does surrender to God, but more usually it is the difficulties of the Christian faith that engage his muse.

In pursuing those difficulties the poet casts his net wide. Not only is he receptive to some of the main issues of Christian theology, past and present, but he also takes account of the 'problematics' of 'theism' considered philosophically. Indeed, theism becomes a central pre-occupation of R. S. Thomas's middle and later poetry, even *the* central preoccupation. And for this reason it is necessary to make at least a cursory detour into what may be called the intellectual background.

'The theist', it has been well if jestingly observed, 'loses every battle but the last.'[33] Christianity exhibits a dual history. There is the history of its various churches: organizations that expanded and competed with each other while offering their supporting populations structures and styles of worship. But there is also a speculative history, the prolonged theological search for a 'proof' of the existence of God as adumbrated in the scriptures. In the Middle Ages St Anselm (1033–1109), Thomas Aquinas (1225–74), Duns Scotus (1266–1308) and others endeavoured to establish the credentials of a Prime Mover once and for all. Medieval scholastics created and sustained a Europe-wide industry, housed in the first universities, that argued the pros and cons of this particular school of thought or that. Subjected to this onslaught, however, God became progressively more abstract; and the more subtle the arguments became, the more vulnerable they were to criticism, so that in time theology gave rise to a secular philosophy that rounded on its progenitor, denying the possibility of such a Being.

The culmination of the theological tradition, and the beginning of the next, occurred in the writings of René Descartes (1591–1650). Descartes' method was to strip theological and philosophical propositions of all their attendant assumptions, then see what could be logically salvaged. In so doing he set new standards for philosophical inquiry. Famously, in the *Discours de la Méthode*, he boiled the whole of philosophy down to a single statement, the legendary 'cogito': *Je pense, donc je suis*, I think therefore I am. By itself, however, the cogito was an unproductive instrument. What Descartes in fact wanted to do was establish an objective system of reliable knowledge, and to do that he soon found himself reintroducing the concept of God. But far from closing theological debate, as he also hoped to have done, Descartes threw it wide open. Not only was the cogito itself suspect, but the procedures he used to extrapolate further 'irrefutable' propositions were shown to be equally faulty, including his own 'proofs' of God; and within a century of his death the entirely secular Scottish philosopher David Hume (1711–76) began advancing powerful arguments that disposed of the Deity as either a useful or a meaningful concept.

Hume may be regarded as the father of philosophical atheism. His assault on religion was twofold. First he sought to show that, like other human institutions, it not only had, but was entirely explicable within terms of, a 'natural' history. That is, religion didn't need the existence of God to explain itself, but was rather the product of psychological needs rooted in 'the incessant hopes and fears, which actuate the human mind'.[34] Secondly, using analytical tools every bit as powerful as Descartes', he demonstrated the logical absurdity of two main props of Christianity: revelation and miracles. There is no way, he said, that what seems like a revelation can in fact be proved to be a revelation. The same pertains to miracles, with the added proviso that since our understanding of how the world works is gained empirically, the real import of a 'miracle' should be to furnish additional data which may or may not cause us to revise that understanding. But more than that, Hume's investigation of recorded 'miracles' showed that in every case conditions of verifiability were either compromised or non-existent.

Not only was Christianity 'at first attended with miracles', Hume mockingly concludes in his *Enquiry Concerning Human Understanding* (1748), 'but even at this day cannot be believed by any reasonable person without one.' Yet despite his attempts to underpin the rationalistic and scientific ideology of the Enlightenment, Hume's arguments have not always prevailed. Although he has inspired generations of like-minded thinkers, in particular the logical positivists of the earlier twentieth century, to others matters are not so cut and dried. Hume's empirical procedures are seen to work, but they are only that: procedures. They account for the how of the world, but not its what and its why. Is there not yet, as Gilbert Ryle put it, 'a ghost in the machine'?[35]

This riddle, in one form or another, has besotted most philosophers. Immanuel Kant (1724–1804), responding to the challenge set by Hume, erected, in a series of *Critiques*, a monumental counter-philosophy the overall effect of which was to deny Hume's reductivism precisely in the realm of thought. Concepts and ideas, Kant taught, can indeed be used to explain the world in purely 'material' terms, but they do not take adequate account of themselves. Rather in the field of reason, and possibly, since the two are related, in the field of ethics as well, there must exist a template for our ideas that is more likely than not to be 'God'-given. But how 'new' was this? In the eleventh century St Anselm proposed a beautiful proof of God that still keeps philosophers awake. Even a fool, Anselm claimed, must acknowledge that 'God', *were* he to exist, must be a being than which nothing greater exists. But then he asks, which is greater: to exist in the mind, or to exist in reality? By definition reality must be greater. Therefore the fool, by admitting that God exists in the mind, denies reality, in which case his argument cannot be right.

Since Kant, various attempts have been made both to repudiate the idea of God, and to legitimate it. Characteristically, contemporary philosophy sets as its agenda a series of specific 'problems', each notionally soluble by increasingly 'technical' means. Accordingly, 'God' has become the object of such discrete disciplines as 'ontology' (the theory of being) and 'epistemology' (the theory of knowledge). At the same time, philosophical procedures have been modified by scientific 'discovery'. One version of God, subjected to the conditions of a specialism, and taking its cue from Blaise Pascal in the seventeenth century, debates the statistical probability of his existence. A more critical example has been Darwin's seemingly irrefutable account of *The Origin of Species*, which has disposed of most 'creationist' notions of God, or the argument 'from design'. Darwin showed that even the best designed phenomena, for example the human eye, were not designed at all, but evolved through time. God as the designer of the biological world is therefore made redundant, although at least one brainy dog, the American John Dewey (1859–1952), readmitted creationism by describing evolution as 'design on the instalment plan'. But while design can be 'pushed back', from the species to the inorganic world of the universe to the background laws of physics, 'God' still falls foul of another contemporary theory that, Hume-like, sees no logical necessity to the time-honoured causal connection between agent and outcome. At best, cause and effect pertain to our world of 'secondary causes', but the inference that the 'universe', or all that there is, is itself an 'outcome' is unfounded.

Conversely, even if the existence of the universe is not an 'outcome', there is still the matter that it does exist. Even just to 'be' is hazardous. Or as Kant put it, 'Whatever, and however much, our concept of an object may contain, we must go outside it, if we are to ascribe existence to that object.'[36]

In fact, apropos God, modern philosophy broadly heads in two contrasting directions. One way, 'God' as a concept is perfectly useless because then he in turn has to be explained – the oldest chestnut of all, perhaps. The other way, the order of existence, which is the only order we know, becomes entirely identified with God. In this version, God simply is the laws of physics, he is all that is. Either way though, God has remained, for the serious-minded, an abstract. Even if as a notion he can be validated, then it is only as a notion.

In a poem called 'Phew!',[37] R. S. Thomas asks:

> Is there a knowledge
> not to be known?

And this in a way is the nub of it. However conceptually sophisticated our arguments, we are, as Kant intimated, constrained by human logic, by the powers of human thought and human perception. There may be whole areas of event of which we are unaware, and which we are conceptually incapable of entering. Science, as the knowledge of second order events, may be fatally limited. We cannot even assume the integrity of the time–space continuum. How do we know, for example, that the universe we inhabit is not alternating, every moment, with some other universe? How do we know that at regular intervals 'our' world doesn't put itself to sleep and transform itself into a flower or a packet of biscuits or something dogs decorate the pavement with, let alone something wholly beyond our imaginations, only to resume its 'original' identity a moment later, as though nothing had happened?

The answer, as Thomas suggests, is we don't know, nor can we. In fact, we know so little that even if we did know everything we still wouldn't have the means of knowing that we know.

The actual arguments advanced by philosophers about God are elaborate and detailed. That Thomas is conversant with them is beyond doubt. His work contains precise references not only to most of the aforementioned figures, but also, inter alia, Plato, Spinoza and Bishop Berkeley, as well as Nietzsche and Wittgenstein. Nor is he a casual name-dropper. Whereas there seems little doubt that he does cherish a 'select band' of thinkers, as he cherishes a select band of poets, there is no question but that the ideas of his chosen few engage him deeply. But as a religious he also operates within another speculative field, that of modern theology: philosophers who have remained committed, nominally or otherwise, to the Christian understanding. Indeed it may be just because Thomas is also engaged here that his attention turns to 'secularists' such as Kant in the first place.

Modern theology is the preserve of the specialist. In the nineteenth century alone there is an entire background of academic theological thought upon which the 'contemporary scene' is dependent. Largely this was a Protestant undertaking. Largely too it was German. Between them, men such as Friedrich Schleiermacher (1768–1834), F. C. Baur (1792–1860), Ludwig Feuerbach (1804–72), D. F. Strauss (1808–74) and Bruno Bauer (1809–82) mounted a far-reaching challenge to conventional Christian wisdom. In complementary manoeuvres, they detached the Bible from its literalist interpretation, while exposing the 'historicity' of scriptural texts. Nor did they conduct their researches in isolation from contemporaneous philosophical and cultural currents. Both the idealist G. W. F. Hegel (1770–1831) and the German literary Romantics impacted on, and were impacted by, this 'second Reformation'.

This new school developed further in the twentieth century, where another (though more heterodox) group of theologians have worked through and applied the implications of what had been 'discovered' by their predecessors, among them Martin Buber (1878–1965),

Rudolf Bultmann (1884–1976), Karl Barth (1886–1968), Paul Tillich (1886–1965), Reinhold Niebuhr (1892–1971) and Hans Küng (b. 1928).

Simultaneously, greater attention has been paid to the doctrines of non-Christian religions: Hinduism, Buddhism and Islam. While the vastly increased rate of global cultural exchange has tended, in the West at least, to diminish the claims of any one religion over its 'rivals', the path-breaking work of Mircea Eliade (b. 1907) in comparing different religious systems has had an opposite effect. That different peoples worship different gods differently indicates not so much the foolishness of choosing any one god so much as a universal human need to express 'spirituality'. Just as Noam Chomsky sought to establish a 'universal grammar' underlying all languages, so too 'comparative religion' indicates common strands, shared by all cultures at all times.

Up until 1963, the Anglican communion, including the Church in Wales, was largely unaffected by such seismic activities. As congregations declined, the entire edifice was steadily sinking without anybody doing very much about it, or even noticing. But then came the bombshell. Bishop John A. T. Robinson's *Honest to God* stunned not only many churchmen, but also its publishers:[38] it climbed to the top of the best-seller lists.

Robinson adumbrated a theology derived precisely from such figures as Bultmann, Barth and Tillich. While in hindsight his book can be seen as a slightly desperate (and ultimately unsuccessful) attempt to revive the flagging fortunes of the Church, it remains a useful introduction to contemporary Anglican thought. It also indicates the extent to which R. S. Thomas's 'personal' search for God has been undertaken within a definable theological context. To begin with there is the deliberate jettisoning of literalist interpretation. The Bible, particularly the Old Testament, but also the New, is to be treated as a form of allegory. In Thomas, as we have already seen, this becomes the Bible as metaphor. Further, God is strongly characterized as a *deus absconditus*, again a key theme in Thomas's later poetry.

'The first thing we must be ready to let go,' the Bishop instructs us, 'is our image of God himself.'[39] Quite specifically, as Thomas also often does, Robinson addresses himself to the question of God's location within a universe 'explained' by science. In the old, primitive days, Robinson tells us, when the physical dimensions of the universe were unknown, God was 'up there' in the clouds somewhere. Then, as Newtonian physics rendered that picture obsolete, God was to be found 'out there' somewhere. But even this adjustment has been superseded by astronomy, so that if God is to be found anywhere today it is either 'in the gaps', or within our very selves. God in other words is everywhere and nowhere – a favourite paradox of the poet. Only by 'turning aside' is he to be discovered. But attached to this notion is the further idea that God, wherever or however he is to be found, embodies 'love', in the tradition of St John the Evangelist. By such means Christ on the Cross, whether regarded as fact or allegory, retains his centrality. By continuing to focus on this trope, God can still be found, and his 'place' in the world recognized.

The preferred techniques for gaining access to this new and revised God are meditation and prayer. And here, Robinson uses a phrase that sounds throughout Thomas's later poetry: '"Meditation"', he writes, paraphrasing another writer, George Macleod, 'can be conducted like a laboratory experiment.' From which perhaps the titles of the two collections, *Laboratories of the Spirit* and *Experimenting with an Amen*.

At the heart of Robinson's inquiry is the restoration of a sense of the great mystery of being, the *mysterium tremendum et fascinans*. Considering St Paul, the great fixer of early Christianity who effectively universalized the specific religion of a Jewish sect, Robinson focuses on the journey to Athens. There, Paul is accosted by an educated mob who demand to know of him the meaning of his message, and whether it is his intention to furnish them with yet more useless idols. But by adroit opportunism, Paul is able to beat them at their own game:

> Then Paul stood in the midst of Mars hill, and said, Ye men of Athens, I perceive that in all things ye are too superstitious. For as I passed by, and beheld your devotions, I found an altar with this inscription: TO THE UNKNOWN GOD. Whom therefore ye ignorantly worship, him declare I unto you.[40]

416

In Thomas too, the unknown God, God the unnameable, plays a central role.

This is not to imply that *Honest to God* has been in any way Thomas's 'crib'. Rather it is to recommend Robinson's book as a useful crib when dealing with the poet; although in its own way it may have led Thomas to some texts and authors he was previously unfamiliar with. Certainly, such was the furore created by *Honest to God*, Thomas can scarcely have been unaware of it at the time.

As one would predict of a clerical poet, Thomas's knowledge and use of the Bible is attested throughout his work. If proof were needed, however, that his interest in religious philosophy predates the appearance of Bishop Robinson, we have only to look back to the poem 'Green Categories' (see above, pp. 295–6), with its juxtaposition of the disparate figures of Iago Prytherch and Kant. Outside the scriptures, the figure R. S. Thomas most consistently identifies with, emotionally as well as intellectually, is neither Kant nor even, say, Paul Tillich – whose sermons, collected in *The Shaking of the Foundations*,[41] have certainly left their mark – but Søren Kierkegaard: a man who exactly straddles the divergent worlds of philosophy and theology.

Born in Copenhagen in 1813, Kierkegaard grew up in the shadow of a father who was both a self-made businessman and an insistent Lutheran. Although Søren enrolled at the University of Copenhagen to study theology, he was quickly sidetracked by other interests. On the one hand he developed a passion for philosophy, particularly the works of Kant and Hegel; on the other he became a fashionable young man-about-town. But then, having fallen in love with Regina Olsen and promised to marry her, he abruptly reneged, and from 1841 onwards lived a life of seclusion, devoting his time and energies to the writing of a dozen or so books – among them the *Concluding Unscientific Postscript to the Philosophical Fragments* (1846) – that have become classics of philosophical theology. From time to time he emerged from the cocoon he had made for himself to launch bitter attacks against the church and its clergy, for having succumbed to worldly values. In turn he was himself vilified in the press. Finally, in 1855, he collapsed in the street one day and died soon after.

Kierkegaard's outstanding contribution to Western thought has been his bequeathing to it the main elements of existentialism. 'My principal thought,' he wrote, 'was that in our age, because of the great increase in knowledge, we had forgotten what it means to *exist*, and what *inwardness* signified, and that the misunderstanding between speculative philosophy and Christianity was explicable on that ground.'[42] To rekindle the proper spirit, Kierkegaard advocated what has passed down to become the *acte gratuit* of twentieth-century existentialists: the spontaneous, logically unstructured gesture or moment that throws all assumptions up in the air; that attains 'freedom' because it risks it.

But Kierkegaard's own most celebrated somersault, what he called 'the leap of faith', was neither unpremeditated nor gratuitous. Rather it was the outcome of a lengthy, and by all accounts painful, philosophical investigation. Possibly it was a feeling of entrapment within his own and others' systems that led him to propound his famous idea. In order to restore the meaning of life, he proposed, it was necessary to exercise the power of choice. And where could that power be more appropriately, more meaningfully exercised than in the individual's relations with God? All recent philosophical writings, he discovered, militated against any sense of immediacy in this respect. The solution therefore was to put 'philosophy' aside and instead embrace the divine. Hence the great leap of faith. But this manoeuvre was justified only at considerable length. Kierkegaard's value to theology is precisely his ability to tackle philosophical issues philosophically. It is his intellectual competence that gives the leap its weight.

Faith is its own reward. Whether for Kierkegaard the bells rang out is uncertain. Other than an occasional exuberance in his writings there is scant evidence. Given the circumstances of his childhood, the leap out seems curiously to have been a leap backwards. But then Kierkegaard did not claim a lasting peace of mind. It was the unsettling or characteristically 'existential' effect of the leap and its consequences that justified it, summed up in the title of one of his books, *Fear and Trembling*,[43] and also in his mataphor, so beloved by Thomas, of the '70,000 fathoms' over which the re-charged soul swirls precariously.

'Truth,' the Dane proclaimed, in opposition to the main tendencies of the scientifically and materially minded society he lived in, 'is subjectivity.' Even if, Kierkegaard maintained, God's existence could be objectively demonstrated, then that would bring us no closer to him.

Any number of psychological theories have been put forward to 'explain' Kierkegaard, among them guilt towards Regina Olsen, and the oppressiveness of bourgeois Protestantism in Denmark. For R. S. Thomas, however, he has provided an outstanding example of the inward voyager embarked on an uncharted journey, the ascetic who chances everything:

> The press sharpened
> Its rapier; wounded, he crawled
> To the monastery of his chaste thought
> To offer up his crumpled amen.
> 'Kierkegaard'[44]

Like Kierkegaard, Thomas is bedevilled by doubts and uncertainties. While these are the penalties of a faith that is not just faith in name, there is a reciprocal tendency in the scepticism of the agnostic. Such scepticism is dismissive of the specific claims made by religion; yet, unlike atheism, it retains a capacity to acknowledge the ultimate mystery of things, or at least the limits of man's knowledge. The agnostic may even experience moments when a greater reality is fleetingly apprehended, the 'something understood' in George Herbert's phrase. Between the agnostic and the writings of Kierkegaard and Thomas therefore there subsists a palindromic relationship that is not to be found, for example, apropos much of the later poetry of T. S. Eliot or, for that matter, the hymns of Ann Griffiths.

After the publication of *Not That He Brought Flowers* in 1968 a four-year interval occurred before the appearance of Thomas's next collection, the ambiguously titled *H'm*. In the same year, 1972, Thomas also published *Young and Old*, supposedly a volume of poems for children, in a series of such volumes commissioned by Chatto and Windus. Both collections mark a fresh beginning for the poet: coming up to sixty, R. S. lays down the themes which will dominate his poetry henceforth. In the same manner that he once quizzed the very being and existence of Iago Prytherch, he now questions the very being and existence of God. In doing so, however, he widens his lens to take account not only of his own peculiar loneliness, but also the whole history of mankind. Of particular concern to him are the evolution of a destructive technology, and the development of a 'science' that seemingly demystifies the mystery of things. Yet at the same time he forces himself to acknowledge that not everything that he finds wrong or evil in the world can be attributed, metaphorically or otherwise, to the Fall in Eden. In particular there are what he will regularly refer to as the 'viruses', natural forces that work against human well-being, even in the brief time allotted to human life. But there is also the deeper theological issue of how it is that an all-powerful and omniscient God can have allowed man as he is to exist in the first place. If God is indeed a moral God, could he not have devised a way in which man could have been given his freedom *and* retained his virtue?

Even in *H'm*, these themes are explored with memorable subtlety and intellectual flexibility. In the first poem, 'Once',[45] Thomas's rearranged poetic persona is brought immediately to the fore:

> God looked at space and I appeared,
> Rubbing my eyes at what I saw.
> The earth smoked, no birds sang;
> There were no footprints on the beaches
> Of the hot sea, no creatures in it.
> God spoke. I hid myself in the side
> Of the mountain.

At once we are plunged into an existentialist rendering of the creation myth. The uninhabited landscape is peculiarly redolent of the modern battlefield, or some great ecological disaster. But there is also the character given to God, in that one word 'looked'. This is not God who encompasses everything in one moment of divine thought, but one who proceeds anthropomorphically. He too rubs his eyes perhaps. But who is the 'I' of these lines? Is it the poet as first man, created out of sequence, before the beasts and the birds? Or is it Satan, evil embodied in the serpent, sliding off into a cave? In which case, if the implied causal relationship between God's looking and the subject's appearing is allowed, then one of God's earliest acts is precisely the creation of evil.

'Once' continues:

>   As though born again
>   I stepped out into the cool dew,
>   Trying to remember the fire sermon,
>   Astonished at the mingled chorus
>   Of weeds and flowers. In the brown bark
>   Of the trees I saw the many faces
>   Of life, forms hungry for birth,
>   Mouthing at me. I held my way
>   To the light, inspecting my shadow
>   Boldly; and in the late morning
>   You, rising toward me out of the depths
>   Of myself. I took your hand,
>   Remembering you, and together,
>   Confederates of the natural day,
>   We went forth to meet the Machine.

The 'I' here, soon to be joined by Eve taken from its side, is less ambiguously human. The first couple go 'forth' from the first land-scape. Yet what is absent is any direct or obvious rendition of the story of the serpent and the apple from the tree of the knowledge of good and evil and Eve's misdemeanour. There is no temptation, no fall, just the inevitability of the 'Machine', in Thomas always a shorthand for the inhuman destructiveness of the modern world. Only by going back to the opening lines do we get any sense of man's culpability. The possibility that man and Satan are one and the same creature haunts the entire poem. And the implications of this are momentous. It implies that God didn't quite follow the script. That Creation is somehow bungled.

This at once tells us how deeply disturbed Thomas is by what he finds, by what he sees. As a Christian he is bound to take account of Genesis. But Genesis, even as metaphor, doesn't square up to his findings. Yet just because, in the manner of the new theology, he is able to treat Genesis as metaphor, he can begin to play with it, to rearrange the Eden story into new contours, to see whether it can be made to make more sense.

This, in the religious poetry of Thomas, is the essential manoeuvre. Not only does he abandon literalism, but he also abandons any kind of interpretative orthodoxy. With a poet's freedom, he licenses himself to deconstruct God's own statements, as they are contained not just in the scriptures, but also in the world as it is. Yet the outcome of this is oddly if only faintly affirmative. In so far as the scriptures and the world are statements made by God, then by treating them as he does, Thomas begins to enter into a dialogue with God. A poem like 'Once', which is inlaid with a great deal of allusive metaphor, is, in Christian terms, a profound meditation, the more so as any 'respect' for God is either withheld, or made conditional. Uncritical respect would be faith in name only, a state of mind or being that, for Thomas, is anathema.

Thomas's, however, is a high-risk strategy. If he is unwilling to grant God respect *de jure*, then God similarly makes life difficult for the priest-poet. In 'Petition',[46] Thomas provides a clear account of where this leaves him. Around him he witnesses 'virtue's defeat', life as a succession of theft and murder and rape. 'Seeking the poem/In the pain,' he refuses to sing naive songs of praise to the Almighty. But because of this his petition as a poet is denied him:

> One thing I have asked
> Of the disposer of the issues
> Of life: that truth should defer
> To beauty. It was not granted.

Through his very forwardness, Thomas is cast into a purgatory of his own making. Why not just sing naive songs of praise instead? But as ever, R.S. balances matters. That truth does not defer to beauty tells us something about beauty, or at least the beauty implied here, the superficial beauty of holiness perhaps. Again, too, there is the description of God, as the 'disposer' of life's issues. Thomas's petition may be refused, but, on this occasion certainly, he is in no doubt where to take it.

Imitating Christ, Thomas places himself deliberately in the wilderness. In 'Invitation',[47] he listens to temptations offered by contrary voices. One calls him back to 'the rain and manure/Of Siloh,' the hill-farms of central Wales maybe, while another beckons him to the streets of the city, where the pound 'sings' and life runs to time 'like an express train'. Rejecting both, Thomas offers to stay where he is.

> blowing
> On the small soul in my
> Keeping with such breath as I have.

But temptation takes other forms as well. In 'No Answer',[48] the challenge is more directly intellectual. In a sparsely contrived interior monologue, the religious life itself is questioned:

> it takes time
> To prepare a sacrifice
> For the God. Give yourself
> To science that reveals
> All, asking no pay
> For it. Knowledge is power;
> The old oracle
> Has not changed. The nucleus
> In the atom awaits
> Our bidding. Come forth,
> We cry, and the dust spreads
> Its carpet. Over the creeds
> And masterpieces our wheels go.

Here, even metaphor, Thomas's habitual means of constructing a poem's argument, is stripped to an ambiguous minimum. The dust can be interpreted as the dust of a deconstructed atom, but it is also the dust of radioactive fall-out. It is not the imagery of these lines that holds our attention so much as the weight of a double censure delivered in a few chiselled statements. Science as an alternative to religion fails morally, through its eventual outcome, and fails as knowledge, because it can only investigate secondary causes. It gives us technology, but that technology, summarized as the invention of

423

the wheel, rides roughshod over what, in Thomas's view, is of more lasting value.

One could quibble, of course. The 'masterpieces' are not defined, but would presumably include, say, certain paintings of the Renaissance, which in turn depended upon a technology of their own. Even a pencil is an engineered tool.[49] Creeds too can be related to man's need to explore and define the world he lives in, which are also the main impulses behind science. Indeed, the multivalency of human intelligence, its ability to destroy as it creates, becomes, in Thomas's poetry, a central problem. But in *H'm*, it is the supposed identification of a *deus absconditus* that, for the poet, features as the main perplexity. In 'Via Negativa'[50] Thomas gives classic utterance to the theology signalled in *Honest to God*:

> Why no! I never thought other than
> That God is that great absence
> In our lives, the empty silence
> Within, the place where we go
> Seeking, not in hope to
> Arrive or find. He keeps the interstices
> In our knowledge, the darkness
> Between stars.

It is from these lines that Thomas has gained his notoriety as 'the poet of the God of the interstices'. It is, however, too easy, and misleading, to equate the apparent negativity they express simply with contemporary society and its long trumpeted 'crisis of faith'. Certainly, throughout *H'm*, Thomas is at pains to depict our present-day moral and spiritual degeneracy. But 'Via Negativa', the negative way, dates back to the fourth century, and the 'secularization' of the Christian church by the Emperor Constantine. Apophantic theology, as it is sometimes called, developed as a direct and oppositionary response to the 'Romification' of the Church of Christ. Very largely it is responsible for the minoritist ascetic and hermit traditions within Christianity. Its main tenets are that God cannot be known through collective worship, or from his attributes, but only through a contemplative study of what he is not.

Through its title, Thomas's poem explicitly belongs to the

apophantic tradition. In a sense it is his declaration of affiliation to it. The famous 'darkness between stars', while expressive of the vastness and therefore the mystery of the created universe, is also a metaphorically compact rendering of God's unknowableness. Since we can neither see nor adequately measure the interstellar spaces except by reference to what is visible (i.e. the stars), God is only located negatively. But this partially disposes of the idea of a *deus absconditus*. God is there all along, only we don't know how to see or find him.

Thomas seemingly invokes the *deus absconditus* when he speaks of 'that great absence' in 'our lives', but even this is double-edged. God in fact is not absent, except in as far as we have elected to make him so. The poem continues:

> His are the echoes
> We follow, the footprints he has just
> Left. We put our hands in
> His side hoping to find
> It warm. We look at people
> And places as though he had looked
> At them, too; but miss the reflection.

These lines reinforce the notion of human complicity in God's alleged absence or retreat. Even if we place ourselves in the wound in God's side, even if we adopt his perspectives on the world and its inhabitants, there is still something missing.

Unexpectedly perhaps, 'Via Negativa' turns out to be a poem about the Fall, and the sorrow of unenlightenment that accompanies the Fall. But what then of redemption? As so often in Thomas's collections, the one poem is offset, or complemented, by a second placed immediately opposite it on the page of the open book, in this case 'Making'.[51] Now, and quite daringly, even heretically, Thomas has God review creation, as a kind of dramatis persona:

> I thought up the flowers
> Then birds. I found the bacteria
> Sheltering in primordial
> Darkness and called them forth
> To the light. Quickly the earth
> Teemed. Yet still an absence

Disturbed me. I slept and dreamed
Of a likeness, fashioning it
When I woke, to a slow
Music; in love with it
For itself, giving it freedom
To love me; risking the disappointment.

At least, the reader assumes initially that this is God speaking, or
reminiscing; the poem can also be read as a monologue of Adam's,
in which case the fashioned 'likeness' becomes not himself but Eve.
Indeed, the presence of a dual identity within the poem emphasizes
the idea of likeness between creator and created, and it is this likeness,
this similarity between God and man, that the poem explores. Both
in their own way are creators, but now it is God who experiences
an 'absence'. In this way his remoteness, as suggested by one reading
of 'Via Negativa', is hugely foreshortened. Rather God, waking and
falling asleep and dreaming just like man, is projected as being
himself susceptible to the need for love.

Again, in 'Making' there is no specific indication of redemption,
but, in an order conditioned by love, actual redemption is of secondary importance because its possibility will always be there. But by
the same token so too is there an endless possibility of 'disappointment'. In an almost magical way, the poem succeeds in extrapolating
a relationship between the divine and the human that, while derived
from Genesis, takes its colouring from St John. If we are guilty of
anthropomorphizing God, Thomas seems to suggest, then that is
because God has anthropomorphized us.

But what of the 'bacteria/ Sheltering in primordial/Darkness'? In
another creation poem in *H'm*, 'Other',[52] God is unable to contain
his disappointment. Indeed he is undone by the risk he has taken:

God secreted
A tear. Enough, enough,
He commanded, but the machine
Looked at him and went on singing.

The title poem too, 'H'm',[53] reflects on a failed endeavour:

and one said
speak to us of love
and the preacher opened
his mouth and the word God
fell out so they tried
again speak to us
of God then but the preacher
was silent reaching
his arms out but the little
children the ones with
big bellies and bow
legs that were like
a razor shell
were too weak to come

Because of passages like this Thomas is sometimes characterized as a poet of uncompromising despair malgré the Christian nature of his imagery and metaphor; even that, like Blake's Milton, he is of the devil's party without knowing it. That however is simplistic. The formless, stream-of-consciousness style of 'H'm', counterpointed by its title, at once expressive of opprobrium and scepticism, alone belies the caricature. Even as we turn the page, we come to 'The Kingdom',[54] where once again an affirmatory note is sounded, albeit circumspectly. The 'Kingdom' of course is the Kingdom of God:

It's a long way off but inside it
There are quite different things going on:
Festivals at which the poor man
Is king and the consumptive is
Healed; mirrors in which the blind look
At themselves and love looks at them
Back; and industry is for mending
The bent bones and the minds fractured
By life. It's a long way off, but to get
There takes no time and admission
Is free, if you will purge yourself
Of desire, and present yourself with
Your need only and the simple offering
Of your faith, green as a leaf.

I say circumspectly because the contents of this paradise are in fact depicted in terms of some of life's unpleasantness. The world's pain is not lightly brushed under the carpet. There is therefore an inherent balance between the poem's images and the use to which they are put. 'The Kingdom' is also circumspect in that, in contrast to 'H'm', the two sentences that compose it are carefully, even elaborately constructed. But there is another sort of balance in the poem as well. The 'simple offering/ Of your faith, green as a leaf' recommends, in a quiet way, Kierkegaard's leap of faith. Thomas also invokes another religious tradition, which is the tradition of such 'transcendental mystics' as Meister Eckhart, who, in the early fourteenth century, well before the advent of either Galilean or Newtonian cosmologies, posited the existence of an 'inner space' and a 'time outside time' in which God resides.[55] That at least is what I take to be the import of the words that commence the poem's second sentence. Thus the leap of faith, in this instance, is not into a precarious unknown, so much as into the kingdom itself.

Like William Blake, Thomas has an uncanny ability to locate heaven and hell in the same place simultaneously. At least, his sensibility inclines that way. The poems of *H'm* are exceptional in their range of often subtly modulated voice, and in their electrifying nuances. Whether the volume adds up, or is even intended to add up, to a whole greater than its parts I doubt. Thomas seems to me just not that kind of poet. He is too alert to the contrary motions of his own thought. The parts collide and agitate each other, but they do not assemble into something architectural or majestic. Any overview is routinely sacrificed on the altar of turbulent tensions.

That turbulence is probably the quality that will ensure Thomas's survival as a poet to be read. In as far as Thomas's poetry has a unity, then that is it. The same turbulence makes it difficult to divide his work into neatly packaged periods or phases; though this has not prevented his critics from attempting just that. Themes and techniques one thought he had laid aside may suddenly resurface. Even *H'm*, with its shift from the political to the 'religious', is not a maintained frontier. Rather it is a meeting point between interiors.

There is a great deal of God in the poems that precede it, as there is a great deal of Wales in the poems that follow.

H'm was succeeded immediately by *Young and Old* (1972), the smaller collection of in fact quite adult poems intended for children. It is rather a volume about children, and about childhood, although one poem, 'Omens',[56] concerning Queen Elizabeth I and the first expeditions against the American Indians, and drawing attention to the dark side of a brutal colonialism not always taught in schools, is as anti the English state as anything Thomas has written. Then too there was the inflammatory *What is a Welshman?* of 1974. In *Laboratories of the Spirit* (1975), however, Thomas advances further into theological territory. Here it is the old theme of God's silence, especially in the face of prayer, as much as his absence, that perturbs the poet. Yet even as he says this, in the opening poem 'Emerging',[57] Thomas gropes his way towards an understanding of God that is more overtly in tune with the 'scientific' culture around him:

> I begin to recognize
> you anew, God of form and number.
> There are questions we are the solution
> to, others whose echoes we must expand
> to contain. Circular as our way
> is, it leads not back to the snake-haunted
> garden, but onward to the tall city
> of glass that is the laboratory of the spirit.

Instead of Kierkegaard, we are presented with Euclid as the true cicerone to Meister Eckhart's other or hidden world. On the face of it this seems as startling a departure as Thomas could make, and certainly it is regularly echoed in poems that follow, both in *Laboratories of the Spirit* and in subsequent collections. 'At It',[58] for instance, from the 1978 collection *Frequencies*, contains the extraordinary pronouncement that

> there will be
> no judgement other than the verdict
> of his calculation, that abstruse

geometry that proceeds eternally
in the silence beyond right and wrong.

Again, in 'The Tree',[59] from the *Later Poems* of 1983, we find Thomas
contemplating God through radiometry (inspired in part no doubt
by the radar station erected on the central heights of Llŷn):

> Nightly
> we explore the universe
> on our wave-lengths, picking up nothing
> but those acoustic ghosts
> that could as well be mineral
> signalling to mineral
> as immortal mind communicating with itself.

'Ghosts' of course is a wonderful metonym. Not only does it capture
the sort of noise detected in the stellar reaches, but also it suggests the
images that fade on the radar screen. There is too the sense of 'the ghost
in the machine', as well as the more obvious association of a human
aftermath. But the real significance of these lines perhaps is that, having
embraced scientific terminology as a viable metaphoric resource, and
incorporated it as such into his poetry, after a while it presents Thomas
with the same spiritual or religious doubt or ambiguity as his more
conventional Christian imagery. Yet in the title poem of the still later
collection *Destinations* (1985), Thomas returns in hope to

> the brightness over
> an interior horizon, which is science
> transfiguring itself in love's mirror.[60]

It is this instability, or unpredictability, in R. S. that keeps particularly his later poetry alive. From one page to the next one never
knows quite what will be encountered, or how the poet will handle
it. 'Poste Restante',[61] in *Laboratories of the Spirit*, returns us suddenly,
and quite violently, to a style and a subject-matter associated with
Manafon. Yet it is also an address to a future reader:

> And so back
> to the damp vestry to the book
> where he would scratch his name and the date

he could hardly remember, Sunday by
Sunday, while the place sank
to its knees and the earth turned
from season to season like the wheel
of a great foundry to produce
you, friend, who will know what happened.

Whatever Thomas acquires as a poet is put into a constantly expanding retrieval system, from which, at the press of a button almost, it may be accessed ready for re-use, but always in a novel way. He is constantly adding, and constantly revising.

These things said, there is a drift towards an acceptance of sorts in some of Thomas's later poetry. George Steiner[62] and other critics have noted how the great creators – Dante, Shakespeare, Goethe, Beethoven, Tolstoy, for example – tend to follow a three-part cycle. Their early productions are addressed to the world as they find it, or are glittering reinvents of established modes; their middle work is laden with darkness; but their late-phase work, if they progress that far, is suggestive of resignation, even redemption. For a while Thomas seems to conform to the same progression. His tone particularly, his voice, becomes steadily more laconic, at times wearily superior even, his attitude that of the purveyor of conflicting ideas rather than one at war among them.

Of particular interest in this respect are his groups of 'painting' poems. Married to an artist, and himself a sharp-eyed observer especially of the natural world, it is scarcely remarkable that Thomas should be drawn to the visual arts. The Welsh landscape itself is sometimes described as though it were a painting; or if not as a painting, then through the 'frame' of a window. Even in his first collection, *The Stones of the Field*, there is the poem 'On a Portrait of Joseph Hone by Augustus John',[63] and in *The Bread of Truth* we have 'Souillac: le Sacrifice d'Abraham':[64]

This is what art could do,
Interpreting faith
With serene chisel.

431

Without either John's picture or the sculpture at Souillac in front of us, these poems lose much of their cogency. At Aberdaron, however, R. S. turned this liability into an asset. In two of his later collections, poems are placed directly opposite photographic reproductions of paintings they analyse. In the first, *Between Here and Now* (1981), it is the French Impressionists who evince Thomas's responses; in the second, *Ingrowing Thoughts*, a variety of Post-Impressionists, Surrealists, Cubists and other Modernists.

It may at first surprise us that Thomas's choice of paintings focuses on secular artists who depict mainly secular, sometimes even mundane scenes. He does not, however, dwell upon their temporality, but looks instead for what is numinous. Thus, simultaneously, he exposes his own high cultural and modernist credentials. In as far as he trespasses on the preserve of art criticism, it is because he is so empowered by his own life-in-art. Although in every case there is something subjective about Thomas's 'readings' of art-works, there is usually a penetrating formal observation as well. It is indeed difficult, having once read Thomas's commentary on, say, de Chirico's *The Oracle*, to lay that commentary aside:

> So mathematicians
> should appear in surrealist
> mourning, shaven-headed
> to reveal the skull
> half in darkness, half in light
> in permanent procrastination
> of the eclipse of thought.[65]

Such lines are not tossed off after a stroll round the gallery. They are rather a communication between two artists working in different mediums at different times.

Contemplation of the painter's medium helps Thomas focus on his own. Predictably of someone willing to regard the scriptures as prima facie metaphor who is also a modernist, Thomas, in his later poetry, is increasingly exercised by the phenomena of words and language. Like the philosopher Ludwig Wittgenstein, to whom he not infrequently alludes, he wants, or rather needs, to find out what, if anything, 'may be said'. There are hints too that Thomas is familiar with structuralist semiotics. 'Directions',[66] one of the non-painter poems in *Between Here and Now*, begins:

> In this desert of language
>   we find ourselves in,
>   with the sign-post with the word 'God'
>   worn away . . .

'Language' and 'sign-post' here are too proximate for us to believe that their contemporary intellectual resonance could escape someone of such serious reading habits as R. S. But even in these sparse lines, there is much more at stake than the mere acknowledgement (or signalling) of what may only be a passing fad. It is language's failure to achieve what for the poet clearly is language's principal responsibility: to bring us closer to the divine.

Since, contra Aristotelian literary precepts, Thomas conceives that the role of the poet is to do just that, the failure of language is of the greatest possible consequence for him. Without the tools he cannot finish the job. In 'Prayer',[67] from *Later Poems*, he brings this to the fore:

> Baudelaire's grave
> not too far
> from the tree of science.
> Mine, too,
> since I sought and failed
> to steal from it,
> somewhere within sight
> of the tree of poetry
> that is eternity wearing
> the green leaves of time.

Thomas confesses that he has allowed himself to be sidetracked. His deliberate use of modern vocabularies, in *Laboratories of the Spirit*, *Experimenting with an Amen* and other late collections, is plainly a mistake. Yet what other option has he, living in the times he does? The reasons for God's absence in his life, or for God's being perennially just beyond his reach, are never simple. Theology has something to do with it, but so too does the nature of language itself. As he succinctly summarizes matters in 'Synopsis',[68] from *Frequencies* (1978),

> the beast that rages
> through history; that presides smiling
> at the councils of the positivists.

The beast is the beast of Armageddon, of Revelations, of Yeats's 'Second Coming'. The positivists are among those who, following Hume and answering Wittgenstein's inquiry before it was made, tell us that what can in fact be said is almost nothing. Yet without the ability to say anything, therefore to think anything, how can God be admitted?

Thomas's inclination to join the philosophers at their work catches up with him. It is all too cerebral. The Kierkegaardian leap of faith becomes more, not less urgent:

> Is there a place
> here for the spirit? Is there time
> on this brief platform for anything
> other than the mind's failure to explain itself?

he asks in another poem from *Frequencies*, 'Balance'.[69] And in yet another he gives 'The Answer':[70]

> There have been times
> when, after long on my knees
> in a cold chancel, a stone has rolled
> from my mind, and I have looked
> in and seen the old questions lie
> folded and in a place
> by themselves, like the piled
> graveclothes of love's risen body.

The love the leap leads to disposes of the questions, of the mind's wrangling; but only, as Thomas concedes, 'at times'.

* * *

It is in the end a search for serenity, as well as a search for God. The two are perhaps the same. In many poems Thomas comes close to both. Scattered throughout all his later collections are synopses of history where Thomas does indeed succeed in finding at least an Olympian stance. There are also autobiographical poems in which, by adopting the same concision, albeit more often than not ironically, he achieves a measure of release from the governing tensions of his life. Yet at other times, writing about himself, Thomas can indulge a rarefied self-pity, as in 'A Life',[71] from *Experimenting with an Amen*:

> Lived long; much fear, less
> courage. Bottom in love's school
> in his class; time's reasons
> too far back to be known.
> Good on his knees, yielding,
> vertical, to petty temptations.
> A mouth thoughts escaped
> from unfledged. Where two
> were company, he the unwanted
> third. A Narcissus tortured
> by the whisperers behind
> the mirror. Visionary only
> in his perception of an horizon
> beyond the horizon. Doubtful
> of God, too pusillanimous
> to deny him. Saving his face
> in verse from the humiliations prose
> inflicted on him. One of life's
> conscientious objectors, conceding
> nothing to the propaganda of death
> but a compulsion to volunteer.

Only the unsparing control of these lines, which are as good an exemplar as any of the archetypal Thomasian technique, of the hidden formal devices, and the seemingly inexhaustible ability to strike the terse phrase that says everything, saves them from dismissal.

But serenity? The more poems Thomas produces, the more they seem like fragments, by simple virtue of their number. Only in two

435

volumes does R. S. endeavour to create an overtly structured whole. The first of these is *The Echoes Return Slow*, where, instead of responding to paintings, the poems respond to an autobiography distilled into gobbets of prose. In the second, *Counterpoint* (1990), untitled verses are separated into four roughly equal sections: 'B. C.', 'Incarnation', 'Crucifixion' and 'A. D.' Here, if anywhere, Thomas attains the summation of his craft and his journey. In poem after poem the esoteric is laid bare to behold:

> Forget it. The Middle Ages
> are over. On a bone
> altar, with radiation
> for candle, we make sacrifice
> to the god of quasars
> and pulsars, wiping
> our robotic hands
> on a disposable conscience.[72]

Or:

> What is the virginity
> of mirrors? Are they surfaces
> of fathoms which mind
> clouds when examining itself
> too closely? Eden in the dream
> of when it was alone.[73]

But the themes and ideas contained in *Counterpoint*, as well as its imagery, though rendered anew, are too obviously identifiable from all the poems that have come before. Only if we approach it after a long rest from the preceding canon can we hope to be freshly engaged, and even then there is a thin but unmistakable glaze to its resignation. Its vapours are, perhaps, a little too well contrived, a little too astringently Delphic.

Yet all that changes. In both *Experimenting with an Amen* and *Counterpoint*, R. S. seems to be reaching an end. The 'amen' is partly for himself, the 'counterpoint' a counterpoint to the life he has had. But in the two most recent volumes, *Mass for Hard Times* and *No*

Truce with the Furies, both published after the death of his wife, Thomas resumes his conventional format: titled poems arranged in sequence, but without an incursive structure. In each case too, as the titles suggest, Thomas seemingly turns away from the very idea of a permanent cease-fire with life's pain. There is no truce with the furies. There is no let-up. Even the traditional consolations of religion are fiercely rebutted, or shown to be hollow. In 'Mass for Hard Times' itself, a longer poem that like so many of Thomas's longer poems is assembled from a handful of shorter ones, the opening statement is marked 'Kyrie':

> Because we cannot be clever and honest
> and are inventors of things more intricate
> than the snowflake – Lord have mercy.
>
> Because we are full of pride
> in our humility, and because we believe
> in our disbelief – Lord have mercy.

The tone here is playfully ironic as well as bitter, the more so if the echo of T. S. Eliot in the first line is permitted. The mass that Thomas celebrates is black enough, but still it is celebrated.

For Thomas in his eighties everything is up in the air again, or for the first time perhaps, and he has earned for himself the freedom to say whatever he wishes. The bleakness endures, but is frequently mingled with an ambitious blitheness. For a poet often accused of narrowness of subject-matter, R. S. is marvellously replete. In the two late collections there are moments when his thin music does falter, or when the frailty of age is camouflaged only by a lingering clarity that may be no more than the force of long habit. But at others the original stream runs vigorous and pure. *No Truce with the Furies* contains, as well as 'The Lost', and also 'Vespers', an elegy to Elsi Thomas comparable to 'A Marriage', the poem 'Geriatric', which begins

> What god is proud
>   of this garden
> of dead flowers, this underwater
>   grotto of humanity,

where limbs wave in invisible
     currents, faces drooping
on dry stalks, voices clawing
     in a last desperate effort
to retain hold?

POSTSCRIPT

CROMWELL'S CURSE

THE POINT WAS MADE BEFORE, but can be made again. It often is unclear when to lay aside an individual poem by R. S. Thomas. And if this is true of many poems individually, how much more true must it be of the whole poet?

In the old Persian tale Scheherazade escaped death by weaving a web of tales around her murderous husband, King Shahriyar. In the *Mabinogion*, the Birds of Rhiannon are blessed with the ability to quicken the dead, and entrance the living. That a modern poet should aspire to, let alone achieve, similar such powers invites incredulity. Nevertheless, that purpose is integral to Thomas's work. Whether in the name of 'God' or in the name of 'Wales', R. S. seeks to deflect us from a soiled world of ordinary temporal and material concern. The priest who seems not to have been greatly exercised by the rescue of souls, as a poet behaves otherwise. If he fails in this, he fails entirely, though the fault may not be his: it is we perhaps who have lost the capacity to be entranced, to be deflected. Imagination's flint cannot strike sparks off a pillow or a lettuce.

Success in modern literature, however, is judged by other means. Thomas's work has already spawned a mass of critical commentary. When a poet as good as R. S. appears, there is joy in academe. Much labour occurs. In the Welsh periodicals especially, but elsewhere too, the learned articles spew forth. Theses are written, monographs prepared. In Germany he goes down well.[1] In America, better. Then there is the whole business of the Nobel Prize.

And all this is necessary. So much is written and published these days we have to have experts to guide us. We have to *know* our taste is properly directed, and the priesthood of lecturers is there to intercede on our behalf.

Here I will consider just one specimen of academic attention, culled from the many that have fed my researches. This is the essay 'Allusions to Welsh Literature in the Writing of R. S. Thomas', by Jason Walford Davies, the younger lecturer who sat on the stage at Hay. It was printed by the Gomer Press for the Bangor-based *New Welsh Review*, and published, in 1995, as the first number of a new journal calling itself *Welsh Writing in English*, and subtitled 'A Year-book of Critical Essays'.

What Jason Walford Davies has to say about R. S. is probably the single most important article about the poet to have appeared in English to date. With exacting detail he lays bare some at least of Thomas's indebtedness to Welsh-language writing, past and present. He shows how, particularly in the earlier collections, Thomas has woven into his poetry and his prose, both directly and indirectly, not only a detailed knowledge of Welsh history, but also countless allusions to Welsh writing at nearly every stage of its development. Further, he demonstrates how many individual lines and passages in Thomas are derived very closely from Welsh originals. In doing so, he confirms the direction which Thomas himself, in the 1940s, insisted is the only direction that 'Anglo-Welsh' writing should take.

This is refreshing. It shows how, in many cases, R. S. achieves his effects, and the extent to which he has immersed himself in the Welsh cultural heritage. But in delivering his discoveries, Walford Davies makes what are, I think, exaggerated claims. While not denying Thomas's indebtedness to other poetries, particularly the poetries of Yeats, Eliot, Ezra Pound and Wallace Stevens, he insists on the primacy of Thomas's Welsh sources; and this narrows the critic's overall purchase on Thomas's work.

Walford Davies offers a number of difficult, even contentious statements. Thomas's 'increasing knowledge of Welsh', he tells us, 'opened a door on an inner identity'. Apropos the influence of Yeats, he can say 'the Welsh allusions reflect, because they well from greater depths, . . . an *inner* civil war.' He asks to what extent 'R. S. Thomas's cultural memory serves a realistically *modern* sense of Wales'. (The italics are the author's, not mine.) And his concluding section begins: 'It is odd to think that this inheritance is completely closed to the vast majority of R. S. Thomas's readers. Even discounting audiences that are not mainly English-language ones, one wonders how well Americans, say, understand these poems.' And not just Americans, of course. Elsewhere in his essay, Walford Davies suggests that the occurrence of, say, Welsh words and Welsh place-names in Thomas's poetry will produce nothing more than 'music' to the non-Welsh ear.

While Thomas's commitment to Welsh is beyond dispute, Walford Davies's particular clothing of it is fraught. He is determined, one feels, to defend and preserve an inner sanctum. The Jungian notion of 'cultural memory' is by no means assured, particularly in the case of someone whose Welsh was acquired relatively late in life. The relationship between 'increasing knowledge' and 'inner identity' is similarly hazardous. I have no problem conceding Thomas's 'inner civil war', indeed it is a main object of the present writing, but that state of mind may as well be created by rival intrusions as by an immanence. Nor would I accept that Thomas's Welsh 'inheritance', whether it is innate or acquired, or, as seems more probable, is both, is necessarily 'completely' closed to non-Welsh readers.

When, in his poem 'The Curse of Cromwell', Yeats gives us the line, 'As the fox in the old fable destroyed the Spartan boy's', it is only the dull reader who, unfamiliar with the presented allusion, does not take the trouble to identify its meaning, but rests contented with its music. Similarly with Thomas. Only the dull reader will ignore the signposts to Welsh history and Welsh culture, at least when they are overt. Indeed, one of the outstanding virtues of Thomas is precisely that he leads us into such areas, and obliges us to explore them with him.

Whether that virtue is intentional or not is another matter. To a degree, Thomas shares his critic's enclavism. Let us though take one example where Walford Davies identifies a Welsh source, in some lines from 'Border Blues' that have already been quoted (see above p. 292):

> I was going up the road and Beuno beside me
> Talking in Latin and old Welsh,
> When a volley of voices struck us; I turned,
> But Beuno had vanished, and in his place
> There stood the ladies from the council houses:

Blue eyes and Birmingham yellow
Hair, and the ritual murder of vowels.

It is scarcely imaginable that any serious reader of this passage should be incurious as to the identity of Beuno; nor, unless Beuno's general identity is ascertained, can it make anything other than phantasmagoric sense. To his real credit, Jason Walford Davies specifically ties these lines to the early Welsh 'Life of St Beuno', *Buchedd Beuno*, where, walking one day by the Severn, Beuno

> heard a voice on the other side of the river, inciting dogs to hunt a hare, and the voice was that of an Englishman, who shouted 'Kergia! Kergia!' which in that language incited the hounds. And when Beuno heard the voice of the hounds, he at once returned, and coming to his disciples, said to them, 'My sons, put on your garments and your shoes, and let us leave this place, for the nation of the man with the strange language, whose cry I heard beyond the river urging on his hounds, will invade this place.[2]

Knowledge of this extract undoubtedly enriches our understanding of Thomas's poem, though not necessarily in Thomas's favour. To equate the council houses' yellow-haired ladies with a putatively bloodthirsty Saxon forebear does not diminish the contemporary slur implicit in 'the ritual murder of vowels'.

It would be narrow-minded to assert that what a poet does with his sources is all that matters. Conversely, to imply that such use is of secondary significance is equally parochial. It would be reassuring to know that Walford Davies, who has little or nothing to say about the immediate import of Thomas's lines, conceives his role as academic critic merely in terms of textual excavation, but his deployment of such phrases as 'inner identity', 'cultural memory' and 'completely closed' inhibits that view.

But perhaps Walford Davies's greater error is to obscure the true dimensions of the very aspect of Thomas's genius that his scholarship quite properly focuses attention upon. The poet's handling of his Welsh sources reveals a mind of formidable refractive powers. But exactly the same can be said about Thomas's handling of his non-Welsh sources. A similar debt is owed not just to English verse, but to his reading in philosophy and theology, as well as of course to his familiarity with the Bible. Another critic, J. P. Ward, in a book-length study of Thomas,[3] singles out the following lines from 'Covenanters'[4] in the *Later Poems*:

> It is here,
> he said, tapping his forehead
> as one would to indicate
> an idiot.

As Ward shows, two Bible verses are present: Luke 16:21 ('the Kingdom of God is within you') and I Corinthians 1:23 ('unto the Greeks, foolishness').

Allusion and the reworking of existing sources are time-honoured literary devices. They are one way of delaying the reader's return to the quotidian world. They also form part of the creative process. *Ex nihilo nihil fit*. In Thomas, it is not just the range of sources that impresses, but the deftness with which he incorporates them into his poetry. His echoes are myriad, his nuances legion. Through that skill, whether or not the reader is always conscious of it, he draws us into Wales; but he also draws us toward a concept of God and into poetry, into culture itself, albeit a distinctly high culture.

But what of Wales?

Perhaps it is too inviting for a relatively unthreatened outsider such as myself to put 'Wales' glibly into 'perspective'. Jason Walford Davies would, I hope, agree though that the critic's essential task is to encourage the reader to go to R. S. Thomas with the application his work demands, even if some aids are required. *The Echoes Return Slow*, for example, which I regard as one of Thomas's finest works, will remain opaque without some biographical background. And if the present book does so encourage and assist the reader, then I shall very nearly have achieved my purpose. But only very nearly, because unless the same reader also considers, or reconsiders, the reality of 'Welsh Wales', and the burdens implicit in belonging to a threatened minority, then I shall yet have failed.

Speaking of my own experience, it has been a profound dismay to witness in various 'remote' parts of the world — remote to us, that is – the decline and sometimes extinction of 'small' peoples and/or their way of life. I think particularly of the tribal groupings in Irian Jaya, and of such people as the H'mong in south-east Asia. In this respect the least salutary encounter has been with the headman of a remnant tribe – the once nomadic Sakhai – on the mountainous border between Thailand and mainland Malaysia.[5] This man, known as Mr Lud, lived with the knowledge that when he died then so too would all hope for his language. The thirty-odd other Sakhai people either had jobs in Malay or Thai towns, or, if they were children, were being energetically bussed to schools by the Thai authorities. Mr Lud alone had a care for the Sakhai tongue, and his sorrow was unspeakable.

While genetically such peoples generally do survive, assimilated into the dominant societies around them, their complex cultures, sometimes in the space of a single generation, have either been taken from them or abandoned. Always, though, it is a case of force majeure prevailing.

Welsh culture and the Welsh tongue have withstood a much longer siege. It may well be that 'Wales' is simply too robust to disappear. I hope so. It should not be assumed however. In this respect nationalism is perhaps a necessary evil. I do not like Welsh nationalism in its more strident, racially prejudicial and religiously bigoted manifestations, any more than I like any other militant nationalism, including my own. Nationalism does not bring out the best in anyone. But I can very well see that, without a critical reappraisal on the part of the essentially English authorities, and yes, on the part of some 'recalcitrant' Welsh too, you cannot have the one without the other.

The alternative is the striking out of yet another culture, another realm of consciousness, from the register of human cultures and consciousnesses. Fine maybe if they are someone else's, but if they were yours? Currently it is estimated there are some six thousand discrete languages in the world. Within a generation or two it is likely this number will have been reduced to six hundred, with further contractions to follow. But how many are we eventually aiming for? How large, or how small, *is* the bare essential rump? Only rump has the wrong resonance. The Rump Parliament was eventually replaced by a broader reconstituted assembly; though not before Oliver Cromwell had dissolved parliament altogether. If we whittle humanity down to a cultural and linguistic rump there will never again be anything but a rump.

ACKNOWLEDGEMENTS

MEIC STEPHENS and Professor M. Wynn Thomas kindly read the manuscript of this book and made many invaluable corrections and suggestions. The author, while taking full responsibility for all surviving errors of fact and judgement, is indebted to them, and to the following, who, in a variety of ways, have made *Furious Interiors* possible:

Deborah Adams, the copy-editor; Mary and Ian Allen of Botwnnog; Henry, Marquess of Anglesey; The Revd Christopher Armstrong, Vicar of Aberdaron; Joseph Bain of Tenby; The Revd T. J. Blewitt, Vicar of Hanmer; Michael and Hazel Bolton of Manafon; James Boulton of the National Trust, Llandeilo Office; Roger L. Brown of Welshpool; The Revd John Butler, Anglican chaplain at Univeristy College of North Wales (Bangor); John Cave of Llanigoch, Holyhead; Professor John Cottingham of Reading University; Anthony Curtis; the late Susan Cowdy, President of the Bardsey Island Trust; Madeleine Dick of the National Trust, Plas-yn-Rhiw; The Very Revd Wyn Evans, Dean of St David's; Dr Barbara Everett of Somerville College, Oxford; Peter Fullerton, of Magdalen College, Oxford; Raymond Garlick of Carmarthen; David and Lorraine Greeson-Walker of Manafon; Mike James of the Torch and Sherman Theatres; Ruth Hall of Manafon; Wyn Hobson, proof-reader; Peter Hope Jones of Menai Bridge; Alwyn Hughes of Aberdaron; Ivy Hughes of Eglwysfach; The Revd Andrew Jones of St Michael's College, Lampeter; Ethel L. Jones of Holyhead; Philip Gwyn Jones at HarperCollins; Andrew McAlister of Bloodaxe Books; Alaistair McGee, BBC Wales; Robert Nisbet of Haverfordwest; Edwin Roland Owens, author, and warden of the Breakwater Country Park, Holyhead; Ianto Owens of Llangwm; Emma Pama of Aldworth; Martin Richards, Chairman of the Bardsey Island Trust; Dr Gareth Roberts of Milford Haven; Gareth Roberts, National Trust Warden for Pen Llŷn; Mary Roberts of Aberdaron; The Revd Michael Roberts, Vicar of Chirk; Thomas Roberts, archivist at University College of North Wales (Bangor); Canon John Rowlands, Warden of St Michael's College, Llandaff; Richard Spencer, of St Michael's College, Llandaff; Professor M. Wynn Thomas of Swansea University; The Revd Randolph Thomas, Vicar of Carmarthen; Dafydd ap Tomos of Plas Glyn-y-Weddw;

Boyd Tonkin of the *New Statesman*; Neville Walker of Talarn Green; Ellen Williams, Information Officer at University College of North Wales (Bangor); Gail Williams of Milford Haven; Canon Howard Williams; Karel and Annwyl Williams of Aberystwyth; Megan Williams of Rhiw; M. B. Williams of Milford Haven; Charlotte Windsor at HarperCollins; Christopher Wintle of King's College, London; the staffs of the London Library, the County Library at Haverfordwest, and the Public Library, Milford Haven; and last, but always first, Kimiko Tezuka-Wintle.

J.W.

NOTES

As many readers may have access only to R. S. Thomas's *Collected Poems: 1945–1990*, J. M. Dent, 1993 I have provided page references to that volume for those poems included in it, using the abbreviation *C P*. Full details of R. S. Thomas's published works are given in the bibliography.

Where I have quoted from such Welsh prose writings of R. S. Thomas as do not already exist in a published English translation, I have provided a translation in the main body of the book. Except for some phrases and half-sentences the original Welsh is given below.

ONE · THE UNION'S EDGE

1 Edited by Gwenno Hywyn, Gwasg Gwynedd, 1985.

2 The South Wales Miners' Federation, a powerful body in the coal valleys in the period leading up to the post-war nationalization of the coal industry.

3 'Welsh Landscape', from *An Acre of Land*; *C P*, p. 37.

4 *C P*, p. 202.

5 *Sade, Fourier, Loyola* by Roland Barthes, Editions du Seuil, Paris, 1971, trans. from the French by Richard Miller, Jonathan Cape, London, is an example of the structuralist tendency to emphasize the internal coherence of a literary work. For a sensible discussion of this subject see John Sturrock, *Structuralism*, 1st edition Paladin, London, 1986, 2nd revised edition Fontana Press, London, 1993.

6 Subsequently Professor. During a conversation with the author in April 1996, M. Wynn Thomas remarked that for many years his endeavours to win a wider critical readership for R. S. Thomas had often been like 'listening to my own voice inside an echo chamber'.

7 Poetry Wales Press, 1985.

8 Later published as an article, 'Only The Mind To Fly With: Birds in R. S. Thomas's Poetry', in *Poetry Wales*, 1995.

9 *Laboratories of the Spirit*; *CP*, p. 306.

10 Mr Jason Walford Davies's translation of *Neb* and other autobiographical writings were, at the time of going to press, scheduled for publication by J. M. Dent in August 1996: too late therefore for the present author to consult.

11 *What is a Welshman?*; *C P*, p. 262.

12 *A Portrait of the Artist as a Young Man*, first appeared in 25 instalments in the *Egoist*, a London magazine, 1914–15. First volume from New York, 1916.

13 John Davies, *At the Edge of Town*, Gomer Press, 1981.

14 See T. H. Parry-Williams's poem 'Hon':

> *Ac mi glywaf grafangau Cymru'n*
> *dirdynnu fy mron,*
> *Duw a'm gwaredo, ni allaf ddianc*
> *rhag hon.*

Quoted in R. Gerallt Jones, *T. H. Parry-Williams*, Writers of Wales series, University of Wales Press, 1978.

15 Idiosyncratically an Oxbridge BA can be converted into an MA without any further academic labour. The Oxford Professor of Poetry is elected by Oxford MAs.

16 Matthew Arnold's ten-year tenure of the Oxford poetry chair began in 1857. As with the US presidency, the modern professor's term is restricted to four years.

17 An engaging state-of-the-art essay on this theme is Stephen Pinker's *The Language Instinct*, William Morrow and Company Inc., New York, 1994. Pinker's rejection of 'linguistic determinism' (the theory that language controls thought) is, however, too determined. He will not allow 'thought controls language controls thought'.

18 Anthony Conran, *The Cost of Strangeness*, Gomer Press, Llandysul, 1982, p. 2.

19 *Winter Pollen: Occasional Prose*, London, 1994.

20 Charles Cotton, 'A Voyage to Ireland in Burlesque', 1670.

21 Quoted in W. J. Hughes, *Wales and the Welsh in English Literature*, Hughes and Son Publishers, London and Wrexham, 1924.

22 Kingsley Amis, *Memoirs*, London, 1994.

23 Kingsley Amis, 'A True Poet', *Spectator*, 13 January 1956.

24 Robert Bolt, *A Man for All Seasons*, London, 1960.

25 Transcript made by the author.

26 *Selected Letters of Philip Larkin*, ed. Anthony Thwaite, London, 1992, p. 341.

27 James Howell, *British Proverbs Englished*, 1659, quoted in *The Travellers' Dictionary of Quotation*, ed. Peter Yapp, London, 1983.

28 *The Invention of Tradition*, eds. Eric Hobsbawn and Terence Ranger, Cambridge, 1983.

29 Translation by Steve Short, in *Aneirin: The Gododdin*, Felinfach, 1994; for the original text and more literal translation, see A. O. H. Jarman, *Aneirin: Y Gododdin*, vol. 3 of Gomer Press's Welsh Classics, Llandysul, 1988.

30 Translation from Anthony Conran, *The Penguin Book of Welsh Verse*, 1967.

31 Text and translation from Rachel Bromwich, *Dafydd ap Gwilym: a Selection of Poems*, vol. 1 of Gomer Press's Welsh Classics, Llandysul, 1982.

TWO · BORN LOST

1 *No Truce with the Furies*.

2 *Poetry for Supper; C P*, p. 95.

3 Raymond Garlick, in conversation with the author, July 1995.

4 Reprinted in William V. Davis ed., *Miraculous Simplicity*, Fayetteville, University of Arkansas Press, 1993, pp. 1–20.

5 *Neb*, p. 7: *Bod cynhyrchiol ydi dyn; mae wedi gorchuddio wyneb y ddaear. Paham ofni diffrwythder, felly? Y funud hon mae gwragedd yn esgor*

ymhob cwr o'r byd. Felly y bu yng
Nghaerdydd ar 29ain o Fawrth
1913; un enedigaeth ymhlith miloedd.
Ychwanegiad i boen y byd; merch yn
ubain ac wedyn baban yn llefain, ac
yn dal i lefain am yn hir. Y mae yna
glwyfau yn y byd hwn, a bydd plant
bach yn syrthio'n ysglyfaeth iddynt.
Meningitis! *Y mae yna luniau'n*
dangos plentyn sydd heb fod yn llawn
llathen. Ond y mae ei ddillad yn ddel.

6 *Planet*, 80, April/May 1990, pp.
   28–52; reprinted in William V.
   Davis, op. cit.

7 *C P*, p. 83.

8 *C P*, p. 129.

9 *C P*, p. 127.

10 *C P*, p. 142.

11 *C P*, p. 136.

12 London, 1948.

13 *C P*, p. 193.

14 *C P*, p. 350.

15 *C P*, p. 394.

16 *The Echoes Return Slow*, p. 76.

17 M. Wynn Thomas ed., *The Page's
   Drift: R. S. Thomas at Eighty*, Seren
   Books, Bridgend, 1993.

18 This epithet was given critical
   prestige by C. B. Cox, 'Welsh Bards
   in Hard Times: Dylan Thomas and
   R. S. Thomas', in Boris Ford ed.,
   *The New Pelican Guide to English
   Literature*, Hardmonsworth, 1983.

19 *Neb*, p. 7: *Daeth meddygon i fod;
   dynion cas a fyddai'n gwthio llwy i
   lawr y corn gwddf.*

20 *Neb*, p. 8: *Dychrynodd drwyddo a
   rhedeg i chwilio am ei fam dan
   sgrechian. Onid yw'r byd yn gas wrth
   hogyn? Pam yr oedd eisiau i fachgen
   llawer hŷn ymosod arno a'i bwnio? Ai
   sumbol o atgasedd y werin tuag at
   gachgi a darpar-fardd?*

21 *Neb*, p. 8: *Ach-y-fi! . . . A'r rhieni'n
   bell yn mwynhau eu hunain. Felly*

*daeth ofn yn rhan o'i brofiad. Ac eto
byddai wynebau caredig yn y drws o
dro i dro, aelodau o griw y llong yn
picio i mewn i ofalu'i fod yn iawn. Sut
y medr plentyn gael gan bobl mewn oed
ddeall holl arswyd chwilod du?*

22 *The Echoes Return Slow*, p. 6.

23 Translated in Sandra Anstey ed.
   R. S. Thomas: Selected Prose,
   Bridgend, 1983, new edition
   1995.

24 Ibid.

25 *Neb*, p. 12: *Gaeaf oedd hi, ac er bod
   Caergybi yn lle digon tyner, roedd
   pwll ar y mynydd wedi rhewi drosto
   gydag ychydig o eira o'i gwmpas. Roedd
   y tri ohonynt yno'n hwyr yn y
   prynhawn a hithau'n dechrau nosi.
   Yng nghanol y pwll roedd darn bach
   heb rewi. Roedd dau ohonynt yn edrych
   i lawr o ryw foncyn, a'r trydydd o'r
   golwg rywle tu ôl iddynt. Yn sydyn
   ymddangosodd ffigur o'u blaen gan
   redeg at fin y dŵr clir. Gwaeddodd
   y ddau ohonynt yr un pryd gan
   rybuddio'r llall i fod yn ofalus. Ond
   y funud nesaf ymunodd ef â nhw o
   gyfeiriad cwbl wahanol, a diflannodd
   y ddrychiolaeth yr un pryd. Buasai'r
   ddau'n barod i gytuno mai breuddwyd
   oedd, onibai i'r ddau ohonynt weiddi'r
   un pryd.*

26 *Neb*, p. 10.

27 *Neb*, p. 9.

28 Jonathan Swift, *Poems from the
   Holyhead Journal*, 1727.

29 As described by Mrs Ethel Jones,
   interview with author, October
   1995.

30 *Paths Gone By*, in Anstey, op cit.,
   p. 133.

31 'Night and Morning', in *The Stones
   of the Field*; omitted from *C P*.

32 *Paths Gone By*, in Anstey, op cit.,
   p. 132.

33 'Autobiographical Essay', in William V. Davis, op cit., p. 2.

34 *Neb*, pp. 12–13: *Ambell gyda'r nos, byddai'i rieni'n dymuno mynd allan. 'A fyddi di'n iawn dy hun?' Wrth gwrs y byddai. Cas ganddo gyfaddef fel arall. Ar ôl iddynt fynd, byddai distawrwydd yn meddiannu'r tŷ. Yn ara' deg sylweddolai mai ar ei ben ei hun yr oedd. Ac eto, a oedd o? Nid peth marw ydi tŷ. Bydd yn ochneidio ac yn gwichian ac yn sibrwd. Gwrandawai. Onid oedd rhywun yn y llofft? Beth oedd y sŵn hwnnw fel dyn yn anadlu? Âi at waelod y grisiau a throi'r golau ymlaen. Ac eto roedd pen-draw'r llofft yn y cysgod. Galwai. Dim ateb. Dringai'r grisiau o ris i ris, ac wedi cyrraedd pen y staer gwrando eto. Yn sydyn neidiai gam neu ddau ymlaen gan daranu â'i draed a gweiddi: 'Bw!' Dim byd. Neb. Dôi i lawr y grisiau gyda pheth gollyngdod, ac ailddechrau darllen o flaen y tân hyd nes y dôi'i rieni adref.*

35 *Neb*, p. 13: *O ble cafodd y bachgen y syniad o wneud delw, rhoi dillad amdani a'i gosod ar gadair ym mhen y staer? A phan ddaeth ei rieni i mewn dyna lle'r oedd y ffigur yn disgwyl amdanynt yn y cysgodion, Ac wrth gwrs ei fam oedd y cyntaf i esgyn y grisiau a chael sioc ei bywyd. Sgrechiadau wedyn a ffwdan fawr, a'i dad yn dweud y drefn am y fath ffwlbri. Ac eto roedd y cwbl yn ddigon diniwed. Buasent wedi aros gartref yn llawen, onibai iddo eu sicrhau y byddai'n iawn.*

36 *Neb*, p. 13: *A bachgen hapus oedd o ar y cyfan. O leiaf dyna a ddywedai wrtho ei hun wedi cyrraedd oed dyn. Y wlad a'i gwnaeth felly. Er gwaethaf natur nerfus a phryderus ei*

fam, roedd o'n rhydd i grwydro'r ynys o ben bore tan fachlud haul.

37 *Neb*, pp. 14–15: *Yma mae o'n crio, wedi cael cweir gan fachgen cryfach. Fan acw mae'n canu nerth ei ben wrth weld y tonnau'n carlamu dros y traeth ar ddiwrnod o dywydd mawr, a'r ewyn ar wib fel haid o wylanod. Y mae yn y sinema; mae ar gae chwarae; mae'n llygadu merch heb fentro dweud gair wrthi, heb gyffwrdd â hi fel ag y gwnâi bechgyn mwy powld.*

38 *Neb*, p. 18: *Trwy orfod chwilio am y gair iawn i gyfieithu'r Lladin fe ddysgodd yr angen am wneud hyn mewn barddoniaeth hefyd.*

39 *Neb*, p. 13: *Yn yr ysgol byddai'n gwneud cerdd a'i hestyn i'w gymydog yn y ddesg nesaf, a hwnnw, wedi'i ddarllen, yn ei hestyn yn ôl gan sibrwd: 'Poet Laureate.' A oedd y llall yn goeg? Derbyniai'r cyw bardd y clod fel ei haeddiant.*

40 *Neb*, p. 18: *A lle bendigedig oedd o i wylio'r adar yn mynd heibio yn yr hydref ar eu ffordd i'r de, petai'n gwybod hynny ar y pryd.*

41 *Neb*, p. 14: *Cymerodd Gymraeg yn ei flwyddyn gyntaf yn yr ysgol uwchradd, pwnc ymhlith pynciau eraill. Nid arhosodd dim byd ar ei gof ac eithrio un pennill pitw am afal: . . .*

42 *Neb*, p. 14: *Er syndod i lawer cafwyd gwybod y diwrnod hwnnw fod llawer o'r staff yn medru Cymraeg, er iddynt swnio'n ddigon digri i blant oedd wedi arfer eu clywed yn siarad yr iaith fain bob diwrnod arall.*

43 *Neb*, p. 17: *Doedd o ddim yn addolwr cyson yn yr eglwys o bell ffordd. Yn wir roedd gan ei fam yr arfer sâl o gychwyn am dro ar nos Sul yn union fel y byddai'r gynulleidfa'n hel am yr eglwys. Creai hyn embaras i'r bachgen, yr un fath â phan âi i'r eglwys hefo'i*

fam. Roedd hi'n sicr o fod ar ôl, gyda'r canlyniad eu bod yn gorfod cerdded holl hyd yr eglwys er mwyn cael sedd.

44 See note 29.

45 *Oldie*, October 1995, no. 79.

46 *The Echoes Return Slow*, pp. 10–11.

47 Ibid., p. 15.

48 *Neb*, p. 19: *A daeth ei fam hefo fo! Dan yr esgus ei bod yn awyddus i weld bod ganddo lety da ac ati, daeth hi hefyd i rannu'i ddiwrnod cyntaf oddi cartref. Ond trwy drugaredd, gan ei fod yn gwbl anadnabyddus, ni safai'r myfyrwyr eraill mewn rhengoedd i gael hwyl am ben y babi bach yn cyrraedd hefo'i nyrs. Dyna oedd ei deimladau ar y pryd.*

49 *Neb*, p. 19: *Wedyn yn ei wely, ar ôl mynd i gysgu, deffrôdd a chlywed rhywun yn ei gusanu drosodd a throsodd.*

50 See Barry Morgan, *The History of the Church Hostel and Anglican Chaplaincy at University College of North Wales Bangor 1886–1986*, Church in Wales Publications, Penarth, n.d.

51 Ibid., p. 29.

52 In the Church in Wales the primacy is rotated among the constituent dioceses, and not, as in the Church of England, located in one see (i.e., Canterbury).

53 See *Neb*, p. 26.

54 See 'Autobiographical Essay', in William V. Davis, op. cit., p. 4.

55 As described by Anthony Burgess in his autobiography *Little Wilson and Big God*, London, 1987.

56 *Neb*, p. 20: *Pa mor hir fyddai cyn dysgu gwthio merch hir-ymarhous i fyny un ochr y neuadd ac i lawr y llall, a gofyn a gâi o'r ddawns olaf fel esgus i'w hebrwng adref i hostel y merched?*

57 See 'Autobiographical Essay', in

58 *Neb*, p. 21: *Rhyw gyda'r nos aeth allan am dro i Felin Esgob. Roedd y lleuad yn llawn a serennai'r nant dan ei golau fel llifai heibio i'r lein fach a arweiniai i Fynydd Llandygái.*

59 *Neb*, p. 21: *Y tro cyntaf iddo wneud hyn, wedi esgyn rhyw fryncyn a gweld y copaon yn eu gogoniant o'i flaen, torrodd allan i ganu 'Hen Wlad Fy Nhadau' gan daflu'i lais pitw yn erbyn y mynyddoedd mawreddog o'i gwmpas.*

60 Chilmark Press, New York, 1968; reprinted in Sandra Anstey ed., *Selected Prose of R. S. Thomas*, Bridgend, 1986, new edition 1995.

61 *Neb*, pp. 21–2: *Dro arall, ym mis Chwefror, mewn cyfnod o dywydd anarferol o gynnes, dringodd lethr gogleddol Carnedd Llywelyn yn foddfa o chwŷs. Ond wedi cyrraedd y cyfrwy rhwng Llywelyn a Dafydd cafodd fod y llethr pellaf yn wyn dan eira a bod gwynt rhewllyd yn chwythu tuag ato'n ddigon i fynd â'i wynt o ei hun.*

62 *Neb*, p. 22: *O'u cymharu â phrofiadau tebyg i'r rhain, roedd rhywbeth afreal yn ei ymdrechion i gymryd rhan yng ngweithgareddau'r coleg.*

63 For example, in the same *Planet* interview, but also in Sandra Anstey, 'Some Uncollected Poems and Variant Readings from the Early Work of R. S. Thomas', in M. Wynn Thomas, *The Page's Drift*, Seren Books, Bridgend, 1993, p. 23.

64 *Omnibus* XLI no. 2, Easter 1933.

65 *Omnibus* XLII no. 1, Christmas 1933.

66 *Omnibus* XLII no. 3, Summer 1934.

67 *The Echoes Return Slow*, p. 4.

68 *Neb*, p. 27: *... a'r Warden yn ferchetaidd eto, er yn ysgolhaig ac yn*

*medru dweud y drefn lawn mor llym
â Glyn Simon.*

69 See Owain W. Jones, *Saint
Michael's College, Llandaff 1892–
1992*, 1992, published by
St Michael's College.

70 *Neb*, p. 27: *Doedd yno ddim lle i fynd
am dro ond ar hyd y ffordd fawr. Doedd
yno ddim mynyddoedd, dim tir agored.*

71 See *Neb*, p. 27.

72 *Tares; C P*, p. 104.

73 Anstey ed., *Selected Prose*, p. 137.

74 *The Bread of Truth; C P*, p. 151.

75 Quoted in Owain W. Jones,
op. cit.

76 GOE questions set by the Central
Advisory Council of Training for
the Ministry. The examination
papers themselves the author
found in a bound volume in a
cupboard at St Michael's.

77 *C P*, p. 192.

78 Vol. 18, no. 41, Summer 1969.

79 See T. W. Pritchard, *The Parish
Church of St Mary*, pamphlet, 1973.

80 'Autobiographical Essay', in
William V. Davis, op. cit., p. 5.

81 Ibid., p. 8.

82 As reported to the author by the
Revd Michael Roberts, vicar of
Chirk, in October 1995.

83 See *Neb*, p. 38.

84 *Neb*, pp. 31–2: *Hynny a agorodd ei
lygaid i ffaith y dôi'n fwyfwy
ymwybodol ohoni wedyn: doedd yr
Eglwys ddim yn barod i gondemnio
rhyfel, dim ond i annog bechgyn i
wneud eu 'dyletswydd' a gwedd'io
drostynt wedyn. Ond i fachgen gyda
delfrydau i'w cynnal roedd y sefyllfa'n
ddigon eglur. Heddychwr oedd Crist,
ond nid felly'r Eglwys a sefydlwyd yn
ei enw.*

85 *The Echoes Return Slow*, p. 18.

86 *Neb*, p. 30: *Roedd rhai o'r plwyfolion*

*yn wael iawn ac yn haeddu ymweliadau
cyson.*

87 *Neb*, p. 30: *Yn ara' deg, trwy
ddarllen a meddwl, daeth i ddeall mai
hon oedd un o'r problemau mwyaf a
boenodd ddyn ers iddo ddechrau
defnyddio'i ymennydd.*

88 *Neb*, p. 29: *Am y tro cyntaf yn ei
fywyd daeth llyfrau barddoniaeth i'w
feddiant.*

89 *Neb*, p. 29: . . . *a sylweddolodd y
llanc yn frawychus o sydyn lle roedd
o. Felly y dechreuodd yr hiraeth am
Ynys Môn a'r môr, hiraeth a fyddai'n
dylanwadu arno trwy gydol y
blynyddoedd dilynol.*

90 *C P*, p. 83.

91 *C P*, p. 103.

92 *C P*, p. 140.

93 *C P*, p. 153.

94 *C P*, p. 300.

95 *C P*, p. 323.

96 *C P*, p. 384.

97 *C P*, p. 459.

98 *Neb*, p. 32: *Ysai yntau am ei brofi'i
hun yn ei faes o.*

99 'Autobiographical Essay', in
William V. Davis, op. cit., p. 6.

100 *Neb*, p. 36.

101 'Autobiographical Essay', in
William V. Davis, op. cit., p. 8.

102 *Neb*, p. 38.

103 A pamphlet prepared (under
supervision) by the children of
Hanmer and called *A Walk
Through The Village Of Hanmer*
(n.d.) is as informative as it is
charming.

104 Detail recorded in both the
'Autobiographical Essay' and *Neb*.

105 'Autobiographical Essay', in
William V. Davis, op. cit., p. 6.

106 *C P*, p. 30.

107 Translation by Ifor Williams, *Canu
Llywarch Hen*, Cardiff, 1935.

108 See Sandra Anstey, 'Some Uncollected Poems and Variant Readings', op. cit.

109 *CP*, p. 3.

THREE · MANAFON

1 Parliamentary return, compiled by the then incumbent, the Revd Walter Davies (Gwallter Mechain).

2 *The Stones of the Field*; *CP*, p. 11.

3 George Borrow, *Wild Wales*, London, 1862.

4 Jan Morris, *The Matter of Wales*, Oxford, 1984; Penguin, p. 105.

5 *A General View of the Agriculture and Domestic Economy of North Wales*, 1810, and *A General View of the Agriculture and Domestic Economy of South Wales*, 1815.

6 Compiled and edited by Meic Stephens, Oxford, 1986.

7 Collected in *The Stones of the Field*; *CP*, p. 4.

8 *The New Welsh Review*, Vol. III, no. 4, Spring 1991.

9 M. Wynn Thomas ed., *The Page's Drift: R. S. Thomas at Eighty*, Bridgend, 1993, pp. 36ff.

10 Translation by Meirion Pennar, *The Black Book of Carmarthen*, Llanerch Enterprises, Lampeter, 1989, pp. 91–2.

11 The Triads are a feature of Celtic culture that plays a prominent part in early Welsh literature. A Triad is a group of three, such as 'the three fastest warriors'. In bardic practice they were probably used as aides-memoires. Two important collections of Triads have survived, namely *Trioedd Ynys Prydain* ('The Triads of the Island of Britain') and *Trioedd y Meirch*

('Triads of the Horses'). The latter provides the names of horses made famous by their owners. Triads were particularly relished by Iolo Morganwg, and were known to Camden.

12 Meirion Pennar, op. cit., pp. 95–6.

13 *An Acre of Land*; *CP*, p. 36.

14 Coincidentally the phrase 'a new dawn' was later used in the insignia of the Free Wales Army: see p. 271f.

15 *Poetry for Supper*; *CP*, p. 75.

16 Norwich Tapes Ltd, 'The Critical Forum', 1978; quoted by Sandra Anstey, in Wynn Thomas ed. op. cit.

17 *Neb*, pp. 42–3: *Iddo fo roedd y wlad a'i chyffiniau'n brydferth. Dymunai ddal i ganu cerddi o fawl iddynt. Ond sut roedd cysoni bywyd ac agwedd y ffermwyr eu hunain â hyn? Ar ddiwrnod tywyll, oer ym mis Tachwedd ar ei ffordd i ymweld â theulu mewn fferm dros fil o droedfeddi uwchlaw'r môr gwelodd frawd y ffermwr allan yn y cae'n tocio rwdins. Gwnaeth y peth argraff ddofn arno, a phan ddychwelodd i'r tŷ ar ôl yr ymweliad aeth ati i sgrifennu 'A Peasant', y gerdd gyntaf i geisio wynebu realiti'r golygfeydd o'i gwmpas.*

Ai oherwydd caledrwydd y bobl a'u gwaith, ynteu oherwydd rhyw neis-neisrwydd ynddo'i hun y cododd y tyndra oedd i fod yn rhan o'i broblemau ysbrydol a llenyddol am gynifer o flynyddoedd? Ar y pryd roedd yn rhy ifanc ac yn rhy ddibrofiad i wybod bod tyndra'n rhan anhepgor o gelfyddyd. Ac eto roedd deuparth ohono mewn cydymdeimlad â'r bobl hyn oedd yn gorfod bod allan ymhob tywydd yn trin y tir a gofalu am yr anifeiliaid oedd mor anhydrin â'r bobl eu hunain.

18 *Neb*, p. 40: *Roedd hefyd gapel Cymraeg yn Yr Adfa, ac at y gweinidog yno yr aeth gyntaf am gymorth hefo'i Gymraeg. D. T. Davies oedd hwnnw, un o'r de, ond ymhen ychydig symudodd, ac aeth y Rheithor newydd at weinidog Penarth, y capel rhwng Manafon a Llanfair, a gofyn help hwnnw. H. D. Owen oedd hwn, yn enedigol o Benrhosgarnedd. Bendith oedd hyn gan y golygai fod y dysgwr yn dod i siarad iaith y gogledd.*

19 *Neb*, p. 50: *Ond heblaw Nanmor, sy'n un o ardaloedd mwyaf hyfryd Cymru, yr oedd lleoedd eraill i ymweld â nhw: Cwm Twrch ym Maldwyn, er enghraifft, ym mhlwyf Garthbeibio, lle rhedai'r afon i lawr mewn cyfres o raeadrau i gyfarfod ag Afon Banw. Wedyn roedd Tal-y-llyn, a'r môr ei hun yn Aberdyfi lle byddent yn mynd â Gwydion weithiau i gael blas ar y tonnau. Ac wrth fynd o gwmpas fel hyn, dechreuodd ffurfio darlun cyfun o Gymru, ei mynyddoedd, ei rhostir a'i nentydd ewynnol.*

20 Edward Thomas, *Collected Poems*, London, 1979.

21 *Neb*, pp. 41–2: *Y funud honno rhagwelodd y tymhorau o'i flaen, gyda'r tywydd yn troi o law i hindda ac o wres i eira. Ac felly y bu. Doedd yna ddim byd arall i edrych arno ond y tir a'r wybren dan y tymhorau cyfnewidiol.*

22 *Neb*, p. 42: *Dyna paham roedd ei dad mor falch, pan glywodd iddo gael ei benodi i'r plwyf, am nad oedd dim byd gwell gan hwnnw na physgota mewn afon.*

23 *Neb*, p. 42: *Aeth yr afon yn rhan o'u bywyd, weithiau'n dawel, bryd arall yn rhuthro heibio'n frown gan y mawn lle codai; ardal o fân dyddynnod a defaid yn disgwyl am iddo'u darganfod.*

24 *Neb*, pp. 49–50: *I wneud pethau'n waeth i'r rheithor, roedd yn gorfod cadw tân yn yr eglwys i'w chynhesu trwy gydol y cyfnod. Roedd y clochydd a arferai wneud tân yno ers blynyddoedd wedi mynd i oed, a chan ei fod yn ddyn trwm ac yn gorfod mynd i lawr grisiau dan yr eglwys i gynnau'r tân, roedd y rheithor wedi'i ddarbwyllo i roi'r gorau i'r gwaith, rhag ofn iddo gael codwm. 'Mi gawn ni rywun arall' dywedodd. Ond doedd neb wedi cynnig, a bellach roedd gaeaf gwaethaf y ganrif wedi dechrau. Yn ogystal â hynny byddai'r pibellau yn y rheithordy mawr yn rhewi bob nos, ac fe âi'r bore heibio tra'r oedd o a'i wraig yn eu dadmer. Weithiau byddai'r cymylau trymion yn symud a dôi'r haul am awr neu ddwy. Ond ni wnaeth yr wybren glir ddim ond achosi rhew gwaeth nag erioed. Un noson disgynnodd y tymheredd hyd at −10°F., hynny yw deugain gradd o rew. Craciai'r tŷ ar hyd y nos fel y tynhâi'r rhew ei afael, ac erbyn y bore roedd y ffenestri i gyd wedi'u gorchuddio gan redyn, na fedrai neb weld trwyddynt. Roedd dŵr y tŷ wedi rhewi a hyd yn oed yr afon yn ei chael hi'n anodd i symud. A thrwy hyn oll bu rhaid cadw'r bychan yn gynnes a'i ddifyrru yn y tŷ, gan ei bod yn rhy oer o lawer i feddwl am fynd â fo allan. Wedyn ar ôl diwrnod o ddisgwyl dôi sŵn pelen eira'n taro'r ffenestr, a dyna lle byddai Roy, mab y nyrs, wedi dychwelyd o'r ysgol. Roedd lluwchfeydd o ddeunaw troedfedd yn Nolanog y gaeaf hwnnw, a dôi straeon am bobl y gweundir yn gorfod cerdded milltiroedd*

i'r pentref agosaf i brynu bara. Bu agos i'r adar newynu, roedd y caeau'n llawn o olion traed y llwynogod, a thynnwyd y rhisgl oddi ar y rhan fwyaf o'r coed gan y cwningod yn eu hymdrechion i gael bwyd. Pan ddaeth y dadmer o'r diwedd gyda'i law trwm, craciodd yr iâ yn yr afon fel ergyd gwn, a dechreuodd talpiau mawr, gwyn garlamu heibio i'r rheithordy.

25 *Neb*, p. 47: *Fel y cynyddodd y gobeithion na fyddai'r rhyfel yn parhau'n hir, mynegodd gwraig y rheithor ei hawydd am gael plentyn.*

26 See p. 143.

27 *The Echoes Return Slow*, pp. 40–1.

28 Cyril Connolly, *Enemies of Promise*, London, 1938.

29 *The Echoes Return Slow*, p. 37.

30 *Neb*, p. 44: *Teimlodd hyd yn oed y Saes-Gymry o'r De eu bod o dras gwahanol i'w cyd-filwyr. Sgrifennodd rhai ohonynt i'r papurau a'r cylchgronau i fynegi'r teimlad hwn. O'r herwydd, adferwyd y cylchgrawn* Wales *dan olygyddiaeth Keidrych Rhys i roi llwyfan iddynt yn Saesneg. Yr oedd y pwyslais ar Gymreictod: straeon gyda chymeriadau Cymraeg, ymadroddion Cymraeg a dyfyniadau o'r beirdd clasurol.*

31 *Neb*, pp. 44–5: *Darllenodd yn Y Faner erthygl gan Saunders Lewis a orffennai gyda'r geiriau: 'O flodyn y dyffryn, deffro'. Fe'i cynhyrfwyd trwyddo. Aeth i Lanfarian i ymweld â Saunders heb air o gyflwyniad. Derbyniwyd ef yn garedig a dechreuodd sgyrsio yn Saesneg am ei ddelfrydau a'i gynlluniau, ond cyn pen dim fe'i harweiniwyd gan Saunders i ddal ymlaen yn ei Gymraeg bratiog.*

32 Novelist, born in 1924.

33 Leading Welsh poet, born 1904.

34 Essayist, and important figure in the Eisteddfod movement, 1888–1961.

35 *Neb*, p. 45: *I'w gynorthwyo yn ei ymdrechion i ddysgu Cymraeg mynychai gyfarfodydd gweinidogion Llanfair a'r cylch, y Frawdoliaeth fel y'i gelwid. I Llanfair yn nes ymlaen daeth Islwyn Ffowc Elis. Galwodd y rheithor heibio ryw ddydd i'w wahodd i ddod hefo fo am dro i'r gweundir o gwmpas Cwm Nant yr Eira, ond gwrthododd Islwyn. Roedd yn rhy brysur yn ceisio gwasanaethu'i Gymru ef. A oedd y ddwy Gymru'n un, tybed? Roedd wedi cwrdd ag Euros Bowen unwaith neu ddwy, a sgrifennodd ato rûan am gymorth hefo'r Gymraeg. Cafodd wahoddiad caredig i aros yn Llangywair am wythnos. Wrth gerdded glannau Llyn Tegid, soniodd fel y byddai'r goleuni'n gorwedd yn wahanol ar lethrau Arenig i'r ffordd y gwnâi ym Manafon. Safodd Euros a dweud yn ei ffordd argyheoddedig: 'Mae hyn yn profi'ch bod yn Gymro,' Un am aros ar ei draed tan oriau mân y bore oedd Euros, ond dysgodd ei ymwelydd lawer am Gymru a'r Gymraeg yr wythnos honno. Roedd Euros yn awyddus i fynd â fo i weld Llwyd o'r Bryn, ond erbyn meddwl, penderfynodd y byddai'i ryferthwy Gymraeg yn ormod i'r dysgwr.*

36 *Neb*, p. 45: *Yn ddiweddarach daeth cenedlaetholwr o'r Alban, Douglas Young, i annerch cyfarfod yn Rhosllannerchrugog. Aeth y rheithor yno a'i gyfarfod ar ôl ei araith. Yn ddiweddarach, yn dilyn adolygiad ganddo yn* Wales *o lenyddiaeth y deffroad yn yr Alban, cafodd y rheithor wahoddiad i fynd yno am wythnos i annerch cyfarfodydd am hanes a llenyddiaeth Cymru.*

37 Reprinted in Sandra Anstey ed.,

R. S. Thomas: Selected Prose,
Bridgend, 1983, new edition
1995.

38 Ibid.

39 Islwyn = William Thomas (1832–
78), a Monmouthshire man;
Ceiriog = John Ceiriog Hughes
(1832–87), a Denbighshire man.
Welsh-language poets
often are known by their 'bardic'
names.

40 Much has been written about what
Anglo-Welsh means, what it
should mean, and what it shouldn't
mean. A sensible authority is
Raymond Garlick: see
Bibliography.

41 *Pace* Anthony Conran, in his *The
Cost of Strangeness*, Llandysul, 1982.

42 John Ackerman, *A Dylan Thomas
Companion*, London, 1991, p. 154.

43 Quoted in Bruce Griffiths, *Saunders
Lewis*, University of Wales Press
Writers of Wales series, Cardiff,
1979, p. 19.

44 Ibid., p. 41.

45 Saunders Lewis, *Is There an
Anglo-Welsh Literature?*, Cardiff,
1939.

46 Bruce Griffiths, op. cit., p. 119.

47 Translated by Joseph P. Clancy, in
Selected Poems: Saunders Lewis,
Cardiff, 1993.

48 See entry on *Wales* (magazine) in
Meic Stephens ed., *The Oxford
Companion to the Literature of Wales*,
Oxford, 1986.

49 *Wales*, Vol. VII, no. 26, Summer
1947.

50 R. Gerallt Jones, *T. H.
Parry-Williams*, University of
Wales Press, Writers of Wales
series, Cardiff, 1978.

51 *The Bread of Truth*; *C P*, p. 138.

52 *Neb*, p. 46: *Rhyw ddiwrnod soniodd*

*Islwyn wrtho am gynllun i fynd i
Drawsfynydd i rwystro'r fyddin rhag
ymestyn ei gwersyll yno. Roedd y peth
yn gwbl gyfrinachol ac roeddent yn
gorfod newid y dyddiad oherwydd i
rywun brepian. Ond daeth y dydd a
chychwynnodd y rheithor ben bore am
y Traws. Wrth fynd i lawr am
Ddolgellau gwelodd dwr bychan yn
sefyll tu allan i gaffe gan yfed coffi.
Roedd D. J. Williams yn eu plith.
Pan gyrhaeddodd roedd Gwynfor yno
a Waldo a llawer un arall, ond yn
brin o'r cant oedd wedi addo dod. Er
hynny yr oedd digon, a dechreuasant
gymryd eu lle ar y lôn i'r gwersyll er
mwyn ei gau. Llwyddasant yn eithaf
da, trwy drefnu newid lleoedd o dro i
dro. Wedi i Gwynfor egluro ar un
adeg y byddai'n rhaid i ryw bedwar
fynd ar ôl y pedwar oedd o'u blaen:
'Wela i,' meddai Waldo. 'Ar ôl bwyd
yr ail bedwar.'*

53 David Jones is commemorated by
R. S. Thomas in his poem
'Remembering David Jones', in
Later Poems C P, p. 429.

54 *Wales*, Vol. V, no. 7.

55 i.e., a merry evening.

56 Literally a 'summer dwelling', a
hafod more usually refers to an
upland farm abandoned during
winter by farmers living below; a
system of farming, i.e.
transhumance, that developed
during the Middle Ages.

57 Traditional Welsh song: 'stanzas'
sung to the accompaniment of a
harp in such a way that the vocalist
and instrumentalist pursue separate
melodies until the music's closing
bar.

58 *Wales*, Vol. VI, no. 3.

59 Ibid.

60 For example: all true Scotsmen

wear kilts; if a Scotsman is not wearing a kilt he is not a Scotsman. See Antony Flew, *Thinking About Thinking*, London 1989.

61 1892–1978, né Christopher Murray Grieve. For an account of the man and his work see Alan Bold, *MacDiarmid*, London 1988.

62 *Y Geiriadur Mawr: The Complete Welsh–English English–Welsh Dictionary*, Llandysul and Llandybie, 1994, offers the following definitions: *bwlch* – gap, pass, notch; *cwm* – valley, glen; *talar* – headland.

63 i.e., Robert Ambrose Jones, 1851–1906. A Methodist who launched bitter attacks against English-language chapels, and against anglicization in general.

64 i.e., *Y Faner*.

65 'Y Gwladwr' was published in *Y Fflam* in 1950; 'Mae Ganddo Bleidlais' in *Barn* in 1984.

66 *Wales*, Vol. VIII, no. 29.

67 Translation from Sandra Anstey ed., *Selected Prose*, Bridgend, 1983, new edition 1995.

68 Translation ibid.

69 *C P*, p. 24.

70 'Adar y Plwyf' ('Birds of the Parish'), in *Y Llan*, 28 September 1945.

71 Translation taken from Tony Brown, '"On the Screen of Eternity": Some Aspects of R. S. Thomas's Prose', *The Powys Review*, no. 21, 1988; reprinted in Sandra Anstey ed., *Critical Writings on R. S. Thomas* (2nd edn), Bridgend, 1992.

72 Poet, critic and teacher born in 1926. Although English by birth he was drawn to Wales by his republican ideals.

73 *Planet*, no. 80.

74 *Some Versions of Pastoral*, London, 1935, p. 3.

75 Ibid., p. 11.

76 Ibid., pp. 114–15.

77 Ibid., p. 137.

78 Job 5:23.

79 Job 15:7.

80 Job 15:11.

81 Job 8:9.

82 Job 34:3.

83 *C P*, p. 13.

84 'The Tiger'.

85 *C P*, p. 1.

86 *C P*, p. 8.

87 *C P*, p. 16.

88 'If', taken from *A Choice of Kipling's Verse*, ed T. S. Eliot, London, 1941.

89 *C P*, p. 22.

90 *C P*, p. 25.

91 *An Acre of Land*, p. 8; not included in *C P*.

92 *C P*, p. 32.

93 Full name Gruffudd Llwyd ap Dafydd ab Einion Llygliw, c. 1380–1420: poet.

94 *C P*, p. 36.

95 *C P*, pp. 42–55.

96 See Anthony Conran, op cit., p. 106 for a more detailed account.

97 *C P*, p. 10.

98 *C P*, p. 15.

99 *C P*, p. 17.

100 *C P*, p. 62.

101 *C P*, p. 67.

102 *C P*, p. 65.

103 *C P*, p. 58.

104 *C P*, p. 61.

105 *C P*, p. 63.

106 *C P*, p. 68.

107 *C P*, p. 59.

FOUR · THE DRAGON APPARENT

1 See Kenneth O. Morgan, *Rebirth of a Nation: Wales 1880–1980*, Oxford, 1981, chap. 9.

2 Quoted in John Davies, *A History of Wales*, Harmondsworth, 1993, p. 599.

3 Ibid., p. 597.

4 Speech, 20 July 1957.

5 Roy Clews, *To Dream of Freedom: The Struggle of M. A. C. and the Free Wales Army*, Talybont, 1980.

6 Ibid., p. 36.

7 Ibid., p. 38.

8 Ibid., pp. 126–7.

9 Derrick Hearne, *The ABC of the Welsh Revolution*, Talybont, 1982, p. 211.

10 Ibid., p. 73.

11 Ibid., p. 81.

12 Ibid., pp. 262–4.

13 *The Welsh Extremist: a Culture in Crisis*, London, 1971.

14 Ibid., p. 12.

15 Ibid., p. 17.

16 Ibid., p. 24.

17 Ibid., p. 26.

18 Ibid., p. 31.

19 Ibid., p. 32.

20 Ibid., p. 36.

21 Ibid., p. 110.

22 Ibid., p. 108.

23 Ibid., p. 32.

24 Ibid., p. 64.

25 Ibid., p. 116.

26 Ibid., p. 112.

27 Ibid., p. 123.

28 Ibid., p. 125.

29 Mario Basini, 'The harsh high priest of our national culture', *Western Mail*, 5 April 1995.

30 Naim Attallah, 'R. S. Thomas', in the *Oldie*, October 1995.

31 Reprinted in William V. Davis ed., op. cit., pp. 32–3.

32 See for instance John Hutchinson, *Modern Nationalism*, London, 1994.

33 *Neb*, p. 64: *Ar ben hyn dyma'r adeg, yn y chwe degau, pan waethygodd y sefyllfa wleidyddol, a dechreuodd rhai o'r Cymry iau ddefnyddio dulliau mwy uniongyrchol yn erbyn yr ormes Seisnig. Cafodd dynion fel Emyr Llewelyn eu trin yn ddigon ffiaidd gan yr heddlu, ac ymatebodd y bardd o Eglwys-fach trwy sgrifennu cerddi mwy gwlatgar. Wrth reswm, fe'i cyhuddwyd o gulni gan y beirniaid Saesneg. Hwn oedd cyfnod rhai o'i gerddi mwyaf chwerw yn erbyn y Saeson. Ond ni weithredodd yn uniongyrchol, gan gofio cyngor Saunders Lewis pan ddywedodd na ddylid disgwyl gormod o weithredoedd gan awdur, am mai trwy ei waith y câi ddylanwadu ar eraill.*

34 *Neb*, pp. 76–7: *Ni chaiff neb osgoi cwmni dysgedigion y byd heb fod ar ei golled. Ar yr un pryd rhaid cofio'r gwahaniaeth rhwng ysgolheigion a phobl greadigol. Hawdd ydi treulio diwrnod cyfan gyda thelyneg a methu'n y diwedd. Ond yn ystod yr un amser bydd efrydydd neu ysgolhaig wedi darllen llyfr cyfan, efallai, a'i gofio hefyd. Cof sâl, fel arfer, sydd gan y meddwl creadigol. Bydd yn anghofio'r pethau sydd ar wyneb bywyd, ond yn ddiarwybod iddo sudda pethau eraill i'w is-ymwybod i ffurfio yno* matrix *neu bwll y gall dynnu ohono rywdro yn y dyfodol. Fel hyn y daw cynifer o'r cerddi llwyddiannus i fod.*

35 'Autobiographical Essay' in William V. Davis ed; op. cit; p. 12.

36 Ibid., p. 12.

37 *Neb*, pp. 58–9: *Roedd Eglwys-fach mewn rhan ddymunol o Gymru wledig. Pentref ffordd fawr ydoedd, ryw bum*

*milltir o'r môr fel yr hed y frân, gydag
Afon Dyfi'n mynd heibio iddo. Codai'r
bryndir yn syth y tu ôl i'r ffordd fawr
a rhedai nentydd ewynnol i lawr y
cymoedd am y gwastadeddau prin
rhwng môr a mynydd. Ardal Gymreig
ei golwg oedd hi, gyda bryniau Meirion
yn codi yn y gogledd ac ambell gip ar
Gadair Idris o'r tir uchel. Ar ôl
ystorm, os gostegai'r gwynt, roedd sûn
y môr i'w glywed o'r gorllewin. Ac
yn well na hynny, unwaith bob dydd
dôi'r llanw i fyny'r afon a chlywid
aroglau'r môr yn yr ewyn.*

38 See *Neb*, p. 59.

39 *Neb*, p. 59: A hyd yn oed ymhlith
gwerin y pentref bu cryn gyd-briodi
hefo Saeson o loedd fel Sir Henffordd.

40 'Letter to Mary Gisbourne'.

41 *Neb*, p. 60: A rhyngddynt oll roedd
y Ficer, fel cocyn hitio, pe dymunent
ei drin felly. Roedd wedi syrffedu ar
fryntni Manafon. Ond wrth edrych
yn ôl, gwelodd fod mwy o esgus gan y
ffermwyr yno am eu hymarweddiad
garw. Doedden nhw ddim wedi cael
llawer o addysg na phrofiad o'r byd
gwâr. Ond dyma i chi yn Eglwys-fach
haenen o bobl a gafodd y ddau, ac
felly'n llai abl i bledio anwybodaeth.
Dysgodd y ficer o dipyn i beth am hen
wendidau dynolryw, fel snobyddiaeth,
cenfigen ac ariangarwrch. Ond
sylweddolodd hefyd yr her oedd o'i
flaen. Roedd ganddo gynulleidfa fwy
soffistigedig rûan, ac yr oedd rhaid
cynllunio'i bregethau'n ofalus i ddelio
hefo'r sefyllfa newydd. Ni fedrai ddal
i sôn am fyd natur o hyd ond ceisio
wynebu rhai o broblemau'r dydd a'r
meddwl dynol.*

42 Conversation between author and
Raymond Garlick, July 1995.

43 *Neb*, pp. 61–2: Ychydig wedi iddo
ymgartrefu yno, daeth athro o*

*Gaergrawnt i ddarlithio ar Chekhov,
ac aeth y ficer yno gan ddisgwyl
gwledd. Ond, och. Ni chododd y
darlithydd mo'i ben o'i lyfr bach am
awr gyfan, y ddarlith fwyaf sych a
glywodd y ficer erioed. Diflannodd ei
frwdfrydedd dros fynchu darlithoedd.
Ac ni chafodd fawr o hwyl yn y llyfrgell
ychwaith. Roedd y llyfrau yno, wrth
gwrs, ond buan y sylweddolodd nad
ysgolhaig oedd o, yn barod i dreulio
oriau yn y lle mawr, sychlyd hwnnw,
pan oedd diwrnod bendigedig o braf yn
ei alw allan.*

44 *Neb*, p. 64: Ond ni fedrwch ddianc
yn gyfan gwbl. Deil geiriau a syniadau
pobl i redeg trwy'r meddwl, a chafodd
ddigon o'r rheiny gan Saeson
Egwlys-fach. Doedd neb tebyg i'r Sais.
Cymaint o fendith fu hwnnw i weddill
y byd! 'Byddai'n dda gennyf fi glywed
rhywun heblaw Sais yn dweud hynny'
fyddai'i ateb. Ond llais yn yr
anialwch oedd, onibai am Gwydol
Owen yn y llythyrdy. Pan fu farw
Churchill, gwelodd amryw o'r Saeson
fai ar y ficer am beidio â gweddo drosto
yn yr eglwys. Pan laddwyd Kennedy
daeth rhai o'r bobl hunan-bwysig i'r
eglwys mewn dillad duon i ddangos eu
bod o'r un dras. Pan fyddai priodas
neu angladd ffasiynol deuent i'r
eglwys yn eu dillad benthyg gan y
Brodyr Moss!*

45 *The Echoes Return Slow*, p. 52.
46 Ibid., p. 46.
47 Ibid., p. 47.
48 Ibid., p. 48.
49 *C P*, pp. 69–72.
50 *C P*, p. 123.
51 *C P*, p. 180.
52 See p. 159.
53 *C P*, p. 73.
54 *C P*, p. 77.
55 *C P*, p. 96.

56 *C P*, p. 146.

57 *C P*, p. 92.

58 *C P*, p. 164.

59 *C P*, p. 169.

60 *C P*, p. 178.

61 *C P*, p. 134.

62 *C P*, p. 139.

63 *C P*, p. 152; see pp. 389–90.

64 *C P*, p. 111.

65 *C P*, p. 129.

66 *Poetry for Supper*; *C P*, p. 81.

67 *The Bread of Truth*; *C P*, p. 130.

68 *CP*, p. 86.

69 W. B. Yeats, *Collected Poems*, London, 1950, p. 401.

70 *C P*, p. 157.

71 William V. Davis ed., *Miraculous Simplicity*, p. 31.

72 Reprinted in Sandra Anstey ed., *R. S. Thomas: Selected Prose*, Bridgend, 1983.

73 Ibid., p. 64.

74 See in particular 'R. S. Thomas: Priest and Poet': transcript of a television documentary made by John Ormond and broadcast by the BBC on 2 April 1972, in *Poetry Wales*, Spring 1972.

75 Anstey ed., *Selected Prose*, p. 65.

76 Reprinted ibid.

77 Ibid., pp. 82–3.

78 Ibid., p. 83.

79 Ibid., p. 84.

80 Reprinted in Anstey ed., *Selected Prose*.

81 *Neb*, p. 62.

82 Ibid.

83 William Condry, *Wildlife, My Life*, Llandysul, 1995, pp. 158–9.

84 *Neb*, pp. 74–5: *O'u blaen yn disgwyl amdanynt roedd Andalucia, talaith fynyddig o dyddynod gwynion a ddangosai ddylanwad y Mwriaid. Fe'u temtiwyd yn fawr i yfed o'r nentydd ewynnol a ddôi i lawr o'r mynyddoedd i'r pentrefi, ond mynnodd R. S. eu bod yn llenwi casgen gan rywun dibynadwy a rhoi tabledi ynddi rhag ofn y dwymyn. Roedd harddwch rhai o'r pentrefi'n bur dwyllodrus, Grazalema'n hynod felly. Ond cawsant eu rhybuddio cyn cyrraedd hwnnw i beidio â chyffwrdd â'r caws lleol oherwydd y llefrith geifr oedd ynddo.*

85 *C P*, p. 204.

86 'Autobiographical Essay', in Davis ed., *Miraculous Simplicity*, p. 14.

87 Several details concerning the creation of RSPB Ynyshir were clarified in a correspondence between the author and Mr James Boulton of the National Trust office at Llandeilo.

88 *Neb*, p. 63: *Bu hanes diddorol i warchod y barcutiaid yng Nghymru. O fod yn aderyn pur gyffredin yn Lloegr y Canol Oesau, roedd wedi cilio i fryniau diarffordd Cymru ac erbyn dechrau'r ganrif hon wedi gostwng i dri neu bedwar pâr. Yn gynnar yn y ganrif dechreuodd ambell Sais gymryd diddordeb ynddynt a byddai rhai o ffermwyr a bugeiliaid Sir Aberteifi'n cofio am y bobl hyn wrth eu henwau. Erbyn i'r pwyllgor gwarchod gael ei ffurfio, roedd eu nifer wedi cynyddu dipyn bach, ond eu bod mewn perygl o hyd. Ond Saeson oedd y rhan fwyaf o aelodau'r pwyllgor, gyda Captain Vaughan, cyn aelod o'r llynges, yn bennaeth. Yn aml iawn, wrth siarad â'r ffermwyr roedd yn anodd iddynt ddeall beth oedd gennych, nes eich bod yn arfer y gair Saesneg 'kite'. Nid oedd yn brofiad anghyffredin chwaith clywed ffermwr yn gwadu'u bod nhw yn ei ardal o gwbl, ac un ohonynt yn hedfan uwch ei ben tra byddai'n siarad!*

89 For what follows, see M. Honora

Keating, *Plas-yn-Rhiw*, a 1957 booklet regularly reprinted by the National Trust; and Pat Cheney, 'The Keatings of Plas-yn-Rhiw', in *Country Quest*, July 1987.

90 Thus a consensus of local memory.

91 See *Neb*, p. 54.

92 See *Neb*, pp. 103–4.

93 *The Echoes Return Slow*, p. 90.

94 Ibid., p. 68.

95 *Neb*, p. 85: *Roedd wedi cyrraedd cyrchfan ei bererindod bersonol ei hun.*

96 *The Echoes Return Slow*, p. 68.

97 *Frequencies*; *C P*, p. 339.

98 *C P*, p. 282.

99 W. B. Yeats, *Collected Poems*, pp. 210–11.

100 *C P*, p. 503.

101 The author is indebted to Dr Gareth Roberts for this tentative diagnosis.

102 *C P*, p. 464.

103 'The Image of Wales in R. S. Thomas's Poetry', *Poetry Wales*, VII, no. 2, Spring 1972.

104 Ibid.

105 Nigel Jenkins 'Harri Webb' in *Poetry Wales* vol. 30 no. 4, April 1995.

106 *Guardian*, 4 March 1964.

107 *Daily Telegraph*, 7 November 1975.

108 Byron Rogers, 'Prisoner of the English Tongue', *Sunday Telegraph*, 30 July 1995.

109 'Saving a young life'. The only answer Thomas gives that is not jocular: while the poet was still on Pen Llŷn a local headmaster, John Morris, drowned while attempting to save one of his pupils from the same fate.

110 *Sunday Telegraph*, 5 September 1993.

111 *Western Mail*, 5 April 1995.

112 *Western Mail*, 19 September 1995.

113 *Independent on Sunday*, 25 September 1995.

114 Important interviews with R. S. Thomas are to be found in *Planet*, no. 80, April/May 1990, with Ned Thomas and John Barnie; in *The Anglo-Welsh Review*, no. 74, 1983, with J. B. Lethbridge; and in the transcript of John Ormond's BBC documentary (see above, note 74).

115 See *Neb*, p. 77.

116 *Neb*, p. 78: *Petai'n gorfod dewis rhwng cadeirlan fawreddog ac eglwys fach wledig, yr ail a ddewisai bob amser. Am yr eglwysi cadeiriol gyda'u rhodres a'u baneri rhyfel, a'r organ yn taranu digon i ddryllio'r to — sawrai'r rheiny bob amser o genedlaetholdeb a militariaeth Lloegr. Iddo fo, pobl a ddaliodd i ddotio at bethau felly oedd y Saeson gan fwyaf. Ond y pethau bach plaen, dirodres a apeliai ato fo. Dyna a'i hysgogai ym Manafon i sgrifennu am y tyddynnwr yn ei gaeau bychain. Dyna pam yr ysgrifennodd lith i gylchgrawn fel Y Fflam yn canmol addoldai fel Soar-y-Mynydd a Maes-yr-Onnen.*

117 *Neb*, p. 85: *Eithr wrth ei gael ei hun mewn cymuned gwbl Gymraeg yn Aberdaron, ni welai fod angen pwysleisio'i Gymreictod bellach, dim ond derbyn y peth fel ffaith hollol naturiol. Cymraeg oedd iaith y rhan fwyaf o'r trigolion, a doedd dim dwywaith amdani yn eu cartrefi nac yn eu cyfarfodydd.*

118 *Neb*, p. 85: *Erbyn yr haf roedd llond y penrhyn o bobl ddieithr, gydag Aberdaron dan ei sang, y Saeson yn llyfu'u hufen iâ neu'n sefyll mewn hwt er mwyn prynu papur newydd i wthio'u*

pennau iddo. Roedd Mynydd Mawr gyferbyn ag Ynys Enlli, ac nid nepell o adfeilion Capel Mair a'i ffynnon. Roedd y golygfeydd yn wyrthiol, ond yr olygfa fwyaf cyffredin oedd y cerbydau yn rhesi a'r modurwyr â'u pennau yn eu papurau yn llyncu newyddion pitw'r byd materol. Ac uwchben hyn oll, bron bob dydd byddai'r llu awyr yn ymarfer yn swnllyd i'w ryfeddu. Daeth yn amlwg i R. S. fod yma dyndra. Ar un llaw roedd golwg dragwyddol y grug a'r creigiau a'r môr, ond uwchben ac ymhobman arall roedd arwyddion bod yr ungeinfed ganrif yn mynnu cael sylw hyd at ddifa popeth oedd ar ôl o'r Oesoedd Canol.

119 *Neb,* p. 86: *Byw mewn ardal draddodiadol Gymraeg fel Pen Llŷn, siarad yr iaith bob dydd, ac eto yn ei fynegi'i hun mewn iaith estron. Canys felly y gwelai'r iaith oedd ar wefusau'r ymwelwyr. Yn ddistaw bach melltithiai'u hiaith nhw. Ond po fwyaf yr arhosai yn y cylch mwyaf oll o berygl a welai i'r Gymraeg. Hynny a'i trodd yn fwy o wladgarwr nag erioed yn ei fywyd, os nad yn ei waith llenyddol.*

120 *Neb,* pp. 89–90: *Bu Aberdaron heb ficer am flwyddyn; felly roedd y bobl yn falch o gael hyd yn oed rhywun fel R. S. Ni wnaeth yntau, chwaith, ddirgelwch o'r ffaith mai wedi dod yno, fwy neu lai, i ymddeol roedd o. Rhaid bod yn glir ar y mater hwn. Ymhob un o'r plwyfi y bu ynddynt gwnaeth R. S. ei waith mor gydwybodol ag oedd yn bosibl. Doedd o ddim yn boblogaidd nac yn bregethwr o fri. Ond ymwelai â'i blwyfolion yn gyson, yn enwedig y cleifion . . . Er hynny trefnai R. S. ei amser fel ag i gael cryn ryddid. Astudiai yn y bore,*

gan deimlo mai'r ystafell oedd lle offeriad ar adeg felly.

121 *The Anglo-Welsh Review,* No. 74, 1983. Interviewed by J. B. Lethbridge, Thomas said: 'I take a solid book of any sort, philosophy or something, and read it every morning. Then if the idea comes for a poem, of course, I put the book aside and write the poem. But that's the kind of pattern, I still keep that up as much as I can'. (p. 53).

122 *Neb,* pp. 94–5: *Ac ystrier gwasanaethau'r eglwys. Faint o bobl a wyddai sut i addoli, wrth benlinio a chau llygaid a'u cynnig eu hunain i Dduw? Roedd nod ymneilltuaeth ar ormod ohonynt. Er ei barch ar gynifer o weinidogion anghydffurfiol, synnai R. S. at eu hagwedd eofn braidd tuag at y Duwdod. Pan fyddent yn gweddio, yn rhy aml yr oeddynt fel petaent yn meddwl bod Duw'n clustfeinio tu allan i'r drws. A'r miwsig! Duw a'n helpo! Faint o gynulleidfaoedd yr Eglwys sy'n gallu canu? Faint o'r organyddion sy'n medru meistroli'u hofferyn? Sôn am gythraul canu; roedd o'n rhemp ym Manafon. Dyna un peth a wnaeth iawn iddo am fynd i Eglwys-fach. Medrai Patricia Mappin ganu'r organ a dewis darnau clasurol i'w perfformio cyn dechrau'r gwasanaeth. Ond hyd yn oed wedyn, ni fu R. S. erioed yn hoff o emynau, sef penillion o'r drydedd radd wedi'u gosod ar gyfer tonau tebyg. Llawer gwell ganddo fyddai llafarganu yn null y mynaich, ond doedd o ddim yn ddigon o gerddor ei hun i ddysgu'r fath ganu i'r gynulleidfa. Dyna un arall o ddiffygion ei hyfforddiant yn y coleg diwinyddol.*

123 *Neb*, p. 107: *Adnod annwyl dros ben
ganddo oedd honno o lyfr
Deuteronomium, y seithfed adnod o'r
seithfed bennod: 'Nid am eich bod yn
lluosocach na'r holl bobloedd yr hoffodd
yr Arglwydd chwi, ac y'ch dewisodd;
oherwydd yr oeddych chwi yn an-amlaf
o'r holl bobloedd.' Neges galonogol iawn
i genedl fach fel y Cymry; ond ar y
cyfan diau i'w eiriau syrthio ar dir
digon caregog.*

124 See *Neb*, p. 108.

125 *Neb*, p. 109: *Pan ddatgelir clefyd y
Cymry, maen nhw'n gwylltio. Gwaeth
na gelyniaeth y Saeson i'r iaith estron
yn eu plith ydi gelyniaeth cynifer o
Gymry Cymraeg i'w mamiaith pan
â'n hanfod.*

126 *Neb*, pp. 110–11: *Dagrau'r peth ydi
mai'r unig ffordd i ennill rhyddid ydi
trwy ymladd drosto. Dyna wers hanes.
Er mai heddychwr oedd R. S., fel y
gweddai i offeiriad fod, ni wyddai am
un enghraifft i'r gwrthwyneb, ac
eithrio'r India. A hyd heddiw y
bobl a ddefnyddiodd drais a wnaeth
yr argraff ddyfnaf ar eu gormeswyr.
Faint o arweinyddion y llywodraethau
yn yr Affrig a'r India na fu am gyfnod
yng ngharcharau'r Saeson . . .*

127 *Neb*, p. 111: *Bydd pwy bynnag a
welodd hebog tramor yn disgyn fel
mellten ar ei brae'n sicr o deimlo rhyw
wefr, sy'n ei wneud yn ddigon
gostyngedig. Dyma feistri byd natur.
Un o reolau di-feth y byd hwnnw ydi
bod bywyd yn gorfod marw er mwyn
bywyd. Os oes ffordd arall ar y ddaear
hon, ni welodd Duw'n dda i'w chanlyn.*

128 *Neb*, p. 117: *Gwlad y peilonau a'r
gwifrau, gwlad mastiau'r teledu a
pholion yr heddlu, gwlad y ffyrdd
newydd yn llawn pobl ddieithr yn ei
heglu hi am y môr ydi Cymru
heddiw, . . .*

129 *Neb*, p. 123: *Bydd pobl yn eich siomi
ond ni bydd Cymru byth yn
anffyddlon. Y mae hi yno bob amser
yn ei holl forwynod difrycheulyd, er
gwaetha'r holl bethau ysgeler a wnawn
iddi.*

130 *Neb*, p. 130: *Y mae posibilrwydd
barn yn eglur ar y gorwel.*

131 *Neb*, pp. 130–1: *Wrth fyw mewn
bwthyn pedwar canmlwydd oed, a
meddwl am ddeiliaid y bwthyn hwnnw
drwy gydol y canrifoedd, fe ddychmygai
weld eu hwynebau'n ei wylio o'r cerrig
yn y muriau. Wrth glywed sûn
tragwyddol y tonnau'n torri ar y traeth
ym Mhorth Neigwl, neu ymateb yn
llawen i ddawns yr heulwen trwy'i
ystafell, ac wedyn troi'r radio ymlaen
a chlywed am enghraifft newydd o
ffo-lineb neu fwystfileidd-dra dyn –
bydd hyn oll yn peri i R. S. hel
meddyliau sydd, ys dywedodd
Wordsworth, yn rhy ddwfn i ddagrau.
Pa beth sy'n gweddu i ddyn bellach
ond ailadrodd, ddydd ar ôl dydd:*
Miserere me, Domine?

132 R. S. responding to a question
posed by Ned Thomas in the
Planet no. 80 interview; see
William V. Davis ed., op. cit., p.
24.

133 See, for example, *Blwyddyn yn Llŷn*,
'A Year in Llŷn', p. 72.

134 *Absalom and Achitophel*, part I.

135 *Sunday Telegraph*, 5 September
1993.

136 In fact R. S. has conducted services
since retirement, so at some point
he must have applied for and
received a licence from his bishop.

137 Pamphlet issued by the Bardsey
Island Trust in 1978.

138 See p. 14.

FIVE · FURIOUS INTERIORS

1 From 'Y Bardd a'r Brawd Llwyd', translated by Rachel Bromwich in *Dafydd ap Gwilym: a Selection of Poems*, Llandysul, 1982/93, as:

> Are not hymns and sequences
> no other than *englynion* and odes?
> and the psalms of the prophet
>   David
> are but *cywyddau* to holy God.

2 See Sandra Anstey ed., *Critical Writings on R. S. Thomas*, Poetry Wales Press, Bridgend, first edition, 1982, p. 136.

3 *R. S. Thomas: ABC Neb*, ed. Jason Walford Davies, Gwasg Gwynedd, Caernarfon, 1995, pp. 93–4: *Efallai mai'r enghraifft fwyaf adnabyddus o'r gair hwn ydi'r un sy'n ei gysylltu â'r rhif naw: 'Naw wfft iddo', ffordd arall o ddangos ein dirmyg o rywbeth neu rywun, neu o esgus nad oes arnom ofn . . . A gaf ddal ar y cyfle, felly, i sôn am rai o'm casbethau i? Ac wedi cael eich caniatâd, estynnaf yr un cyfle i chwi. Dyma nhw: Naw wfft i ragrith y Sais y soniais i amdano eisoes. Does neb wedi dioddef mwy yn sgîl hyn na ni'r Cymry . . . Naw wfft i'r Sais-Gymry ac i'r rhai sydd naill ai wedi llyncu abwyd Prydeindod neu wedi dewis ochri hefo fo'n agored . . . Naw wfft i'r bobl sydd â digon o bres i brynu cerbyd drud, i redeg dau ohonynt, i fod yn berchen ar ddwy neu dair set deledu, sy'n bwrw gwyliau costus dramor ond sy'n gadael i achosion Cymraeg a'r wasg Gymraeg ddihoeni. Naw wfft i'r bobl sy'n hel esgusion pitw am beidio â mynychu cyfarfodydd a ralïau pwysig, gan wybod yn iawn pa effaith a gaiff eu habsenoldeb a'u diffyg cefnogaeth. Naw wfft i'r Cymry sy'n esgeulus o fyd*

natur ac o olygfeydd arbennig ein gwlad, gan adael y dasg o ofalu amdanynt yn nwylo'r Saeson sy'n eu mwynhau a'u gwerthfawrogi.

4 Ibid., pp. 94–5: *Naw wfft i'r rhai sy'n mynd yn ôl ar eu gair. Nid yw'n hawdd cyflawni addewid bob amser. Felly ni ddylid gwneud un yn ysgafn ac yn ddifeddwl. Ond, wedi gwneud addewid, dylid ei gadw hyd eithaf ein gallu, yn enwedig addewid i blentyn, oherwydd bod gan blentyn gof hir, ac wedi mynd yn oedolyn bydd yn cofio am yr addewid nas cyflawnwyd. Sy'n dod â ni at gwestiwn ysgariad, sydd, gwaetha'r modd, mor gyffredin yn ein plith bellach. Beth bynnag sy'n digwydd gerbron y gyfraith – mewn addoldy neu swyddfa gofrestru – y peth sylfaenol mewn priodas ydi'r llw o ffyddlondeb a gymer y naill i'r llall, na fedr nac eglwys na chapel ond rhoi sêl eu bendith arno. Ac oherwydd bod cynifer yn manteisio ar gydsyniad cymdeithas hunanol, faterol i dorri'r adduned honno, gan beri dioddefaint a chyni i blant bach yn aml, naw wfft i'r rheini hefyd. O'r braidd na thueddwn i ddweud mai'r rhain yw'r gwaethaf ohonynt i gyd. Ond mae yna un ar ôl, y pwysicaf oll rydw i'n credu, a fi fy hun ydi hwnnw. Felly oherwydd f'aml fethiannau a'm llwfrdra a'm rhagrith, caf orffen drwy ddweud: Naw wfft i mi hefyd.*

5 Published by the Gomer Press as one in a series, *Changing Wales*, edited by Meic Stephens.

6 Ibid., 5.

7 Ibid., 11.

8 Ibid., 31.

9 See Chapter 2, note 60.

10 Sandra Anstey ed., *R. S. Thomas: Selected Prose*, Bridgend, 1983, p. 100.

11 i.e., 'In Abercuawg the cuckoos sing'
   Canu Llywarch Hen ('The Song of
   Old Llywarch') is a cycle of poems,
   composed in the *englynion* form and
   dating most probably from the
   ninth century.
12 Quoted by R. S. Thomas, in Anstey
   ed., op. cit., p. 160.
13 *Planet*, no. 41, 1978; reprinted in
   Anstey ed., op. cit., p. 175f.
14 *CP*, p. 340.
15 W. B. Yeats, *Collected Poems*,
   Macmillan, London, 1950,
   p. 350.
16 *CP*, p. 152.
17 *CP*, p. 525.
18 *CP*, p. 194.
19 *Nippon Keizai Shimbun*, 2 February
   1996.
20 *CP*, p. 194.
21 *CP*, p. 197.
22 *CP*, p. 257.
23 *CP*, p. 261.
24 M. Wynn Thomas, 'Keeping His
   Pen Clean: R. S. Thomas and Wales',
   in William V. Davis, *Miraculous
   Simplicity*, Fayetteville, University of
   Arkansas Press, 1993.
25 Translation by A. M. Allchin in *Ann
   Griffiths: The Furnace and the
   Fountain*, Cardiff, 1987.
26 As well as Allchin, op. cit., the
   reader may wish to refer to John
   Ryan, *The Hymns of Ann Griffiths*,
   Tŷ ar y Graig, Caernarfon,
   1980.
27 Also sometimes known as Williams
   Pantycelyn, 1717–91, a Welsh
   Methodist and hymn-writer
28 1755–1814.
29 *CP*, p. 281.
30 *CP*, p. 470–5.
31 A. M. Allchin, op. cit., p. 20.
32 Ibid., p. 34.
33 J. L. Mackie, *The Miracle of Theism:*

*Arguments for and against the Existence
   of God*, Oxford, 1982, p. 143.
34 David Hume, *Dialogues Concerning
   Natural Religion*, London 1779,
   published posthumously and
   without printer's name; refer to
   Penguin Classics edition, London,
   1990.
35 Gilbert Ryle, *The Concept of Mind*,
   Hutchinson, London, 1949.
36 Quoted in J. L. Mackie, op. cit.
37 In *The Way of It*; *CP*, p. 322.
38 John A. T. Robinson, *Honest to God*,
   SCM Press, London, 1963.
39 Ibid., p. 124.
40 Acts 17: 22–3.
41 SCM Press, London, 1949.
42 Quoted in Patrick Gardiner,
   Kierkegaard, Oxford, 1988, p. 34.
43 1843, trans. 1949.
44 'Kierkegaard', in *Pietà*; *CP*,
   p. 162.
45 *CP*, p. 208.
46 *CP*, p. 209.
47 *CP*, p. 212.
48 *CP*, p. 214.
49 See Henry Petroski, *The Pencil: A
   History*, New York, 1989: an
   eye-opening investigation into the
   technology behind a supposedly
   simple artefact.
50 *CP*, p. 220.
51 *CP*, p. 221.
52 *CP*, p. 235.
53 *CP*, p. 232.
54 *CP*, p. 233.
55 See C. F. Kelley, *Meister Eckhart on
   Divine Knowledge*, Yale University
   Press, 1977.
56 *CP*, p. 241.
57 *CP*, p. 263.
58 *CP*, p. 331.
59 *CP*, p. 417.
60 *CP*, p. 456.
61 *CP*, p. 272.

62 In *The Death of Tragedy*, London,
   1961, and elsewhere.
63 *C P*, p. 15.
64 *C P*, p. 147.
65 *C P*, p. 443.
66 *C P*, p. 374.
67 *C P*, p. 436.
68 *C P*, p. 357.
69 *C P*, p. 362.
70 *C P*, p. 359.
71 *C P*, p. 516.
72 *Counterpoint*, p. 49.
73 *Counterpoint*, p. 12.

POSTSCRIPT · CROMWELL'S CURSE

1 The first issue of a now defunct
   literary magazine, *Babel*, 1982, was
   entirely devoted to R. S.
2 Translation by Jason Walford Davies
   in article cited.
3 J. P. Ward, *The Poetry of R. S. Thomas*,
   Bridgend, 1987, p. 122.
4 *CP*, p. 404.
5 Justin Wintle, 'In search of the shy
   tribe of Thailand', *Financial Times*,
   19 December 1992.

BIBLIOGRAPHY

Works by R. S. Thomas

POETRY: COLLECTIONS

1946   *The Stones of the Field*, Druid Press, Carmarthen
1952   *An Acre of Land*, Montgomeryshire Printing Company, Newtown
1953   *The Minister*, Montgomeryshire Printing Company, Newtown
1955   *Song at the Year's Turning*, Hart-Davis, London
1958   *Poetry for Supper*, Hart-Davis, London
1961   *Tares*, Hart-Davis, London
1963   *The Bread of Truth*, Hart-Davis, London
1966   *Pietà*, Hart-Davis, London
1968   *Not That He Brought Flowers*, Hart-Davis, London
1972   *H'm*, Macmillan, London
1972   *Young and Old*, Chatto and Windus, London
1973   *Selected Poems*, Hart-Davis, MacGibbon, London
1974   *What is a Welshman*, Christopher Davies, Llandybie
1975   *Laboratories of the Spirit*, Macmillan, London
1977   *The Way of It*, Ceolfrith Press, Sunderland
1978   *Frequencies*, Macmillan, London
1981   *Between Here and Now*, Macmillan, London
1983   *Later Poems 1972–83*, Macmillan, London
1985   *Ingrowing Thoughts*, Poetry Wales Press, Bridgend
1985   *Destinations*, Celandine Press, Halford
1986   *Experimenting with an Amen*, Macmillan, London
1987   *Welsh Airs*, Seren Books, Bridgend
1988   *The Echoes Return Slow*, Macmillan, London
1990   *Counterpoint*, Bloodaxe Books, Newcastle-upon-Tyne
1992   *Mass for Hard Times*, Bloodaxe Books, Newcastle-upon-Tyne
1993   *Collected Poems 1945–1990*, J. M. Dent, London
1995   *No Truce with the Furies*, Bloodaxe Books, Newcastle-upon-Tyne

PROSE: BOOKS & PAMPHLETS

1964   *Words and the Poet*, University of Wales Press, Cardiff – see
       Lectures, Broadcasts, etc.
1968   *The Mountains*, Chilmark Press, New York
1983   *Selected Prose*, ed. Sandra Anstey, Poetry Wales Press, Bridgend:
       includes both above items
1985   *Neb*, Gwasg Gwynedd, Caernarfon
1988   *Pe medrwn yr iaith ac ysgrifau eraill*, eds. Tony Brown and Bedwyr
       Lewis Jones, Christopher Davies, Abertawe
       The Echoes Return Slow, Macmillan, London
1990   *Blwyddyn yn Llŷn*, Gwasg Gwynedd, Caernarfon
1992   *Cymru or Wales?*, Gomer Press, Llandysul
1995   *A B C Neb*, ed. Jason Walford Davies, Gwasg Gwynedd,
       Caernarfon
1996   *R.S. Thomas: Autobiographies*: *Neb*, *Blwyddyn yn Llŷn*, *Y Llwybrau
       Gynt* and *Hunanladdiad y Llenor*, trans. Jason Walford Davies, J.M.
       Dent, London

SELECTED OCCASIONAL PROSE

(Note: * denotes inclusion in *Selected Prose*, ed. Anstey, 1983: see above.)
1944   Letter to Keidrych Rhys, in *Wales*, III. 4, pp. 106–7
1945   'Adar y Plwyfi', in *Y Llan*, 28 September
       'Adar y Gaeaf', in *Y Llan*, 28 December.
       'The Depopulation of the Welsh Hill Country', in *Wales*, V.7 *
1946   'Arian a Swydd', in *Y Fflam* I.1
       'Replies to *Wales* Questionnaire 1946', in *Wales*, VI.3
       'Some Contemporary Scottish Writing', in *Wales*, VI.3*
1947   '*Break in Harvest and Other Poems* by Roland Mathias', in *Wales*,
       VII.26 [review]
1948   'A Welsh View of the Scottish Renaissance', *Wales*, VIII.30
       'Anglo-Welsh Literature', in *The Welsh Nationalist*, December
       'Dau Gapel', in *Y Fflam* V (English version 'Two Chapels' in
       Selected Prose)
       '"The Guests" by Dilys Cadwaladr', in *Wales*, VIII.29
       [translation]
1952   'Llenyddiaeth Eingl-Gymreig', in *Y Fflam*, XI (trans. as
       'Anglo-Welsh Literature')*

1956   'A Cymric Survey: *A History of Welsh Literature* by Thomas Parry, trans. H. Idris Bell', in *New Statesman*, 24 March [review]

1958   'The Welsh Parlour', in *Listener*, 16 January

1959   'The Qualities of Christmas', in *Wales*, XLVI*

1960   '*Dragons and Daffoldils: Contemporary Anglo-Welsh Verse* ed. John Stuart Williams and Richard Milner', in *Listener*, 8 September [review]

1962   '*The Oxford Book of Welsh Verse* by Thomas Parry', in *Listener*, 26 April [review]

1963   Letter to the Editor, in *The Listener*, 14 November

1966   'A Frame for Poetry', *TLS*, 3 March

1967   'Adaryddiaeth – Beth amdani?', in *Barn*, 5
       'Preface' to *MacDiarmid: The Scottish National Library Exhibition Catalogue*, Edinburgh
       '*Barbarous Knowledge* by Daniel Hoffman; *W. B. Yeats and Georgian Ireland* by Donald T. Torchiana; *T. S. Eliot: Moments and Patterns* by Leonard Unger; *The Craft and Art of Dylan Thomas* by William T. Moynihan', in *Critical Quarterly*, IX.4 [review]

1968   Contribution (answer to questionnaire) 'Poets on the Vietnam War', in *The Review*, 18

1969   'The Making of a Poem', in *Conference of Library Authorities in Wales and Monmouthshire 35th, Barry, 1968*, ed. L. M. Rees, Swansea, 1969*
       Letter in *Anglo-Welsh Review*, 18

1972   *Y Llwybrau Gynt 2* [*The Paths Gone By*], ed. A. Oldfield-Davies, Gwasg Gomer, Llandysul: text of radio talk and part of a series*
       'Ynys Enlli', in *Barn*, 121

1974   '*Bury My Heart at Wounded Knee* by Dee Brown', in *Barn*, 135*
       'Where do we go from here?', in *Listener*, 8 August*

1976   *Abercuawg* – see Lectures, Broadcasts, etc.*

1977   'Gwahaniaethu', in *Y Faner*, 19 August
       'Hunanladdiad Y Llenor', in *Taliesin*, 35: translated as 'The Creative Writer's Suicide', in *Planet*, 41, 1978
       'O'n cwmpas', in *Y Faner*, 4 March
       'Yr "Union Jack"', [Letter to the Editor] in *Y Faner*, 20 May

1978   'Dwyieithedd? – Dim Perygl!', [Letter] in *Y Faner*, 25 August

1979   Letter in support of devolution and signed by others, in *The Western Mail*, 27 February

1980   'Pe medrwn yr iaith', in *Y Faner*, 11 January
       'Llanw Llŷn', in *Y Faner*, 7 November

1981   'Neges R. S. Thomas', in *Y Faner*, 17 July

1983   'Cau ceg er mwyn chwe chant', in *Y Faner*, 30 April

1986   'Autobiographical Essay', in *Contemporary Authors: Autobiographical Series* vol. 4, pp. 301–13, Gale Detroit: reprinted in *Miraculous Simplicity: Essays on R. S. Thomas*, ed. William V. Davis, University of Arkansas Press, Fayetteville, 1993

EDITORIAL: INCLUDING INTRODUCTIONS

1961   *The Batsford Book of Country Verse*, Batsford, London

1963   *The Penguin Book of Religious Verse*, Penguin Books, London

1964   *Selected Poems of Edward Thomas*, Faber & Faber, London

1967   *A Choice of George Herbert's Verse*, Faber & Faber, London

1971   *A Choice of Wordsworth's Verse*, Faber & Faber, London

[Note: the Introductions to 1963 and 1971 are reprinted in *Selected Prose*, ed. Anstey, 1983]

LECTURES, BROADCASTS, INTERVIEWS

1952   *The Minister* broadcast by BBC Radio Wales – see Poetry Collections

1961   'The World of Books', BBC Radio Home Service, 29 July: contribution published as 'The Making of Poetry' in *The Listener* 17 August

1963   The W. D. Thomas Memorial Lecture at University College Swansea, November: published as *Words and the Poet*, University of Wales Press, Cardiff, 1964*

1968   'St David's', in *Ten to Eight*, BBC Radio 4, 1 March: text published as 'St David's' in *By Request from Ten to Eight on Radio 4*, BBC Books, London

1972   'R. S. Thomas: Priest and Poet', film by John Ormond broadcast by the BBC, 2 April: transcript in *Poetry Wales*, Spring 1972

1976   'Abercuawg', address to the 1976 National Eisteddfod: published under the same title by the Gomer Press, Llandysul, 1976 (English version in *Selected Prose*)*

       'R. S. Thomas Reading His Own Poems', Oriel Records, Welsh Arts Council

1983   'R. S. Thomas talks to J. B. Letbridge', in *Anglo-Welsh Review*, 74

1990   'Probings: an Interview with R. S. Thomas', Ned Thomas and

John Barnie, in *Planet*, 80, April/May: reprinted in *Miraculous Simplicity* ed. William V. Davis, University of Arkansas Press, Fayetteville, 1993

1996   A lecture delivered by R. S. Thomas at King's College, London on 8 February and called 'Wales: a Problem of Translation': will be published by the College toward the end of the same year

Selected critical studies of R. S. Thomas

Ackerman, John, 'R. S. Thomas: Poet for Our Time', in *Anglo-Welsh Review*, 85, 1987

Allchin, A. M. 'An Inexplicable Note of Hope', in *New Welsh Review*, v. 4, 1993

Anstey, Sandra, ed., *Critical Writings on R. S. Thomas*, Poetry Wales Press, Bridgend, 1983; new edition with revised table of contents, Seren Books/ Poetry Wales Press Bridgend, 1983, rev. 1995 (bibliography includes Welsh-language critical essays)

Bianchi, Tony, 'R. S. Thomas and his Readers', in Tony Curtis ed., *Wales: The Imagined Nation*, Poetry Wales Press, Bridgend, 1986

Brown, Tony: 'Language, Poetry and Silence: Some Themes in the Poetry of R. S. Thomas', in W. Tydeman ed., *The Welsh Connection*, Gomer Press, Llandysul, 1987.

Conran, Anthony, 'R. S. Thomas and the Anglo-Welsh Crisis', in *Poetry Wales*, VII.4, 1972

Cox, C. B., 'Welsh Bards in Hard Times: Dylan Thomas and R. S. Thomas', in Boris Ford ed., *The New Pelican Guide to English Literature*, vol. 8, Penguin Books, London, 1983

Davies, Jason Walford, 'Allusions to Welsh Literature in the Writing of R. S. Thomas', in *Welsh Writing in English; a Yearbook of Critical Essays*, vol. I, 1995

Davies, Walford, 'R. S. Thomas: the Poem's Harsher Conditions', in *The New Welsh Review*, III.3, 1991

Davis, William V. ed., *Miraculous Simplicity: essays on R. S. Thomas*, University of Arkansas Press, Fayetteville, 1993

Dyson, A. E., *Yeats, Eliot and R. S. Thomas: Riding the Echo*, Macmillan, London 1981

Merchant, W. Moelwyn, *R. S. Thomas*, in 'Writers of Wales' series, University of Wales Press, Cardiff, 1979, revised 1989

New Welsh Review, special 'R. S. Thomas at Eighty' issue, 20, Spring, 1993

Philips, D. Z., 'Poetry and Philosophy: A Reply', in *New Welsh Review*, III.4, Spring, 1991 (with a rejoinder by Walford Davies)

——*R. S. Thomas: Poet of the Hidden God: Meaning and Meditation in the Poetry of R. S. Thomas*, Macmillan, London, 1986

Poetry Wales, special R. S. Thomas editions, Spring, 1972 and Spring, 1993

Reading, Peter, 'Doubting Thomas', in *TLS*, 3 October 1983

Stacey, Tom, 'Andrew Young, R. S. Thomas and the Parson Poets', in *Essays by Divers Hands*, Transactions of the Royal Society of Literature, New series, XLII, 1982

Thomas, M. Wynn, ed., *The Page's Drift: R. S. Thomas at Eighty* (essays), Seren Books Poetry Wales Press, Bridgend 1993

——'R. S. Thomas: War Poet', in *Welsh Writing in English: A Yearbook of Critical Essays*, II, 1996

Ward, J. P., *The Poetry of R. S. Thomas*, Poetry Wales Press, Bridgend, 1987

Wintle, J., '"My Prince Died in 1282"', in *New Statesman*, 25 August 1995

Selected further reading: Wales, its history and its literature

Allchin, A. M., *Ann Griffiths: The Furnace and the Fountain*, University of Wales Press, Cardiff, 1987

Aneirin, *Canu Aneirin*, ed. Ifor Williams, University of Wales Press, Cardiff, 1938

——*Y. Gododdin*, dual text, ed. and trans. A. O. H. Jarman, Gomer Press, Llandysul, 1990

——*Y. Gododdin*, trans. Steve Short, Llanerch, Felinfach, 1994

Arnold, Matthew, *On the Study of Celtic Literature and Other Essays*, ed. Ernest Rhys, Everyman, London 1910/76

Black Book of Carmarthen, The, ed. and trans. Meirion Pennar, Llanerch Enterprises, Lampeter, 1989

Borrow, George, *Wild Wales: Its People, Language and Scenery*, London, 1862

Clews, Roy, *To Dream of Freedom: the Struggle of MAC and the Free Wales Army*, Y Lolfa, Talybont, 1980

Conran, Anthony, *The Cost of Strangeness: Essays on the English Poets of Wales* (includes a chapter on R. S. Thomas), Gomer Press, Llandysul, 1982

Conran, Anthony and Williams, J. E. Caerwyn, eds. and trans., *The Penguin Book of Welsh Verse*, Penguin Books, London, 1967

Curtis, Tony, ed., *Wales: The Imagined Nation*, Poetry Wales Press, Bridgend, 1986

Dafydd Ap Gwilym, *Gwaith Dafydd ap Gwilym*, ed. Thomas Parry, University of Wales Press; Cardiff, 1952

——*Poems*, dual text, ed. and trans. Rachel Bromwich, Gomer Press, Llandysul, 1982/93

Davies, D. Hywel, *The Welsh Nationalist Party 1925–1945*, University of Wales Press, Cardiff, 1983

Davies, John, *A History of Wales*, Allen Lane, London, 1993; English version of 2-volume *Hanes Cymru*, Allen Lane, London, 1990

Davies, R. R., *The Revolt of Owain Glyn Dŵr*, O U P, Oxford, 1995

Garlick, Raymond, *An Introduction to Anglo-Welsh Literature*, University of Wales Press, Cardiff, 1972

Garlick, Raymond and Mathias, Roland, eds., *Anglo-Welsh Poetry 1480– 1980*, Poetry Wales Press, Bridgend, 1984

Griffiths, Bruce, *Saunders Lewis*, 'Writers of Wales' series, University of Wales Press, Cardiff, 1989

Hearne, Derrick, *The A B C of the Welsh Revolution*, Y Lolfa, Talybont, 1982

Hughes, W. J., *Wales And The Welsh In English Literature*, Hughes and Sons, Wrexham, 1924

Hywel Dda, *The Law*, ed. and trans., Dafydd Jenkins, Gomer Press, Llandysul, 1986

Iolo Goch: *Poems*, ed. and trans. Dafydd Johnston, Gomer Press, Llandysul, 1993

Jones, Glyn, *The Dragon Has Two Tongues*, J. M. Dent, London, 1968

Jones, R. Gerallt, *T. H. Parry-Williams 1887–1978*, 'Writers of Wales' series, University of Wales Press, Cardiff, 1978

Lewis, Saunders, *Selected Poems*, trans. Joseph P. Clancy, University of Wales Press, Cardiff, 1993

Lloyd, J. E., *A History of Wales from the Earliest Times to the Edwardian Conquest*, 2 vols., Longman Green, London, 1911

Mabinogion, The, trans. Jeffrey Gantz, Penguin Books, London, 1976

Mathias, Roland, *A Ride Through The Wood: Essays on Anglo-Welsh*

Literature, (includes a chapter of R. S. Thomas), Poetry Wales Press, Bridgend, 1985

Morgan, Gerald, *The Dragon's Tongue: the Fortunes of the Welsh Language*, Triskel Press, Narberth, 1966

Morgan, Kenneth O., *Rebirth of a Nation: Wales 1880–1980*, OUP, Oxford, 1981

Morgan, Prys, 'From a Death to a View: The Hunt for the Welsh Past in the Romantic Period', in Eric Hobsbawn and Terence Ranger eds. *The Invention of Tradition*, CUP, Cambridge, 1983

Morris, Jan, *The Matter of Wales: Epic Views of a Small Country*, OUP, Oxford, 1984

——*A Machynlleth Triad/Triawd Machynlleth*, Penguin Books, London, 1994

Parry, Thomas, *History of Welsh Literature*, trans. H. Idris Bell, OUP, Oxford, 1955

Smith, Dai, *Aneurin Bevan and the World of South Wales*, University of Wales Press, Cardiff, 1993

Stephens, Meic, ed., *The Oxford Companion to the Literature of Wales*, OUP, Oxford, 1986

Taliesin, *The Poems of Taliesin*, trans. J. E. Caerwyn Williams, 1968

——*Poems*, trans. Meirion Pennar, Llanerch, Felinfach, 1988

Thomas, M. Wynn, *Internal Difference: Literature in Twentieth-Century Wales* University of Wales Press, Cardiff, 1992 (contains two chapters on R. S. Thomas)

——'Hidden Attachments: aspects of the two literatures of modern Wales', in *Welsh Writing in English: a Yearbook of Critical Essays*, vol.I, 1995

Thomas, Ned, *The Welsh Extremist: A Culture in Crisis*, Gollancz, London, 1971

Williams, Gwyn, *An Introduction to Welsh Poetry*, Faber & Faber, London, 1953

Williams, Gwyn A., *When Was Wales? A History of the Welsh*, Penguin Books, London, 1985

Williams, J. E. Caerwyn, *The Poets of the Welsh Princes*, 'Writers of Wales' series, 2nd edition, University of Wales Press, Cardiff, 1994

Williams, John Stuart and Stephens, Meic, eds., *The Lilting House: an Anthology of Anglo-Welsh Poetry*, with an Introduction by Raymond Garlick, J. M. Dent, London, 1969

INDEX OF R. S. THOMAS'S WORKS

GENERAL INDEX

Note: Works by R. S. Thomas that are quoted or cited have been separately indexed (see above). Works by other authors are indexed below under the names of their authors.